15 Maui's Top Experiences

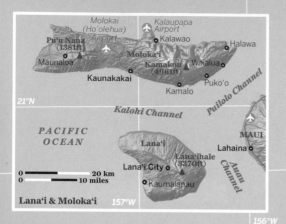

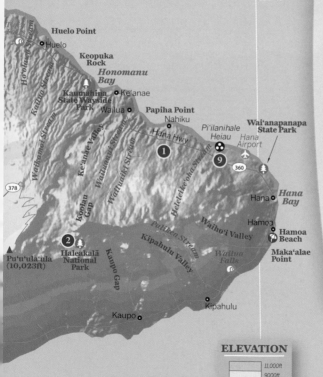

ELEVATION

	11,000ft
	9000ft
	7000ft
	5000ft
	4000ft
	3000ft
	2000ft
	1000ft
	0

Maui

156°30'W

Pailolo Channel

PACIFIC OCEAN

0 ————————— 10 km
0 ————————— 5 miles

Nakalele Point
Light Beacon

Slaughterhouse Beach
30
Honokohau

21°N
Kapalua

Napili **12**
Kahakuloa

340
Kapalua West Maui Airport

Kahana
14

Honokowai

15 Kaʻanapali
Waiheʻe

30
Honolua Stream

Pauwela Point
Uaoa Bay

Hoʻokipa Beach Park
Paʻuwela

HA Baldwin Beach Park
36

11
Paʻia
Haʻiku

36

Eke Crater
(4751ft)
Kahului Bay

**ʻIao Needle
(2250ft)**
Wailuku
Kanaha Pond

Kahului
Kahului Airport

Baldwin Ave

365

5 Puʻu Kukui
(5788ft)

ʻIao Valley State Park
ʻIao Stream

4
Waikapu

311
Haleakalā Hwy

37
Makawao

Lahaina **5**

13

Honoapiʻilani Hwy

30

380
30

Pukalani
37

Olowalu

377

Kuihelani Hwy

Mokulele Hwy

Kealia Pond

MAUI

Maʻalaea
Kihei

ʻAuʻau Channel

Maʻalaea Bay

Papawai Point
McGregor Point

6

Kula

Piʻilani Hwy

Kula Hwy

Keokea

31
Wailea

37
7

Polipoli Spring State Recreation Area

Kealaikahiki Channel

Maluʻaka Beach
3
Makena
ʻUlupalakua Ranch

Puʻu Olai
(360ft)

Molokini Crater
8

10

Big Beach

Puʻu Mahoe
(2660ft)

1790 Lava Flow

ʻAlalakeiki Channel

La Pérouse Bay

1790 Lava Flow

31
Piʻilani Hwy

Kaulana Bay

Luamakika
(1482ft)

Kanapou Bay

Puʻu Moiwi
(1161ft)

Kahoʻolawe

20°30'N

156°30'W

This Is Maui

Admit it – you're grinning already, even before you step on the plane. It starts with the idea of Maui...the anticipation. Maybe you can hear the twang of a steel guitar and feel the balmy breezes. But it's once you arrive that the real thrill begins.

The beaches themselves would be reason enough for all this excitement.
Maui's entire west coast is fringed with golden sands, some backed by resorts, some full of beach towels and boogie boards, others as naked as the day they were born.

Maui boasts world-class conditions for anything that involves a wave.
Yet each of its shores has a different temperament. You can ride monster breaks if you're a pro or learn to surf in gentle waves if you're not. Snorkel with sea turtles. Kayak with dolphins. Pin a sail to your board and fly with the wind.

Exploring on land is equally awesome.
Strap on a pair of boots and hike the crunchy moonscape surface of the world's largest dormant volcano. Twist your way along the jungly cliff-hugging Hana Hwy, soaking up waterfalls and swimming holes. Or take it airborne on an adrenaline-charged swoop down Hawaii's longest zipline.

Diversity is a big part of the allure.
Maui's resorts are world-renowned. Out of the limelight but equally worthy are the cozy B&Bs, offering the opportunity to experience island life up close. As for the food scene, it's proudly locavore from the fresh catch reeled in by Hana fishers to the grass-fed beef raised in Upcountry pastures. Foodies could spend their whole vacation touring farms and dining at chef-driven restaurants.

A harborful of sailboats offers more splashy fun.
Take a sunset cruise, sail to a sunken volcano, see humpback whales eye to eye. And just in case your thirst for adventure or quietude is so great that not even Maui can slake it, a quick leap across the channel delivers you into the arms of Maui's smaller siblings, Lana'i and Moloka'i.

> **"**
> You can ride monster breaks or learn to surf in gentle waves
> **"**

Ka'anapali Beach (p65)
ANN CECIL/LONELY PLANET IMAGES ©

West Maui

Side Trips:
Lana'i &
Moloka'i   p233

'Iao Valley &
Central Maui

p57

Road to Hana

p31   p91   p145   p199

Lahaina

p217

Kihei & South Maui   p115   p175   Hana & East Maui

North Shore & Upcountry   Haleakalā National Park

Contents

Plan Your Trip

On the Road

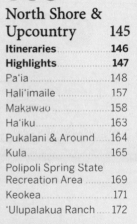

D0395689

Discover

Contents

Maui

Throughout this book, we use these icons to highlight special recommendations:

The Best...
Lists for everything from beaches to wildlife – to make sure you don't miss out

 Local experts reveal their top picks and secret highlights

Detour
Special places a little off the beaten track

These icons help you quickly identify reviews in the text and on the maps:

Beaches

Eating

Sights

Drinking

Sleeping

Information

This edition written and researched by

Glenda Bendure, Ned Friary, Amy C Balfour

Our Story

A beat-up old car, a few dollars in the pocket and a sense of adventure. In 1972 that's all Tony and Maureen Wheeler needed for the trip of a lifetime – across Europe and Asia overland to Australia. It took several months, and at the end – broke but inspired – they sat at their kitchen table writing and stapling together their first travel guide, *Across Asia on the Cheap*. Within a week they'd sold 1500 copies. Lonely Planet was born.

Today, Lonely Planet has offices in Melbourne, London and Oakland, with more than 600 staff and writers. We share Tony's belief that 'a great guidebook should do three things: inform, educate and amuse'.

Our Writers

NED FRIARY

Coordinating author, 'Iao Valley & Central Maui, North Shore & Upcountry, Haleakalā National Park, Road to Hana, Hana & East Maui, Side Trips: Lana'i & Moloka'i, Maui Today, History, Family Travel, Directory & Transport Ned first experienced Maui after a long teaching stint in the urban jungle of Osaka, Japan. So taken by the splendor of these tropical islands, Ned, along with Glenda, went on to author Lonely Planet's first Hawaii guidebook. He's gone back to Maui to work on Lonely Planet guides scores of times since, exploring the island from the depths of Molokini to the summit of Haleakalā. Maui's raw natural beauty, creative energy and emphasis on the outdoors, plus the organic and the ecofriendly, never fail to inspire.

GLENDA BENDURE

Coordinating author, 'Iao Valley & Central Maui, North Shore & Upcountry, Haleakalā National Park, Road to Hana, Hana & East Maui, Side Trips: Lana'i & Moloka'i, Maui Today, History, Family Travel, Directory & Transport Glenda has been a frequent visitor to Hawaii for nearly three decades. She loves digging into each island, driving the roads, hiking the trails, snorkeling the waters and tasting everything there is to taste till the *poke* bowl is empty. But if you're a first-time visitor to Hawaii and ask her which island you should choose, she'll point to Maui every time. Together she and Ned wrote the first five editions of Lonely Planet's *Hawaii*, and authored the previous edition of Lonely Planet's *Maui*.

AMY C BALFOUR

Lahaina, West Maui, Kihei & South Maui, The People of Maui, Hawaii's Cuisine, Hawaiian Arts & Crafts, Green Maui, Outdoor Adventures Amy first visited Hawaii as a toddler. According to family lore she was so happy to arrive, she 'sprinkled' all over the customs agent. For this book, she zipped down the West Maui mountains, clutched the wheel on the Kahekili Hwy, sunset-cruised off Ka'anapali, snapped photos of a roaring blowhole, snorkeled beside a green turtle, hiked a jungly mountain trail and enjoyed her most decadent Thanksgiving dinner ever – a no-worries feast at the Ka'anapali Beach Hotel. Amy has worked on nine books for Lonely Planet, including *Los Angeles Encounter*, *California*, *Caribbean Islands* and *Arizona*.

Published by Lonely Planet Publications Pty Ltd
ABN 36 005 607 983
1st edition – Sep 2011
ISBN 978 1 74220 448 2
© Lonely Planet 2011   Photographs © as indicated 2011
10 9 8 7 6 5 4 3 2 1
Printed in China

How to Use This Book

These symbols will help you find the listings you want:

- 🏖 Beaches
- ◉ Sights
- ⊕ Activities
- ⊖ Courses
- 📷 Tours
- 🎉 Festivals & Events
- 🛏 Sleeping
- 🍴 Eating
- 🍷 Drinking
- 🎭 Entertainment
- 🛍 Shopping
- ℹ Information/Transport

These symbols give you the vital information for each listing:

- ☏ Telephone Numbers
- ⊙ Opening Hours
- P Parking
- ⊖ Nonsmoking
- ✳ Air-Conditioning
- @ Internet Access
- 🛜 Wi-Fi Access
- 🏊 Swimming Pool
- 🥗 Vegetarian Selection
- 📖 English-Language Menu
- 👪 Family-Friendly
- 🐾 Pet-Friendly
- 🚌 Bus
- 🚢 Ferry
- M Metro
- S Subway
- ⊖ London Tube
- 🚋 Tram
- 🚆 Train

Reviews are organised by author preference.

Look out for these icons:

- **FREE** No payment required
- 🌿 A green or sustainable option

Our authors have nominated these places as demonstrating a strong commitment to sustainability – for example by supporting local communities and producers, operating in an environmentally friendly way, or supporting conservation projects.

Map Legend

Sights
- ◉ Beach
- ◉ Buddhist
- ◉ Castle
- ◉ Christian
- ◉ Hindu
- ◉ Islamic
- ◉ Jewish
- ◉ Monument
- ◉ Museum/Gallery
- ◉ Ruin
- ◉ Winery/Vineyard
- ◉ Zoo
- ◉ Other Sight

Activities, Courses & Tours
- ◉ Diving/Snorkelling
- ◉ Canoeing/Kayaking
- ◉ Skiing
- ◉ Surfing
- ◉ Swimming/Pool
- ◉ Walking
- ◉ Windsurfing
- ◉ Other Activity/Course/Tour

Sleeping
- ◉ Sleeping
- ◉ Camping

Eating
- ◉ Eating

Drinking
- ◉ Drinking
- ◉ Cafe

Entertainment
- ◉ Entertainment

Shopping
- ◉ Shopping

Information
- ☺ Post Office
- ℹ Tourist Information

Transport
- ✈ Airport
- ⊗ Border Crossing
- 🚌 Bus
- ⊕ Cable Car/Funicular
- ◉ Cycling
- ◉ Ferry
- Ⓜ Metro
- ⊕ Monorail
- P Parking
- S S-Bahn
- ◉ Taxi
- ◉ Train/Railway
- ◉ Tram
- ◉ Tube Station
- Ⓤ U-Bahn
- • Other Transport

Routes
- Tollway
- Freeway
- Primary
- Secondary
- Tertiary
- Lane
- Unsealed Road
- Plaza/Mall
- Steps
- Tunnel
- Pedestrian Overpass
- Walking Tour
- Walking Tour Detour
- Path

Boundaries
- International
- State/Province
- Disputed
- Regional/Suburb
- Marine Park
- Cliff
- Wall

Population
- ◉ Capital (National)
- ◉ Capital (State/Province)
- ◉ City/Large Town
- ◉ Town/Village

Geographic
- ◉ Hut/Shelter
- ◉ Lighthouse
- ◉ Lookout
- ▲ Mountain/Volcano
- ◉ Oasis
- ◉ Park
-)(Pass
- ◉ Picnic Area
- ◉ Waterfall

Hydrography
- River/Creek
- Intermittent River
- Swamp/Mangrove
- Reef
- Canal
- Water
- Dry/Salt/Intermittent Lake
- Glacier

Areas
- Beach/Desert
- Cemetery (Christian)
- Cemetery (Other)
- Park/Forest
- Sportsground
- Sight (Building)
- Top Sight (Building)

Tours

000 Map pages

Sleeping

Road to Hana

Ready for an adventure? Of all the heart-stoppingly dramatic drives in Hawaii, this is the Big Kahuna. A roller-coaster of a ride, the Hana Hwy (p202) winds down into jungly valleys and back up towering cliffs, curling around 600 twists and turns along the way. Some 54 one-lane bridges cross nearly as many waterfalls – some of them eye-popping torrents and others so gentle they beg a dip. But the ride's only half the thrill. Get out and swim in a Zen-like pool, stroll a ginger scented trail and explore the wonders along the way.

Haleakalā National Park

Picture yourself huddled at predawn, blanket wrapped around you in the frozen air, surrounded by hundreds of people. Everything seems surreal and there's a sense that something unworldly is about to unfold. Then a soft, orange glow pierces the darkness on the summit. Rich tones of amber and ocher light up on the crater floor below (p189), inviting exploration.

Snorkeling at Maluʻaka Beach

Don your mask and snorkel on the shores of stunning Maluʻaka Beach (p139) in Makena and start swimming in the direction of the tour boats. Before you get halfway you'll likely spot a magnificent green sea turtle nibbling algae on the ocean floor. Welcome to 'Turtle Beach' – where the underwater scenery is nothing short of mesmerizing.

'Iao Valley State Park

Nowhere is Maui's verdant, moody beauty better captured than at 'Iao Valley (p109), where the 'Iao Needle – a phallic-shaped, emerald-green pinnacle – shoots straight up from the valley floor. The pinnacle is the centerpiece of this mystical state park. Snuggled sensuously into deep folds of lush rain-forested mountains, 'Iao is such a sumptuous sight it's easy to understand why Hawaiian kings placed a kapu (taboo) on the valley, forbidding commoners from laying eyes on it. Luckily for you, the kapu has been lifted. You brought your camera, right?

4

The Best...
Hikes

SLIDING SANDS (KEONEHE'EHE'E) TRAIL
You'll think you're walking on the moon on this descent into Haleakalā Crater. (p184)

WAIHE'E RIDGE TRAIL
Provides the kind of breathtaking views you'd expect to see from a helicopter. (p89)

PIPIWAI TRAIL
Cascading waterfalls and bamboo forest entice hikers on this rainforest walk. (p195)

HONOLUA RIDGE & MAHANA RIDGE TRAILS
Combines a scenic mountain ridge with a trek back to the coast. (p81)

SKYLINE TRAIL
A daylong descent from the summit of Haleakalā through a dreamy cloud forest. (p187)

Old Lahaina Luau  5

They had us at aloha, but who are we to refuse the cool mai tai and sweet-smelling lei that followed? At Maui's most authentic luau (Hawaiian feast; p52), Hawaiian history, culture and culinary prowess are the focus, presented like a gift from the most hospitable of hosts. Highlights? The unearthing of the *imu*-cooked pig, the dancing of the *hula kahiko* and, of course, the savoring of the feast – a spread of hearty salads, fresh fish, and grilled and roasted meats. But it's the sense of shared community that will linger longest in your memory.

GREG ELMS/LONELY PLANET IMAGES ©

GREG ELMS/LONELY PLANET IMAGES ©

6 Whale Watching

Seems humpback whales find Maui romantic, too. Every winter, thousands of them frolic off Maui's western coast, courting, mating, calving and breaching. If you're in Maui at the same time, treat yourself to a whale-watching cruise. Whales are also readily spotted from cliffside lookouts such as Papawai Point (p65), from west-facing beaches and from your oceanfront condo – just about any place will do. Snorkelers and divers who stick their heads underwater at the right time can even hear them singing: love songs, we presume!

Upcountry Drive

Upcountry (p165) bursts to the brim with rolling pastures and bountiful gardens. This region supplies Maui's locavore cuisine and is heaven to foodies. Sample cheeses at Surfing Goat Dairy, munch on scones at Ali'i Kula Lavender, sip Maui-grown coffee at Grandma's Coffee House, join a pick-your-own organic lunch tour at O'o Farm then visit Tedeschi Vineyards and raise a toast to green Maui.

Jacaranda trees, Kula

Diving Molokini Crater

Hawaiian legend says that Molokini (p303) was a beautiful woman turned to stone by a jealous Pele, the goddess of fire and volcanoes. Today Molokini is the stuff of legends in the diving community. The crescent-shaped rock, which sits about three miles from the South Maui coast, is the rim of a volcanic crater. The shallow waters cradled within are a hospitable spot for coral and a calling card for more than 250 fish species. For an iconic Hawaiian dive, this is the place.

Pi'ilanihale Heiau

Standing in front of Hawaii's largest temple (p213) – five stories high – it's impossible not to feel dwarfed by the scale. The remote setting on a windswept coast adds to the sense of being in a sacred place. Be still. You can almost hear the footsteps of the ancients and see the high priest walking up the terraced stone steps to offer sacrifices to the gods. The surrounding Polynesian gardens – swaying coconut palms, sturdy breadfruit trees – add depth to the vision of how it must have looked centuries ago.

The Best...
Ocean Adventures

DIVING AT MOLOKINI
The crystal waters of this submerged volcano teem with all manner of sea creatures. (p303)

KAYAKING AT MAKENA BAY
A paddle here takes you through waters frequented by humpback whales. (p130)

SNORKELING AT MALU'AKA BEACH
See for yourself why this pretty strand is dubbed 'Turtle Beach.' (p138)

WINDSURFING AT KANAHA BEACH PARK
This windward beach shimmers with sailriders. (p94)

SURFING AT HONOLUA BAY
Like O'ahu's famed North Shore, Honolua Bay is a surfer's dream. (p80)

STAND UP PADDLE BOARDING IN WAILEA
The latest craze on Maui. (p133)

Big Beach (Oneloa), Makena State Park

Close your eyes and conjure up the idyllic Hawaiian beach. An endless expanse of gleaming sands, no development in sight, unbelievably blue water, a surfer scanning for the next perfect wave. Open your eyes – you're at Big Beach (p139), the heart of Makena State Park. If one beach captures the spirit of Maui, this is it: wild, vast and in a completely natural state. But unvisited, no. This is where Mauians come to celebrate Maui the way it used to be. Join them. Worship the waves. Applaud the sunsets. Big Beach is big enough for everyone.

The Best...
Views

10

11 Hoʻokipa & Paʻia

If you're on the pro windsurfing circuit, meet your buddies at Hoʻokipa Beach Park (p148). The rest of us can grab a voyeur's seat on the adjacent hillside and watch the death-defying action. Want the ultimate North Shore experience? Follow Hoʻokipa's windsurfing theatrics by immersing yourself in the funky vibe of nearby Paʻia (p148). Maui's hippest burg, hang-loose Paʻia, will woo you with artsy shops, cool surfer haunts and the island's hottest cafe scene. You could bump into just about anyone here, from Willie Nelson to the Dalai Lama. Windsurfer, Hoʻokipa Beach Park

Masters of Hawaiian Slack Key Guitar Concert Series

You'll feel like you're part of a family jam session at this intimate slack key guitar concert series (p78). Slack key tuning, with its simultaneous playing of bass and melody, virtually defines Hawaiian music. The host, Grammy Award–winning musician George Kahumoku Jr, interweaves the music with an upbeat banter on growing up, Hawaiian-style. The weekly guest list features some of the finest slack key guitar players on the planet.

SEIDEN ALLAN/PHOTOLIBRARY

Surfing West Maui

This is Hawaii, of course you're going to catch some waves. The best part is, you don't have to be Laird Hamilton to enjoy the Maui surf. Just stick to Lahaina and West Maui, where the waves are more accessible, and you'll be hanging 10 in no time. Up-and-at-'em surf schools cluster near Kamehameha Iki Park (p42) in Lahaina, ready to launch newbies on easy waves beside the breakwall. Got your surf legs? Head to Launiupoko Beach Park (p60) for a picture-perfect day. Surfer, Honolua Bay (p80)

Waiheʻe Ridge Trail

Hiking doesn't get much better than the Waiheʻe Ridge Trail (p89), an inviting footpath that climbs the rugged green slopes of the West Maui Mountains. The trail is alternately covered and exposed, winding through a dense grove of guava trees before darting up a grassy ridgeline with birds-eye views of cloud-topped peaks and overgrown valleys. After 2.5 miles of gentle climbing, the lonely summit is a sweet reward.

DEBRA BEHR/ALAMY

Sunset Cruise

No one likes a braggart, but every now and then it's OK to sit back, smile and say, 'Life is good.' A sunset catamaran cruise (p67) off the Ka'anapali coast is one of those times. The two-hour tour launches from shore and sets a course along the coast, following the winds and the views. The best tours include tropical drinks, hearty appetizers and cheerful crews who really seem to care that you have a good time. As the coastline turns rugged and Lana'i slips past, lean into the breeze, shake off your cares and toast your undeniable good fortune. Ka'anapali Beach (p65)

The Best...
Local Cuisine

ALOHA MIXED PLATE
Affordable local fare pairs with a million-dollar view at this seaside eatery. (p47)

CAFÉ O'LEI
Order the blackened mahi-mahi with papaya salsa and just see if you can resist coming back the next day. (p127)

DA KITCHEN
Maui's ultimate plate lunch joint dishes up carb-loaded plates with two-scoop rice. (p99)

SAM SATO'S
It's all about the noodles at this quintessential local eatery. (p106)

BRUDDAH HUTT'S BBQ
You'll feel like you're at an aloha picnic at this outdoor barbecue in Hana. (p226)

Maui's
Top Itineraries

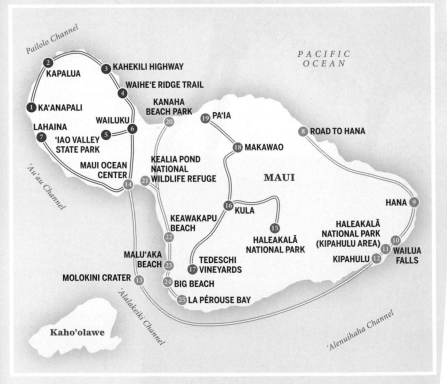

Pailolo Channel

PACIFIC
OCEAN

2 **KAPALUA**

3 **KAHEKILI HIGHWAY**

WAIHE'E RIDGE TRAIL

4

1 **KA'ANAPALI**

**KANAHA
BEACH PARK**

LAHAINA

WAILUKU

20

19 **PA'IA**

8 **ROAD TO HANA**

7

**'IAO VALLEY
STATE PARK**

5

6

18 **MAKAWAO**

**MAUI OCEAN
CENTER**

**KEALIA POND
NATIONAL
WILDLIFE REFUGE**

MAUI

14

21

HANA **9**

16 **KULA**

**KEAWAKAPU
BEACH**

15

**HALEAKALĀ
NATIONAL PARK
(KIPAHULU AREA)**

22

**HALEAKALĀ
NATIONAL PARK**

10

**MALU'AKA
BEACH**

**TEDESCHI
VINEYARDS**

KIPAHULU

11

**WAILUA
FALLS**

12

MOLOKINI CRATER

13

23

17

24 **BIG BEACH**

25 **LA PÉROUSE BAY**

'Au'au Channel

'Alalakeiki Channel

Kaho'olawe

'Alenuihaha Channel

● **Ka'anapali to Lahaina** Four days
● **Road to Hana to Ma'alaea** Six days
● **Haleakalā National Park to Pa'ia** Eight days
● **Kanaha Beach Park to La Pérouse Bay** Ten days

Ka'anapali to Lahaina

Ka'anapali Beach (p65)

ANN CECIL/LONELY PLANET IMAGES ©

4 DAYS

❶ Ka'anapali (p64)
Plunge into Maui with a plunge into the sea at **Ka'anapali Beach**. Snorkel out to **Pu'u Keka'a** (Black Rock) to check out Maui's dazzling underwater scenery.

❷ Kapalua (p79)
Start day two over chocolate macnut pancakes at the **Gazebo** restaurant in Napili. Next delve into Kapalua's menu of adventures that range from **arboretum hikes** to **zipline** leaps. In the afternoon, swimmers should head to **Kapalua Bay**, bodysurfers to **DT Fleming Beach**.

❸ Kahekili Hwy (p85)
It's time to hit the road with an adventurous drive around the northern tip of Maui. Seek out **Nakalele Blowhole**, and don't miss **Ohai Viewpoint**.

❹ Waihe'e Ridge Trail (p89)
In the afternoon lace up your hiking boots. Lofty mountain views and waterfalls are just starters on this ridge trail that goes deep into the West Maui Mountains

❺ 'Iao Valley State Park (p109)
This oh-so-pretty park offers cool streams, misty mountains and Maui's emerald jewel, the 'Iao Needle.

❻ Wailuku (p106)
Follow 'Iao's tasty views with a tasty meal in Maui's time-honored capital.

❼ Lahaina (p34)
Enjoy a stroll around Maui's captivating old whaling town, loll under the USA's largest banyan tree, and then feast your stomach and your eyes at the **Old Lahaina Luau**.

⟳ THIS LEG: 55 MILES

Road to Hana to Ma'alaea

6 DAYS

Honomanu Bay (p206), Road to Hana

GREG ELMS/LONELY PLANET IMAGES ©

8 Road to Hana (p202)

Take off on the most magical drive in all Hawaii, with waterfalls and lush scenery galore. Swing down to **Ke'anae Peninsula**, be humbled by Hawaii's largest temple at **Kahanu Garden** and unwind on **Wai'anapanapa State Park**'s beach.

9 Hana (p220)

This wide spot in the road is well worth a poke around. Enjoy lunch at **Bruddah Hutt's BBQ** and a visit to Hana's museum. Then keep moving – there's still lots to see!

10 Wailua Falls (p228)

This roadside cascade is a top contender for Maui's most gorgeous waterfall.

11 Haleakalā National Park (p194)

(Kipahulu area) The road continues to **'Ohe'o Gulch** with its 24 pools, each backed by its own little waterfall. Make time to hike to the 200ft plunge of **Makahiku Falls**.

12 Kipahulu (p229)

Seek out the grave of aviator Charles Lindbergh before heading off on the Pi'ilani Hwy for a romp through cowboy country.

13 Molokini Crater (p303)

On day six, dive into the pristine waters of this sunken crater that harbors brilliant fish and coral.

14 Maui Ocean Center (p111)

Right where the Molokini boat docks sits one of the finest tropical aquariums on the planet. Go and identify all those colorful fish you've just seen.

🔶 **THIS LEG: 130 MILES**

Haleakalā National Park to Paʻia

Haleakalā National Park (p178)

JOHN ELK III/LONELY PLANET IMAGES ©

⑮ Haleakalā National Park (p178)

Grab a coat and picnic lunch, and head out early (3am!) to catch the sunrise atop this magnificent volcano. Follow with a hike into the belly of the beast and climb around those cool cinder cones.

⑯ Kula (p165)

On the way down the mountain, stop at **Sunrise Country Market** and see how many varieties of protea flowers you can count in its garden. For Upcountry's sweetest green scene, wind over to **Aliʻi Kula Lavender** and munch on lavender scones as you soak up the rainbow-lit coastal views.

⑰ Tedeschi Vineyards (p173)

Let the heady scent of fermenting grapes fill your head on a winery tour at 'Ulupalakua Ranch. Follow with a swagger over to the tasting room to swig the final products.

⑱ Makawao (p158)

Browse the *paniolo*-meets-Picasso shops in this artsy cowboy town. Then enjoy a melt-in-your-mouth cream puff from **Komoda Store & Bakery**.

⑲ Paʻia (p148)

Surfer culture, hip cafes and the island's coolest shops await in this former plantation town. The best place to begin is at **Hoʻokipa Beach Park**, watching pro windsurfers rip on wicked waves.

⏩ THIS LEG: 65 MILES

10 DAYS

Keawakapu Beach (p118)

GREG ELMS/LONELY PLANET IMAGES ©

⑳ Kanaha Beach Park (p94)

When the wind picks up it's show time! A circus parade of rainbow sails whips across the bay as kitesurfers strut their stuff. It's mind-blowing to watch, and there are instructors waiting right on the beach if *you're* ready to fly.

㉑ Kealia Pond National Wildlife Refuge (p110)

Take a walk on the wild side, getting up close to rare waterbirds along a half-mile boardwalk over marsh and dunes.

㉒ Keawakapu Beach (p118)

The star of Kihei's many beaches, this soft-sand beauty is tops for long swims.

㉓ Malu'aka Beach (p139)

Slip on a snorkel and swim out to the coral gardens to discover why this one's dubbed Turtle Beach: green sea turtles munch away on the bottom as you swim past.

㉔ Big Beach (Oneloa; p139)

Pack a picnic – once you get to this magnificent stretch of untouched beach you won't want to leave. But it's OK: you can swing back by to catch one of the best sunsets Maui has to offer after you finish driving south.

㉕ La Pérouse Bay (p142)

The day's sightseeing ends at the road's end. Breathe in the wild windswept scenery. Clamber over twisted lava flows. Now go back for that Big Beach sunset.

⊙ THIS LEG: 40 MILES

Get Inspired

 ## Books

o **Middle Son** (2000) Deborah Iida describes 1950s Maui through the eyes of a sugar plantation laborer.

o **Maui** (2000) A stunning photo book from famed Pacific photographer Doug Peebles.

 ## Films

o **The Devil at 4 O'Clock** (1961) Spencer Tracy and Frank Sinatra hang out at Lahaina's Pioneer Inn.

o **50 First Dates** (2003) Drew Barrymore and Adam Sandler get lovey-dovey on Maui.

o **Hereafter** (2011) Clint Eastwood's film shot scenes on Lahaina's Front St.

♫ Music

o **Maui On My Mind** (2010) Jeff Peterson, with cowboy roots in the Upcountry, took Hawaii's 2010 Hoku Award for Best Slack Key Album.

o **Peace Love Ukulele** (2011) Hot uke whiz Jake Shimabukuro takes ukulele to the next level.

o **Ke'alaokamaile** (2003) One of the finest of many albums from Maui-born singer, chanter and hula teacher Keali'i Reichel.

o **Hapa** (1992) Let the Maui duo Hapa woo you with beautiful harmonies, including the classic *Haleakalā Ku Hanohano*.

 ## Websites

o **Maui Visitors Bureau** (www.gohawaii.com/maui) Pretty pictures on the official tourist office site.

o **Maui News** (www.mauinews.com) Maui's main daily newspaper has a visitors guide.

o **Maui Web Cams** (www.mauihawaii.org/webcams) Check out the beach scene live.

o **KPOA Radio** (www.kpoa.com) Listen to live streaming of Hawaiian music, Maui style.

 ## Short on time?

This list will give you an instant insight into Maui.

Read *The Wave* (2010), where Susan Casey chronicles Laird Hamilton's big wave riding on Maui.

Watch *Ho'okolo Wa'a: Turning the Canoe* (2010) by Danny Miller showcases Maui's environmental movement.

Listen *Legends of Hawaiian Slack Key Guitar – Live From Maui* (2007) won George Kahumoku Jr a Grammy for slack key guitar album of the year.

Log-on Whalesong Project (www.whalesong.net) lets you listen to humpback whales along Maui's shores.

Surfer, Jaws (p153)
PHOTO RESOURCE HAWAII/ALAMY

Maui Month by Month

January

⭐ Hyundai Tournament of Champions

In this season opener (p83) for the PGA tour in early January, the prior year's champions tee-off in Kapalua for a multi-million dollar purse.

February

Between December and April, about 10,000 humpback whales converge along the West Maui coast to breed and give birth in the shallow waters. February is the best month to view them.

🐋 Whale Day Celebration

A whale of a bash, this parade and beachside celebration (p122) in Kihei in mid-February honors Maui's favorite winter visitor – the splashy North Pacific humpback whale.

April

🐋 Banyan Tree Birthday Party

Celebrate Maui's most renowned tree with a wild birthday party (p44) under its sprawling branches, which cover an entire square. Held on the weekend closest to April 24.

✕ East Maui Taro Festival

Hana, Maui's most Hawaiian town, throws the island's most Hawaiian party (p224) in late April, with everything from hula dances and a topnotch Hawaiian music festival to a demo for carving a poi pounder.

Top Events

🐋 **Whale Day Celebration**
February

✕ **East Maui Taro Festival** April

⭐ **Maui Film Festival** June

⭐ **Ki Hoʻalu Slack Key Guitar Festival** June

🐋 **Halloween in Lahaina** October

Maui Film Festival
PHOTOGRAPHER: RANDY JAY BRAUN/MAUI FILM FESTIVAL

May

 Maui Onion Festival

Whalers Village in Ka'anapali hosts this festival (p68) celebrating Maui's famous pungent bulb. The mighty onion takes center stage in cooking events and raw-onion-eating contests (gasp) on the first weekend of May.

June

 Maui Film Festival

In mid-June, movie lovers gather in Wailea (p135), where the golf course is transformed into the 'Celestial Theater' and Hollywood stars show up for added bling.

 Kapalua Wine & Food Festival

Hawaii's hottest chefs vie for attention in this culinary extravaganza of cooking demonstrations and wine tasting (p83) in late June.

 Ki Ho'alu Slack Key Guitar Festival

Slack key guitar music doesn't get any better than this. The event (p98), held in late June, brings in all the big-name players from throughout the state. Plan to spend the day at the Maui Arts & Cultural Center in Kahului.

July

 Makawao Rodeo & Panioli Parade

Roping contests, daredevil bull-riding events and a colorful parade showcase Upcountry's *paniolo* (cowboy) past on the weekend closest to Independence Day (p160).

 Lana'i Pineapple Festival

Pineapples, the symbol of hospitality, are feted on the island of Lana'i on the weekend of July 4 (p239) with live music, hula dances, fireworks and cooking contests.

September

 Maui County Fair

Maui is a garden land, so it's no surprise that its old-fashioned agricultural fair (p104) in late September is a bountiful event with orchids, luscious produce and all sorts of good food.

October

 Halloween in Lahaina

Lahaina hosts Maui's biggest street festival (p55) on Halloween night, attracting a whopping 20,000 revelers with music, dancing and costume contests.

November

 Hula O Na Keiki

Talented *keiki* (children) are the headliners at this annual hula and chant competition (p68) held at the Ka'anapali Beach Hotel in mid-November, with arts and crafts and workshops.

December

 Holiday Lighting of the Banyan Tree

On the first weekend of December, Lahaina illuminates America's oldest banyan tree with thousands of bright, colorful holiday lights (p45). Even Santa stops by for this one.

Need to Know

Language
English, Hawaiian

ATMs
In banks, some groceries, shopping malls and convenience stores.

Credit Cards
Visa and MasterCard widely accepted.

Visas
Generally not required for stays of up to 90 days.

Cell Phones
Use GSM 1900 or CDMA 800; frequencies differ from other countries. Only tri- or quad-ban models work in US.

Wi-Fi
Common in midrange and top-end hotels; available in some condo units. Free with purchase at many cafes and at most McDonald's.

Internet Access
Most towns have cafes offering internet for about $3 for 20 minutes. Available at libraries with a $10 non-resident library card.

Tipping
15-20% for restaurant waitstaff; 15% for taxi drivers; $2 per bag at airports and hotels.

When to Go

Tropical climate, wet & dry seasons

Lahaina
GO Dec-Apr

Pa'ia
GO all year

Hana
GO all year

Kihei
GO all year

Haleakalā
National Park
GO all year

High Season
(mid-Dec– mid-Apr)
- Highest accommodation prices
- Coincides with Christmas holidays
- Prices stay high through whale season

Shoulder
(Jun–Aug)
- Coincides with school vacation schedules
- Book rental car early; fleets may be reduced

Low Season
(Apr & May, Sep–mid-Dec)
- Between whale season and summer
- Slow between Thanksgiving and Christmas
- Look for online specials and cheap airfares

Advance Planning

- **Three months before** Make flight and hotel reservations, particularly if arriving over the holidays, during whale season or the weekend of a big event (watch out for those golf tournaments!).

- **One month before** Secure reservations for popular activities, such as a whale-watching cruise, outrigger canoe tour or the Old Lahaina Luau.

- **One week before** Make fine-dining reservations, particularly during the holidays. It's also a good idea to make reservations for popular activities such as ziplining or a guided tour of the Road to Hana.

Your Daily Budget

Budget less than $150
- B&B or inn within a town: $80–100
- Excellent groceries for do-it-yourself meals; fast food
- Walking tour, lazy beach days
- Maui Bus

Midrange $150–350
- Hotel room or condo: $100–275
- Rental car: $40–50
- Good midrange restaurant
- Snorkeling, hiking, scenic drives

Top End over $350
- Hotel or resort from $275
- Rental car: $60–75
- Three-course meal in top restaurant
- Diving, ziplining, spa treatment, sunset cruise

Exchange Rates

Australia	A$1	$0.99
Canada	C$1	$1.01
Europe (euro)	€1	$1.32
Japan	Y100	$1.20
New Zealand	NZ$1	$0.76
UK	£1	$1.55

For current exchange rates see www.xe.com

What to Bring
- **Sunscreen & hat** It's the tropics baby! It's also usually sunny, so be kind to your skin.
- **Snorkel, mask & fins** There's fantastic snorkelling from Makena north to Kapalua.
- **Binoculars** You'll want them for roadside whale watching in winter.
- **Warm jacket** It's chilly on top of Haleakalā all day, but downright frigid before sunrise.
- **Hiking boots or shoes with good traction** Jungle-like trails are often slick with rain and mushy fruit.

Arriving on Maui
- **Kahului International Airport**

Private shuttle To Kihei $31–35, Lahaina $45–50.

Taxi To Kihei/Lahaina from $35/75.

Rental car $40–80 per day; rental booths at airport.

Maui Bus Upcountry Islander 40 and Haiku Islander 35 stop at airport. Transfers required for West and South Maui. $1 per ride.

Getting Around
- **Rental car** Due to limited public transportation, renting a car is recommended. Major rental companies are located at Kahului Airport.
- **Maui Bus Public** Bus provides daily service to limited destinations within and between cities in Central, West and South Maui and Upcountry; $1 per trip.
- **Resort shuttles** Complimentary; run regularly within most major resort areas.
- **Taxis** Cluster near malls and shopping areas but don't expect to flag one down on the street. Drop charge $3.50, additional miles $3 per mile.

Accommodations
- **B&Bs & inns** Homes or small lodgings. Owner usually lives on-site. Fruit, pastries and bread are typically served for breakfast.
- **Condominiums** Individually owned units grouped in one complex. Typically include a full kitchen.
- **Hotels** Price is usually based on room size and view, with bigger rooms and full ocean views garnering top rates.
- **Resorts** Sprawling complexes, often luxurious, with myriad restaurants, several pools, nightly entertainment and children's programs. Expect daily charges for parking and wi-fi.

Be Forewarned
- **Rental car break-ins** Maui is notorious for smash-and-grabs. Don't leave valuables in the car.
- **Rental car availability** If you see a good rate online before your trip, book the car. Unexpected shortages and rate spikes are not uncommon.

Lahaina

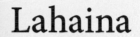

Locals stop to point out rainbows in Lahaina, a one-time whaling village tucked between the West Maui mountains and the ocean, and so inviting that humpback whales return yearly to raise their young. Ancient Hawaiian royals were the first to converge on this sunny spot, followed by whalers and missionaries. Today it's a base for eco-minded chefs, passionate artists and dedicated surf gods willing to share their knowledge with goofy-footed newbies.

Near the harbor, wooden storefronts that once housed saloons, dance halls and brothels are now crammed with art galleries, souvenir shops and, well, still plenty of watering holes. As for the whalers, they've been replaced by a new kind of leviathan hunter: photo-snapping whale watchers as dedicated as Ahab in their search for a spout. Between January and March, they don't have to look very hard.

Lahaina Harbor

31

PHOTOGRAPHER: KORDCOM KORDCOM/PHOTULIBRARY

Lahaina Itineraries

MALA OCEAN TAVERN ⑥
Mala Wharf
① ⑤ OLD LAHAINA LUAU
LAHAINA JODO MISSION ④
Honoapiilani Hwy
Ala Moana St
Lahaina Station
Wainee St
Front St
Lahainaluna Rd
PACIFIC OCEAN
② ⑤ LAHAINALUNA RD
WO HING MUSEUM ③
⑤
⑥ LAHAINA GRILL
• Lahaina
SUNRISE CAFÉ ①
② BALDWIN HOME
④ PACIFIC WHALE FOUNDATION
HARBOR ①
③ BANYAN TREE DELI & BAKERY
Au'au Channel
Shaw St
② SURFING LESSONS

One Day

① **Harbor** (p34) Start the day in the heart of Lahaina at this lively harbor where catamarans jostle for attention, the **Best Western Pioneer Inn** hums with period ambience and the USA's largest banyan tree spreads its branches across **Banyan Tree Sq**.

② **Baldwin Home** (p37) Step into this simple house for scenes from a medical missionary's life then walk to **Hale Pa'ahao** and peer into one of the old prison cells to see where bad-boy whalers did time for breaking the law.

③ **Banyan Tree Deli & Bakery** (p49) For a quick but filling lunch, order a scrumptious pastrami sandwich at this bakery near the harbor.

④ **Pacific Whale Foundation** (p43) Hop aboard a catamaran to see 40-ton humpback whales up close and personal.

⑤ **Lahainaluna Rd** (p34) Back on land, a short walk along shop-lined Front St should include a pause at Lahainaluna Rd. It's a prime spot to watch the sun drop behind Lanai in a blaze of orange and red.

⑥ **Lahaina Grill** (p47) A few more steps will drop you at the doorstep of this sparkling grill, where fine wine, fresh fish and easy conversation make for a memorable meal. And don't skip the triple berry pie.

● THIS LEG: 1 MILE

Two Days

1 **Sunrise Café** (p49) Start your second day with chocolate waffles topped with strawberries and whipped cream. After breakfast, walk behind the cafe to the edge of the point and look down into the ocean. To your right is the mighty **Hauloa Stone**, a chair-shaped rock used as a birthing stone by ancient Hawaiians and considered to have healing powers.

2 **Surfing Lessons** (p42) To learn the Hawaiian art of wave riding, there's no better place to take a lesson than on the gentle waves at the Lahaina Breakwall. Kids will enjoy the courses at Goofy Foot Surf School and bigger folk can get pro tips from former champ Nancy Emerson.

3 **Wo Hing Museum** (p35) After your time in the surf, spend the afternoon browsing the shops and galleries on Front St then step inside this ornate museum to glimpse a 1912 Chinese meeting hall. Black-and-white films shot in Maui by Thomas Edison play in the cookhouse out back.

4 **Lahaina Jodo Mission** (p38) To escape the crowds, head north to this mission, where a meditative 12ft Buddha marks the centennial of Japanese immigration to Hawaii.

5 **Old Lahaina Luau** (p52) Traditional hula dances trace Hawaii's history, and a hearty buffet celebrates its culinary past. Think *kalua* pig, *laulau*, taro salad and lots, lots more.

6 **Mala Ocean Tavern** (p47) Toast your time in Lahaina at this convivial seaside restaurant and bar serving 12 specialty martinis. Cheers!

⊙ THIS LEG: 2.3 MILES

Lahaina Highlights

1 **Best Hawaiian Experience: Old Lahaina Luau** (p52) Celebrate Hawaiian culture with traditional hula, tropical cocktails and a feast fit for kings.

2 **Best View: Seaside Front St** (p34) Dawdling sailboats and a languid Lana'i are the shimmering backdrop.

3 **Best Activity: Whale-watching cruise** (p43) Odds are good that you'll see a whale in winter. Most companies offer a free second chance if you don't.

4 **Best Green Space: Banyan Tree Sq** (p35) Lahaina's landmark banyan is a tree-climber's dream.

5 **Best Fine Dining: Lahaina Grill** (p47) Attentive service, an expansive wine list and exquisitely prepared seafood – *mahalo* (thank you) for the memories.

Dancer, Old Lahaina Luau (p52)
PHOTOGRAPHER: GREG ELMS/LONELY PLANET IMAGES ©

Discover Lahaina

History

In ancient times Lahaina – then known as Lele – housed a royal court for high chiefs and was the breadbasket (or, more accurately, the breadfruit basket) of West Maui. After Kamehameha the Great unified the islands, he chose the area as his base, and the capital remained there until 1845. The first Christian missionaries arrived here in the 1820s and within a decade Hawaii's first stone church, missionary school and printing press were in place.

Lahaina became the dominant port for whalers, not only in Hawaii but in the entire Pacific. The whaling years reached their peak in the 1840s, with hundreds of ships pulling into port each year. When the whaling industry fizzled in the 1860s, Lahaina became all but a ghost town. In the 1870s sugarcane came to Lahaina and it remained the backbone of the economy until tourism took over in the 1960s.

Sights

Lahaina's top sights cluster around the **harbor** (Map p40), with other sights either on Front St or within a few blocks of it. This makes Lahaina an ideal town to explore on foot. The top free sight? The sunset view from Front St, at its intersection with Lahainaluna Rd.

FREE **OLD LAHAINA COURTHOUSE** Museum (Map p40; ☎667-9193; www.visit lahaina.com; 648 Wharf St; ☀9am-5pm) Tucked in the shadows of a banyan tree, Lahaina's 1859 courthouse is a repository of history and art. Its location beside the bustling harbor is no coincidence. Smuggling was so rampant during the whaling era that officials deemed this the ideal spot for customs operations, the courthouse and the jail – all neatly wrapped into a single building. It also held the governor's office, and in 1898 the US annexation of Hawaii was formally concluded here. Gifts and a downtown map are available at the 1st floor **visitor center**.

The basement holds the old jail, now used as a gallery by the **Lahaina Arts Society** (http://lahaina-arts.com; ☀9am-5pm), and the cells that once held drunken sailors now display artwork. The paintings,

Banyan Tree Sq
PHOTOGRAPHER: GREG ELMS/LONELY PLANET IMAGES ©

jewelry and woodwork are creations of island artists who operate the gallery as a cooperative. The entrance to the jail is outside, on the north side of the building.

On the 2nd floor, the **Lahaina Heritage Museum** (Map p40; www.lahainarestoration. org; admission free; ⊙9am-4pm) celebrates the town's culture and history. Changing exhibits might focus on anything from ancient Hawaiian society to 19th-century whaling.

🌿**BANYAN TREE SQUARE**   Park
(Map p40; cnr Front & Hotel Sts) A tree has stature when throngs of citizens gather each year to celebrate its birthday! Marking the center of Lahaina, this awesome banyan tree sprawls across the entire square and ranks as the largest banyan tree in the US. Planted as a seedling on April 24, 1873 to commemorate the 50th anniversary of missionaries in Lahaina, the tree has become a virtual forest unto itself, with 16 major trunks and scores of horizontal branches reaching across the better part of an acre. Tarzan and the Swiss Family Robinson would feel right at home among its aerial roots and sturdy branches. On weekends artists and craftsmen set up booths beneath it.

FORT RUINS   Ruins
(Map p40; cnr Wharf & Canal Sts) A crumbly wall made of coral blocks stands at attention just south of the courthouse – all that remains of a fort built in 1832 to keep rowdy whalers in line. Each day at dusk a Hawaiian sentinel would beat a drum to alert sailors to return to their ships. Stragglers who didn't make it in time were imprisoned here. At the height of its use the fort had some 47 cannons, most salvaged from foreign ships that sank in Lahaina's tricky waters.

When the fort was dismantled in the 1850s, its stone blocks were used to build Hale Pa'ahao, the new prison.

WO HING MUSEUM   Museum
(Map p40; www.lahainarestoration.org/wohing. html; 858 Front St; admission $2; ⊙10am-4pm) Built in 1912 as a meeting hall for the benevolent society Chee Kung Tong,

Local Knowledge

NAME: BRAYZLEE ILIKEA DUTRO

OCCUPATION: HULA DANCER, OLD LAHAINA LUAU

RESIDENCE: LAHAINA

What is hula? Is it entertainment or storytelling? Hula is both...we tell stories with our hand motions. The entertainment part [is] how we do it. How we dance and we smile.

Do the hand motions mean something? When you chant your words, you want to tell your story with your motion that you're doing. Like sometimes, if you go like this [rolls hand] that means it could be the waves.

Why is the kahiko dance your favorite part of the show? You get to do the chanting while you're dancing and while telling your story with your hand motions. And you just get to feel more of the hula.

How is the Old Lahaina Luau different from others? We are a traditional hula show, which means that we don't do any Samoan fire dancing. And we shouldn't because hula and Hawaiians came from Polynesia. We're traditional Hawaiian. We tell the story from the beginning to when the missionaries came.

How long have you been hula dancing? Since I was about four years old.

Is there anything at the Old Lahaina Luau geared to kids? We have three stations. One [has] our different hula instruments, and then we do a little hula lesson afterwards with them. Then we also have another station called the *ahupua'a*, and we teach them about how the Hawaiians...live from the mountains to the sea – who takes care of which part of the land, and what the women did. And then we have...the *'ulu maika*, kind of a rock game and you can roll the rock in between two sticks.

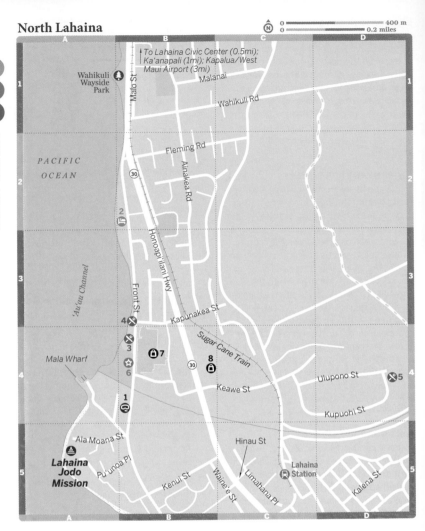

this two-story temple provided Chinese immigrants with a place to preserve their cultural identity, celebrate festivities and socialize in their native tongue. After WWII, Lahaina's ethnic Chinese population spread far and wide and the temple fell into decline. Now restored and turned into a cultural museum, it houses period photos, a ceremonial dancing-lion costume and a Taoist shrine.

Don't miss the tin-roof cookhouse out back, which holds a little theater showing fascinating films of Hawaii shot by Thomas Edison in 1898 and 1906, soon after he invented the motion-picture camera. These grainy black and white shots capture poignant images of old Hawaii, with *paniolo* (Hawaiian cowboys) herding cattle, cane workers in the fields and everyday street scenes. The wall behind the screen holds a collection of opium bottles unearthed during an excavation of the grounds.

North Lahaina

FREE **HALE PA'AHAO**   Museum
(Map p40; www.lahainarestoration.
org/paahao.html; cnr Prison & Waine'e Sts;
⏱10am-4pm Mon-Sat) As far as prisons go,
this stone-walled calaboose doesn't look
too imposing. A remnant of the whaling era, Hale Pa'ahao (Stuck-in-Irons
House) was built in 1852 and looks much
as it did 150 years ago. One of the tiny
cells displays a list of arrests in 1855.
The top three offenses were drunkenness (330 arrests), 'furious riding' (89)
and lascivious conduct (20). There's no
record of how much of that furious riding
might have been done in a drunken state!
Other transgressions of the day included
profanity, aiding deserting sailors and
drinking 'awa (kava).

BALDWIN HOME   Museum
(Map p40; www.lahainarestoration.org/baldwin.
html; 120 Dickenson St; adult $3; ⏱10am-4pm)
Reverend Dwight Baldwin, a missionary
doctor, built this house in 1834, making
it the oldest Western-style building in
Lahaina. It served as both his home and

the community's first medical clinic. The
coral and rock walls are a hefty 24in thick,
which keeps the house cool year-round.
The exterior walls are now plastered over,
but you can get a sense of how they originally appeared by looking at the **Masters'
Reading Room** next door.

It took the Baldwins 161 days to get
here from their native Connecticut, sailing
around Cape Horn at the southern tip of
South America. Dr Baldwin's passport
and Bible are on display, as well as
representative period furniture. A doctor's
'scale of fees' states that $50 was the
price for treating a 'very great sickness',
while a 'very small sickness' cost $10. It's
only a cold, Doc, I swear.

WAINE'E (WAIOLA) CHURCH   Church
(Map p40; 535 Waine'e St) The first stone
church in Hawaii, Waine'e Church was
built in 1832 then hit with a run of bad
luck. In 1858 the belfry collapsed. In 1894
royalists, enraged that the minister supported Hawaii's annexation, torched the
church to the ground. A second church,
built to replace the original, burned in
1947, and the third blew away in a storm a
few years later. One might get the impres-
sion that the old Hawaiian gods didn't
take kindly to the house of this foreign
deity! The fourth version, now renamed
Waiola Church, has stood its ground since
1953 and still holds Sunday services.

The adjacent **cemetery** holds as much
intrigue as the church. Here lie several
notables, including Governor Hoapili,
who ordered the original church built;
Reverend William Richards, Lahaina's first
missionary; and Queen Ke'opuolani, wife
of Kamehameha the Great and mother of
kings Kamehameha II and III.

LIBRARY GROUNDS   Park
(Map p40; 680 Wharf St) Although they don't
reveal themselves at first glance, the
grounds surrounding the library hold
a cluster of historic sites. The yard, for
example, was once a royal taro field where
Kamehameha III toiled in the mud to
instill in his subjects the dignity of labor.

On the ocean side of the library sat the
first Western-style building in Hawaii, the

DISCOVER LAHAINA SIGHTS

Brick Palace, erected by Kamehameha I around 1800 so he could keep watch on arriving ships. Despite the name, this 'palace' was a simple two-story structure built by a pair of ex-convicts from Botany Bay. All that remains is the excavated foundation.

Walk to the northern shoreline and look down. There lies the **Hauola Stone**, a chair-shaped rock that the ancient Hawaiians believed emitted healing powers to those who sat upon it. It sits just above the water's surface, the middle of three lava stones. In the 14th and 15th centuries royal women sat here while giving birth to the next generation of chiefs and royalty.

About 100ft to the south stands the **Lahaina Lighthouse**, the site of the first lighthouse in the Pacific. It was commissioned in 1840 to aid whaling ships pulling into the harbor. The current structure dates from 1916.

FREE **HALE KAHIKO** Cultural Park (Map p40; Lahaina Center, 900 Front St; ⊙9am-6pm) Yep, they paved paradise and put up a parking lot at the Lahaina

Center Mall, but a patch of earth was kindly set aside for Hale Kahiko, an authentic replication of thatched *hale* (houses) found in ancient, pre-Western Hawaiian villages.

The three houses here were hand-constructed true to the period using ohia-wood posts, native pili grass and coconut-fiber lashings. Each replica *hale* depicts a different function: one serves as family sleeping quarters, one as a men's eating house and the third as a workshop where women make tapa (a coarse cloth made from pounded bark). Inside you'll find gourd containers, woven baskets and other essentials of Hawaiian life.

The grounds are planted in native plants that Hawaiians relied upon for food and medicine.

LAHAINA JODO MISSION Mission (Map p36; www.lahainajodomission.org; 12 Ala Moana St; admission free) A 12ft-high bronze Buddha sits serenely in the courtyard at this Buddhist mission, looking across the Pacific toward its Japanese homeland. Cast in Kyoto, the Buddha is the largest of

Buddha statue, Lahaina Jodo Mission

its kind outside Japan and was installed here in 1968 to celebrate the centennial of Japanese immigration to Hawaii. The grounds also hold a 90ft pagoda and a whopping 3.5-ton temple bell, which is rung 11 times each evening at 8pm. Inside the temple are priceless Buddhist paintings by Haijin Iwasaki.

HALE PA'I   Printing Press
(off Map p40; ☏ 667-7040; www.lahaina restoration.org/halepai.html; 980 Lahainaluna Rd; donations appreciated; ⊙ 10am-4pm Mon-Fri) A two-mile drive from downtown Lahaina leads to Hale Pa'i, a white cottage on the grounds of Lahainaluna High School. This small building housed Hawaii's first printing press. Although its primary mission was making the Bible available to Hawaiians, the press also produced, in 1834, Hawaii's first newspaper. Named *Ka Lama* (The Torch), it held the distinction of being the first newspaper west of the Rockies.

So heavily used was the original Rampage Press that it wore out in the 1850s, but several items it printed are on display. There's also an exhibit explaining the history of Hawaii's 12-letter alphabet and a reprint of an amusing 'Temperance Map' ($5), drawn by an early missionary to illustrate the perils of drunkenness. Don't be alarmed if an ear-splitting siren breaks your 1850s reverie; it's not an attack, just the high school's 'bell' for changing classes. The adjacent school was founded in 1831, and students operated the press.

It's wise to call in advance. Hale Pa'i is staffed by volunteers so hours can be iffy.

 **Activities**

Lahaina is not known for its beaches, which are generally shallow and rocky, although it is a good place to take a surf lesson. For swimming and snorkeling, head up the coast to neighboring Ka'anapal. For boat tours, whale watching and other cruises, see p43.

The Best…
Activities for Kids

1 Pacific Whale Foundation cruise (p43)

2 Banyan tree (p35)

3 Old Lahaina Luau (p52)

4 Atlantis Submarine (p43)

5 Sugar Cane Train (p44)

Diving & Snorkeling
Dive boats leave from Lahaina Harbor, offering dives suitable for all levels.

LAHAINA DIVERS   Diving
(Map p40; ☏ 667-7496, 800-998-3483; www. lahainadivers.com; 143 Dickenson St; 2-tank dives from $109; ⊙ store 8am-5pm) Maui's first PADI five-star center offers a full range of dives, from advanced night dives to 'discover scuba' dives for newbies. The latter go to a reef thick with green sea turtles – a great intro to diving.

MAUI DIVE SHOP   Diving, Snorkeling
(Map p36; ☏ 661-5388, 800-542-3483; www. mauidiveshop.com; 315 Keawe St; 2-tank dives from $140; ⊙ 7am-6pm) This full-service operation offers daily scuba and snorkeling trips. Everywhere we went, locals recommended the custom-built *Alii Nui*, Maui Dive Shop's new 65ft catamaran available for small-group snorkeling and sunset excursions (snorkel/sunset $129/99). The company has eight shops across Maui; this branch is located in Lahaina Gateway.

For cheap snorkel-set rentals, try **Snorkel Bob's** (Map p36; ☏ 661-4421; www. snorkelbob.com; 1217 Front St; ⊙ store 8am-5pm).

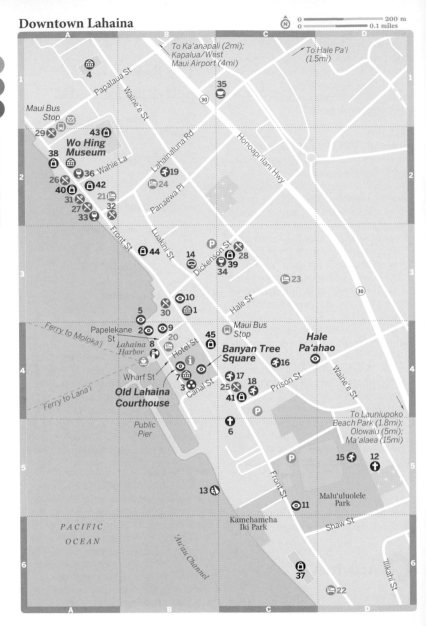

N
0   200 m
0   0.1 miles

To Ka'anapali (2mi);
Kapalua/West
Maui Airport (4mi)

To Hale Pa'i
(1.5mi)

DISCOVER LAHAINA

Maui Bus
Stop

Wo Hing
Museum

Lahainaluna Rd

Honoapi'ilani Hwy

Papalaua St

Waine'e St

Wahie La

Lahainaluna Rd

Panaewa Pl

Front St

Luakini St

Dickenson St

Hale St

Papelekane St

Lahaina
Harbor

Ferry to Moloka'i

Ferry to Lana'i

Hotel St

Wharf St

Old Lahaina
Courthouse

Maui Bus
Stop

Banyan Tree
Square

Hale
Pa'ahao

Canal St

Prison St

Waine'e St

To Launiupoko
Beach Park (1.8mi);
Olowalu (5mi);
Ma'alaea (15mi)

Public
Pier

Front St

Malu'uluolele
Park

PACIFIC
OCEAN

Kamehameha
Iki Park

Shaw St

'Ilikahi St

'Au'au Channel

Kayaking

MAUI KAYAKS   Kayaking
(Map p40; ☎ 874 4000; www.mauikayaks.com;
505 Front St; ⏰ 8am-4pm) This locally owned
operation takes guided kayaking and
kayaking-snorkel tours along the western
coast of Maui ($69 to $139). The Lahaina
Paddle trip doubles as a whale-watching
excursion in season (adult/child 8-11
$69/52). Kayak rentals are also available
(two hours/day $20/35).

Downtown Lahaina

Stand Up Paddle Surfing

Everybody's trying to stand up paddle surf (SUP) these days, as a quick glance at Maui's west coast quickly confirms. Beginners should consider a lesson. The graceful sport – which requires a long-board, a paddle and some balance – is easy to learn, but Maui's currents can be tricky for newcomers.

Maui Wave Riders　　Stand Up Paddle Surfing
(Map p40; ☏875-4761; www.mauiwaveriders. com; 133 Prison St; ☉7am-3pm) Limits class size to six students per instructor. Also offers surfing lessons.

Surfing

Never surfed before? Lahaina is a great place to learn, with first-class instructors, gentle waves and ideal conditions for beginners. The section of shoreline known as **Lahaina Breakwall** (Map p40), north of **Kamehameha Iki Park**, is a favorite spot for novices. Surfers also take to the waters just offshore from Launiupoko Beach Park.

Several companies in Lahaina offer surfing lessons. Most guarantee you'll be able to ride a wave after a two-hour lesson or the class is free. Rates vary depending upon the number of people in the group and the length of the lesson, but for a two-hour class expect to pay about $65 in a small group or $150 for private instruction.

Goofy Foot Surf School   Surfing
(Map p40; ☎244-9283; www.goofyfootsurf school.com; 505 Front St; ☺7am-9pm Mon-Sat, 8am-8pm Sun) This top surf school combines fundamentals with fun. In addition to lessons, it runs day-long surf camps and rents boards to experienced surfers.

**Nancy Emerson's School
of Surfing**   Surfing
(Map p40; ☎244-7873; www.mauisurfclinics. com; Suite 224B, 505 Front St; ☺8am-8pm) The oldest surfing school on the island is owned by Nancy Emerson, who was winning international surfing contests by the time she was 14.

Royal Hawaiian Surf Academy   Surfing
(Map p40; ☎276-7873; www.royalhawaiian surfacademy.com; 117 Prison St; ☺7:30am-5pm) The professionals at Royal Hawaiian were profiled in MTV's brief-run reality show *Living Lahaina*.

Tennis

There are public tennis courts at **Lahaina Civic Center** (off Map p36) and **Malu'uluolele Park** (Map p40). Both have lights to enable night playing.

Left: Surf lessons, Lahaina **Below:** Sugar Cane Train (p44)

PHOTOGRAPHERS: (LEFT) GREG ELMS/LONELY PLANET IMAGES ©;
(BELOW) KARL LEHMANN/LONELY PLANET IMAGES ©

Tours

Ocean Tours

Catamarans and other vessels in Lahaina Harbor cater to the tourist trade, and outfitters staff booths along the harbor's edge. The ferry to Lana'i docks behind the Pioneer Inn. Most companies offer discounts or combo deals on their websites.

PACIFIC WHALE FOUNDATION
Eco-Tour

(Map p40; ☎808-667-7447, 800-942-5311; www.pacificwhale.org; 612 Front St; adult/child 7-12 from $32/16; ☻6am-10pm; 👪) The well-versed naturalists on this nonprofit foundation's cruises are the island's best. Several types of trips, all focusing on Maui's spectacular marine environment, leave from Lahaina Harbor. Immensely popular are the whale-watching cruises, which depart several times a day in winter. In the unlikely event you don't spot whales, your next trip is free.

TOP CHOICE TRILOGY EXCURSIONS
Snorkel Tour

(Map p40; ☎874-5649, 888-225-6284; www.sailtrilogy.com; 180 Lahainaluna Rd; adult/child 3-15 $190/95; ☻7am-7pm) This family-run operation specializes in personable eco-friendly catamaran tours that let you get your feet wet. The early trip (6am to 4pm) from Lahaina to Lana'i's Hulopo'e Beach includes a barbecue lunch and snorkeling time. The 10am boat offers dinner and sails back to Lahaina at sunset. In winter there's whale watching along the way and you can spot spinner dolphins year-round.

ATLANTIS SUBMARINE
Underwater Tour

(☎661-7827, 800-548-6262; www.atlantissubmarines.com; 658 Wharf St; adult/child under 13 $99/45; 👪) Visit a world usually reserved for divers aboard this 65ft sub that dives to a depth of 130ft to see coral, tropical fish and the sunken *Carthaginian*,

43

a sailing brig that played a leading role in the 1965 movie *Hawaii*. Tours depart from 9am to 2pm. Check in at the Wharf St office.

REEFDANCER Glass-Bottom Boat
(📞667-2133; www.mauiglassbottomboat.com; Lahaina Harbor; adult/child 6-12 1hr $35/19, 1½hr $45/25; ⏰departures 10am-2:15pm; 👪) A good option for younger kids, this glass-bottomed boat has a submerged lower deck lined with viewing windows. The views aren't as varied as on a submarine, but the underwater scenes are still eye candy and you won't feel claustrophobic.

Cocktail, Dinner & Sunset Cruises

During whale season, cocktail cruises often double as whale-watching excursions. Pacific Whale Foundation, for instance, offers a sunset cocktail whale-watch cruise. The following boats book whale-watching excursions in season.

AMERICA II Yacht Cruise
(📞667-2195; www.sailingonmaui.com; Slip 6, Lahaina Harbor; sunset sail adult/child under 12 $40/20) No cocktails and only token snacks, but this slick racing yacht sailed in the famed America's Cup. If the wind is blowing, your cruise really feels like an adventure. In winter, cruises are timed to include whale watching.

LAHAINA CRUISE COMPANY Sunset Cruise
(📞667-6165; www.thelahainacruisecompany. com; Slip 3, Lahaina Harbor; cocktail cruise $30, dinner cruise adult/child 7-12 $68/49) Unsure about your sea legs? Consider this company for your sunset cruise. Its 70ft-long *Kaulana* is the largest and most stable catamaran in the harbor. The sunset cruise features two complimentary cocktails and appetizers, while the dinner cruise on the 120ft-long *Maui Princess* includes open-air table service and live music.

SCOTCH MIST II Sunset Cruise
(📞661-0386; www.scotchmistsailingcharters. com; Slip 2, Lahaina Harbor; sunset charter $1200 or per person $60) The *Scotch Mist II* serves champagne, wine, beer and chocolate-covered macadamia nuts on its sunset cruise. The beautiful boat is also a 50ft sailing yacht that's fast and seductive. Book in advance as the boat (which is available for group charters) carries just two dozen passengers per sail. Snorkel cruises are also available seasonally.

SPIRIT OF LAHAINA Sunset Cruise
(📞662-4477; www.spiritoflahaina.com; Slip 4, Lahaina Harbor; dinner cruise adult/child $76/45, cocktail cruise adult/child 3-11 $55/33) The sunset dinner cruise includes a family-style meal delivered to your table plus cocktails, Hawaiian music and a hula show. Take away the dinner, and you've got the cocktail cruise.

On Land

SUGAR CANE TRAIN Historic Train
(Map p36; 📞661-0080; www.sugarcanetrain. com; 17 Kaka'alaneoe Dr; adult/child 3-12 $23/16; ⏰Lahaina departures 11:05am, 1pm, 2:30pm, 4pm; 👪) The restored century-old steam train that once carried cane from the fields to Lahaina's sugar mill now carries tourists on a 45-minute ride between Lahaina, Ka'anapali and Pu'uokilli'i, departing from Lahaina Station and running right beside the Honoapi'ilani Hwy. The ride is a bit pokey and there's not really much to see, but younger kids and steam-train buffs will want to hop aboard.

 Festivals & Events

Lahaina's top festivals draw huge crowds, with Front St closed to traffic during these events. For updated details on Lahaina festivities, contact the **Lahaina Town Action Committee** (📞event hotline 667-9194; www.visitlahaina.com).

Ocean Arts Festival Arts Festival
Fete the annual humpback whale migration in mid-March at Banyan Tree Sq during this weekend-long celebration with Hawaiian music, hula and games. Also features marine-minded art.

Banyan Tree Birthday Party Historic Celebration
Branch out a bit! Lahaina's favorite tree gets a two-day birthday party, complete with a

birthday cake and nature-minded art plus piñatas for the *keiki* (children). It's held on the weekend closest to April 24.

King Kamehameha Celebration — Hawaiian Parade

Traditionally dressed Hawaiian riders on horseback, marching bands and floral floats take to Front St to honor Kamehameha the Great on this public holiday in mid-June. An awards ceremony and arts festival follow at Banyan Tree Sq.

Fourth of July — Fireworks

Bands perform tunes on the lawn of the public library from 5pm and fireworks light up the sky over the harbor at 8pm.

Halloween in Lahaina — Street Festival

Front St morphs into a costumed street festival on Halloween night. Forget parking; take a bus or taxi to this one.

Holiday Lighting of the Banyan Tree — Christmas Celebration

Lahaina lights Hawaii's biggest tree on the first weekend in December with thousands of colorful lights, accompanied by music, carolers and a craft show. And, of course, Santa shows up for the *keiki*.

Sleeping

Despite the throngs of tourists filling its streets, Lahaina is surprisingly sparse on places to stay. West Maui's resort hotels are to the north, where the beaches are better. On the plus side, Lahaina's accommodations tend to be small and cozy. Between Lahaina and Ma'alaea Harbor to the south are an oceanside campground (p61) and a stylish hillside B&B (p60). See p63 for midrange B&Bs between Lahaina and Ka'anapali.

TOP CHOICE **PLANTATION INN** — Boutique Hotel **$$$**

(Map p40; ☎667-9225, 800-433-6815; www.theplantationinn.com; 174 Lahainaluna Rd; r incl breakfast $169-245, ste $265-290; P ❄ ☎ ☎) Alohas are warm at the 19-room Plantation Inn, a genteel oasis set back from the hustle and bustle of Lahaina's waterfront. Inside the stylish Lanai rooms, flat-screen TVs and DVD players blend seamlessly with plantation-era decor. Victorian-style standard rooms come with four-poster beds. The highlight? Complimentary breakfast from Gerard's that's served by the pool; we say *mahalo*

Best Western Pioneer Inn (p46)

GREG ELMS/LONELY PLANET IMAGES ©

GREG ELMS/LONELY PLANET IMAGES ©

for the savory, piping-hot eggs Florentine. The property is not on the beach, but guest privileges are provided at its sister property Ka'anapali Beach Hotel (p69).

LAHAINA INN   Boutique Hotel   **$$**
(Map p40; ☏ 661-0577, 800-222-5642; www.lahainainn.com; 127 Lahainaluna Rd; r $145-175, ste $195; P ❄ 🛜) Rooms are tiny, but they strut their stuff like the chicest of boutique hotels with artsy prints, hardwood floors and a touch of greenery. And there's always the balcony if you need more space. Pastries and coffee are available in the morning in the lobby. Gourmands take note: the 12-room inn is perched above the highly recommended Lahaina Grill, and the bar is a welcoming place to enjoy a glass of wine before heading out. Per day, parking is $6 and wi-fi is $10.

LAHAINA SHORES   Condo   **$$$**
(Map p40; ☏ 661-3339, 866-934-9176; www.lahainashores.com; 475 Front St; studio/1br from $290/355; P ❄ 🛜 🏊) Adjacent to some of Lahaina's hottest restaurants, this seven-story property is the only oceanfront condo complex in central Lahaina

operated hotel-style with a front desk and full services. The adjacent beach is a good place for beginner surfers and a venue for nighttime entertainment. All the units are roomy, and even the studios have full kitchen and lanai (veranda). Parking is $8 and wi-fi is $10 each per day.

BEST WESTERN PIONEER INN   Hotel   **$$**
(Map p40; ☏ 661-3636, 800-457-5457; www.pioneerinnmaui.com; 658 Wharf St; r $150-180; ❄ @ 🛜 🏊) Between the ship figureheads and swinging saloon doors, this historic harborfront hotel packs loads of whaling-era personality. While the common space abounds in character, the rooms are disappointingly bland and lacking water views. But heck, you're in the hub of Lahaina, so who's hanging out in a room?

OUTRIGGER AINA NALU   Condo   **$$**
(Map p40; ☏ 667-9766, 800-688-7444; www.outrigger.com; 660 Waine'e St; studio/2br from $185/275; P ❄ 🏊) Tropical trees shoot through 2nd-floor walkways, giving this complex a Kipling-esque ambience. Though not on the beach, it's just one block from the Wharf Cinema Center.

Hotel-style guest services available in the lobby; wi-fi available in the pool area only. Parking is $15 per day.

MAKAI INN Condo **$$**
(Map p36; ☎662-3200; www.makaiinn.net; 1415 Front St; r $105-180; P @ ☜) The furnishings could exude a bit more luster at this well-worn inn, but the ambience is welcoming and the oceanside setting shines. All units have full kitchens and louvered windows to catch the breeze.

Eating

Kalua pork. Spicy ahi *poke*. Juicy burgers. Macadamia nut-crusted fish. Triple berry pie. Need we continue? Lahaina has the finest dining scene on Maui. But remember, fine food draws hungry hordes. Many folks staying in Ka'anapali pour into Lahaina at dinnertime and traffic jams up. Allow extra time.

TOP CHOICE **LAHAINA GRILL** Hawaii Regional **$$$**
(Map p40; ☎667-5117; www.lahainagrill.com; 127 Lahainaluna Rd; mains $36-52; ⊙dinner) The windows at the Lahaina Grill frame a simple but captivating tableau: beautiful people enjoying beautiful food. Trust us (and the crowd gazing in from the sidewalk) – there's something special about this restaurant. Once inside, expectations are confirmed by the service and the food. The menu relies on fresh local ingredients given innovative twists and presented with artistic style. Seafood standouts include the Maui onion seared ahi with vanilla-bean jasmine rice, and Big Island prawns in roasted Kula corn salsa. The finishing brush stroke? Always the triple berry pie.

TOP CHOICE **ALOHA MIXED PLATE** Hawaiian **$**
(Map p36; ☎661-3322; www.alohamixedplate.com; 1285 Front St; mains $7-13; ⊙10:30am-10pm) This is the Hawaii you came to find: friendly, open-air and right on the beach. The food's first-rate, the prices affordably local. For a thoroughly Hawaiian experience, order the Ali'i Plate, packed with *laulau, kalua* pig, *lomilomi* salmon, poi and *haupia* (see the food glossary, p284) – and, of course, macaroni salad and rice. On your next visit tackle the awesome coconut prawns.

MALA OCEAN TAVERN Eclectic **$$$**
(Map p36; ☎667-9394; www.malaoceantavern.com; 1307 Front St; lunch $12-24, dinner $17-19; ⊙11am-10pm Mon-Fri, 9am-10pm Sat, 9am-9pm Sun) A favorite of Maui's smart set, Mark Ellman's stylish bistro fuses Mediterranean and Pacific influences with sophisticated flair. Recommended tapas include the kobe beef cheeseburger slathered with caramelized onions and smoked apple bacon, and the 'adult' mac & cheese with mushroom cream and three fancy fromages. For entrees, anything with fish is a sure pleaser, and everyone raves over

Favorite Chilly Treats

I scream, you scream, we all scream for...shave ice. And gelato. And yes, even ice cream. Downtown Lahaina whips up delectable versions of all three of these cool refreshments. For over-the-top (literally) shave ice, amble up to the counter at **Ululani's Hawaiian Shave Ice (Map p40; 819 Front St)** and take your pick of tropical flavors. At **Ono Gelato Company (Map p40; 815 Front St)** a few doors down, there's always a crowd gazing at the sinful array of silky gelatos – all prepared with Maui cane sugar. **Scoops (Map p40; 888 Front St)** serves locally made Lappert's ice cream, but we'll make the choice easy: Kauai Pie, a luscious mix of Kona coffee ice cream, coconut, macadamia nuts and fudge.

the decadent 'caramel miranda' dessert. At sunset, tiki torches on the waterfront lanai add a romantic touch.

KIMO'S
Hawaiian $$$

(Map p40; ☎661-4811; www.kimosmaui.com; 845 Front St; lunch $8-16, dinner $23-36; ⏰11am-10:30pm) This is our favorite ocean patio on Front St. A locally beloved standby, Hawaiian-style Kimo's keeps everyone happy with reliable food, a superb water view and a family friendly setting. Entrees include fresh fish, oversized prime rib cuts and good ol' teriyaki chicken. At lunch, if you're seeking lighter fare, don't miss the delicious Caesar salad. Mai tais are served in fun glass totems.

COOL CAT CAFÉ
Diner $$

(Map p40; ☎667-0908; www.coolcatcafe.com; Wharf Cinema Center, 658 Front St; mains $9-15; ⏰10:30am-10:30pm; 🚸) Burgers and sandwiches at this upbeat diner are named for 1950s icons, honoring the likes of Marilyn Monroe, Buddy Holly and Elvis Presley (although Patsy 'Klein' may be intrigued by the spelling). The 6½ ounce burgers are made with 100% Angus beef and consistently rank as Maui's best. The view overlooking Banyan Tree Sq isn't bad either.

WINDOW 808
Hawaiian $

(Map p40; www.thewindow808.com; 790 Front St; mains $3.50-8; ⏰9:30am-9:30pm) This open-air taco shack serves the best mahi fish tacos that we tasted on Maui – savory bundles of fresh goodness that rise to celestial with a few drops of its potent green sauce. The kalua pork is also nicely seasoned. Great budget option. To find it, enter the table-dotted courtyard just south of the intersection of Lahainaluna Rd and Front St. Cash only.

PACIFIC'O
Hawaii Regional $$$

(Map p40; ☎667-4341; www.pacificomaui.com; 505 Front St; lunch $13-16, dinner $30-42; ⏰11:30am-4pm & 5:30-10pm) Contemporary cuisine with added bling jumps off the menu at this chic seaside restaurant. The food is bold and innovative – where else can you try a crispy coconut roll with seared scallops and lime pesto? Lunch is a tamer affair, with salads and sandwiches but the same in-your-face ocean view. Live dinnertime jazz on the weekend cranks the hip atmosphere up a notch.

I'O
Hawaii Regional $$$

(Map p40; ☎661-8422; www.iomaui.com; 505 Front St; mains $28-39; ⏰dinner) For Lahaina's best fine dining with a waterfront setting, come here. I'O is the handiwork of Maui's most acclaimed chef, James McDonald. The nouveau Hawaii cuisine includes scrumptious creations such as seared fresh catch in lobster curry and slow braised short ribs from Maui Cattle Company. McDonald is so obsessed with freshness that he started a farm in Kula to grow his own veggies. There's a fierce martini menu, too.

Eclectic fare at Mala Ocean Tavern (p47)

BANYAN TREE DELI & BAKERY
Bakery, Deli $
(Map p40; 662-3354; 626 Front St; mains under $10; 7am-6pm) Muffins, banana bread and mango macadamia nut scones are just a few of the breakfast strumpets preening in the display case at this new pastry and sandwich shop. In the morning, repeat guests file in for these tasty treats, a pattern repeated at lunchtime for the top-notch pastrami sandwiches. Friendly proprietor and free wi-fi round out the appeal.

THAI CHEF
Thai $$
(Map p40; 667-2814; Old Lahaina Center, 878 Front St; mains $11-18; lunch Mon-Fri, dinner Mon-Sat) Hidden in the back of an aging shopping center, this place looks like a dive from the outside, but the food's incredible. Start with the fragrant ginger coconut soup and the fresh summer rolls and then move on to savory curries that explode with flavor. It's BYOB so pick up a bottle from the nearby Foodland.

PENNE PASTA CAFÉ
Italian $$
(Map p40; 661-6633; 180 Dickenson St; mains $8-18; 11am-9:30pm Mon-Fri) To keep prices down, renowned chef Mark Ellman, who also operates upscale Mala, chose a side-street location and streamlined the menu to pastas, pizzas and sandwiches. That said, the food's anything but boring: garlic ahi atop a bed of pesto linguine, roasted squash with almonds, warm focaccia and, of course, creamy tiramisu for dessert.

SUNRISE CAFÉ
Cafe $
(Map p40; 661-8558; 693 Front St; mains $5-11; 6am-4:40pm) The dawn patrol loves this cozy hole-in-the-wall near the harbor. Breakfasts have pizzazz: smoked salmon with eggs, Maui onions and lemon caper hollandaise, or maybe a croissant with cheese and fresh fruit. Lunch covers the gamut of gourmet sandwiches to roast beef plates. Cash only.

GERARD'S
French $$$
(Map p40; 661-8939; www.gerardsmaui.com; 174 Lahainaluna Rd; mains $33-50; dinner) Chef Gerard Reversade takes fresh Lahaina-caught seafood and infuses it

Island Insights

For ahi *poke* (marinated raw fish) that's fresh, cheap and tasty, locals head to Foodland grocery stores. Their seafood counters may not be the fanciest digs in town, but service is friendly and fast. Best part? Free samples! If you want your *poke* as a meal ask for a *poke* bowl, which comes with a hefty helping of rice. The spiced ahi *poke* is outstanding and is one of our favorite to-go meals.

with flavors from the French countryside in savory dishes such as the Pacific bouillabaisse. The island-style French cuisine and the extensive wine lists have earned Gerard's top-of-the-line accolades. Add a quiet candlelit porch, and it makes for a romantic evening.

STAR NOODLE
Pan-Asian $$
(Map p36; 667 5400; www.starnoodle.com; 286 Kupuohi St; lunch $9-12, dinner $9-25; 10:30am-3pm & 5:30-10pm) Grazers can nibble on an eclectic array of Asian-fusion share plates at this chic noodle shop. Those seeking heartier fare can dive into garlic noodles, *kim chee ramen* and a local saimin (noodle soup; Spam included). The food is lightly seasoned, so heat fiends will need to ask for hot sauce.

Need to stock up? **Foodland** (Map p40; 661-0975; www.foodland.com; Old Lahaina Center, 878 Front St; 6am-midnight) and **Safeway** (Map p36; 667-4392; www.safeway.com; Lahaina Cannery Mall, 1221 Honoapi'ilani Hwy; 24hr) supermarkets have everything you need for self-catering, as well as good delis. For discounts, you can use your phone number in place of a customer card in Foodland, and Safeway accepts customer club cards from the mainland.

🍷 Drinking

Front St is the center of the action. Check the entertainment listings in the free weeklies *Lahaina News* and *MauiTime Weekly*, or just stroll the streets. In addition to places listed here, many of Lahaina's waterfront restaurants have live music at dinnertime.

ALOHA MIXED
PLATE   Open-air Restaurant
(Map p40; ☎661-3322; 1285 Front St; ⏱10:30am-10pm) Let the sea breeze whip through your hair while lingering over a heady mai tai – come between 2pm and 6pm and they're $3. After sunset, you can listen to Old Lahaina Luau's music beating next door.

BEST WESTERN PIONEER INN   Pub
(Map p40; ☎661-3636; 658 Wharf St; ⏱7am-10pm) If Captain Ahab himself strolled through the swinging doors, no one would look up from their grog. With its whaling-era atmosphere and harborfront lanai, the captain would blend right in at this century-old landmark. For us landlubbers,

the afternoon happy hour (3pm to 6pm most days) keeps it light on the wallet.

LAHAINA COOLERS   Cafe
(Map p40; ☎661-7082; www.lahainacoolers.com; 180 Dickenson St; ⏱8am-1am) This eclectic open-air cafe attracts 30-somethings who come to mingle, munch *pupu* (snacks) and sip wine coolers. As the town's late-night bar, it's the place to head after the dance floor has emptied. Hungover? Come here in the morning for *kalua* pork huevos rancheros.

MOOSE MCGILLYCUDDY'S   Bar
(Map p40; ☎667-7758; www.moosemcgillycuddys.com; 844 Front St; ⏱7:30am-1:30am Tue-Sat, 7:30am-midnight Sun & Mon) College kids? Bachelorettes? Dancing fools? Here's your party. This vibrant bar and restaurant attracts a convivial crowd out to drink and dance till they drop. With two dance floors, McGillycuddy's jams with live music Friday to Sunday and DJs nightly. The bar is also known for $1 drinks (cocktails and draft beers) on Tuesday and Saturday nights, with $5 cover.

Cheeseburger in Paradise

Righteous & Rowdy

Lahaina owes much of its period appearance to two diametrically opposed groups of New Englanders who landed in the 1820s.

In 1823 William Richards, Lahaina's first missionary, converted Maui's native governor, Hoapili, to Christianity and persuaded him to pass laws against 'drunkenness and debauchery.' However, after months at sea, sailors weren't looking for a prayer service when they pulled into port – to them there was 'no God west of the Horn.' Missionaries and whalers almost came to battle in 1827 when Governor Hoapili arrested a whaler captain for allowing women to board his ship. The crew retaliated by shooting cannonballs at Richards' house. The captain was released, but laws forbidding liaisons between seamen and Hawaiian women remained in force.

It wasn't until Governor Hoapili's death in 1840 that laws prohibiting liquor and prostitution were no longer enforced and whalers began to flock to Lahaina. Among the sailors who roamed Lahaina's streets was Herman Melville, who later penned *Moby Dick*.

CHEESEBURGER IN PARADISE Open-air Restaurant
(Map p40; ☎661-4855; www.cheeseburgerland. com; 811 Front St) Perched above the sea at the corner of Front St and Lahainaluna Rd, this open-air place is a lively – and lovely – spot to watch the sunset. The music's Jimmy Buffett–style, and the setting is pure tropics, from the rattan decor to the homemade pina coladas. Live soft rock from 4:30pm to 10pm nightly

COOL CAT CAFÉ Cafe
(Map p40; ☎667-0908; Wharf Cinema Center, 658 Front St; ☺10:30am-10:30pm) The breezy setting and '50s decor would make Elvis feel right at home. Whether you're looking for fountain drinks or hard-hitting cocktails, this is the perfect spot to wet the whistle as the sun sets over the harbor. Live music nightly and rotating list of $3 daily cocktails.

MAUIGROWN COFFEE Coffee Shop
(Map p40; ☎661-2728; www.mauigrown coffee.com; 277 Lahainaluna Rd; ☺6:30am-5pm Mon-Sat) Your view from the lanai at Maui-Grown's historic bungalow? A sugar plantation smokestack and the cloud-capped West Maui Mountains. With 100% Maui grown coffee, life can be good at 7am.

TIMBA Nightclub
(Map p40; ☎661-9873; www.timbamaui.com; 505 Front St; ☺9pm-2am Thu-Sat) This sleek club above Pacific'O is as chic as it gets in Maui. Sultry lighting, posh lounges, ocean breezes, groovin' house tracks – come here to step it up in style. Unfortunately, style isn't free in Lahaina – there's a $10 to $15 cover on weekends. No baseball caps or MMA (mixed martial arts attire).

CAPTAIN JACK'S Bar
(Map p40; ☎667-0988; Wharf Cinema Center, 672 Front St; ☺8am-midnight) This watering hole had just opened at press time, so we can't confirm its reputation – although a pirate-themed bar does have an inherent cool. From the looks of the low-key crowd and the sports events splashed across its nine TV screens, this is a chill spot to sip a beer and catch a game.

⭐ Entertainment

When it comes to hula and luau (feast), Lahaina offers the real deal. Catching a show is sure to be a vacation highlight. You can also enjoy free hula shows at **Lahaina Cannery Mall** (Map p36; www. lahainacannery.com; 1221 Honoapi'ilani Hwy)

TRAVEL DIVISION IMAGES/ALAMY

at 7pm Tuesday and Thursday, and hula shows for the *keiki* at 1pm Saturday and Sunday.

TOP CHOICE **OLD LAHAINA LUAU**   Luau
(Map p40; ☏667-1998; www.oldlahaina luau.com; 1251 Front St; adult/child 2-12 $95/65; ◷5:15-8:15pm Oct-Mar, 5:45-8:45pm Apr-Sep; ⊛) From the warm aloha greeting to the extravagant feast and the mesmerizing hula dances, everything here is first rate. No other luau on Maui comes close to matching this one for its authenticity, presentation and all-around aloha. The feast is outstanding, with high-quality Hawaiian fare that includes *kahlua* pork, *'ahi* poke, *pukehu* steak and an array of salads and sides. What you won't find? The long lines of a resort-hotel luau. It's held on the beach at the north side of town. One caveat: it often sells out a month in advance, so book ahead.

FEAST AT LELE   Luau
(Map p40; ☏667-5353; www.feastatlele. com; 505 Front St; adult/child 2-12 $110/80; ◷5:30-8:30pm Oct-Mar, 6-9pm Apr-Sep) Food takes center stage at this intimate Polynesian luau held on the beach in front of I'O restaurant. Dance performances in Hawaiian, Maori, Tahitian and Samoan styles are each matched to a food course. With the Hawaiian music, you're served *kalua* pork and *pohole* ferns; with the Maori, duck salad with *poha* berry dressing. A true gourmet feast.

'ULALENA   Modern Dance
(Map p40; ☏661-9913; www.ulalena.com; Old Lahaina Center, 878 Front St; adult $60-165, child 3-12 $25-80; ◷6:30-8pm Mon-Fri) This Cirque du Soleil–style extravaganza has its home at the 680-seat Maui Theatre. The theme is Hawaiian history and storytelling; the medium is modern dance, brilliant stage sets, acrobatics and elaborate costumes. An entertaining, high-energy performance.

Shopping

Classy boutiques, tacky souvenir shops and flashy art galleries run thick along Front St. You'll find lots of shops under one roof at the **Wharf Cinema Center** (Map p40; ☏661-8748; www.thewharf cinemacenter.com; 658 Front St) and **Lahaina Cannery Mall** (Map p36; ☏661-5304; www. lahainacannery.com; 1221 Honoapi'ilani Hwy).

A new strip mall, **Lahaina Gateway** (Map 36; ☎ 877-7073; www.lahainagateway.com; 305 Keawe St) is located across Hwy 30 from the Cannery. Here you'll find a large Barnes & Noble (www.barnesandnoble.com) and a branch of Maui Dive Shop (www.mauidiveshop.com).

Every Friday night is 'Art Night' in Lahaina. Dozens of galleries have openings, some with entertainment, wine and hors d'oeuvres. It's a perfect time to stroll the Front St art scene, meet artists and nibble a little cheese. The action goes from 7pm to 10pm and it's all free – that is, unless you see a treasure that takes your fancy.

TOP CHOICE — LAHAINA ARTS SOCIETY
Arts & Crafts

(Map p40; http://lahaina-arts.com; 648 Wharf St) A nonprofit collective representing nearly 100 island artists, this extensive gallery covers two floors in the Old Lahaina Courthouse. Works range from avant-garde paintings to traditional weavings. Many of Maui's best-known artists got their start here, and there are some gems among the collection.

LAHAINA PRINTSELLERS
Art, Maps

(Map p40; www.printsellers.com; 764 Front St) Hawaii's largest purveyor of antique maps, including fascinating originals dating back to the voyages of Captain Cook. It also sells affordable reproductions if you don't have a large wad of cash on you. The location is inside Lahaina Giclee, a gallery selling a wide range of fine quality Hawaiian *giclee* (zhee-clay) digital prints.

VILLAGE GIFTS & FINE ARTS
Crafts, Gifts

(Map p40; cnr Front & Dickenson Sts) This one-room shop in the Masters' Reading Room sells prints, wooden bowls and

glasswork, with a portion of the proceeds supporting the Lahaina Restoration Foundation.

Old Lahaina Book Emporium
Books

(Map p40; www.oldlahainabookemporium.com; 834 Front St) Bookworms, you're in for a feast at Maui's top independent bookstore; new and used volumes, plus vintage Hawaiiana.

Crazy Shirts
Clothing

(Map p40; www.crazyshirts.com; 865 Front St) Stylish Hawaii-motif T-shirts and hoodies for sale.

Lahaina Scrimshaw
Craftwork

(Map p40; 845 Front St) Contemporary and antique artwork on fossil walrus teeth, mammoth ivory and bone.

Maui Hands
Arts & Crafts

(Map p40; 612 Front St) Excellent selection of island-made crafts.

Hale Zen
Home Decor

(Map p40; 180 Dickenson St) The Zen is more Balinese than Hawaiian, but this welcoming shop is well-stocked with candles, lotions and gifts as well as crafted furniture and cute children's clothes.

Kamehameha Iki Park (p42)
PHOTOGRAPHER: ANDY JACKSON/ALAMY

Peter Lik Gallery Photography
(Map p40; 712 Front St) Vibrant colors, stunning
landscapes – nature is king in the stylish lair of
Australian photographer Peter Lik.

ℹ Information

Emergency

Police (📞244-6400) For non-emergencies.

Police, fire and ambulance (📞911) For
emergencies only.

Medical Services

The Maui Memorial Medical Center in Wailuku is
the nearest hospital in case of emergencies.

Longs Drugs (📞667-4384; www.cvs.com;
Lahaina Cannery Mall, 1221 Honoapi'ilani Hwy;
🕐7am-midnight) Lahaina's largest pharmacy.

Maui Medical Group (📞661-0051; www.
mauimedical.com; 130 Prison St; 🕐8am-7pm
Mon-Fri, 8am-5pm Sat & Sun) This clinic handles
non-emergencies.

Money

Bank of Hawaii (www.boh.com; Old Lahaina
Center, 130 Papalaua St)

Post

Downtown post office station (Old Lahaina
Center, 132 Papalaua St; 🕐9am-4pm Mon-Fri)

Tourist Information

Lahaina Visitor Center (📞667-9193; www.
visitlahaina.com; Old Lahaina Courthouse, 648
Wharf St; 🕐9am-5pm)

ℹ Getting There & Away

The Honoapi'ilani Hwy (Hwy 30) connects Lahaina
with Ka'anapali and points north, with Ma'alaea to
the south and with Wailuku to the east. Ferries to
Lana'i and Moloka'i dock at Lahaina Harbor.

ℹ Getting Around

To/From the Airport

To get to Lahaina from the airport in Kahului, take
Hwy 380 south to Hwy 30; the drive takes about
45 minutes. If you're not renting a car, **Executive
Shuttle** (📞669-2300, 800-833-2303; www.
mauishuttle.com; 1/2 passengers $43/45)
provides the best deal on taxi service between
Lahaina and the airport.

Bicycle

For bike rentals head to **West
Maui Cycles** (📞661-9005;
1087 Limahana Pl; per day $15-
60; 🕐9am-5pm Mon-Sat,
10am-4pm Sun), which has
quality hybrid and mountain
bikes, as well as cheaper
cruisers fine for kicking
around town.

Bus

The Maui Bus (www.
mauicounty.gov) runs
between Kahului and Lahaina
($1, one hour) on the Lahaina
Islander 20 route. This bus

Sunset cruise (p44), Lahaina Harbor

Halloween, Lahaina Style

Lahaina is party central. So it's no surprise that by the 1990s its modest kiddie-oriented Halloween parade had boomed into an all-out blast. The event was rechristened 'Mardi Gras of the Pacific,' spiced up with elaborate floats and outrageous costumes, and promoted far and wide. It grew into Maui's biggest bash, attracting upwards of 30,000 revelers to the jam-packed Front St for the October 31 celebration. After island families complained that risqué attire and heavy drinking had made the festival unsuitable for children, organizers dropped the Mardi Gras title and ratcheted it back down a notch. Consider it a fine-tuning of sorts. It seems to have struck a happy medium – these days about 20,000 partygoers come out for 'Halloween in Lahaina,' a street festival of music, dance and costume contests.

stops at Ma'alaea, where connections can be made to Kihei and Wailea. Another route, the Ka'anapali Islander 25, connects Lahaina and Ka'anapali ($1, 30 minutes). Both routes depart from the Wharf Cinema Center hourly from 6:30am to 8:30pm.

Car & Motorcycle

For Harley-Davidson motorcycle rentals, try **Eagle Rider** (☏662-4877; www.eaglerider. com; 94 Kupuohi St; motorcycle hire per day incl helmet $149), located near the Lahaina Gateway Center.

Front St has free on-street parking, but there's always a line of cruising cars competing for spots. There's one free lot on tiny Luakini St between Lahainaluna Rd and Dickenson – but get there early, it fills fast. Your best bet is the large parking lot at the corner of Front and Prison Sts where there's free public parking with a three-hour limit. There are also several private parking lots, averaging $8 per day, with the biggest one being Republic Parking on Dickenson St. Otherwise, park at one of the shopping centers and get your parking ticket validated for free by making a purchase.

Taxi

For a taxi in Lahaina, call **Ali'i Cab** (☏661-3688), **LA Taxi** (☏661-4545) or **Paradise Taxi** (☏661-4455). It's about $15 to $16 one-way between Lahaina and Ka'anapali.

West Maui

Simply put, West Maui is where the action is. Whether you want to snorkel beside lava rocks, zipline down the mountains, thwack a golf ball, hike through the jungle or sail beneath the setting sun, the adventures are as varied as the landscape. Ka'anapali is the splashy center of it all, a look-at-me town luring travelers with world-class golf courses, stylish resorts, oceanfront dining and a dazzling, mile-long crescent of beach.

Further north, Hawaiian history and swanky exclusivity have formed an intriguing, sometimes uneasy, alliance in Kapalua, where a world-class resort preens between a lush mountain watershed, a PGA golf course, an ancient burial ground and several gorgeous beaches. To escape any semblance of a 'scene,' hunker down in Kahana or Napili, lovely seaside communities known for their condos and budget-friendly prices. For off-the-grid excitement, only one adventure will do – a breezy, sometimes hair-raising, drive around the untamed northern coast.

Kapalua Beach (p80)

57

West Maui Itineraries

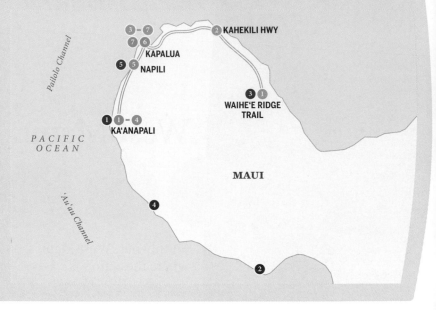

Two Days

1 Ka'anapali Beach (p65) Begin by jumping into the water at West Maui's hottest spot for sand and sun. For snorkeling, swim toward Pu'u Keka'a (Black Rock) and head for the tip of the rock, home to abundant fish and colorful coral.

2 Whalers Village Museum (p66) Dry off and don your slippers for this intriguing museum, which explores West Maui's role in the whaling trade as well as the hard but exciting life of a 19th-century whaler.

3 Teralani Sailing (p67) For a different angle on the sand and sea, hop aboard a catamaran for a motor-free cruise of the coast. Teralani's open bar goes down smoothly, too.

4 Ka'anapali Beach Walk (p67) A stroll beside the lovely beach on the Ka'anapali Beach Walk is a scenic way to end the day. Stop to watch the **cliff-diving and torch-**

lighting ceremony off Pu'u Keka'a then follow with a tropical drink at beachside **Leilani's**.

5 Gazebo (p77) Wake up with a splash on day two at this waterfront gem in unspoiled Napili. Pineapple pancakes, perhaps?

6 Kapalua Adventures (p81) Sign up for a zipline swoop or catch a shuttle up to the Maunalei Arboretum trailhead for a jungle hike down to the sea.

7 Sansei Seafood Restaurant & Sushi Bar (p84) Step into stylish duds and head to this snazzy sushi bar and restaurant tucked between Kapalua's golf courses and the Ritz-Carlton.

⊙ THIS LEG: 8 MILES

Four Days

1 **Waihe'e Ridge Trail** (p89) If you have four glorious days in West Maui, plan your first two days as above. Start day three by stretching your legs on this lofty ridgeline path with misty mountain views. This is one of those hikes that produces I-want-to-go-back memories.

2 **Kahekili Hwy** (p85) After your descent, hop into the car and head off around the rugged northern tip of the island on this serpentine highway. With one-way bridges and blind turns, this is West Maui's most adventurous road trip. Keep your hiking shoes on – there's a lot more than roadside views on this one.

3 **Plantation House** (p84) Start day three here with an 'Oh-my-gosh-I-can't-believe-how-good-this-is' crab cake Benedict. The backdrop for your meal? A sweeping panorama of the Ritz-Carlton, Moloka'i and, of course, the ever-present golf fiends.

4 **Kapalua Golf** (p82) Speaking of golfers, follow in the footsteps of Tiger Woods by knocking around the greens of Maui's premier golf course.

5 **Oneloa Beach** (p80) Not a golfer? Then grab your beach towel and find your way to Oneloa Beach, a true hidden gem – as uncrowded and pretty as they come.

6 **Merriman's Kapalua** (p84) In the afternoon, stroll over to the patio here for happy hour. Your reward? $3 cocktails and a cliff-top perch above gorgeous Kapalua Beach.

7 **Pineapple Grill** (p84) End your West Maui adventure at Kapalua's hottest restaurant, dining on what may be the best Hawaiian fusion fare on the island. And one fab view to go with it!

⟶ THIS LEG: 26 MILES

West Maui Highlights

1 **Best Beach: Ka'anapali Beach** (p65) Snorkel beside Pu'u Keka'a (Black Rock) then strut your stuff resort-style at 'Dig-Me Beach.'

2 **Best View: Papawai Point** (p65) Thar she blows at this cliffside perch, a primo whale-watching spot.

3 **Best Hike: Waihe'e Ridge Trail** (p89) Climb into the clouds on this scenic 5-miler with sweeping north coast views.

4 **Best Water Activity: Balancing on a board** (p60) Surfing, boogie boarding and stand up paddling: everyone's catching waves.

5 **Best Hawaiian Entertainment: Masters of Hawaiian Slack Key Guitar Concert Series** (p78) These old-style jams are a cultural celebration that make everyone feel like 'ohana (family).

Snorkelers, Pu'u Keka'a (Black Rock, p65)
PHOTOGRAPHER: KARL LEHMANN/LONELY PLANET IMAGES ©

Discover
West Maui

Lahaina to Ma'alaea

The drive between Lahaina and Ma'alaea offers fine mountain scenery, but in winter everyone is craning their necks seaward to spot humpback whales cruising just offshore. Stand up paddle surfers are also a common sight.

Olowalu Petroglyphs
PHOTOGRAPHER: KARL LEHMANN/LONELY PLANET IMAGES ©

Puamana Beach Park & Launiupoko Beach Park

PUAMANA BEACH PARK   Beach
This shady beach park (Map p62), 1.5 miles south of Lahaina, is rocky but sometimes has good conditions for beginning surfers – otherwise it's mostly a quick stop for a seaside view, particularly at sunset. Not a great spot for lying out.

LAUNIUPOKO BEACH PARK   Beach
This is a better stop, where even the restrooms glow with murals of young surfers hitting the waves. The south side of the beach (Map p62) has small waves ideal for beginning surfers, while the north side ratchets it up a notch for those who have honed their skills. You're also likely to see paddle surfers plying through Launiupoko's surf. The park is an ideal spot for families; *keiki* (children) have a blast wading in the large rock-enclosed shoreline pool and good picnic facilities invite you to linger. Launiupoko is at the traffic lights at the 18-mile marker.

Sleeping

For B&Bs in Maui, remember to reserve a room ahead of time. Showing up late at night, unannounced and without reservations, is not a good idea.

HO'OILO HOUSE   B&B $$$
(Map p62; ☎667-6669; www.hooilohouse.com; 138 Awaiku St; r $229-289; P✱@☎≋) One word describes this lush getaway on the slopes of the West Maui mountains: Zenful. Six Asian- and Maui-themed rooms hug the A-framed center, a big-windowed community room with a grand view of Lana'i. Stylish furnishings differ from room to room – many contain Balinese imports – but all have a private lanai (veranda)

and an eclectically designed outdoor shower. Breakfast includes fresh muffins and bread, cereal, granola and fruit, which is often plucked from the 2-acre property's orchard (pesticide free). Proprietors Dan and Amy installed solar panels in 2011, and they anticipate that the panels will generate 90% to 95% of the house's power.

Olowalu

The West Maui Mountains form a scenic backdrop, giving Olowalu its name, which means 'many hills.' The tiny village is marked by the Olowalu General Store and the Olowalu Juice Stand.

Sights & Activities

You'll notice snorkelers taking to the water near the 14-mile marker. Don't bother. The coral reef is shallow and silty, and the 'Sharks May Be Present' signs lining the beach are the real thing: there were three shark attacks off Olowalu between 1993 and 2002.

OLOWALU PETROGLYPHS Petroglyphs **(Map p62)** A short walk behind the general store leads to petroglyphs (ancient Hawaiian stone carvings). Park just beyond the water tower at the back of the store and look for the signposted gate. It's a quarter-mile walk up an open road to the petroglyph site. The path is easy to follow; just keep the cinder cone straight ahead of you as you go.

As with most of Maui's petroglyphs, these figures are carved into the vertical sides of cliffs (rather than on horizontal lava as they are on the Big Island). Most of the Olowalu figures have been damaged, but you can still make some out.

Watch your footing at the site itself, where there are some loose rocks and a narrow viewing platform.

Sleeping & Eating

CAMP OLOWALU Camping **$** **(Map p62; ☎ 661-4303; www.campolowalu.com; 800 Olowalu Village Rd; campsite per adult/child 6-12 $10/5)** Bordered by the ocean on one side and a dense thicket of gnarled trees on the other, the setting is pure *Survivor*.

The Best...
West Maui for Kids

1 Swimming hole, Launiupoko Beach Park (p60)

2 Hula show, Ka'anapali Beach Hotel (p69)

3 Cliff divers, Pu'u Keka'a (p72)

4 Whalers Village Museum (p66)

But simple amenities— cold-water showers, outhouses, picnic tables, drinking water – and a friendly caretaker kick things up a notch. A-frame cabins with six cots are also available for $20 per person.

**OLOWALU JUICE STAND** Food Truck **$** **(Map p62; Olowalu Village Rd; smoothies $5; ⏰ 9am-5:30pm)** Papaya. Banana. Ginger. Guava. Lime. Mango. Tangerine. Hmm, what are we forgetting? Oh yes, how could we? Pineapple! Smoothies made with squeezed-on-the-spot sugarcane juice are whipped up at this food truck at the north side of **Olowalu General Store** (Map p62). Fresh fruit is also available for sale.

Ukumehame Beach Park & Around

At the 12-mile marker is **Ukumehame Beach Park** (Map p62). Shaded by ironwood trees, this sandy beach is OK for a quick dip, but because of the rocky conditions most locals stick with picnicking and fishing. Dive and snorkel boats anchor offshore at **Coral Gardens**. This reef also creates **Thousand Peaks** toward its west end, with breaks favored by long-boarders and beginner surfers.

The pull-off for the western end of the **Lahaina Pali Trail** (p113) is just south of the 11-mile marker, on the inland side of the road.

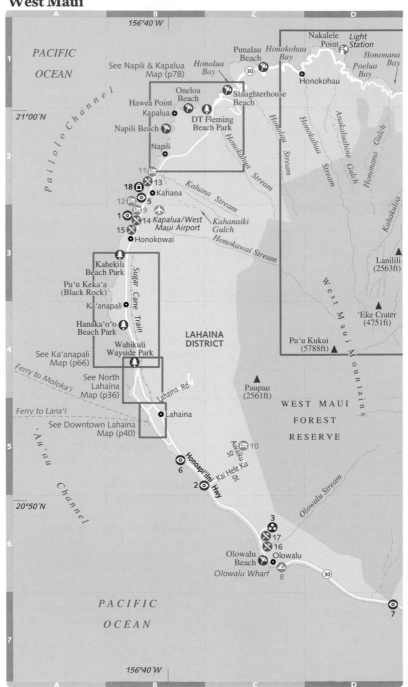

Lahaina to Ka'anapali

The stretch between Lahaina and Ka'anapali offers a couple of roadside beach parks plus two good B&Bs.

Wahikuli Wayside Park

Two miles north of Lahaina, **Wahikuli Wayside Park** (Map p66) occupies a narrow strip of beach flanked by the busy highway. Although the beach is mostly backed by a black-rock retaining wall, there's a small sandy area. Swimming conditions are usually fine, and when the water's calm, you can snorkel near the lava outcrops at the park's south end. The park has showers and restrooms.

Sleeping

The following B&Bs are near each other in a residential neighborhood between Lahaina and Ka'anapali, inland of Hwy 30. You're not on the beach, but it's just a five-minute drive away.

GUEST HOUSE　　　　B&B **$$**
(Map p66; ☎661-8085, 800-621-8942; www.mauiguesthouse.com; 1620 Ainakea Rd; s/d incl breakfast $169/189, P ❄ @ 🛜 🏊) Now fronted by an inviting salt water pool, the welcoming Guest House provides amenities that put nearby resorts to shame. Every room has its own hot tub and 42in plasma TV. Stained-glass windows and rattan furnishings reflect a tropical motif. The long list of free perks runs from beach towels and snorkel gear to a stocked community kitchen and guest shower you can use before your midnight flight.

HOUSE OF FOUNTAINS　　B&B **$$**
(Map p66; ☎667-2121, 800-789-6865; www.alohahouse.com; 1579 Lokia St; r incl breakfast $150-170; P ❄ 🛜 🏊) The hand-carved outrigger canoe that hangs above the common room is a showstopper. But Hawaiian flourishes don't end there. Hula rattles and warrior masks brim from every corner, and there's even a turtle painted on the bottom of the pool. The six guest rooms are nicely fitted with queen beds, refrigerators and DVD players. It's a child-friendly place – the owners have kids. German is a second language here.

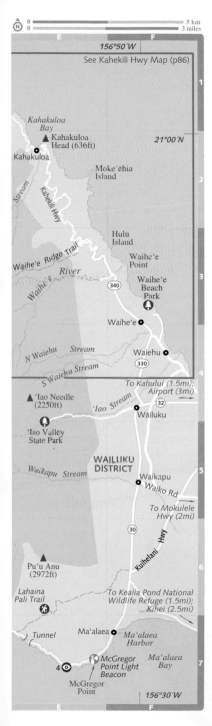

West Maui

Hanaka'o'o Beach Park

The long, sandy **Hanaka'o'o Beach Park** (Map p66), extending south from Ka'anapali Beach Resort, has a sandy bottom and water conditions that are usually safe for swimming. However, southerly swells, which sometimes devel-op in summer, can create powerful waves and shorebreaks, while the occasional *kona* (leeward) storm can kick up rough water conditions in winter. Snorkelers head down to the second clump of rocks on the south side of the park, but it really doesn't compare with sites further north. The park has full facilities and is one of only two beaches on the entire West Maui coast that has a lifeguard. Hanaka'o'o Beach is also called 'Canoe Beach,' as West Maui outrigger canoe clubs practice here in the late afternoon. A small immigrant cemetery dating from the 1850s marks the entrance.

Ka'anapali

Honeymoon. Reunion. Three-day frolic. Ka'anapali is a place to celebrate. Maui's flashiest resort destination boasts 3 miles of sandy beach, a dozen oceanfront hotels, two 18-hole golf courses and an ocean full of water activities. You can sit at a beachfront bar with a tropical drink, soak up the

Ka'anapali Beach
PHOTOGRAPHER: ANN CECIL/LONELY PLANET IMAGES ©

Whale Spotting

During the winter, humpback whales occasionally breach as close as 100yd from the coast, and 40 tons of leviathan suddenly exploding straight up through the water can be a real showstopper!

Beach parks and pull-offs along the road offer great vantages for watching the action. The very best spot is **Papawai Point** (Map p62), a cliffside perch jutting into the western edge of Ma'alaea Bay, and a favored humpback nursing ground (not to mention a great place to catch a sunset). During winter, the Pacific Whale Foundation posts volunteers at the parking lot to share their binoculars and point out the whales.

Papawai Point is midway between the 8- and 9-mile markers. Note that the road sign reads simply 'scenic point,' not the full name, but there's a turning lane into it, so slow down and you won't miss it.

gorgeous views of Lana'i and Moloka'i across the channel and listen to guitarists strum their wiki-wacky-woo.

 ## Beaches

TOP CHOICE **KA'ANAPALI BEACH**   Beach
Home to West Maui's liveliest beach scene, this gorgeous stretch of sand unfurls alongside Ka'anapali's resort hotels, linking the Hyatt Regency Maui with the Sheraton Maui 1 mile north. Dubbed 'Dig-Me Beach' for all the preening and strutting that goes on, it's a vibrant spot. Surfers, boogie boarders and parasailers rip across the water, and sailboats pull up on shore. Check with the hotel beach huts before jumping in, however, as water conditions vary with the season and currents are sometimes strong.

For the best snorkeling, try the underwater sights off **Pu'u Keka'a**, also known as Black Rock. This lava promontory protects the beach in front of the Sheraton Maui. Novices stick to the sheltered southern side of the landmark rock – where there's still a lot to see – but the shallow coral here has been stomped to death. If you're a confident swimmer, the less-frequented horseshoe cove cut into the tip of the rock is the real prize, teeming with tropical fish, colorful coral and sea turtles. There's often a current to contend with off the point, which can make getting to the cove a bit tricky, but when it's calm you can swim right in. Pu'u Keka'a is also a popular shore-dive spot; any of the beach huts can set you up.

KAHEKILI BEACH PARK   Beach
To escape the look-at-me crowds clustered in front of the resorts, head to this idyllic golden-sand beach at Ka'anapali's less-frequented northern end. The swimming's better, the snorkeling's good and you'll find plenty of room to stretch without bumping into anyone else's beach towel. The park has everything you'll need for a day at the beach – showers, restrooms, a covered picnic pavilion and barbecue grills. Access is easy and there's lots of free parking.

Snorkelers will find plenty of coral and marine life right in front of the beach. Sea turtle sightings are common. If you want to go a bit further afield, you can swim north to Honokowai Point and then ride the mild current, which runs north to south, all the way back.

The wide beach, backed by swaying palms and flowering morning glory, is also ideal for strolling. It's a 15-minute walk south to Pu'u Keka'a. Or you could walk north along the beach for about 20 minutes to **Honokowai Point** and have lunch in the village.

Ka'anapali

Ka'anapali

◉ **Sights**
1 Hanaka'o'o Beach Park.....................B3
2 Ka'anapali Beach..............................A2
3 Kahekili Beach Park............................ A1
4 Pu'u Keka'a (Black Rock) A2
5 Wahikuli Wayside Park.....................B4
6 Whalers Village Museum A2

Activities, Courses & Tours
    Ka'anapali Dive Company..........(see 17)
7 Royal Lahaina Tennis Ranch A1
    Skyline Eco-Adventures............(see 15)
    Teralani Sailing .... (see 6)
    Tour of the Stars........................(see 11)
8 Trilogy Ocean Sports A2

🛏 **Sleeping**
9 Guest House B4
10 House of Fountains B4
11 Hyatt Regency Maui Resort &
    Spa..A3
12 Ka'anapali Beach Hotel....................A2
13 Outrigger Maui Eldorado...................A2
14 Sheraton Maui A2

✖ **Eating**
    China Bowl ....(see 15)
15 CJ's Deli...A2
    Hula Grill & Barefoot Bar............(see 18)
    Son'z at Swan Court..................(see 11)

🎭 **Entertainment**
    Drums of the Pacific ....(see 11)
    Hyatt Regency Maui Resort &
    Spa.. (see 11)
    Ka'anapali Beach Hotel..............(see 12)
    Leilani's...(see 18)
16 Marriott's Maui Ocean Club................A3
    Sheraton Maui ....(see 14)
17 Westin Maui Resort & Spa A2
    Whalers Village ....(see 18)

🎁 **Shopping**
18 Whalers Village A2

To get to the beach from the Honoapi'ilani Hwy, turn *makai* (toward the ocean) 0.2 miles north of the 25-mile marker onto Kai Ala Dr, then bear right.

 Sights

TOP
CHOICE **WHALERS VILLAGE
MUSEUM**   Museum

(☎ 661-5992; www.whalersvillage.com/museum. htm; Level 3, Whalers Village, 2435 Ka'anapali Pkwy; admission free; ☺ 10am-6pm) During the Golden Age of Whaling (1825–60), Lahaina was a popular stop for whaling ships traveling between Japan and the Arctic. This fascinating museum reveals the hardships and routines of life at sea. Authentic period photographs, ship logs, harpoons and intriguing interpretive plaques sound the depths of whaling history. Particularly eye-opening is the life-size forecastle displayed in back. How 20 crewmen could live for weeks in this tiny room – without coming to blows or losing their minds – is one of life's eternal mysteries. Also worth a look is the intricate rigging between the sails on the built-to-scale replica of an 1850s-era whaling ship. Consider the skill required to maneuver

DISCOVER WEST MAUI

such a complex vessel through rough and dangerous seas!

Interest piqued? Look for the full-size **sperm whale skeleton** at the front entrance to the shopping center.

KA'ANAPALI BEACH WALK
Walking Trail

Smell the salt air, take in the opulent resort sights and check out the lively beach scene along the mile-long walk that runs between the Sheraton and Hyatt hotels. In addition to the action on the beach, both the Hyatt and the Westin are worth a detour for their dazzling garden statuary and landscaping replete with free-form pools, rushing waterfalls and swan ponds. A walk through the Hyatt's rambling lobbies is a bit like museum browsing – the walls are hung with heirloom Hawaiian quilts and meditative Buddhas. Don't miss the pampered black African penguins who love to waddle beside their four-star penguin cave.

At the southern end of the walk the graceful 17ft-high bronze sculpture *The Acrobats*, by Australian John Robinson, makes a dramatic silhouette at sunset. In the early evening, you'll often be treated to entertainment from the beachside restaurants.

 **Activities**

 TERALANI SAILING
Catamaran Cruises

(661-7245; www.teralani.net; Whalers Village, 2435 Ka'anapali Pkwy; trips $59-119; vary)
This friendly outfit offers a variety of sails on two custom-built catamarans that depart from the beach beside Whalers Village. The easygoing sunset sail offers an inspiring introduction to the gorgeous West Maui coast. Snorkel sails and whale-watching outings are additional options, but no matter which you choose, you'll find a friendly crew, an open bar and decent food.

KA'ANAPALI DIVE COMPANY
Diving

(800-897-2607; www.goscubamaui.com; Westin Maui Resort & Spa; 1-tank dives $65;

The Best…
Beaches

7am-5pm) If you've never been diving before, these are the people you want to see. Its introductory dive ($95) for novices starts with instruction in a pool and moves on to a guided dive from the beach. It also offers beach dives for certified divers. No rentals. Walk up, or make reservations through the 800 number (the American Express Tours and Activities line).

TRILOGY OCEAN SPORTS
Watersports

(661-7789; www.sailtrilogy.com; Ka'anapali Beach Walk; 8am-5pm) From its beach hut in front of the Ka'anapali Beach Hotel, it can get you up and riding a board with a two-hour surfing lesson ($70). Snorkel sets and boogie boards rent for $15 a day, and it offers a sunset catamaran cruise (adult/teen 13-18/child 3-12 $59/40/27).

SKYLINE ECO-ADVENTURES
Ziplining

(878-8400; www.zipline.com; Fairway Shops, 2580 Keka'a Dr; 4hr outing incl breakfast or lunch $150; departs on the hour 7am-2pm) Got a need for speed? The Ka'anapali course takes you 2 miles up the wooded cliffsides of the West Maui Mountains and sets you off on a free-glide along eight separate lines above waterfalls, stream beds and valleys. Eco-stewardship is a mission of

the company, and guides discuss local flora and fauna. If it's drizzly and windy? Hold on tight and no cannonballs!

KA'ANAPALI GOLF COURSES   Golf
(☎ 661-3691; www.kaanapali-golf.com; 2290 Ka'anapali Pkwy; greens fee $195-235, after 1pm $95-120; ⏰ vary seasonally) Of the two courses, the more demanding is the Royal Ka'anapali Golf Course, designed by Robert Trent Jones. It's tournament grade with greens that emphasize putting skills. The Ka'anapali Kai Golf Course is shorter and more of a resort course. The setting isn't as spectacular as the courses in Kapalua, but it tends to be less windy down this way and the rates are a relative bargain.

TOUR OF THE STARS   Stargazing
(☎ 667-4727; 200 Nohea Kai Dr; admission $25-30) Enjoy stellar stargazing atop the Hyatt resort. These 50-minute viewings are limited to 10 people, use a 16in-diameter telescope and are held at 8pm, 9pm and 10pm on clear nights. Romantic types

should opt for the couples-only viewing at 11pm Friday and Saturday, which rolls out champagne and chocolate-covered strawberries.

ROYAL LAHAINA TENNIS RANCH   Tennis
(☎ 667-5200; 2780 Keka'a Dr; per person per day $10; ⏰ pro shop 8am-noon & 2-6pm Mon-Fri, 8am-noon & 2-5pm Sat & Sun) Named the 2010 'Facility of the Year' by the United States Tennis Association, this is the largest tennis complex in West Maui, with six courts lit for night play. Rackets and shoes can be rented. Private lessons and group clinics are available.

⭐ Festivals & Events

Maui Onion Festival   Food Festival
(www.whalersvillage.com) Held at Whalers Village the first weekend in May, this popular celebration highlights everything that can be done with Maui's famed Kula onions. The Maui Onion Grower Association brings in more than

Left: Hula performance, Ka'anapali Beach Hotel (p72); **Below:** Exhibits, Whalers Village Museum (p66)

PHOTOGRAPHER: GREG ELMS/LONELY PLANET IMAGES ©

800lb of onion for the festival's renowned fried onion rings. Also look for cooking demonstrations by Maui's top chefs.

Hula O Na Keiki   Hula Competition
(www.kbhmaui.com) Children take center stage at this hula dance competition in November, which features some of the best *keiki* dancers in Hawaii.

Na Mele O Maui   Hawaiian Music
(www.kaanapaliresort.com) The 'Song of Maui' features children's choral groups singing Native Hawaiian music honoring Hawaii's last monarch, Queen Lili'uokalani, who was a renowned music composer and cultural revivalist. This aloha-rich event is held in early December at the Maui Arts & Cultural Center.

 **Sleeping**

The following accommodations are on the beach or within walking distance of it. Some rates, in response to the ongoing recession, are lower than in years past.

In addition to these resorts, there are nearby B&Bs (p63) between Ka'anapali and Lahaina.

TOP CHOICE **KA'ANAPALI BEACH HOTEL**   Resort **$$**
(☏ 661-0011, 800-262-8450; www.kbhmaui.com; 2525 Ka'anapali Pkwy; r from $159; P ❄ @ 🖥 📶 ♨ 👶) Guests are welcomed like old friends at the beloved Ka'anapali Beach Hotel. The property is a little older than its neighbors and the style is far from posh, but it has its own special charms: warm staff, nightly hula shows, an outdoor tiki bar, tidy grounds framed by palm trees and an enviable location on a gorgeous stretch of beach. Isn't this why you came to Maui? Family-friendly activities, from lei-making to ukulele singalongs, assure that the *keiki* will never be bored. Bring a camera and a hankie to your farewell lei ceremony. Parking is $9 per day and wi-fi $10 per day (but free in the lobby).

OUTRIGGER MAUI ELDORADO
Condo $$

(☎ 661-0021, 888-339-8585; www.outrigger.com; 2661 Keka'a Dr; studio/1br from $145/259; P ❄ @ ≋) How close are you to the fairways at the Maui Eldorado? One sign says it all: 'Beware of flying golf balls in the lanai areas.' And it's true, you can literally step off your lanai and onto the fairways at this quiet condo development bordering the Royal Ka'anapali Golf Course. Units are not on the beach, but the complex isn't far from the ocean, and the resort shuttle stops out front. The best rooms are the large studios which have kitchens set apart from the bedroom area. Parking is $7 per day. Wi-fi available in the lobby.

SHERATON MAUI
Resort $$$

(☎ 661-0031, 866-716-8109; www.sheraton-maui.com; 2605 Ka'anapali Pkwy; r from $525; P ❄ @ 🛜 ≋ 🛅) Hmm, darling. Shall we snorkel beside turtles? Or watch whales breach from the room? Or maybe catch the sunset cliff dive? The choices are many at this sleek hotel, which sprawls across 23 acres at the north end of the

Ka'anapali Beach Walk. The beach itself bumps against Pu'u Keka'a (Black Rock), renowned for its snorkeling and silhouette. Rooms have rich wood tones and Hawaiian prints; grounds have night-lit tennis courts, a fitness center, a lava-rock swimming pool and the spa at Black Rock. The $25 daily resort fee includes parking, local and Lahaina shuttle service and wi-fi (available in a few common areas only).

HYATT REGENCY MAUI RESORT & SPA
Resort $$$

(☎ 661-1234, 800-492-1234; www.maui.hyatt.com; 200 Nohea Kai Dr; r from $404; P ❄ @ 🛜 ≋ 🛅) The lobby atrium is tricked out with cockatoos in palm trees and extravagant artwork, the grounds given over to gardens and swan ponds. Kids of all ages will thrill in the water world of meandering pools, swim-through grottos and towering water slides. Angle for a room in the revamped Lahaina Tower; we were less-than-impressed with the tired furnishings in the Napili Tower, yet to be upgraded. The $25 daily resort fee includes parking and wi-fi.

Hyatt Regency Maui Resort & Spa

Eating

Don't limit yourself to Ka'anapali's restaurants. Many of Maui's top chefs are just a skip down the road in Lahaina.

TOP CHOICE HULA GRILL & BAREFOOT BAR
Hawaii Regional $$$

(☎667-6636; hulagrillkaanapali.com; Whalers Village, 2435 Ka'anapali Pkwy; bar & grill $8-20, dinner $10-32; ⊙bar 11am-11pm, dining room 5-9:30pm) The Barefoot Bar is your Maui postcard: coconut-frond umbrellas, the sand beneath your sandals and the guy strumming the guitar. It's the ambience that impresses most, and there's no better place on the beach walk to sip mai tais and nibble *pupu* (snacks) by the sea. The Kapulu Joe pork sandwich with macnut slaw (add a dash of chili water) is reliably good, and the beer battered mahimahi taco hits the spot too. Dinner inside at the restaurant kicks it up a notch with spicy kiawe-grilled seafood

SON'Z AT SWAN COURT
Eclectic $$$

(☎667-4506; Hyatt Regency Maui Resort & Spa, 200 Nohea Kai Dr; mains $32-50; ⊙dinner) Between the waterfalls, the swan pond and the tiki torches, this is Ka'anapali's most romantic night out. The award-winning cuisine includes the expected fine-dining steak and lobster selections, but many appetizers and mains highlight the best of Maui, from the ravioli with Surfing Dairy goat cheese to Maui Cattle Company tenderloin with local coffee marinade. Incredible wine list, too.

CJ'S DELI
Cafe $

(☎667-0968; www.cjsmaui.com; Fairway Shops, 2580 Keka'a Dr; mains $8-12; ⊙7am-8pm) For day trips to East Maui, pick up a Hana Lunch Box ($12) at this New York–style deli-cafe. It comes with a sandwich, Maui chips, a homemade Hana bar, soda and a returnable cooler. If you're dining in, salads, burgers and paninis are also on the menu, plus meatloaf and pot roast. Eggs and pancakes are available until 11am. No alcohol is served; BYOB is OK.

Island Insight

According to traditional Hawaiian beliefs, Pu'u Keka'a, the westernmost point of Maui, is a place where the spirits of the dead leap into the unknown to be carried to their ancestral homeland. The rock is said to have been created during a scuffle between the demigod Maui and a commoner who questioned Maui's superiority. Maui chased the man to this point, froze his body into stone then cast his soul out to sea. Today, daring teens wait their turn to leap off the rock for a resounding splash into the cove below.

CHINA BOWL　　　Chinese　$$
(☎661-061; www.chinaboatandbowl.com; Fairway Shops, 2580 Keka'a Dr; mains $9-24; ☺10:30am-9:30pm Mon-Sat, 11am-9:30pm Sun) This family friendly place wok-fries authentic Szechuan dishes with fiery peppers as well as Mandarin fare for tamer palates. The health conscious will be happy to know MSG is banned from the kitchen. The kids' meal features a meal with a drink ($6.25).

Drinking & Entertainment

Bars in Whalers Village and many resorts offer live music in the evening. Luau and hula shows are also popular. Check www.mauitimes.com for performers and schedules.

Live Music

The places listed here, as well as the Hula Grill & Barefoot Bar, have live music throughout the afternoon and evening. It's typically Jimmy Buffett–style guitar tunes, but is occasionally spiced up with some ukulele strumming.

LEILANI'S　　Acoustic, Classic Rock
(☎661-4495; Whalers Village, 2435 Ka'anapali Pkwy; ☺11am-11pm) This open-air bar and restaurant right on the beach is the place to linger over a cool drink while catching a few rays. It also has a good grill and *pupu* menu. Live music Friday through Sunday.

Westin Maui Resort & Spa　　Hawaiian
(☎667-2525; www.westinmaui.com; 2365 Ka'anapali Pkwy) You're likely to find live music at the Westin any night of the week. Check the website for times and the specific restaurant offering live music.

Marriott's Maui Ocean Club　　Acoustic
(☎667-8220; 100 Nohea Kai Dr) Longboards has a solo guitarist from 5:30pm to 8pm Monday through Friday.

Hyatt Regency Maui
Resort & Spa　　Acoustic
(☎661-1234; 200 Nohea Kai Dr) There's live music poolside at Umalu from 6:30pm to 8:30pm nightly. Free torch lighting between 5:30pm and 6pm.

Hula, Luau & Theater

KA'ANAPALI BEACH HOTEL　　Hula
(☎661-0011; www.kbhmaui.com; 2525 Ka'anapali Pkwy) Maui's most Hawaiian hotel cheerfully entertains anyone who chances by between 6:30pm and 7:30pm with a free hula show. Enjoy mai tais and brews at the adjacent Tiki Bar with music and dancing nightly in the Tiki Courtyard.

SHERATON MAUI　　Cliff Dive
(☎661-0031; 2605 Ka'anapali Pkwy) Everybody swings by to watch the torch-lighting and cliff-diving ceremony from Pu'u Keka'a (Black Rock) that takes place at sunset. There's also live music in the late afternoon at the Cliff Dive Bar.

DRUMS OF THE PACIFIC Luau
(667-4727; Hyatt Regency Maui Resort & Spa, 200 Nohea Kai Dr; adult/teen 13-20/child 6-12 $96/61/49; ⏱5-8pm) Ka'anapali's best luau includes an *imu* ceremony (unearthing of a roasted pig from an underground oven), an open bar, a Hawaiian-style buffet and a South Pacific dance and music show.

WHALERS VILLAGE Hula, Dance
(661-4567; www.whalersvillage.com; 2435 Ka'anapali Pkwy) Ka'anapali's shopping center hosts free hula and Polynesian dance performances from 7pm to 8pm on Monday, Wednesday and Saturday. Check the website for a monthly calendar of all events and classes.

 **Shopping**

You'll find more than 50 shops at the **Whalers Village** (661-4567; www.whalers village.com; 2435 Ka'anapali Pkwy; ⏱9:30am-10pm) shopping center:

ABC Store Sundries
(www.abcstores.com) Stop here for sunblock and great beach totes.

Crazy Shirts T-Shirts
(662-8785) This Hawaiian company has been selling stylish T-shirts for 40 years.

Honolua Surf Beachwear
(www.honoluasurf.com) The place to pick up Maui-style board shorts and other casual beachwear.

Honolua Wahine
Women's Swimwear
(www.honoluasurf.com) Get your bikinis here.

Lahaina Printsellers
Art, Maps
(www.printsellers.com) Packable Hawaiian prints and maps.

Martin & MacArthur
Hawaiian Crafts
(www.martinandmacarthur. com) Museum-quality

Hawaiian-made wood carvings, paintings and other crafts.

ℹ **Getting Around**

The **Maui Bus** (www.mauicounty.gov) connects Whalers Village Shopping Center in Ka'anapali with the Wharf Cinema Center in Lahaina hourly from 6am to 8pm, and also runs north up the coast to Kahana and Napili hourly from 6am to 8pm.

The free Ka'anapali Trolley runs between the Ka'anapali hotels, Whalers Village and the golf courses about every 20 minutes between 10am and 10pm.

Cabs often line up beside the trolley and Maui bus stop in front of Whalers Village on Ka'anapali Pkwy.

The resort hotels offer free beach parking, but the spaces allotted are so limited they commonly fill by mid-morning. Your best bet for beach parking is at the south end of the Hyatt, which has more slots than other hotels. Another option is the pay parking at Whalers Village ($2 per 30 minutes; free parking validation, based on purchase amount, varies by merchant).

Cliff diver, Sheraton Maui
PHOTOGRAPHER: GREG ELMS/LONELY PLANET IMAGES ©

Honokowai

Condo-laden Honokowai may not have the glamour of pricier Ka'anapali to the south, but it has its virtues. It's convenient, affordable and low-rise, and the ocean views are as fine as in the upscale resorts. Another perk: in winter this is the best place in West Maui to spot passing whales right from your room lanai. The main road, which bypasses the condos, is Honoapi'ilani Hwy (Hwy 30). The parallel shoreline road is Lower Honoapi'ilani Rd, which leads into Honokowai.

Sights

HONOKOWAI BEACH PARK   Beach
The real thrills here are on land, not in the water. This family-friendly park (Map p62) in the center of town has cool playground facilities and makes a nice spot for a picnic. Forget swimming, though. The water is shallow and the beach is lined with a submerged rock shelf. Water conditions improve at the south side of town, and you could continue walking along the shore down to lovely **Kahekili Beach Park** at the northern end of Ka'anapali.

Activities

Boss Frog   Snorkel Gear
(Map p62; ☎665-1200; www.bossfrog.com; 3636 Lower Honoapi'ilani Rd; per day from $1.50; ☺8am-5pm) Offers great prices for rental mask, snorkel and fins.

 Sleeping

NOELANI   Condo $$
(Map p62; ☎669-8374, 800-367-6030; www.noelani-condo-resort.com; 4095 Lower Honoapi'ilani Rd; studios from $157, 1br/2br/3br from $197/290/357; P ≋) Get to know your neighbors at the weekly mai tai party at this compact hideaway, a 50-unit complex that's so close to the water you can sit on your lanai and watch turtles swimming in the surf. The units cover a

Takeout plate lunch, Honokowai Okazuya

GREG ELMS/LONELY PLANET IMAGES ©

wide range, from cozy studios to three-bedroom suites, but all have ocean views. Two heated pools, a Jacuzzi, a small exercise room and concierge services are additional perks.

HALE KAI Condo $$
(Map p62; 669-6333, 800-446-7307; www.halekai.com; 3691 Lower Honoapi'ilani Rd; 1br/2br/3br $160/210/350; P 🛜 ≋) This two-story place abounds in Hawaiian accents, from the room decor to the lava-rock exterior. It's perched on the water's edge: step off your lanai and onto the sand. Good for groups, the three-bedroom corner unit has a cool loft, wraparound ocean-view windows and all the character of a Hawaiian beach house.

Eating

FARMERS MARKET DELI Deli $
(Map p62; 669-7004; 3636 Lower Honoapi'ilani Rd; sandwiches under $6; ⏱7am-7pm; 🍴) Stop here to pick up healthy takeout fare. The salad bar (with free samples) includes organic goodies and hot veggie dishes. The smoothies are first-rate, and Maui-made ice cream is sold by the scoop. The place becomes even greener on Monday, Wednesday and Friday morning, when vendors sell locally grown produce in the parking lot.

TOP CHOICE **HONOKOWAI OKAZUYA** Plate Lunch $$
(Map p62; 665-0512; 3600 Lower Honoapi'ilani Rd; mains $10-18; ⏱10am-9pm Mon-Sat) The appeal is not immediately apparent. The place is tiny, prices are high and the choices seem weird (*kung pao* chicken AND spaghetti with meatballs?). But then you hunker down at the counter and nibble a forkful of piping-hot Mongolian beef. Hmm, it's OK. Chomp chomp. You know, that's pretty interesting. Gulp gulp. What is that spice? Savor savor – until the whole darn container is empty. This place – primarily takeout – is all about the cooking, with plate lunch specialties taking a gourmet turn. Cash only.

JAVA JAZZ & SOUP NUTZ Eclectic $$
(667-0787; www.javajazz.net; Honokowai Marketplace, 3350 Lower Honoapi'ilani Rd; breakfast & lunch $6-12, dinner $10-30; ⏱6am-10pm) With a menu as eclectic as its decor, this arty cafe never disappoints. Breakfast packs 'em in with everything from bagels to frittata; lunch revolves around Greek salads and innovative sandwiches. Dinner gets downright meaty with the tastiest flame-grilled filet mignon you'll find anywhere on Maui.

Kahana

Trendy Kahana, the village north of Honokowai, boasts million-dollar homes, upscale beachfront condominiums and Maui's only microbrewery. It's a popular place to head for a night out.

Sights & Activities

The sandy **beach** fronting the village offers reasonable swimming. Park at seaside **Pohaku Park** (Map p62) and walk north a couple of minutes to reach the beach. Pohaku Park itself has an offshore break called S-Turns that attracts surfers.

Maui Dive Shop Diving, Snorkeling
(Map p62; 669-3800; www.mauidiveshop.com; Kahana Gateway, 4405 Honoapi'ilani Hwy; 2-tank dives $140, snorkel-set per day $6; ⏱8am-6pm) Come here for information about a full range of dives and to rent snorkel gear.

Sleeping

KAHANA VILLAGE Condo $$
(Map p62; 669-5111, 800-824-3065; www.kahanavillage.com; 4531 Lower Honoapi'ilani Rd; 2br/3br from $290/445; P 🛜 ≋) With their A-frame ceilings, airy lofts and oceanfront views, 2nd-story units have a fun 'vacation' vibe. The breezy appeal of the interior is well-matched outside with lush tropical flora and weekly mai tai parties with live Hawaiian music. Some condos have views of Lana'i while others face Moloka'i. Every unit has a lanai, full kitchen, and washer and dryer.

ANN CECIL/LONELY PLANET IMAGES ©

 Eating & Drinking

ROY'S KAHANA BAR
& GRILL   Hawaii Regional **$$$**
(Map p62; 669-6999; www.roysrestaurant.
com; Kahana Gateway, 4405 Honoapi'ilani
Hwy; mains $27-40; dinner) From its lofty
2nd-floor perch, Chef Roy Yamaguchi's
Maui flagship beckons like a guiding star,
drawing gourmands to a promised land of
exquisitely prepared island and regional
fare. Yamaguchi runs a little empire of
restaurants, and this location rakes in
a crowd with savory dishes such as the
sashimi-like blackened ahi with Chinese
mustard, and a local rib eye with a bacon
and blue cheese cream sauce. Aloha!

MAUI BREWING
COMPANY   Brewpub **$$**
(Map p62; 669-3474; www.mauibrewingco.
com; Kahana Gateway, 4405 Honoapi'ilani
Hwy; mains $12-25; 11am-midnight) Maui
Cattle Company burgers. *Kalua* pork
pizza. Mahimahi fish and chips. Pub grub
takes a Hawaiian twist at this cavern-
ous brewpub hunkered in the corner of
Kahana Gateway. The company, honored
as one of Hawaii's top green businesses in
2008, implements sustainable practices
where it can (see p297). The Bikini Blonde
lager, Big Swell IPA and Coconut Porter
are always on tap, supplemented by a half
dozen or so seasonal brews.

CHINA BOAT   Chinese **$$**
(Map p62; 669-5089; 4474 Lower Honoapi'ilani
Rd; mains $9-20; 11:30am-2pm Mon-Sat &
5pm-10pm daily) If you want to see where
islanders bring the kids for an affordable
dinner, come here. The menu includes
both tame Mandarin and fiery Szechuan
favorites, as well as a few Japanese
dishes, with nearly 100 choices.

Hawaiian Village Coffee   Cafe **$**
(Map p62; www.hawaiianvillagecoffee.com;
Kahana Gateway, 4405 Honoapi'ilani Hwy; snacks
under $7; 6am-8pm Sun-Thu, to 9pm Fri & Sat;
) Off-duty surfers shoot the breeze at this
low-key coffee shop. Surf the net on one of three
computers in back (20 minutes for $3).

Napili

Napili is a sun-kissed center of calm, a
bayside oasis flanked by the posh bar-
ricades of Kapalua to the north and the
hustle of Kahana and Ka'anapali to the
south.

DISCOVER WEST MAUI

 Beaches

NAPILI BEACH — Beach

The deep golden sands and gentle curves of Napili Beach (Map p78) offer good beachcombing at any time and excellent swimming and snorkeling when it's calm. Big waves occasionally make it into the bay in winter, and when they do it's time to break out the skimboards – the steep drop at the beach provides a perfect run into the surf.

Sleeping

Napili Bay is surrounded by older condos and small, mellow resorts. Come here to escape the Ka'anapali crowds and to enjoy low-cost proximity to Kapalua.

TOP CHOICE — NAPILI SURF BEACH RESORT

Beach Resort, Condo $$

(Map p78; ☎669-8002, 800-541-0638; www.napilisurf.com; 50 Napili Pl; studio/1br from $171/260; P⎘☎) Regulars bring appetizers to the Wednesday mai tai party at this friendly, well-maintained property tucked on a gentle curve of sand on Napili Bay. One of the best deals in West Maui, a stay here includes complimentary maid service and wi-fi, not to mention the tasty free mai tais. Full kitchens are nice if you want to eat in, but the Gazebo is next door and the Sea House is a beach stroll away. The kicker? Each guest is welcomed with a fresh half-pineapple chilling in the refrigerator. Cash or check only.

TOP CHOICE — HALE NAPILI — Condo $$

(Map p78; ☎669-6184, 800-245-2266; www.halenapilimaui.com; 65 Hui Dr; studio/1 br from $160/260; P⎘☎) The aloha of the Hawaiian manager ensures lots of repeat guests at these tidy condos smack on the beach. The place is a welcome throwback to an earlier era, when everything in Maui was small and personable. The 18 neat-as-a-pin units have tropical decor, full kitchens and oceanfront lanai.

MAUIAN — Condo $$$

(Map p78; ☎669-6205, 800-367-5034; www.mauian.com; 5441 Lower Honoapi'ilani Rd; studio with kitchen from $199, r $179; P@☎) Most Napili condos wear their age gracefully, but not the sassy Mauian, a 44-room condo/hotel hybrid kicking up her stylish heels like a teenager. Bamboo ceilings, frond prints, crisp whites and browns, Tempur-Pedic mattresses – rooms are sharp, stylish and comfortable, and come with a lanai with big views. Units do not have TVs, phones or wi-fi, but all three are available in the common area.

NAPILI KAI BEACH RESORT — Independent Hotel $$$

(Map p78; ☎669-6271, 800-367-5030; www.napilikai.com; 5900 Lower Honoapi'ilani Rd; r/studio from $250/320; P@☎) Spread across several acres at the northern end of Napili Bay, this pampering resort offers classic appeal. The units, which tastefully blend Polynesian decor with Asian touches, have oceanview lanai and, in most cases, kitchenettes. For modern style and wi-fi, reserve a room in the renovated Puna II building. Some units have air-con, ask when booking. Wi-fi available in the lobby.

Outrigger Napili Shores — Condo $$$

(Map p78; ☎669-8061, 800-688-7444; www.outrigger.com; 5315 Lower Honoapi'ilani Rd; studio/1br from $285/339; P@☎) Two words: the Gazebo. West Maui's superstar breakfast joint is on the premises, giving guests a head start on the line. Freshly renovated, every unit looks spanking new.

Eating

TOP CHOICE — GAZEBO — Cafe $

(Map p78; ☎669-5621; Outrigger Napili Shores, 5315 Lower Honoapi'ilani Rd; mains $8-11; ☺7:30am-2pm) Locals aren't kidding when they advise you to get here early to beat the crowds and the line. But a 7:10am arrival is worth it for this beloved open-air restaurant – literally a gazebo on the beach – with a gorgeous waterfront setting. The tiny cafe is known for its breakfasts, and sweet tooths love the white

N 0 ——————— 1 km
0 ——————— 0.5 miles

PACIFIC
OCEAN

To Kahekili
Hwy (10mi);
Kahului (22mi)
Honolua-Mokule'ia   Kalaepiha Honolua
Bay Marine Life   Point   Bay
Conservation District

Makaluapuna
Point

Mokule'ia
Bay

Hawea
Point
Oneloa
Bay

Honokahua
Bay

Plantation Club
Kapalua
Plantation
Golf Course

Honokohau

Light
Beacon

KAPALUA

Plantation Estates Dr

Office Rd

Kapalua Bay
Golf Course

Kapalua
Dr

Bay Club Pl

Village Rd

Honokahua Stream

Kahauiki Gulch

Napili Bay

Pineapple Hill Dr

Napili Pl

Hui Dr

NAPILI

Simpson Way

Honoapi'ilani Hwy

Honokeana
Bay

Hui Rd

Lower
Honoapi'ilani Rd

Napilihau St

Kaopala Gulch

To Kahana Gateway
Shopping Center (0.6mi)

chocolate macnut pancakes. Meal-size salads, hearty sandwiches and the *kalua* pig plate steal the scene at lunch.

SEA HOUSE RESTAURANT   Hawaii Regional $$$

(Map p78; ☎669-1500; www.napilikai.com; Napili Kai Beach Resort, 5900 Lower Honoapi'ilani Rd; breakfast $9-12, lunch $9-14, dinner $25-37; ⏰breakfast, lunch, dinner) Pssst. Want a $9 meal framed by a million dollar view? Sidle up to the bar at this tiki-lit favorite, order a bowl of the smoky seafood chowder then watch as the perfectly framed sun drops below the horizon in front of you. Bravo! If you stick around, and you should, seafood and steak dishes are menu highlights.

MAUI TACOS   Mexican $

(Map p78; www.mauitacos.com; Napili Plaza, 5095 Napilihau St; mains under $10; ⏰9am-8pm)

Here's proof that Mexican fare can be island-style healthy. The salsas and beans are prepared fresh daily, transfat-free oil replaces lard, and fresh veggies and local fish feature on the menu.

⭐ Entertainment

MASTERS OF HAWAIIAN SLACK KEY GUITAR CONCERT SERIES   Live Music

TOP CHOICE

(Map p78; ☎669-3858; www.slackkey.com; Napili Kai Beach Resort, 5900 Lower Honoapi'ilani Rd; admission $40; ⏰7:30pm Wed) Top slack key guitarists Ledward Kaapana and Dennis Kamakahi appear regularly at this exceptional concert series, and George Kahumoku Jr, a slack key legend in his own right, is the weekly host. As much

Napili & Kapalua

a jam session as a concert, this is a true Hawaiian cultural gem that's worth going out of your way to experience. Reservations recommended.

Kapalua & Northern Beaches

Kapalua is a posh resort sprung from the soil of a onetime pineapple plantation. Long known as a world-class golf destination, Kapalua is now making an all-out effort to broaden its appeal. An awesome zipline is taking people skyward for new thrills, trails in a once-restricted forest have opened to the public and the dining scene is among the island's best. The nightlife doesn't exactly sizzle, but the beaches – all with public access – sure do.

If you're turned off by well-manicured glitz, swoop past the resort and take a winding drive along the rugged northern coast. The untamed views are guaranteed to replenish your soul.

If uninterrupted sunshine is your goal, note that Kapalua can be a bit rainier and windier than points south.

 Beaches

TOP CHOICE **DT FLEMING BEACH PARK** Beach
Dr Beach crowned this mile-long swath of sand (Map p78) 'America's Best Beach' in 2006. We think the doctor diagnosed this one right.

Surrounded by ironwood trees and backed by an old one-room schoolhouse, this sandy beach appears like an outpost from another era. In keeping with its Hawaiian nature, the beach is the domain of wave riders. Experienced surfers and bodysurfers find good action here, especially in winter. The shorebreaks can be brutal, however, and this beach is second only to Ho'okipa for injuries. The reef on the right is good for snorkeling in summer when the water is very calm.

Fleming has restrooms, showers, grills, picnic tables and a lifeguard. The access road is off Honoapi'ilani Hwy (Hwy 30), immediately north of the 31-mile marker.

The Coastal Trail and the Mahana Ridge Trail (p81) intersect here.

ONELOA BEACH   Beach

Also on the Coastal Trail, this white-sand jewel (Map p78) is worth seeking out. Fringed by low sand dunes covered in beach morning glory, it's a fine place to soak up a few rays. On calm days swimming is good close to shore, as is snorkeling in the protected area along the rocky point at the north side of the beach. When there's any sizable surf, strong rip currents can be present.

The only trick? Finding it and snagging a parking spot. The half-mile strand – Oneloa means 'long sand' – is backed by gated resort condos and restricted golf greens, and beach access requires a sharp eye. Turn onto Ironwood Lane and turn left into the parking lot opposite the Ironwoods gate. Get here early or around lunchtime, when people are heading out.

KAPALUA BEACH   Beach

This gorgeous strand (Map p78) gets the seal of approval! Not only do tourists sun on the beach here, but endangered monk seals occasionally haul out on the soft, white sand to snooze the afternoon away as well.

This crescent-shaped beach, with its clear view of Moloka'i across the channel, is a sure bet for a fun day in the water. Long rocky outcrops at both ends of the bay make Kapalua Beach the safest year-round swimming spot on this coast. You'll find colorful snorkeling on the right side of the beach, with abundant tropical fish and orange slate-pencil sea urchins.

Take the drive immediately north of Napili Kai Beach Resort to get to the beach parking area, where there are restrooms and showers. A tunnel leads from the parking lot north to the beach. This is also a start point for the Coastal Trail (p81).

SLAUGHTERHOUSE BEACH & HONOLUA BAY   Beach

This marine conservation district comes with Jekyll-and-Hyde mood swings: wild and wicked in the winter, calm and tranquil in the summer. But no matter its mood, it's always ideal for some sort of activity.

The narrow Kalaepiha Point separates **Slaughterhouse Beach** (Mokule'ia Bay; Map p78) and **Honolua Bay** (Map p78). Together they form the Honolua–Mokule'ia Bay Marine Life Conservation District.

Like O'ahu's famed North Shore, Honolua Bay is a surfer's dream. It, too, faces northwest and when it catches the winter swells it has some of the gnarliest surfing anywhere in the world. It's so hot it's been cover material for surfing magazines.

In summer snorkeling is excellent in both bays, thanks in part to prohibitions on fishing in the preserve. Honolua Bay is the favorite, with thriving reefs and abundant coral along its rocky edges. As an added treat, spinner dolphins sometimes hang near the mouth of the bays, swimming just beyond snorkelers. When it's calm, you can snorkel around Kalaepiha

Surfer, Honolua Bay
PHOTOGRAPHER: KARL LEHMANN/LONELY PLANET IMAGES ©

Point from one bay to the other, but forget it after heavy rains: Honolua Stream empties into Honolua Bay and the runoff clouds the water.

The land fronting Honolua Bay is owned by Maui Land & Pineapple. The company allows recreational access to the bay for no fee. A few families have the right to live on this land, but they cannot charge an access fee or restrict visiting hours. Once you reach the bay, review the signage about protecting the coral, then enter via the rocky coastline. Do not enter the water via the concrete boat ramp, which is very slippery and potentially hazardous.

When the waters are calm the bays offer superb kayaking. Slaughterhouse Beach is also a top-rated bodysurfing spot during the summer. Its attractive white-sand crescent is good for sunbathing and beachcombing – look for glittering green olivine crystals in the rocks at the south end of the beach.

Just north of the 32-mile marker, there's public parking and a concrete stairway leading down the cliffs to Slaughterhouse Beach. A half-mile past the 32-mile marker there's room for about six cars to park adjacent to the path down to Honolua Bay.

Activities

Hiking

Whether you're after an easy coastal stroll or a hardcore trek through tropical flora, **Kapalua** (☎665-4386; www.kapalua. com) has got a trail for you. The **Maunalei Arboretum Trail** cuts through a forest planted by DT Fleming, the arborist who developed Maui's pineapple industry. Access is strictly via a free shuttle (☎665-9110) that departs from the Kapalua Resort Center at 8am, 9:30am, 11am and 2pm and returns from the trailhead at 9:50am, 11:20pm, 2:20pm and 5:20pm.

For a one-way hike that ends at the resort, pick up the **Honolua Ridge Trail** (1.25 miles) from the Maunalei Arboretum Trail. You'll enjoy a spectacular mountain vista along the ridge before dipping back

The Best...
Sunset Cocktails

1 Barefoot Bar, Hula Grill (p71)

2 Patio, Merriman's Kapalua (p84)

3 Teralani cruise (p67)

4 Sea House Restaurant (p78)

5 Cliff Dive Bar, Sheraton Maui (p72)

into the jungle-like forest for a view of Pu'u Kukui (5788ft), one of the wettest spots in the world, averaging 325in annually. Pass through a stand of Sugi trees then pick up the **Mahana Ridge Trail** (5.75 miles). When you reach the golf course restrooms, look left for the wooded trail just above the restroom building. At the sharp roadside bend, after the telephone poles, either turn right onto the dirt path to descend to DT Fleming Beach (look for the small sign) or follow the road left to return to the adventure center.

The old Village Golf Course, now overgrown and reincarnated as the **Village Walking Trails**, offers stunning scenery as it rises up the mountain slopes. The easy **Coastal Trail** (1.75 miles) links Kapalua Beach with Oneloa Beach, then crosses below the Ritz-Carlton to end at DT Fleming Beach. During your walk, be sure to stay on the designated path to avoid disturbing nesting birds. The Coastal Trail passes ancient burial grounds and the jagged Dragon's Teeth formation, both located north of the Ritz-Carlton and the trail. These sites are of cultural significance to Native Hawaiians and should not be inspected up-close. Respect the signage.

For maps, liability waivers and shuttle pick-ups, check in at the Kapalua Resort Center.

Golf

KAPALUA GOLF Golf
(☎669-8044, 877-527-2582; www.kapalua.com;
Bay/Plantation greens fee before 1pm $208/268,
after 1pm $138/158; ☉1st tee 6:40am) Kapalua
boasts two of the island's top championship golf courses, both certified by
Audubon International as sanctuaries
for native plants and animals. How's that
for green greens? The **Bay course (Map
p78; 300 Kapalua Dr)** is the tropical ocean
course, meandering across a lava peninsula. The challenging **Plantation course**
(Map p78; 2000 Plantation Club Dr) sweeps
over a rugged landscape of hills and deep
gorges.

Kapalua Golf Academy Golf Lessons
(Map p78; ☎665-5455; www.kapalua.com; 1000
Office Rd; 1hr private lesson $125, half-day school
$195; ☉8am-4pm) Hawaii's top golf academy is
staffed by PGA pros.

Tennis

KAPALUA TENNIS Tennis
(Map p78; ☎665-9112; 100 Kapalua Dr; per
person per day $10, racket rental $6; ☉staffed
8am-noon & 3-6pm Mon-Fri, 8am-4pm Sat & Sun)
Maui's premier full-service tennis club
has 10 Plexipave courts and an array of
clinics. If you're on your own, give the club
a ring and they'll match you with other
players for singles or doubles games.

Watersports

**KAPALUA DIVE
COMPANY** Diving, Kayaking
(Map p78; ☎669-3448; www.kapaluadive.com;
Kapalua Bay; dives from $85; kayak tours $85;
☉8am-5pm) Offers a range of water activities, including kayak-snorkel tours and a
full menu of dives. Rent a basic snorkel
set for $15/day; you can use a credit card
or driver's license for rental deposit. Look
for its beach shack on Kapalua Beach.

Left: Snorkelers, Honolua Bay (p80); **Below:** Plantation course, Kapalua Golf

Ziplining

KAPALUA ADVENTURES
Ziplining

(Map p78; ☎665-3753; www.kapaluaadventures.com; Office Rd; tour from $149; ⏱7am-7pm) Ready to soar across the West Maui Mountains – for nearly 2 miles? This adventure includes eight ziplines in all, two of them extending a breathtaking 2000ft in length. The tour has a dual track, allowing you to zip side by side with a friend. Full-moon trips are offered three times per month. Kapalua Adventures is located inside the discreetly signed Kapalua Resort Center south of the Honolua Village Center.

 Festivals & Events

Hyundai Tournament of Champions
Golf Tournament

(www.pgatour.com) Watch Tiger and friends tee off at the PGA Tour's season opener in early January at the Plantation course, vying for a multimillion-dollar purse.

Celebration of the Arts
Arts Festival

(www.celebrationofthearts.org) This festival in April at the Ritz-Carlton celebrates traditional Hawaiian culture with storytelling, hula demonstrations, films, arts and music.

Kapalua Wine & Food Festival
Food & Wine Festival

(www.kapalua.com) A culinary extravaganza held over four days in late June at the Ritz-Carlton, the festival features renowned winemakers and Hawaii's hottest chefs offering cooking demonstrations and wine tastings.

 Sleeping

KAPALUA VILLAS
Condo $$$

(Map p78; ☎665-9170, 800-545-0018; www.outrigger.com; 2000 Village Rd; 1br/2br from $209/279; ❄@🛜🏊) These swank condos – let's call them fortresses of luxury – are clustered into three separate compounds. The Golf Villas line the Bay

83

Golf Course while the Bay and Ridge Villas overlook the beach. The one-bedroom units sleep up to four; the two-bedroom units sleep six. For up-close whale watching, try the spacious Bay Villas. The $25 daily resort fee includes parking, wi-fi and use of the resort shuttle.

RITZ-CARLTON KAPALUA
Resort Hotel $$$

(Map p78; ☎669-6200, 800-262-8440; www.ritzcarlton.com; 1 Ritz-Carlton Dr; r from $595; ❄@🤙🅿) This luxe hotel's low-key elegance attracts the exclusive golf crowd. On a hillside fronting the greens and the sea, this hotel has a heated multilevel swimming pool shaded by palm trees, a spa and a fitness club. Rooms boast oversize marble bathrooms, goose-down pillows...you get the picture. The $25 daily resort fee covers parking, wi-fi and use of the fitness center and resort shuttle. Internet access at the business center is 75¢ per minute.

 Eating & Drinking

TOP CHOICE HONOLUA STORE
Plate Lunch $

(Map p78; ☎665-9105; www.kapalua.com; 502 Office Rd; lunch $6-9; ⏱store 6am-8pm, deli to 3pm) This porch-wrapped bungalow was once the general store for the Honolua Pineapple Plantation. On the outside, the store looks almost the same as it did when it opened in 1929. Today, the place is a nod to normalcy in the midst of lavish exclusiveness. The deli is known for its reasonable prices and fantastic plate lunches. The $5.75 hobo lunch (one main and a scoop of rice) is one of Maui's best lunch deals. Wraps are hearty affairs, and even the Spam *musubi* (a rice ball topped with sautéed Spam and wrapped with dried seaweed) is can't-miss (well, it's better than expected). There's also a coffee bar with pastries.

TOP CHOICE PLANTATION HOUSE
Hawaii Regional $$$

(Map p78; ☎669-6299; www.theplantation house.com; Plantation Golf Course clubhouse,

2000 Plantation Club Dr; breakfast & lunch $12-18, dinner $28-42; ⏱8am-3pm & 6-9pm) Breakfast at this open-air eatery is the stuff that memories and poems are made of. The crab cake Benedict? A fluffy, hollandaise-splashed affair that will have you kissing your plate and plotting your return. Adding to the allure are stellar views of the coast and Moloka'i, as well as the world-famous golf course below. For dinner, fresh fish is prepared with Mediterranean flair and a Mauian finish – think Hawaiian fish with couscous and roasted Maui onions.

SANSEI SEAFOOD RESTAURANT & SUSHI BAR
Japanese $$$

(Map p78; ☎669-6286; www.sanseihawaii.com; 600 Office Rd; sushi $3-16; mains $22-43; ⏱5:30pm-10pm) The innovative sushi menu is reason enough to dine here, but the non-sushi house specials shouldn't be overlooked. The tempura rock shrimp in garlic aioli flawlessly blends Japanese and French flavors, and the spicy Dungeness crab ramen with truffle broth is another prize. Order before 6pm and all food is discounted by 25%. No reservation? Queue up for one of the 12 seats at the sushi bar – folks start gathering outside about 4:50pm.

PINEAPPLE GRILL
Hawaii Regional $$$

(Map p78; ☎669-9600; www.pineapplekapalua.com; Kapalua Bay Golf Course clubhouse, 200 Kapalua Dr; lunch $11-17, dinner $26-47; ⏱lunch & dinner) This beauty's got it all, from a sweeping hilltop view to a sleek exhibition kitchen that whips up creative fusion fare. Tantalize the taste buds with the likes of lobster-coconut bisque, wasabi-seared fish and a pork chop with a Maui Gold Pineapple glaze.

MERRIMAN'S KAPALUA
Hawaii Regional $$$

(☎669-6400; www.merrimanshawaii.com; 1 Bay Club Pl; happy hour menu $9-24; ⏱happy hour 3-5pm) We like Merriman's for happy hour. Perched on a scenic point between Kapalua Bay and Napili Bay, this tiki- and palm-dotted spot is a gorgeous place to unwind after braving the Kahekili Hwy.

Kahekili Highway

They call this narrow, serpentine, blind-curving thread of pavement a highway? That's some optimistic labeling, for sure. This challenging road, which hugs the rugged northern tip of Maui, needles around hairpin turns, careens over one-lane bridges and teeters beside treacherous cliffs. It's one of Maui's most adventurous drives, and undisputedly its most challenging.

The area's so ravishingly rural that it's hard to imagine trendy West Maui could hold such untouched countryside. The key to its preservation is the Kahekili Hwy (Route 340), which narrows to the width of a driveway, keeping construction trucks and tourist buses at bay.

Not for the faint of heart, sections slow to just 5mph as the road wraps around blind curves; a lengthy stretch around the village of Kahakuloa is a mere one lane with cliffs on one side and a sheer drop on the other – if you hit oncoming traffic here you may be doing your traveling in reverse! But if you can handle that, this largely overlooked route offers all sorts of adventures, with horse and hiking trails, mighty blowholes and delicious banana bread. Don't be fooled by car rental maps that show the road as a dotted line – it's paved and open to the public the entire way. There are no services, so gas up beforehand. Give yourself a good two hours' driving time, not counting stops.

Property between the highway and the coast is both privately and publicly owned. Trails to the shore are often uneven, rocky and slippery, and the coast is subject to dangerous waves. If you decide to explore, take appropriate precautions, and get access permission when possible.

Sights in this section are arranged in geographical order from west to east.

Punalau Beach

Manicured golf courses and ritzy enclaves drop away and the scenery gets wilder as you drive toward the island's north-ernmost point. Ironwood-lined Punalau Beach, 0.7 miles after the 34-mile marker, makes a worthy stop if you're up for a solitary stroll. Swimming is a no-go though, as a rocky shelf creates unfavorable conditions for water activities.

Nakalele Point

Continuing on, the terrain is hilly, with rocky cattle pastures punctuated by tall sisal plants. At a number of pull-offs, you can stop and explore. Lush pastures are quite enticing, willing you to traipse down the cliffs and out along the rugged coastline.

At the 38-mile marker, a mile-long trail leads out to a **light station** at the end of windswept Nakalele Point. Here you'll find a coastline of arches and other formations worn out of the rocks by the pounding surf.

Nakalele Blowhole (p87)
PHOTOGRAPHER: SEAN CAFFREY/LONELY PLANET IMAGES ©

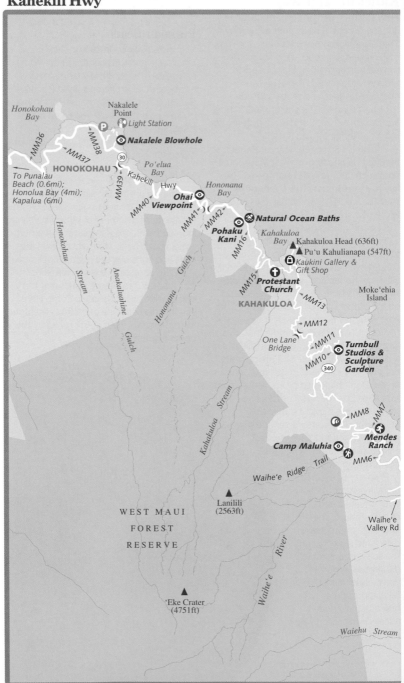

The **Nakalele Blowhole** roars when the surf is up but is a sleeper when the seas are calm. To check on its mood, park at the boulder-lined pull-off 0.6 miles beyond the 38-mile marker. You can glimpse the action, if there is any, a few hundred yards beyond the parking lot. Feeling adventurous? It's a 15-minute scramble down a jagged moonscape of lava rocks to the blowhole, which can shoot up to 100ft. This should go without saying, but really, don't sit on top of the blowhole! In fact, keep a safe distance.

Eight-tenths of a mile after the 40-mile marker look for the **Ohai Viewpoint**, on the *makai* side of the road. The viewpoint won't be marked but there's a sign announcing the start of the Ohai Trail. Don't bother with the trail – it's not particularly interesting. Instead, bear left and walk out to the top of the point for a jaw-dropping coastal view that includes a glimpse of the Nakalele Blowhole. If you have kids, be careful – the crumbly cliff has a sudden drop of nearly 800ft!

Natural Ocean Baths & Bellstone

After the 42-mile post the markers change; the next marker is 16 and the numbers go down as you continue on from here.

One-tenth of a mile before the 16-mile marker, look seaward for a large dirt pull-off and a well-beaten path that leads 15 minutes down lava cliffs to **natural ocean baths** on the ocean's edge. Cut out of slippery lava rock and encrusted with olivine minerals, these incredibly clear pools sit in the midst of roaring surf. Some have natural steps, but if you're tempted to go in, size it up carefully – people unfamiliar with the water conditions here have been swept into the sea and drowned. If the rocks are covered in silt from recent storm runoffs, or the waves look high, forget about it – it's dangerous. Although the baths are on public land, state officials do not recommend accessing them due to the hazardous conditions, including slippery rocks, large and powerful surf, waves on ledges and strong currents.

The huge boulder with concave marks on the inland side of the road just before the pull-off is a bellstone, **Pohaku Kani**. If you hit it with a rock on the Kahakuloa side, where the deepest indentations are, you might be able to get a hollow sound. It's a bit resonant if you hit it just right, though it takes some imagination to hear it ring like a bell.

Kahakuloa

An imposing 636ft-tall volcanic dome guards the entrance to Kahakuloa Bay like a lurking, watchful dragon. They say this photogenic landmark, known as **Kahakuloa Head**, was a favorite cliff-diving spot of Chief Kahekili. Before the road drops into the valley, there's a pull-off above town providing a bird's-eye view.

The bayside village of Kahakuloa, tucked at the bottom of a lush valley and embraced by towering sea cliffs, retains a solidly Hawaiian character. Kahakuloa's isolation has protected it from the rampant development found elsewhere on Maui. Farmers tend taro patches, dogs wander across the road, and a missionary-era Protestant church marks the village center. One of Hawaii's most accomplished ukulele players, Richard Ho'opi'i, is the church minister.

You won't find stores here, but villagers set up hard-to-miss roadside stands selling fruit and snacks to day-trippers. For shave ice ($3), hit Ululani's hot-pink stand. For free samples of 'ono (delicious) banana bread, stop at Julia's lime-green shack (www.juliasbananabread.com). After one taste and some talk-story on the porch, we bet you'll buy a loaf for the road ($6). It tastes fresh for days and makes for a terrific no-fuss breakfast.

Kahakuloa to Waihe'e

On the outskirts of Kahakuloa, near the 14-mile marker, the hilltop **Kaukini Gallery & Gift Shop** (✆244-3371; www.kaukinigallery.com; ◷10am-5pm) sells works by more than 120 island artists, with watercolors, jewelry, native-fiber baskets, pottery and more. A locator map on the front lanai tells you how many more narrow miles you need to drive in either direction to reach relative safety.

Past the 10-mile marker look for **Turnbull Studios & Sculpture Garden** (✆244-9838; www.turnbullstudios.org; ◷10am-5pm Mon-Fri), where you can view Bruce Turnbull's ambitious bronze and wood creations, as well as the works of other area artists...very cool stuff. If you pass the giraffe, you've gone too far. Turn around when you can.

Continuing around beep-as-you-go blind turns, the highway gradually levels out atop sea cliffs. For an Eden-like scene, stop at the pull-off 0.1 miles north of the 8-mile marker and look down into the ravine below, where you'll see a cascading **waterfall** framed by double pools.

Kahakuloa Head

For a real *paniolo* (cowboy) experience, saddle up at **Mendes Ranch** (📞871-5222; www.mendesranch.com; 3530 Kahekili Hwy; 2hr ride $110; ⏱rides 8:15am & 11:30pm), a working cattle ranch near the 7-mile marker. The picture-perfect scenery on these rides includes everything from jungle valleys to lofty sea cliffs and waterfalls.

Waihe'e Ridge Trail

This fabulous trail has it all: tropical flora, breezy ridgelines, lush valley landscapes and lofty views of Maui's wild northern coast and the central valley. Best part? The well-defined trail is less than 5 miles roundtrip and only takes about three hours to complete.

The path is a bit steep, but it's a fairly steady climb and not overly strenuous. It's best to tackle this one before 8am in order to beat the clouds, which can obscure the view from the top later in the morning.

Starting at an elevation of 1000ft, the trail, which crosses reserve land, climbs a ridge, passing from pasture to forest. Guava trees and groves of eucalyptus are prominent, and the aroma of fallen fruit may accompany you after a rainstorm. From the 0.75-mile post, panoramic views open up, with a scene that sweeps clear down to the ocean along the Waihe'e Gorge and deep into pleated valleys.

As you continue on, you'll enter ohia forest with native birds and get distant views of waterfalls cascading down the mountains. The ridge-top views are similar to those you'd see from a helicopter, and you'll probably see a handful of them dart into the adjacent valley like gnats on a mission.

There are several benches along the trail to stop and soak in the scenery and the remarkable stillness. Birdsong, chirping insects, a rushing stream, muffled bits of hiker conversation below – these are the only interruptions. The trail ends at a small clearing on the 2563ft peak of Lanilili. Here you'll find awesome views in all directions as well as a picnic table.

Solos, seniors and in-shape kids should be fine on this hike. If you have access to hiking poles, bring them. The trail gets muddy and steep in spots.

The Best…
Outdoor Activities

1 Snorkeling Pu'u Keka'a (p65)

2 Picnicking on the Waihe'e Ridge Trail (p89)

3 Ziplining the West Maui Mountains (p67)

4 Scrambling for a view of the Nakalele Blowhole (p87)

5 Whale-watching on a sunset cruise off Ka'anapali Beach (p67)

6 Hiking the Honolua Ridge and Mahana Ridge Trails (p81)

To get to the trailhead, take the one-lane paved road that starts on the inland side of the highway just south of the 7-mile marker. It's almost directly across the road from the big gate at Mendes Ranch. The road (open 7am to 6pm) climbs to the Boy Scouts' Camp Mahulia and winds through open pasture, so keep an eye out for cattle that mosey across the road. The trailhead, marked with a Na Ala Hele sign, is a mile up on the left just before the camp.

For complete details, visit http://hawaiitrails.ehawaii.gov, the state's trail and access website.

Waihe'e to Wailuku

Soon after the Waihe'e Ridge Trail, the Kahekili Hwy runs through the sleeper towns of Waihe'e and Waiehu before arriving in Wailuku. There's not much to do here, but if you're up for a round of golf, the county-run **Waiehu Municipal Golf Course** (📞243-7400; 200 Halewaiu Rd; greens fee $55, optional cart $20) offers an affordable and easily walkable 18 holes on the coast. On-site are a small cafe, pro-shop and public restrooms.

'Iao Valley & Central Maui

Once all but overlooked by travelers, this wind-whipped region has hit the map big time, morphing into action-central for anything with a sail. Kanaha Beach takes home gold for kitesurfing and windsurfing, bursting into color each day with a glorious mile-long sea of sails. But you don't have to get all your thrills on the water. Central Maui has exceptional green treats, most notably lush 'Iao Valley, a sight so spectacular it was once reserved for royalty; two rare water-bird sanctuaries; and the most dazzling tropical aquarium you'll ever see.

Central Maui also cradles the island's most fertile agricultural land with fields of waving sugarcane stretching clear across the central plains from Kahului to Ma'alaea. Bustling Kahului boasts Maui's largest farmers market, and homespun Wailuku serves up the region's tastiest lunch scene.

'Iao Valley State Park (p109)

ʻIao Valley & Central Maui Itineraries

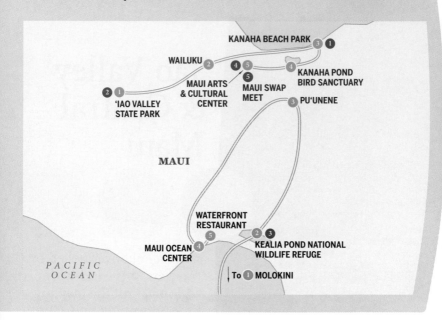

KANAHA BEACH PARK

WAILUKU

MAUI ARTS
& CULTURAL
CENTER

MAUI SWAP
MEET

KANAHA POND
BIRD SANCTUARY

ʻIAO VALLEY
STATE PARK

PUʻUNENE

MAUI

WATERFRONT
RESTAURANT

MAUI OCEAN
CENTER

KEALIA POND NATIONAL
WILDLIFE REFUGE

PACIFIC
OCEAN

To ① MOLOKINI

One Day

① ʻIao Valley State Park (p109)
Start your day ogling the island's most photographed landmark, ʻIao Needle. Follow your photo snaps with a walk along the park's cool streamside trails.

② Wailuku (p104) Lucky you, it's lunchtime, and there's no better place than Wailuku for an island-style meal. The only hard part is choosing: spicy Vietnamese, those famous **Sam Sato's** noodles or perhaps Hawaiian fare from **Takamiya Market**. Work off your lunch with a poke around the town's antique shops and a visit to **Bailey House Museum**.

③ Kanaha Beach Park (p94) Next make your way to Kahului's crowning glory, and watch the scores of colorful sails ripping across Kanaha's waves. If you want to try your hand, windsurfing and kitesurfing instructors give lessons right at the beach.

④ Kanaha Pond Bird Sanctuary (p94)
Inland from the beach lies this unexpectedly peaceful respite. Unexpected because it's right along the highway where cars and trucks barrel along, yet once you walk through the gate into the wetlands it's all Zen: just you and some of the rarest birds on the planet.

⑤ Maui Arts & Cultural Center (p101)
An evening show at this state-of-the-art center might well be one of the highlights of your trip. Slack key guitar masters, ukulele virtuosos, Willie Nelson at his finest.

➡ **THIS LEG: 28 MILES**

Two Days

1 **Molokini** (p112) On day two, it's time to take your adventures beneath the surface. Hop on a boat at Ma'alaea Harbor for a snorkel cruise or dive outing to this awesome volcanic crater, renowned for its crystal waters and wildly abundant sea life. If it's winter, there's a good chance you'll spot humpback whales along the way.

2 **Kealia Pond National Wildlife Refuge** (p110) Get your land legs back by meandering along Maui's longest boardwalk for a close-up look at the fascinating ocean, marsh and pond sights unfolding at your feet.

3 **Pu'unene** (p110) Roll down your windows and smell the sweet air of Maui's sugar town. Start at the **Alexander & Baldwin Sugar Museum** to get up to speed on the island's sugar history, then drive around the back of the sugar mill for a little detour to discover the remains of a forgotten plantation town.

4 **Maui Ocean Center** (p111) Now it's time to come eye to eye with huge stingrays and menacing reef sharks at this tropical aquarium. Yikes, aren't you glad you didn't see any of these guys at Molokini! A glass tunnel takes you right through the center of the shark tank – how cool is that?

5 **Waterfront Restaurant** (p113) Top off day two with a sunset dinner at Central Maui's best seafood eatery. Grab a seat on the breezy lanai and gaze out at Ma'alaea Harbor, where fishing boats pull up each afternoon and unload their catch. What to order? Catch of the day, natch.

▶ **THIS LEG: 38 MILES**

'Iao Valley & Central Maui Highlights

1 **Best Beach: Kanaha Beach Park** (p94) This wind-whipped beach is a mecca for kiteboarding and windsurfing.

2 **Best View: 'Iao Valley State Park** (p109) The emerald pinnacle is Maui's top postcard scene.

3 **Best Nature Walk: Kealia Pond Boardwalk** (p110) A unique ecosystem unfolds at your feet.

4 **Best Entertainment Venue: Maui Arts & Cultural Center** (p101) A cornucopia of aloha-filled festivals, concerts and theater.

5 **Best Place to Meet the Locals: Maui Swap Meet** (p102) The island's finest place to buy from farmers and artisans.

Windsurfer, Kanaha Beach Park (p94)
PHOTOGRAPHER: ANDY JACKSON/ALAMY

Discover 'Iao Valley & Central Maui

Kahului

All roads lead to Kahului, the commercial heart of Maui. It's home to the island's gateway airport and cruise-ship harbor. Just about everything that enters Maui comes through this workaday town thick with warehouses and shopping centers. Hardly a vacation scene, you say. True, but if you dig a little deeper you'll find more to your liking. You have to go island-style to have fun here: talk story with the locals at the Saturday swap meet, take in a concert on the lawn of the cultural center or join the wave-riding action at Kanaha Beach. There's a lot more to Kahului than first meets the eye.

 ## Beaches

KANAHA BEACH PARK Beach
This mile-long beach (Map p96) is surf city, with hundreds of brilliant sails zipping across the waves. Both windsurfing and kitesurfing are so hot here that the beach is divvied up, with kitesurfers converging at the southwest end, known as **Kite Beach**, and windsurfers hitting the water at the northeast end. There's no better place to learn both sports.

A section in the middle of the beach is roped off for swimmers, but this place is really all about wind power. Facilities include restrooms, showers and shaded picnic tables.

 ## Sights

KANAHA POND BIRD SANCTUARY
Wildlife Sanctuary
(Hwy 37; admission free; ☺sunrise-sunset) This easy-access roadside sanctuary provides a haven for rare Hawaiian birds, including the *ae'o* (Hawaiian black-necked stilt), a wading bird with long, orange legs that feeds along the pond's marshy edges. Even though this graceful bird has a population of just 1500 in the entire state, you can count on spotting it here.

An **observation deck** just a short walk beyond the parking lot offers the ideal lookout for seeing stilts, native coots and black-crowned night herons. Close the gate

Ae'o (Hawaiian black-necked stilt)
PHOTOGRAPHER: ART DIRECTORS & TRIP/ALAMY

and walk into the sanctuary quietly; you should be able to make several sightings right along the shoreline.

 MAUI NUI BOTANICAL GARDENS
Gardens

(☑ 249-2798; www.mnbg.org; 150 Kanaloa Ave; admission free; ⏱8am-4pm Mon-Sat) If you're interested in the subtle beauty of native Hawaiian plants, this garden is a gem. Come here to view rare species and to identify plants you've heard about but haven't yet seen, such as *wauke* (paper mulberry, used to make tapa), *'ulu* (breadfruit) and *'iliahi* (sandalwood). Don't expect it to be overly flowery, however. What you won't see here are the riotous colors of exotic tropicals that now dominate most Hawaiian gardens. To delve even deeper into the key role of native plants in Hawaiian culture join one of the **guided tours** (suggested donation $5; ⏱10am-11:30am Tue & Fri).

KAHULUI HARBOR
Harbor

Kahului's large protected harbor serves many functions. It's the island's only deepwater port, so all boat traffic, from cruise ships to cargo vessels, docks here. But don't think it's all business. You'll find one of the harbor's most attractive scenes at **Hoaloha Park**, where you can watch outrigger canoe clubs practice in the late afternoon.

FREE Schaefer International Gallery
Museum

(☑ 242-2787; www.mauiarts.org; 1 Cameron Way; ⏱11am-5pm Wed-Sun) This gallery at the Maui Arts & Cultural Center features fascinating exhibits on Hawaiian culture, hula and art.

🏃 Activities

Windsurfing

Windswept Kahului is the base for Maui's main windsurfing operations. Board-and-rig rentals cost around $50/325 per day/week. If you're new to the sport, introductory classes are readily available, last a couple of hours and cost $90. The

The Best...
Nature Spots

1 'Iao Valley State Park (p109)

2 Kealia Pond Boardwalk (p110)

3 Maui Ocean Center (p111)

4 Maui Nui Botanical Gardens (p95)

5 Kanaha Pond Bird Sanctuary (p94)

business is competitive, so ask about discounts.

Reliable shops that rent gear and arrange lessons:

Hi-Tech Surf Sports (☑ 877-2111; www.htmaui.com; 425 Koloa St; ⏱9am-6pm)

Hawaiian Island Surf & Sport (☑ 871-4981; www.hawaiianisland.com; 415 Dairy Rd; ⏱8.30am-6pm)

Second Wind (☑ 877-7467; www.secondwindmaui.com; 111 Hana Hwy; ⏱9am-6pm)

Kitesurfing

Kitesurfing, also known as kiteboarding, has taken off big-time in Kahului. The action centers on Kite Beach, the southwest end of Kanaha Beach Park. If you've never tried it before, you can learn the ropes from some of the very pros who've made kitesurfing such a hot wave ride. Vans set up at Kite Beach to offer lessons: expect to pay about $275 for a half-day intro course. Check out the scene live at kitebeachcam.com.

Action Sports Maui (☑ 871-5857; www.actionsportsmaui.com)

Aqua Sports Maui (☑ 242-8015; www.mauikiteboardinglessons.com)

Kiteboarding School Maui (☑ 873-0015; www.ksmaui.com)

'Iao Valley & Central Maui

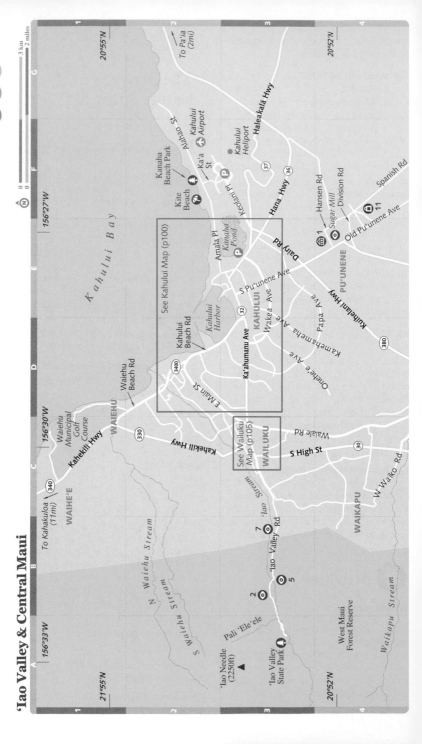

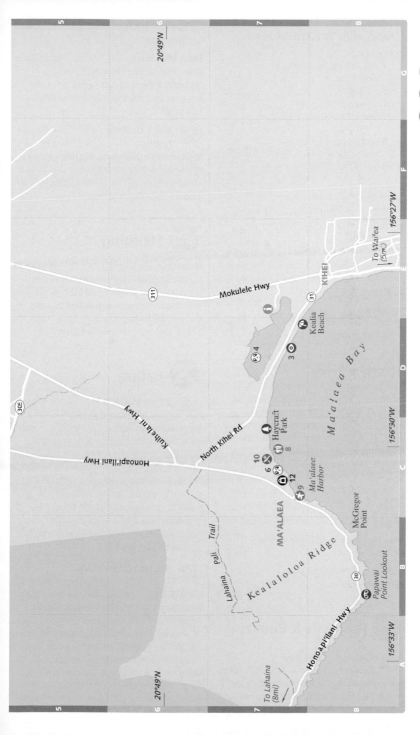

97

'Iao Valley & Central Maui

Helicopter Rides

Several companies offer helicopter tours of Maui. All operate out of the **Kahului Heliport** (Map p96; 1 Kahului Airport Rd), alongside Kahului Airport. Thirty-minute tours of the jungly West Maui Mountains cost around $150 and one-hour circle-island tours cost about $275. Discounts abound.

Companies advertise in the free tourist magazines, with all sorts of deals.

AlexAir (☏ 871-0792; www.helitour.com)

Blue Hawaiian (☏ 871-8844; www.bluehawaiian.com)

Sunshine (☏ 871-7799; www.sunshinehelicopters.com)

 **Festivals & Events**

TOP CHOICE **Ki Ho'alu Slack Key Guitar Festival**   Music Festival (www.mauiarts.org) At this event held on the lawn of the Maui Arts & Cultural Center in June,

top slack key guitarists from throughout Hawaii take the stage.

Maui Marathon   Road Race (www.mauimarathon.com) Held in mid-September, this road race begins in Kahului and ends 26.2 miles later at Whalers Village in Ka'anapali.

TOP CHOICE **Maui 'Ukulele Festival**   Music Festival (www.ukulelefestivalhawaii.org) Held outdoors at the Maui Arts & Cultural Center on a Sunday in mid-October, this aloha event showcases uke masters from Maui and beyond.

 **Sleeping**

Maui Seaside Hotel   Hotel $$
(☏ 877-3311; www.seasidehotelshawaii.com; 100 W Ka'ahumanu Ave; r from $125; ❋ @ ≋) If you have some dire need to spend the night in Kahului, this is the better of its aging hotels. It's a plain Jane but the rooms are clean.

 Eating

TOP CHOICE **CYNNAMON'S**   Food Truck $
(Kahului Beach Rd, at boat ramp; meals $8; ◷ 10am-1pm Tue-Sat) The queen of island food trucks, this family operation sells only freshly caught fish. It's no coincidence it's in front of the boat dock; the hubby reels in the fish, and Cynnamon grills it to perfection for a lunchtime crowd. Top choices include the panko-crusted mahi plate lunch and the fresh ahi *poke* (marinated raw fish) made on-site while you wait.

TOP CHOICE **BISTRO CASANOVA**   Mediterranean $$
(☏ 873-3650; www.casanovamaui.com; 33 Lono Ave; mains $14-32; ◷ 11am-9:30pm Mon-Sat) An offshoot of the popular Casanova in Makawao, this is Kahului's classiest dining, with a solid tapas menu, good Maui-raised steaks and plenty of organic Kula veggies. The setting is upscale and urban. Reservations are recommended at dinner, when the bistro can fill with a pre-theater

Green Power

Windy central Maui is a major league player in the field of alternative energy, producing some 20% of Maui's electricity needs from the windmills above Ma'alaea and a bagasse plant at Pu'unene's sugar mill. The mill's power plant is a thorough recycler, burning residue sugarcane fibers, called bagasse, to run the mill and pump excess juice into the island's electrical grid. But it's the windmills that hold the greenest future and a planned expansion of the wind farm could soon double the number of turbines at Ma'alaea.

crowd en route to a show at the Maui Arts & Cultural Center.

DA KITCHEN Hawaiian **$$**
(www.da-kitchen.com; 425 Koloa St; plate lunches $9-14; ⊙9am-9pm) Hawaiian decor and unbeatable island grinds make this a favorite meal stop. The *kalua* pork is, as they say, 'so tender it falls off da bone,' and the more expensive plate lunches are big enough to feed two. Expect a crowd at lunch but don't be deterred as the service is quick.

CAMPUS FOOD COURT Food Court **$**
(www.mauiculinary-campusdining.com; Maui College, 310 W Ka'ahumanu Ave; mains $5-8; ⊙11am-1:30pm Mon-Fri) With names like Farm to Table and the Raw Fish Camp, you know this isn't your average campus fare. This food court, run by students in Maui College's acclaimed culinary arts program, is well worth a detour. You might also want to check out the **Class Act** (☏984-3280) fine dining restaurant, where students create a multi-course locavore meal.

THAILAND CUISINE Thai **$$**
(www.thailandcuisinemaui.com; Maui Mall, 70 E Ka'ahumanu Ave; mains $10-16; ⊙10:30am-3:30pm & 5-9:30pm; ✈) *Maui News* readers voted this family-run eatery as Maui's best ethnic restaurant. And yes, it lives up to the reputation. Start with the shrimp summer rolls, then move on to aromatic green curries or perhaps the ginger grilled mahimahi.

Performers, Maui Arts & Cultural Center (p101)

Kahului

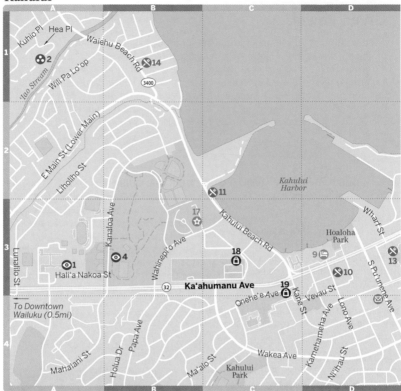

Kahului

Drinking

WOW-WEE MAUI'S KAVA
BAR & GRILL   Bar

(www.wowweemaui.com; 333 Dairy Rd; ⊙11am-9pm Mon-Sat, to 6pm Sun; @) This hip cafe is *the* place to try kava served in a coconut shell. A ceremonial drink in old Hawaii, this spicy elixir made from the *Piper methysticum* plant gives a mild buzz. Wow-Wee Maui's chocolate bars, some spiked with kava, will also make you swoon. For something more conventional, it makes a killer martini.

MAUI COFFEE ROASTERS   Cafe

(www.mauicoffeeroasters.com; 444 Hana Hwy; @ 🛜) There's good vibes and good java at this coffee shop where locals linger over lattes while surfing free wi-fi. Need to jump-start your day? Step up to the bar and order a Sledge Hammer – a quadruple espresso with steamed half and half.

Entertainment

MAUI ARTS & CULTURAL
CENTER   Concert Hall

(MACC; 🗷242-7469; www.mauiarts.org; 1 Cameron Way) There's always something happening at this snazzy performance complex, which boasts two indoor theaters and an outdoor amphitheater, all with excellent acoustics. As Maui's main venue for music, theater and dance, it hosts everything from ukulele jams to touring rock bands. If you happen to be in the area on the third Thursday of the month, don't miss the Slack Key Masters show hosted by George Kahumoku Jr.

Shopping

Kahului hosts Maui's big-box discount chains of the Wal-Mart and Costco variety, as well as its biggest shopping malls, Queen Ka'ahumanu Center.

TASAKA GURI-GURI   Dessert $

(Maui Mall, 70 E Ka'ahumanu Ave; 2 scoops/quart $1.10/5; ⊙9am-6pm Mon-Sat, 10am-4pm Sun) For the coolest treat in town, queue up at this hole-in-the-wall shop dishing up homemade pineapple sherbet. The *guri-guri,* as it's called, is so popular that locals pick up quarts on the way to the airport to take to friends on neighboring islands.

If you need to stock up the condo on the way in from the airport, the **Safeway** (170 E Kamehameha Ave; ⊙24hr) in the town center never closes. Like it greener? **Whole Foods** (Maui Mall, 70 E Ka'ahumanu Ave; ⊙8am-9pm) carries island-grown produce, fish and beef, and is a good place to pick up lei.

MAUI SWAP MEET Outdoor Market

(244-3100; Maui College, 310 Ka'ahumanu Ave; admission 50¢; ⊙7am-1pm Sat) Spend a Saturday morning chatting with local farmers and craftspeople at Maui's largest outdoor market. You'll not only find fresh organic Hana fruits, Kula veggies and homemade banana bread, but it's also a fun place to souvenir shop for everything from Hawaiian quilts to Maui-designed Ts. Don't be misled by the term 'swap meet': most stands sell quality local goods and every dollar you spend here stays in the community.

Bounty Music Ukuleles
(www.ukes.com; 111 Hana Hwy) Hawaiian music lovers, take note. Here you'll find all sorts of ukuleles, from inexpensive imported models to handcrafted masterpieces.

① Information

Bank of Hawaii (www.boh.com; 27 S Pu'unene Ave)

Longs Drugs (☑877-0041; Maui Mall, 70 E Ka'ahumanu Ave; ⊙7am-midnight) The town's largest pharmacy.

Maui Visitors Bureau (☑872-3893; www. visitmaui.com; Kahului airport; ⊙7:45am-9:45pm) This staffed booth in the airport's arrivals area has tons of tourist brochures.

Post office (www.usps.com; 138 S Pu'unene Ave)

① Getting There & Around

To/From The Airport

Kahului airport is at the east side of town. Most visitors pick up rental cars at the airport. See p328 for shuttle and taxi information.

Bicycle

Island Biker (☑877-7744; www.islandbikermaui. com; 415 Dairy Rd; per day/week $50/200; ⊙9am-5pm Mon-Fri, to 3pm Sat) Rents quality mountain bikes and road bikes well suited for touring Maui.

Left: Wow-Wee Maui's Kava Bar & Grill (p101);
Below: Ukuleles, Bounty Music
PHOTOGRAPHER: GREG ELMS/LONELY PLANET IMAGES ©

Bus

The Maui Bus connects Kahului with Ma'alaea, Kihei, Wailea and Lahaina; each route costs $1 and runs hourly. There are also free hourly buses that run around Kahului and connect to Wailuku.

Car

Bio-Beetle (☎873-6121; www.bio-beetle. com; 55 Amala Pl; per day/week from $50/275) Offers a green alternative to the usual car rental scene, renting Volkswagens that run on recycled vegetable oil.

Haleki'i-Pihana Heiau State Monument

Overgrown and nearly forgotten, **Haleki'i-Pihana Heiau** (Map p100; Hea Pl; admission free; ☉sunrise-sunset) holds the hilltop ruins of two of Maui's most important heiau (ancient stone temples). The site was the royal court of Kahekili, Maui's last ruling chief, and the birthplace of Keopuolani, wife of Kamehameha the Great. After

his victory at the battle of 'Iao in 1790, Kamehameha marched to this site to worship his war god Ku, offering the last human sacrifice on Maui.

Haleki'i, the first heiau, has stepped stone walls that tower above 'Iao Stream, the source for the stone used in its construction. The pyramid-like mound of **Pihana Heiau** is a five-minute walk beyond, but a thick overgrowth of kiawe makes it harder to discern.

Although it's all but abandoned, a certain mana (spiritual essence) still emanates from the site. To imagine it all through the eyes of the ancient Hawaiians, ignore the creeping suburbia and concentrate instead on the wild ocean and mountain vistas.

The site is about 2 miles northeast of central Wailuku. From Waiehu Beach Rd (Hwy 340), turn inland onto Kuhio Pl, then take the first left onto Hea Pl and follow it to the end.

Wailuku

POP 12,300

Unabashedly local, Wailuku is an enigma. As an ancient religious and political center, it boasts more sights on the National Register of Historic Places than any other town on Maui, but sees the fewest tourists. As the county capital, its central area wears a modern facade of midrise office buildings, while its age-old backstreets hold an earthy mishmash of curio shops, galleries and mom-and-pop stores that just beg for browsing. If you're here at lunchtime you're in luck. Thanks to a combination of low rent and hungry government employees, Wailuku dishes up tasty eats at prices that shame Maui's more touristed towns.

👁 Sights

Ready to get down to some nitty-gritty exploring? Dusty Wailuku offers a bevy of historic treasures. Hawaii's best-known architect, Maui-born CW Dickey, left his mark in this town before moving on to fame in Honolulu. The c 1928 **Wailuku Public Library** (cnr High & Aupuni Sts) is a classic example of Dickey's distinctive Hawaii regional design. Another Dickey creation, the **Territorial Building**, lies right across the street. Within a short walk are four more buildings on the National Register of Historic Places. To

Island Insights

Olympian gold-medal swimmer Duke Kahanamoku (1890–1968) revived the ancient art of surfing. A full-blooded Hawaiian, he traveled the world with his surfboard in hand, introducing the sport to people in Australia, Europe and the US mainland. Today he's considered the father of modern surfing.

discover all the gems in town, pick up a copy of the free *Wailuku Historic District* walking map at the library or the Bailey House Museum.

BAILEY HOUSE MUSEUM　Museum
(📞 244-3326; www.mauimuseum.org; 2375 W Main St; adult/child 7-12 $7/2; ⏰ 10am-4pm Mon-Sat) This evocative museum occupies the 1833 home of Wailuku's first Christian missionary, Edward Bailey. The 2nd story, decorated with Bailey's sparse furnishings, reflects his era.

But it's the Hawaiian section on the ground floor that holds the real intrigue. Check out the display of spears and shark-tooth daggers (ouch!) used in the bloody battles at nearby 'Iao Valley. There's also a notable collection of native wood bowls, stone adzes, feather lei and tapa cloth.

Don't miss the 10ft redwood surfboard that surfing legend Duke Kahanamoku rode and the koa fishing canoe (c 1900), both in an outdoor exhibit near the parking lot.

KA'AHUMANU CHURCH　Church
(cnr W Main & S High Sts) This handsome missionary church is named for Queen Ka'ahumanu, who cast aside the old gods and allowed Christianity to flourish. The clock in the steeple, brought around the Horn in the 19th century, still keeps accurate time. Hymns ring out in Hawaiian at Sunday morning services, but at other times it's a look-from-outside site, as the church is usually locked.

✨ Festivals & Events

E Ho'oulu Aloha　Festival
(www.mauimuseum.org) This old-Hawaii-style festival held in November at the Bailey House Museum features hula, ukulele masters, crafts, food and more. You won't find a friendlier community scene.

Maui County Fair　Fair
(www.mauicountyfair.com) Get a feel for Maui's agricultural roots at this venerable fair held in late September, with farm exhibits, tasty island grinds and a dazzling orchid display.

Wailuku

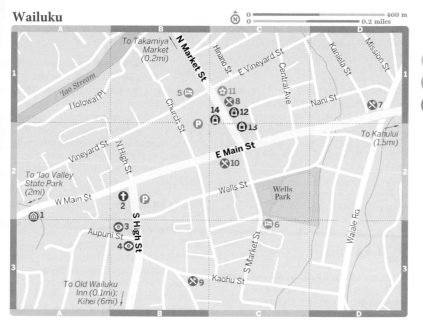

Wailuku

⊙ Sights
1 Bailey House Museum A2
2 Ka'ahumanu Church B2
3 Territorial Building................................ B3
4 Wailuku Public Library B3

🛏 Sleeping
5 Northshore Hostel................................. B1
6 Wailuku Guesthouse C3

⊗ Eating
7 A Saigon Café D1

8 Café O'Lei Wailuku C1
9 Ichiban Okazuya.....................................B3
10 Main Street Bistro C2

✪ Entertainment
11 'Iao Theater....................................... C1

🏬 Shopping
12 Bird-of-Paradise Unique
        Antiques... C1
13 Brown-Kobayashi.................................C2
14 Native Intelligence............................... C1

Wailuku First Friday   Street Fair
Wailuku turns Market St into a street party
complete with live music, poetry slams and a beer
garden on the first Friday evening of the month.

 **Sleeping**

TOP CHOICE **OLD WAILUKU INN**   B&B **$$**
(☎244-5897; www.mauiinn.com; 2199
Kaho'okele St; r incl breakfast $165-195; ❀ @)
Step back into the 1920s in this elegant
period home built by a wealthy banker.
Authentically restored, the inn retains

the antique appeal of earlier times while
discreetly adding modern amenities. Each
room has its own personality, but all are
large and comfy with traditional Hawaiian
quilts warming the beds. The inn, 0.1 mile
south of the library, is hands-down the
finest place to lay your head in Central
Maui.

**WAILUKU
GUESTHOUSE**   Guesthouse **$**
(☎986-8270; www.wailukuhouse.com; 210
S Market St; r $79-109; ❀ 🛜 ⛱) This af-
fordable family-run guesthouse has

simple, clean rooms, each with its own bathroom and private entrance. There's a refrigerator and coffeemaker in the rooms and a park with tennis courts across the street.

NORTHSHORE HOSTEL Hostel **$**
(📞986-8095; www.northshorehostel.com; 2080 E Vineyard St; dm $24, s/d with shared bathroom $55/65; ❄@🛜) The smaller and spiffier of Wailuku's two hostels occupies an old building with a fresh coat of paint. Popular with European travelers, it has separate male and female dorms as well as private rooms, a full kitchen and little perks like free international calls.

 Eating

TOP CHOICE A SAIGON CAFÉ Vietnamese **$$**
(📞248-9560; cnr E Main & Kaniela Sts; mains $9-22; ⊙10am-9:30pm Mon-Sat, to 8:30pm Sun) The oldest and best Vietnamese restaurant on Maui is out of the way, but you'll be rewarded for your effort. Menu stars include the Buddha rolls in spicy peanut sauce and the aromatic lemongrass curries. To get there from N Market St, turn right on E Vineyard St and then right on Kaniela St.

TOP CHOICE TOM'S MINI-MART Shave Ice **$**
(📞244-2323; 372 Waiehu Beach Rd; shave ice $3; ⊙7am-6pm Mon-Sat) Search out this little neighborhood shop in the middle of nowhere for supersmooth shave ice ripe with tropical fruit syrups. You gotta try the mango. To get there take E Main St northeast toward the ocean, turn left on Waiehu Beach Rd and continue north for 0.2 miles.

TOP CHOICE SAM SATO'S Japanese **$**
(📞244-7124; 1750 Wili Pa Loop; mains $5-8; ⊙7am-2pm Mon-Sat) Don't even think of coming during the noon rush – islanders flock here from far and wide for Sato's steaming bowls of saimin-like dry noodles. Maui's number-one noodle house also makes amazing *manju* (Japanese cakes filled with sweet bean paste), which are sold for takeout at the counter until 4pm. To get there take E Vineyard St, go left on Central, right on Mill, left on Imi Kala and left on Wili Pa Loop.

'Iao Theater

CAFÉ O'LEI

WAILUKU   Hawaii Regional   **$**
(☏986-0044; 62 N Market St; mains $8-13;
🕙10:30am-3pm Mon-Fri) Sophisticated
decor, waitstaff in black...Wailuku has
never looked so smart. The food is on
par with top-end restaurants and the
average price is just $10. Don't miss its
signature blackened mahimahi topped
with fresh papaya salsa. The Maui onion
soup, spiked with brandy and topped with
Gruyère cheese, makes a fine starter.

ICHIBAN OKAZUYA   Plate Lunch   **$**
(☏244-7276; 2133 Kaohu St; mains $6-7;
🕙10am-2pm & 4-7pm Mon-Fri) Little more
than a tin-roofed shed, this place tucked
behind the government buildings has
been dishing out tasty Japanese-style
plate lunches to office workers for half a
century, so you'd better believe it has the
recipes down pat.

MAIN STREET BISTRO   Cafe   **$$**
(☏244-6816; www.msbmaui.com; 2051 E Main
St; mains $7-15; 🕙11am-7pm Mon-Fri) Owner
Tom Selman, former top chef at the
esteemed David Paul's, commandeers
the exhibition kitchen here. The creative
menu includes the likes of crab-cake
salad and macnut smoked beef brisket,
with reasonably priced wines to wash it
all down.

TAKAMIYA MARKET   Hawaiian   **$**
(359 N Market St; meals $4-8; 🕙5:30am-6pm
Mon-Sat) This old-time grocer specializes
in all things Hawaiian. Lunchtime features
ahi *poke, laulau* (steamed bundle made
of meat and salted butterfish, wrapped in
taro and *ti* leaves), *kalua* pig and scores
more – wrapped and ready to go.

⭐ Entertainment

'IAO THEATER   Theater
(☏242-6969; www.mauionstage.com; 68 N Mar-
ket St) Beautifully restored after years of
neglect, this 1928 art deco theater, which
once hosted big names such as Frank
Sinatra, is now the venue for community
theater productions.

Local Knowledge

NAME: ALLEN TOM

OCCUPATION: DIRECTOR, HAWAIIAN ISLANDS HUMPBACK WHALE NATIONAL MARINE SANCTUARY

RESIDENCE: KULA

What do you tell visitors? Slow down
when you get to Maui. Don't spend all your
time driving around. It's OK if you miss
something.

Where's a good beach stroll? Kealia Beach
(p111) in front of the boardwalk, there's never
anybody there. If you want a deserted beach,
or a nice long walk, you can walk from Kealia
Beach all the way to Ma'alaea.

What's your favorite Kahului experience?
Go down to Kahului Harbor (p95) around
dusk to see all the canoe paddlers in the
water with the sun setting and the West Maui
Mountains in the background. I think that's
something distinctly Hawaiian. You know
you're not in Kansas anymore.

Any local secrets? The cafeteria at Maui
College (p99). It's open to the public and
actually it's really good. It's operated by the
culinary school. Students run the whole
thing. A lot of them have gone on to careers
not only here but on the mainland.

Special green spots? If you like birds, the
Kealia Pond Boardwalk (p110) is a must. And
then there's the Maui Ocean Center (p111).
If you went out on the water and you really
loved it and want to see more, that's the
place.

Whale-watching advice? If you want
to come when the waters are infested
with whales, February to April is the best
time. There are a lot of cheap whale-
watching cruises out there but my
recommendation is to make sure you
pick one with a naturalist onboard.

The Best...
For Families

1 Maui Ocean Center (p111)

2 Snorkeling trip to Molokini (p112)

3 Shave ice at Tom's Mini-Mart (p106)

4 Whale-watching cruise (p112)

Shopping

Head to N Market St for fun browsing.

Native Intelligence   Hawaiian Gifts
(www.native-intel.com; 45 N Market St) Hula instruments, koa bowls and finely handcrafted items.

Brown-Kobayashi   Antique Shop
(38 N Market St) Museum-quality Asian antiques.

**Bird-of-Paradise Unique
Antiques**   Antique Shop
(56 N Market St) Stuffed to the gills with vintage Hawaiiana.

Information

First Hawaiian Bank (www.fhb.com; 27 N Market St)

Maui Memorial Medical Center (☎244-9056; www.mmmc.hhsc.org; 221 Mahalani St; ☻24hr) The island's main hospital.

Post office (www.usps.com; 250 Imi Kala St)

Dangers & Annoyances

One caution: the town can get rough at night. The public parking lot on W Main St is an after-dark hangout rife with drug dealing and fights, and gets more police calls than any other spot on Maui.

Getting There & Around

The Maui Bus runs free buses between Wailuku and Kahului hourly from 8am to 9pm. Wailuku stops include the state office building and the post office.

Wailuku to 'Iao Valley State Park

'Iao Valley's unspoiled natural beauty belies its brutal past. Filled as it is today with sightseers and picnickers, it's hard to imagine this was once the site of Maui's bloodiest battle. In 1790 Kamehameha the Great invaded Kahului by sea and routed the defending Maui warriors up into precipitous 'Iao Valley. Those unable to escape over the mountains were slaughtered along the stream. The waters of 'Iao Stream were so choked with bodies that the area was called Kepaniwai (Dammed Waters).

Today a steady stream of cars and tour buses marches up 'Iao Valley Rd along the same streamside route to Maui's most celebrated sight, 'Iao Needle.

Sights

**TROPICAL GARDENS
OF MAUI**   Gardens
(Map p96; www.tropicalgardensofmaui.com; 200 'Iao Valley Rd; adult/child under 8 $5/free; ☻9am-4:30pm Mon-Sat) These fragrant gardens, which straddle both sides of 'Iao Stream, showcase a superb orchid collection, endemic Hawaiian plants, brilliant bromeliads and a meditative bamboo grove with a trickling waterfall. See if you can find the world's largest orchid!

**KEPANIWAI PARK & HERITAGE
GARDENS**   Park
(Map p96; 875 'Iao Valley Rd; ☻7am-7pm) Two miles west of Wailuku, this family-oriented park pays tribute to Hawaii's ethnic heritages. Sharing the grounds are a traditional Hawaiian *hale* (house), a New England–style missionary home, a Filipino farmer's hut, Japanese gardens and a Chinese pavilion with a statue of revolutionary hero Sun Yat-sen (who, incidentally, briefly lived on Maui). 'Iao Stream runs through the park, bordered by picnic shelters with barbecue pits. The place is cheerfully alive with families picnicking here on weekends.

JFK PROFILE Landmark

(Map p96; 'Iao Valley Rd) At a bend in the road a half-mile after Kepaniwai Park, you'll likely see a few cars pulled over and their occupants staring off into Pali 'Ele'ele, a gorge on the right where a rock formation has eroded into the shape of a profile. Some legends associate it with a powerful *kahuna* (priest) who lived here during the 1500s, but today it bears an uncanny resemblance to former US president John F Kennedy. If parking is difficult, continue on to 'Iao Valley State Park, as it's only a couple of minutes' walk from there back to the viewing site.

'Iao Valley State Park

Every Hawaiian island has a landmark scene of singular beauty that's duplicated nowhere else. On O'ahu it's Diamond Head and on Maui it's unquestionably 'Iao Needle. Rising above a mountain stream in Maui's lush interior, this sensuous rock pinnacle is the focal point of **'Iao Valley State Park** (Map p96; admission per car $5; 🕙8:30am-5pm). The rainforest park, which starts 3 miles west of central Wailuku, extends clear up to Pu'u Kukui (5788ft), Maui's highest and wettest point.

snatched the merman and threatened to cast him out to sea. 'Iao pleaded that she could not live without the sight of her beloved, so Maui instead turned 'Iao's lover to a needle of stone.

Whether you believe in legends or not, this place looks like something from the pages of a fairy tale. Clouds rising up the valley form an ethereal shroud around the top of 'Iao Needle. With a stream meandering beneath and the steep cliffs of the West Maui Mountains in the backdrop, it's the most photographed scene on Maui.

Just a few minutes' walk from the parking lot, you'll reach a bridge where most people shoot their photos of the needle. A better idea is to take the walkway just before the bridge that loops downhill by the stream; this leads to the nicest photo angle, one that captures the stream, bridge and 'Iao Needle together.

If the water is high you'll see local kids taking bravado jumps from the bridge to the rocky stream below. You might be tempted to join them, but expect to get the stink eye — not to mention that

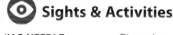

👁 Sights & Activities

'IAO NEEDLE Pinnacle

The velvety green pinnacle (Map p96) that rises straight up 2250ft takes its name from 'Iao, the daughter of Maui. According to legend, Maui and the goddess Hina raised their beautiful daughter 'Iao in this hidden valley, hoping to shelter her from worldly temptations. But a merman (half-man, half-fish) swam into the valley one night and took 'Iao as a lover. When Maui discovered the affair he

Kepaniwai Park & Heritage Gardens
PHOTOGRAPHER: GREG ELMS/LONELY PLANET IMAGES ©

the rocks below are potentially spine-crushing for unfamiliar divers. Better to take your dip in the swimming holes along the streamside path instead. Even there, however, be aware of potential dangers – the rocks in the stream are slippery and there can be flash floods.

WALKING TRAILS   Trails

After you cross the bridge you'll come to two short trails that start opposite each other. Both take just 10 minutes to walk and shouldn't be missed. The upper path leads skyward up a series of steps, ending at a sheltered lookout with a close-up view of 'Iao Needle. The lower path leads down along 'Iao Stream, skirting the rock-strewn streambed past native hau trees with their fragrant hibiscus-like flowers. Look around and you'll be able to spot fruiting guava trees as well. The lower path returns to the bridge by way of a garden of native Hawaiian plants, including patches of taro.

Pu'unene

Sugar is the lifeblood of Pu'unene. End-less fields of sugarcane expand out from the Hawaiian Commercial & Sugar (C&S) Company's mill that sits smack in the center of the village. If you happen to swing by when the mill is boiling down the sugarcane, the air hangs heavy with the sweet smell of molasses.

 Sights

ALEXANDER & BALDWIN
SUGAR MUSEUM   Museum

(Map p96; www.sugarmuseum.com; cnr Pu'unene Ave & Hansen Rd; adult/child 6-12 $7/2; ⏱9:30am-4:30pm) The former home of the sugar mill's superintendent now houses this evocative museum. Exhibits, including a working scale model of a cane-crushing plant, give the skinny on the sugarcane biz. Even more interest-ing, however, are the images of people. The museum traces how the privileged sons of missionaries wrested control over Maui's fertile valleys and dug the amazing irrigation system that made large-scale

plantations viable. Representing the other end of the scale is an early-20th-century labor contract from the Japanese Emigra-tion Company committing laborers to work the canefields 10 hours a day, 26 days a month for a mere $15.

PLANTATION
VILLAGE   HIstorical Buildings

You could drive through Pu'unene every day without realizing a little slice of a by-gone plantation village lies hidden behind the sugar mill. There, a long-forgotten church lies abandoned in a field of waving cane, across from the village's old school-house. Still, the place isn't a ghost town. Out back, just beyond the school, you'll find an old shack that's served as a used **bookstore** (Map p96) since 1913. It's a bit musty and dusty, but still sells books for a mere dime. To get there turn off Mokulele Hwy (Hwy 311) onto Hansen Rd and take the first right onto Old Pu'unene Ave, continuing past the old Pu'unene Meat Market building (c 1926) and the mill. Turn left after 0.6 miles, just past a little bridge. Just before the pavement ends, turn right and drive behind the old school to reach the bookstore, which is open 9am to 4pm Tuesday to Saturday.

Kealia Pond National Wildlife Refuge

A magnet for both birds and bird-watchers, this **refuge** (Map p96; www.fws. gov/kealiapond; Mokulele Hwy; admission free; ⏱8am-4pm Mon-Fri) harbors native water-birds year-round and migratory birds from October to April. In the rainy winter months Kealia Pond swells to 400 acres, making it one of the largest natural ponds in Hawaii. In summer it shrinks to half that size, creating the skirt of crystalline salt that gives Kealia (meaning 'salt-encrusted place') its name. The coastal marsh and dunes nestling Kealia Pond not only provide feeding grounds for native waterbirds but are also a nesting site for the endangered hawksbill sea turtle.

Birding is excellent from the 2200ft **Kealia Pond Boardwalk** (Map p96) – an elevated boardwalk that's turned previously inaccessible marshland into a one-of-a-kind nature walk. Interpretive plaques and benches along the way offer opportunities to stop and enjoy the splendor, and in winter you might be able to spot passing humpback whales. It's located 0.2 miles north of the 2-mile marker on N Kihei Rd.

Birding is also good from the refuge's visitor center off Mokulele Hwy (Hwy 311) at the 6-mile marker. In both places, you're almost certain to spot wading *ae'o* (Hawaiian black-necked stilts) and Hawaiian coots, two endangered species that thrive in this sanctuary. Osprey, magnificent fish hawks, can sometimes be seen dive-bombing for fish at Kealia during the winter months.

Ma'alaea

Wind defines Ma'alaea. Prevailing trade winds sweep from the north, funneling down between the two great rises of Haleakalā and the West Maui Mountains straight at Ma'alaea Bay. It's no coincidence that Maui's first windmill farm marches up the slopes here. By midday you'll need to hold on to your hat.

 **Beaches**

MA'ALAEA BAY Beach
Ma'alaea Bay (Map p96) is fronted by a 3-mile stretch of sandy beach, running from Ma'alaea Harbor south to Kihei. It can be accessed from **Haycraft Park** at the end of Hauoli St in Ma'alaea and from several places along N Kihei Rd including **Kealia Beach** in front of the Kealia Pond Boardwalk.

 Sights

TOP CHOICE **MAUI OCEAN CENTER** Aquarium
(Map p96; www.mauioceancenter.com; 192 Ma'alaea Rd; adult/child 3-12 $27/19; ⏱9am-5pm; ♿) The largest tropical aquarium in the US showcases Hawaii's dazzling marine life with award-winning style. The exhibits are laid out to take you on an ocean journey, beginning with nearshore reefs teeming with colorful tropical fish and ending with deep-ocean sea life. For the spectacular grand finale, you walk along a 54ft glass tunnel right through the center of a massive tank as gliding

Maui Ocean Center

TOR JOHNSON/HAWAII TOURISM AUTHORITY

stingrays and menacing sharks encircle you. It's as close as you'll ever get to being underwater without donning dive gear.

Kid-friendly features abound, including interactive displays on whales in the Marine Mammal Discovery Center, a cool touch-pool and, best of all, *keiki*-level viewing ports that allow the wee ones to peer into everything on their own.

Activities

Cruises

Many of the boats going out to Molokini (see p303) leave from Ma'alaea. Go in the morning. Afternoon trips are typically cheaper, but because that's when the wind picks up it's also rougher and murkier. Snorkel gear is included in the snorkeling cruises; bring your own towels and sunscreen.

TOP CHOICE **PACIFIC WHALE FOUNDATION**   Snorkeling & Whale-Watching Cruises
(Map p96; ☎249-8811; www.pacificwhale.org; Harbor Shops at Ma'alaea; adult/child 7-12 from

$55/35; ☉7am-6pm; ♿) Led by naturalists, these Molokini tours do it right, with onboard snorkeling lessons and wildlife talks. Snacks are provided and kids under 6 are free. Half-day tours concentrate on Molokini. Full-day tours combine snorkeling at Molokini and Lana'i. Also recommended are the whale-watching cruises (adult/child $32/16) that operate several times a day in the winter season.

QUICKSILVER   Snorkeling Cruise
(Map p96; ☎662-0075; www.frogman-maui. com; Slip 103 Ma'alaea Harbor; cruise $95) If you want more of a party scene, hop aboard this sleek double-decker catamaran. Once you're done snorkeling, your crew cranks up Jimmy Buffett and breaks out a barbecue lunch.

Windsurfing & Surfing

Wicked winds from the north shoot straight out toward Kaho'olawe, creating some of the best windsurfing conditions on Maui. In winter, when the wind dies down elsewhere, windsurfers still fly along Ma'alaea Bay.

The bay has a couple of hot surfing spots. The **Ma'alaea Pipeline** (Map p96) freight-trains right and is the fastest surf

Whale-watching cruise

KARL LEHMANN/LONELY PLANET IMAGES ©

Swim with the Fishes

The sharks are circling. Some 20 of them, to be exact. Blacktip reef sharks, hammerheads and, gasp, a tiger shark. And you can jump in and join them. **Shark Dive Maui** (☎270-7075; 2hr dive $199; ⏰8:15am Mon, Wed & Fri) takes intrepid divers on a daredevil's plunge into Maui Ocean Center's 750,000-gallon deep-ocean tank to swim with the toothy beasts as aquarium visitors gaze on in disbelief. You do need to be a certified diver and because it's limited to four divers per outing, advance reservations are essential.

break in all Hawaii. Summer's southerly swells produce huge tubes.

Hiking

LAHAINA PALI TRAIL Hiking
Fine hilltop views of Kaho'olawe and Lana'i are in store along this trail (Map p96), which follows an ancient footpath as it zigzags steeply up through native dryland. After the first mile it passes into open, sun-baked scrub, from where you can see Haleakalā and the fertile central plains. Ironwood trees precede the crossing of Kealaoloa Ridge (1600ft), after which you descend through Ukumehame Gulch. Look for stray petroglyphs and *paniolo* (cowboy) graffiti. Stay on the footpath all the way down to Papalaua Beach and don't detour onto 4WD roads. The 5.5-mile trail should take about 2½ hours each way.

You can hike in either direction, but starting off early from the east side of the mountains keeps you ahead of the blistering sun. The trailhead access road, marked by a Na Ala Hele sign, is on Hwy 30, just south of its intersection with N Kihei Rd. If you prefer to start at the west end, the trailhead is 200yd south of the 11-mile marker on Hwy 30.

Eating

TOP CHOICE **WATERFRONT RESTAURANT** Seafood $$$
(Map p96; ☎244-9028; www.waterfront restaurant.net; Milowai Condominium, 50

Hauoli St; mains $30-42; ⏰5-10pm) Sit on the lanai (veranda), listen to the surf and order fresh-off-the-boat seafood at this harborfront restaurant. The type of fish depends on what's reeled in each day, but the preparation choice – nine tempting options – is yours. Maybe you're in a blackened Cajun mood. Perhaps Sicilian with artichoke hearts and roasted garlic. The food, service and wine selection are among Maui's best.

BEACH BUMS BAR & GRILL Barbecue $$
(Map p96; ☎243-2286; Harbor Shops at Ma'alaea; mains $8-22; ⏰8am-9pm) If barbecue is your thing, you'll love this harborfront eatery, which uses a wood-burning rotisserie smoker to grill up everything from burgers and ribs to turkey and Spam. Come between 3pm and 6pm for $3 drafts of Kona-brewed Longboard Lager.

Hula Cookies Dessert $
(Map p96; www.hulacookies.com; Harbor Shops at Ma'alaea; snacks $3-6; ⏰10am-6pm Mon-Sat, to 5pm Sun) The fresh-baked cookies and Maui-made ice cream are chockful of macadamia nuts, pineapple and coconut. A perfect place to take the kids for a snack after the aquarium.

ⓘ Getting There & Away

Located at a crossroads, Ma'alaea has good connections to the rest of Maui's public bus system. The Maui Bus connects the Harbor Shops at Ma'alaea with Lahaina, Kahului and Kihei. Service depends on the route, but buses operate hourly from around 6am to 8pm.

Kihei & South Maui

Sunsets are a communal affair in South Maui – just look at the throngs crowding the beach wall at Kamaʻole Beach Park II in the late afternoon. It's a scene repeated up and down the coast here every day.

Dubbed Haole-wood for its LA-style strip malls and white-bread resorts, the region is a bit shiny and overbuilt. But dig deeper and you'll find a mixed plate of scenery and adventure, from Kihei to Wailea, Makena and beyond, that's truly unique. You can snorkel reefs teeming with turtles, kayak to remote bays or sail in an outrigger canoe. The coral gardens are so rich you can dive from the shore. And the beaches are undeniably glorious, whether you're looking to relax beneath a resort cabana or wanting to discover your own little pocket of sand. Add reliably sunny weather, quiet coastal trails and a diverse dining scene and South Maui's a pretty irresistible place to strand yourself.

Keawakapu Beach (p118), Kihei

Kihei & South Maui Itineraries

Two Days

1 **Ulua Beach** (p133) In the morning, snorkel north to coral gardens teeming with fish at Maui's favorite snorkel spot. Try to find the *humuhumunukunukukuapua'a* (Hawaii's state fish), which sports more colors than vowels.

2 **Café O'Lei** (p127) There's no better place for lunch than this stylish bistro serving savory Maui-centric fare. The blackened mahimahi with fresh salsa is always a tasty choice.

3 **Hawaiian Islands Humpback Whale National Sanctuary Headquarters** (p120) Showcasing Maui's marine life and its famous annual visitors, the humpback whales. At **Kalepolepo Beach Park** next door, splash beside an ancient Hawaiian fishpond on a kid friendly beach.

4 **Kama'ole Beach Park II** (p119) Join the crowds for a gorgeous sunset.

5 **808 Bistro** (p127) Stroll to the patio for gourmet comfort food and cap the night with dancing at **South Shore Tiki Lounge**.

6 **Makena Landing** (p139) Start your second day kayak paddling south through water thick with green sea turtles. On land, the nearby **Keawala'i Congregational Church** offers a glimpse into Makena's *paniolo* (cowboy) past.

7 **Big Beach** (Oneloa; p139) Walk on the wild side at Makena State Park, home of Big Beach. This magnificent stretch of sand and surf is untouched by development. Bathing suit feeling restrictive? You can always climb the hill to Little Beach where some folks think beachwear is overrated.

⏩ THIS LEG: 30 MILES

Four Days

1 **Lava Java** (p130) If you have four days in South Maui, plan your first two as above. On day three, grab your sweetie and head here for the 2-for-1 morning coffee special.

2 **Malu'aka Beach** (p138) Before the wind picks up, head down to the beach. Nicknamed Turtle Beach, it's the best place on Maui to swim among big green sea turtles. Worked up an appetite? Nearby **Makena Grill** serves scrumptious fish tacos.

3 **'Ahihi-Kina'u Natural Area Reserve** (p142) Cruise through a lava wonderland – and enjoy more snorkeling.

4 **Makena Stables** (p143) Giddy up for a sunset ride up the slopes of 'Ulupalakua Ranch with a Maui-born cowboy whose stories are as fascinating as the terrain.

5 **Kihei Caffe** (p128) In the morning, enjoy a veggie scramble, a big cup of coffee and a side of people-watching on the bustling patio at this cafe in Kihei Kalama Village aka the Triangle.

6 **Maui Dreams Dive Company** (p121) If all that snorkeling has you craving something deeper, take the plunge with this personable bunch of folks specializing in shore dives.

7 **Keawakapu Beach** (p118) On your last evening, pack a towel and relax on Kihei's loveliest strand.

8 **Da Kitchen Express** (p126) End the day with the flavors of Maui: a hearty helping of *kalua* pork and two scoops of rice followed by a rainbow-bright Big Baby from **Local Boys Shave Ice**.

⊙ THIS LEG: 35 MILES

Kihei & South Maui Highlights

1 **Best Beach: Big Beach** (Oneloa; p139) Gleaming sands, wild forests, blue water – aloha from the heart of Makena State Park.

2 **Best Snorkeling: Malu'aka Beach** (p138) Green turtles here, green turtles there, at Turtle Beach these graceful beasts are everywhere.

3 **Best Hawaiian Meal: Da Kitchen Express** (p126) Tender *kalua* pork, creamy macaroni and two scoops rice – tell us we didn't eat the whole thing.

4 **Best Sunset: Keawakapu Beach** (p118) Bring your beach chair – sunsets at this soft-sand crescent are a nightly performance.

5 **Best Lava Landscape: La Pérouse Bay** (p142) Eerie yet beautiful, this craggy black lawn feels like the dark side of the moon.

Big Beach (Oneloa, p139)
PHOTOGRAPHER: ANDY JACKSON/ALAMY

Discover Kihei & South Maui

Kihei

The largest tourist destination in Maui, this busy oceanfront community is a good choice for vacationers on a short trip who want to maximize their beach time and throw in an adventure or two. With 6 miles of beaches, loads of affordable accommodations and dining options, it offers everything necessary for an enjoyable seaside vacation.

To zip from one end of Kihei to the other, take the Pi'ilani Hwy (Hwy 31). It runs parallel to and bypasses the stop-start traffic of S Kihei Rd. Well-marked crossroads connect these two routes.

Beaches

The further south you go, the better the beaches. At the northern end of Kihei, swimming is not advised, but kayaking is good in the morning and windsurfers set off in the afternoon.

TOP CHOICE KEAWAKAPU BEACH Beach
This sparkling stretch of sand (Map p122) is a showstopper. Extending from southern Kihei to Wailea's Mokapu Beach, it's set back from the main road and is less visible than Kihei's main roadside beaches just north. It's also less crowded, and is a great place to settle in and watch the sunset.

With its cushiony soft sand, Keawakapu is also a favorite for sunrise yoga and wake-up strolls and is the perfect spot for an end-of-day swim. Mornings are the best time for snorkeling: head to the rocky outcrops that form the northern and southern ends of the beach. During winter keep an eye out for humpback whales, which come remarkably close to shore here.

There are three beach access points, all with outdoor showers. To get to the south end, go south on S Kihei Rd until it dead-ends at a beach parking lot. Near the middle of the beach, there's a parking lot at the corner of Kilohana Dr and S Kihei Rd; look for a blue shoreline access sign on the *makai* (seaward) side of the street. At the northern end, beach parking can be found in a large unpaved access lot north of the Days Inn Maui Oceanfront.

Keawakapu Beach

KAMA'OLE BEACH PARKS I, II & III
Beach

Kama'ole Beach (Map p122) is having so much fun, it just keeps rolling along. And along. And along. Divided into three sections by rocky points, these popular strands are known locally as Kam I, II and III. All three are pretty, golden-sand beaches with full facilities and lifeguards. There's a volleyball court at Kam I and parking lots at Kam I and III.

Water conditions vary with the weather, but swimming is usually good. For the most part, these beaches have sandy bottoms with a fairly steep drop, which tends to create good conditions for bodysurfing, especially in winter.

For snorkeling, the south end of Kama'ole Beach Park III has some nearshore rocks harboring a bit of coral and a few colorful fish, though it pales in comparison to the snorkeling at beaches further south.

CHARLEY YOUNG BEACH
Beach

Out of view from sightseers cruising the main drag, this side-street neighborhood beach (Map p122) is the least-touristed strand in Kihei. It's a real jewel in the rough: broad and sandy, and backed by swaying coconut palms. You're apt to find fishers casting their lines, families playing volleyball and someone strumming a guitar. It also has some of the better bodysurfing waves in Kihei. Beach parking is on the corner of S Kihei Rd and Kaia'u Pl. To get to the beach, simply walk to the end of Kaia'u Pl and follow the steps down the cliff.

PUNAHOA BEACH
Beach

This discreet postage-stamp-sized beach (Map p122), embraced by a rocky lava shoreline, is Kihei's best bet for swimming with turtles. Forget it, however, if it's not a calm day. The beach is reached via shoreline access at the north side of Punahoa condos. Park streetside on Ili'ili Rd, and it's just a minute away.

KALEPOLEPO BEACH PARK
Beach

Adjacent to the Humpback Whale National Marine Sanctuary Headquarters, this compact park (Map p126) is a nice spot for families with younger kids. A grassy

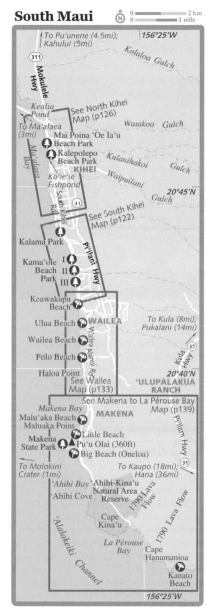

South Maui

lawn is fronted by the ancient **Ko'ie'ie Fishpond** (Map p126), whose stone walls create a shallow swimming pool with calm waters perfect for wading. There are also picnic tables and grills.

119

Launching a canoe, Kihei Canoe Club

GREG ELMS/LONELY PLANETS IMAGES ©

**MAI POINA O'E IA'U
BEACH PARK** Beach
This long sandy beach (Map p126) at
the northern end of Kihei is a popular
morning launch for outrigger canoes and
kayaks. After the wind picks up in the
afternoon, it's South Maui's main venue
for windsurfing.

 Sights

**HAWAIIAN ISLANDS HUMPBACK
WHALE NATIONAL MARINE
SANCTUARY HEADQUARTERS** Museum
(Map p126; 879-2818, 800-831-4888; www.
hawaiihumpbackwhale.noaa.gov; 726 S Kihei Rd;
admission free; 10am-3pm Mon-Fri;) If
you're curious about Maui's most famous
annual visitors, stop by the marine sanctuary headquarters. The center overlooks
the ancient **Ko'ie'ie Fishpond**, and its
oceanfront lookout is ideal for viewing the
humpback whales that frequent the bay
during winter. There are even free scopes
set up for viewing. Displays on whales and
sea turtles provide background, and there
are lots of informative brochures about
Hawaiian wildlife. Swing by at 11am on

Tuesday or Thursday for the free '45-Ton
Talks' on whales.

DAVID MALO'S CHURCH Church
(Map p126; 100 Kulanihako'i St) Philosopher
David Malo, who built this church in 1852,
was the first Hawaiian ordained to the
Christian ministry. He was also coauthor
of Hawaii's first Constitution and an early
spokesperson for Hawaiian rights. While
most of Malo's original church has been
dismantled, a 3ft-high section of the walls
still stands beside a palm grove. Pews
are lined up inside the stone walls, where
open-air services are held at 9am on
Sundays by Trinity Episcopal Church-by-
the-Sea. It's really quite beautiful.

KALAMA PARK Park
Across from the busy pub and restaurant
scene at Kihei Kalama Village, this expansive park (Map p122) has ball fields, tennis
and volleyball courts, a playground, picnic
pavilions, restrooms and showers. A retaining wall runs along most of the shoreline
so the park is best for landlubbers. There is
a small beach behind a whale statue, but a
runoff ditch carries wastewater here after
heavy rains so best swim elsewhere.

 **Activities**

Canoeing & Kayaking

TOP CHOICE **SOUTH PACIFIC KAYAKS & OUTFITTERS** Kayaking
(☎875-4848, 800-776-2326; www.south pacifickayaks.com; 95 Hale Kuai St; 1-/2-person kayaks per day $40/50, tours $65-139; ☺6am-9pm) This topnotch operation leads kayak-and-snorkel tours. It also rents kayaks for those who want to go off on their own, and will deliver them to Makena Landing.

KIHEI CANOE CLUB Canoeing
(Map p126; ☎879-5505; www.kiheicanoeclub. com; Kihei Wharf; donation $25) This paddle club invites visitors to share in the mana (spiritual essence) by joining members in paddling their outrigger canoes on Tuesday and Thursday mornings from about 7:30am to 9am. No reservations are necessary; just show up at the wharf at 7:00am. It's first-come first-served, and spots fill quickly. The donation helps offset the cost of maintaining the canoes.

Diving & Snorkeling

TOP CHOICE **MAUI DREAMS DIVE COMPANY** Diving
(Map p122; ☎874-5332; www.mauidreamsdiveco. com; Island Surf Bldg, 1993 S Kihei Rd; 1-/2-tank dives from $69/99; ☺7am-6pm) Maui Dreams is a first-rate, five-star PADI operation specializing in shore dives. With this family-run outfit, a dive trip is like going

The Best...
South Maui for Kids

1 Ulua Beach (p133)

2 Hawaiian Sailing Canoe Adventures (p134)

3 Kama'ole Beach Park III (p119)

4 Local Boys Shave Ice (p128)

5 Hawaiian Islands Humpback Whale National Marine Sanctuary Headquarters (p120)

out with friends. Nondivers, ask about the introductory dive ($89), and to zoom around underwater, check out its scooter dive ($99 to $129).

BLUE WATER RAFTING Snorkeling
(Map p122; ☎879-7238; www.bluewaterrafting. com; Kihei Boat Ramp; Molokini Express/Kanaio Coast $50/100; ☺departure times vary) In a hurry? Try the Molokini Express trip if you want to zip out to the crater, snorkel and be back within two hours. An adventurous half-day trip heads southward on a motorized raft to snorkel among sea turtles and dolphins at remote coves along the Kanaio coast.

 **Island Insights**

In ancient Hawaii, coastal fishponds were built to provide a ready source of fish for royal families. The most intact fishpond remaining on Maui is the 3-acre **Ko'ie'ie Fishpond** (Map p126), now on the National Register of Historic Places. This fascinating fishpond borders both Kalepolepo Beach Park and the Hawaiian Islands Humpback Whale National Marine Sanctuary Headquarters.

Maui Dive Shop   Diving, Snorkeling
(Map p122; ☎879-3388; www.mauidiveshop.com;
1455 S Kihei Rd; 2-tank dives $140-150, snorkel
rentals per day $6; ☉6am-9pm) This is a good
spot to rent or buy watersports gear, including
boogie boards, snorkels and wetsuits.

Stand Up Paddle Surfing

Stand up paddle surfing (SUP) looks easy,
and it is a learnable sport, but currents off
Maui can carry you down the coast very
quickly. Best to start with a lesson before
renting a board.

**STAND-UP PADDLE SURF
SCHOOL**   Paddle Surfing
(☎579-9231; www.standuppaddlesurfschool.
com; 90 min lesson $159; ☉9am & 11am) This
SUP school is owned by Maria Souza,
the first woman surfer to tow into the
monster waves at Jaws and a champion
paddle-surfer. Small classes and safety
are priorities, and the paddling location is
determined by weather and water conditions. Classes fill quickly, so call a few
days – or a week – ahead.

Walking

KIHEI COASTAL TRAIL   Walking Trail
Follow this trail (Map p122) along coastal
bluffs ideal for whale watching and quiet
meditation. At the start of the trail look for
the burrows of ʻuaʻu kani (wedge-tailed
shearwaters), ground-nesting seabirds
that return to the same sites each spring.
The birds lay a single egg and remain until
November, when the fledglings are large
enough to head out to sea.

The trail starts beyond the grassy lawn
at the south end of Kamaʻole Beach Park
III and winds half a mile south to Kihei
surfside condos, just beyond Kihei Boat
Ramp. The path is made of packed gray
gravel outlined in white coral. Curiously,
when the trail was being built, a storm
washed hundreds of yards of bleached
coral onto the shore here. The coral
was not originally planned for the trail
construction, but the volunteers building
the trail consulted with a Hawaiian kahuna
(priest) and were told ancient trails were
often outlined in white coral so they could

be followed at night. The Hawaiian gods
were thanked for the gift of coral, which
was then incorporated into the trail.

South Kihei

⭐ Festivals & Events

**Whale Day
Celebration**   Outdoor Festival
(www.greatmauiwhalefestival.org; 👪) Organized
by the Pacific Whale Foundation, this family-
friendly bash honors Maui's humpback whales
with crafts, live music and food booths. It's held
at Kalama Park, next to the big whale statue, on
a Saturday in mid-February.

Maui Ohana Pride   Gay Pride
(www.mauigayinfo.com) Maui's gay and lesbian
community gathers to party on the first Sunday in
June. Check the website for current information;
the location and activities vary from year to year.

South Kihei

Sleeping

Condos are plentiful in Kihei, while hotels and B&Bs are few. Some condominium complexes maintain a front desk that handles bookings, but others are booked via rental agents. Be sure to ask about cleaning fees, which vary. Traffic along S Kihei Rd can be noisy, so avoid rooms close to the road.

TOP CHOICE PUNAHOA   Condo **$$**
(Map p122; ☎879-2720, 800-564-4380; www.punahoabeach.com; 2142 Ili'ili Rd; studio $159, 1br $244-269, 2br $274; P ☎) Sip coffee, scan for whales, savor sunsets – it's hard to leave your lanai (veranda) at Punahoa, a classy boutique condo where every unit has a clear-on ocean view. Tucked on a quiet side street, this 15-unit complex offers privacy and warm alohas. It's also next to a gorgeous strand of sand, Punahoa Beach, that's a favorite of turtles and surfers. At sunset, join other

guests on the first-floor communal lanai. Penthouse units have air-conditioning.

TWO MERMAIDS ON MAUI B&B   B&B **$$**
(Map p122; ☎874-8687, 800-598-9550; www.twomermaids.com; 2840 Umalu Pl; studio/1br incl breakfast $115/140; P @ ☎ ☎) I'd like to be, under the sea...yep, the happy-go-lucky Beatles tune springs to mind inside the Ocean Ohana suite, a bright space swirling with whimsical maritime imagery. The Poolside Sweet, with its sunset colors and in-room guitar, might inspire your own inner songwriter. Organic island fruit is provided for breakfast. Both units have kitchenettes, and the Ocean Ohana suite has air-con. Families are welcome.

OCEAN BREEZE HIDEAWAY   B&B **$**
(Map p126; ☎879-0657, 888-463-6687; www.hawaiibednbreakfast.com; 435 Kalalau Pl; r incl breakfast from $80; @ ☎) Bob and Sande have run this welcoming B&B for more than a decade and, with their licensed

activity desk certification, the couple is a treasure trove of insider tips. Their home has two comfortable guest rooms, one with a queen bed and ceiling fans, the other with a king bed and air-con. Both have a private entrance and a refrigerator. Children over 12 are welcome.

MANA KAI MAUI   Condo **$$$**
(Map p122; ☏ 879-1561, 800-525-2025; www.
manakaimaui.com; 2960 S Kihei Rd; r/1br from $190/281; P ✳ @ ≋) Perched on a point overlooking Keawakapu Beach, this complex offers great sunset views. You can swim and snorkel from the beach right outside the door. The on-site rental company manages 50 units, providing all the conveniences of a condo as well as the pluses of a hotel, with a front desk and a full-service restaurant. Request an upper floor for the best views.

MAUI SUNSEEKER   Boutique Hotel **$$**
(Map p126; ☏ 879-1261, 800-532-6284; www.
mauisunseeker.com; 551 S Kihei Rd; r $105-185, ste $125-265, studio $110-195; P ✳ @ 🛜) No,

the new webcam doesn't sweep past the clothing-optional rooftop deck and its hot tub, but it does take in Mai Poina 'Oe la'u Beach Park across the street. Catering to gay and lesbians, this breezy, 17-room motel consists of three adjacent properties. Opt for the one out back, formerly the Wailana Inn; its rooms beam with tasteful decor that outshines other places in this price range. Amenities include refrigerator, microwave and lanai. Helpful staff.

KIHEI KAI NANI   Condo **$$**
(Map p122; ☏ 879-9088, 800-473-1493; www.
kiheikainani.com; 2495 S Kihei Rd; 1br $168; P @ ≋) Rooms and decor may be a little on the old side, but when it comes to amenities this inviting low-rise condo is on par with more expensive properties. On site are a large pool, a laundry room, shuffleboard, barbecue grills and picnic tables – all fringed by colorful tropical landscaping. Kama'ole Beach Park II is across the street.

Left: Stand up paddle surfer; **Below:** Green turtle

KOA LAGOON
Condo **$$$**

(Map p126; ☎879-3002, 800-367-8030; www.koalagoon.com; 800 S Kihei Rd; 1br/2br from $170/200; P ❄ ☎) Watch the whales from your balcony at this seaside complex with just 42 rooms, each with a clear view of the ocean. Other perks include a pretty backyard, a relaxing beach and a heated pool that's seldom crowded. Comfy units – on six floors – are fitted with king beds and everything you'd need including a washer and dryer. A few units have wi-fi.

NONA LANI COTTAGES   Cottages **$$**

(Map p126; ☎879-2497, 800-733-2688; www.nonalanicottages.com; 455 S Kihei Rd; cottages from $150; P ❄) Wooden cottages, lazy hammocks, picnic tables, swaying palms – this place looks like the tropical version of Camp Minnehaha. The eight retro cottages are compact but squeeze in a full kitchen, private lanai, living room with daybed and a bedroom with a queen bed, plus cable TV.

KAMA'OLE BEACH
ROYALE   Condo **$$$**

(Map p122; ☎879-3131, 800-421-3661; www.kbr1maui.com; 2385 S Kihei Rd; 1br/2br from $170/200; P ❄ ☎) The rooftop patio on this six-story condo is awesome (just ignore the putting-green carpet). Views of the ocean are superb, and there's a grill if you want to cook out. Most of the condos in the rental pool are fresh off a renovation that's added a little pizzazz. Request a room on an upper floor to take advantage of that ocean view. Some units have wi-fi.

MAUI COAST HOTEL   Hotel **$$$**

(Map p122; ☎874-6284, 800-663-1144; www.mauicoasthotel.com; 2259 S Kihei Rd; r $209, ste $229-249; ❄ @ ☎) We're not swooning, but among the handful of hotels in Kihei, this is the best. It's clean and comfortable, and the set-back-from-the-road location makes it quieter than other places on the strip. The $18 daily resort fee includes wi-fi, parking and local shuttle service.

125

North Kihei

⊙ Sights

1	David Malo's Church	B4
2	Hawaiian Islands Humpback Whale National Marine Sanctuary Headquarters	A3
3	Kalepolepo Beach Park	A3
	Ko'ie'ie Fishpond	(see 2)
4	Mai Poina 'Oe Ia'u Beach Park	A2

Activities, Courses & Tours

5	Kihei Canoe Club	A1
6	Maui Dive Shop	A5

⊜ Sleeping

7	Koa Lagoon	A3
8	Maui Sunseeker	B3
9	Nona Lani Cottages	B2
10	Ocean Breeze Hideaway	B2

⊗ Eating

11	Eskimo Candy	B5
12	Kihei Farmers Market	A1
	Pizza Madness	(see 6)
	Safeway	(see 17)
13	Saigon Pearl Vietnamese Cuisine	A5
14	Stella Blues	A5

⊝ Drinking

15	Dina's Sandwitch	A1
16	Kiwi Roadhouse	B5

⊙ Shopping

	Maui Quilt Shop	(see 13)
17	Pi'ilani Village	B5

DISCOVER KIHEI & SOUTH MAUI

draped luxury condos, everything is low-rise. Units are spacious, and it's in a quiet location opposite Kama'ole Beach Park III.

DAYS INN MAUI OCEANFRONT   Hotel **$$**
(Map p122; ☏879-7744, 800-263-3387; www. mauioceanfrontinn.com; 2980 S Kihei Rd; r $159; P❄@) Yeah, it's a chain, rooms are pint-sized and the hair dryer looks like it belongs on a 1970s spaceship, but rates are among the cheapest in town, and the property borders beautiful Keawakapu Beach.

Maui Kama'ole   Condo **$$$**
(Map p122; ☏879-2778, 866-975-1864; www. crhmaui.com; 2777 S Kihei Rd; 1br/2br from $225/270; ❄@⊜) At these bougainvillea-

Eating

TOP CHOICE **DA KITCHEN EXPRESS**   Hawaiian **$**
(Map p122; www.da-kitchen.com; Rainbow Mall, 2439 S Kihei Rd; meals $9-16; ⊙9am-9pm) Da kitchen is da bomb. Congenial service, heaping portions, loads of flavor – come here to eat like a king. Tucked at the back of anvil-shaped Rainbow Mall, this eatery is all about Hawaiian plate lunches. The local favorite is Da Lau Lau Plate (with

steamed pork wrapped in taro leaves), but you won't go wrong with any choice, from charbroiled teriyaki chicken to the gravy-laden *loco moco* (rice, fried egg and hamburger patty). We particularly liked the spicy *kalua* pork.

CAFÉ O'LEI
TOP CHOICE

Hawaii Regional **$$$**

(Map p122; ☏891-1368; www.cafeolei restaurants.com; Rainbow Mall, 2439 S Kihei Rd; lunch $7-13, dinner $17-37; ⏰10:30am-3:30pm & 4:30pm-10pm Tue-Sun) With its uninspiring strip mall setting, this bistro looks rather ho-hum at first blush. But step inside. The sophisticated atmosphere, innovative Hawaii Regional Cuisine, honest prices and excellent service knock Café O'Lei into the fine-dining big league. For a tangy treat, order the blackened mahimahi with fresh papaya salsa. Look for unbeatable lunch entrees, with salads, for under $10, and a sushi chef after 4:30pm. Famous martinis, too.

SANSEI SEAFOOD RESTAURANT & SUSHI BAR
Japanese **$$$**

(Map p122; ☏879-0004; www.sanseihawaii.com; Kihei Town Center, 1881 S Kihei Rd, appetizers $3-15, mains $17-32; ⏰5:30pm-10pm, to 1am Thu-Sat) The line runs out the door, but you'll be rewarded for your patience. The creative appetizer menu includes everything from traditional sashimi to lobster and blue-crab ravioli. Hot Eurasian fusion dishes include Peking duck in a *foie gras demi*. Between 5:30pm and 6pm all food is discounted 25%, and sushi is discounted 50% from 10pm to 1am Thursday through Saturday.

808 BISTRO
Eclectic **$$**

(Map p122; ☏879-8008; www.808bistro.com; 2511 S Kihei Rd, #A; breakfast $8-13, dinner $15-20; ⏰7am-noon & 5-9pm) The sandwich maestros behind 808 Deli raised their game with this new open-air eatery. Its creative menu showcases comfort foods prepared with a savory, gourmet spin – think short-rib pot pie and gorgonzola alfredo. Your diet will walk the plank at breakfast with banana bread French toast or the decadent whale pie with ham, hash browns, eggs, cheese and brown gravy. The bistro is waiting for its liquor license, so BYOB is welcome for the foreseeable future.

808 DELI
Cafe **$**

(Map p122; ☏879-1111; www.808deli.net; Suite 102, 1913 S Kihei Rd; sandwiches $7-8; ⏰7am-5pm) As Subway wept and Quizno's cried, 808 Deli tap-danced its way into our sandwich-loving hearts. With fresh breads, gourmet spreads and 17 different sandwiches and paninis, this tiny gourmet sandwich shop across from Kama'ole Beach Park II is the place to grab a picnic lunch. For a spicy kick, try the roast beef with wasabi aioli.

Café O'Lei

KIHEI CAFFE
Cafe $

(Map p122; www.kiheicaffe.com; 1945 S Kihei Rd; mains $6-11; ☉5am-3pm) Kihei Caffe newbie? Here's the deal: step to the side and review the menu before you join the queue. The cashier is chatty, but he keeps that long line moving. Next, fill your coffee cup at the inside thermos, hunt down a table on the patio then watch the breakfast burritos, veggie scrambles and *loco moco* (rice, fried egg and hamburger patty) flash by. And keep an eye on those sneaky birds. Solos, couples, families – everybody's here or on the way.

JOY'S PLACE
Cafe $

(Map p122; www.joysplacemaui.com; Island Surf Bldg, 1993 S Kihei Rd; mains $9-12; ☉8am-3pm Mon-Sat; 🖋) Joy takes pride in her little kitchen where the operative words are organic, free range and locally harvested. The healthiest takeout salads ($9) you'll find anywhere in South Maui, wrap sandwiches made to order, overstuffed sandwiches and daily specials like fresh fish tacos on Saturdays attract a loyal following.

STELLA BLUES
Eclectic $$

(Map p126; 🕿874-3779; www.stellablues.com; Azeka Mauka II, 1279 S Kihei Rd; breakfast $6-13, lunch & dinner $12-28; ☉7:30am-11pm; 🖋) Grateful Dead on the airwaves, a canopy-covered patio, hefty three-egg omelets – Stella Blues is one cool place to start the day. This Kihei favorite never skimps, and the eclectic menu offers something for every mood, from Hawaiian-style macadamia-nut pancakes to Caesar salad, pan-seared fresh fish and Maui Cattle Company burgers.

ESKIMO CANDY
Seafood $$

(Map p126; www.eskimocandy.com; 2665 Wai Wai Pl; mains $8-17; ☉10:30am-7pm Mon-Fri) Tucked on a side street, Eskimo Candy is a fish market with a takeout counter and a few tables. Fresh-fish fanatics should key in on the *poke* (cubed, marinated raw fish), ahi (yellowfin tuna) wraps and fish tacos. *Keiki* (children) will love the pirate theme, and parents will love the under $7 kids menu.

LOCAL BOYS SHAVE ICE
Shave Ice $

(Map p122; Kihei Kalama Village, 1913 S Kihei Rd; shave ice $4-6; ☉10am-9pm) Local Boys dishes up soft shaved ice drenched in a

Local Boys Shave Ice

rainbow of sweet syrups. We like it tropical – banana, mango and 'shark's blood' – with ice cream, *kauai* cream and azuki beans. Load up on napkins, these babies are messy!

PIZZA MADNESS Pizza **$$**
(Map p126; ☏270-9888; 1455 S Kihei Rd; pizzas $7-20; ⊙11am-9:30pm Tue-Sat, to 9pm Sun & Mon) The vibe and decor are a little, well, mad. Picture a giant shark overhead that's chomping on a slice of pizza, surrounded by a dark room and flickering flatscreens. But no matter. Pizza Madness serves the best pizza in Kihei.

SAIGON PEARL VIETNAMESE CUISINE Vietnamese **$$**
(Map p126; ☏875-2088; Azeka Makai, 1280 S Kihei Rd; mains $9-14; ⊙10:30am-9:30pm) The curried lemongrass chicken with jasmine rice awakens the senses. Or have some fun and order *banh hoi* (a roll-your-own Vietnamese version of fajitas that come with mint leaves, assorted veggies and grilled shrimp).

FAT DADDY'S Comfort Food **$$**
(Map p122; www.fatdaddysmaui.com; Kihei Kalama Village, 1913 S Kihei Rd; mains $8-19; ⊙11:30am-10pm) Big plates of tangy barbecued ribs with all the fixings are the specialty at this smart, Texas-style smokehouse. Here, Southwest takes on a Hawaiian accent with Maui Cattle Company beef on the grill.

Pita Paradise Mediterranean **$$**
(Map p122; ☏875-7679; Kihei Kalama Village, 1913 S Kihei Rd; mains $7-22; ⊙11am-9:30pm) Aloha. Yassou. And dig in. Enjoy gyros and kebabs at this low-key Greek favorite in the Triangle.

Shaka Sandwich & Pizza Cheese Steaks, Pizza **$$**
(Map p122; ☏874-0331; 1770 S Kihei Rd; mains $7-27; ⊙10:30am-9pm Sun-Thu, to 10pm Fri & Sat) Come here for the cheese steak sandwiches.

Foodland Grocery
(Map p122; www.foodland.com; Kihei Town Center, 1881 S Kihei Rd) Handy 24-hour supermarket.

Safeway Grocery
(Map p126; www.safeway.com; Pi'ilani Village, 277 Pi'ikea Ave) Another 24-hour supermarket.

Hawaiian Moons Natural Foods Health F
(Map p126; www.hawaiianmoons; Kama'ole Center, 2411 S Kihei Rd; ⊙8am-9pm Mon 9am-9pm Sat & Sun; ☏) A good place healthy picnic lunch.

Kihei Farmers Market Farmers Market
(Map p126; 61 S Kihei Rd; ◷8am-4pm Mon-Thu, to 5pm Fri) Sells island-grown fruits and vegetables – a bit pricey but fresh.

Drinking & Entertainment

Most bars in Kihei are across the street from the beach and have nightly entertainment. Kihei Kalama Village, aka the Bar-muda Triangle (or just the Triangle), is crammed tight with buzzy watering holes.

All bars listed are open by 11am and most close between 1:30am and 2pm. Five Palms closes at 11pm.

SOUTH SHORE TIKI LOUNGE Tiki Bar
(Map p122; ☎874-6444; Kihei Kalama Village; 1913 S Kihei Rd) This cozy tropical shack has a heart as big as its lanai. Drink maestros here regularly win annual *Maui Time Weekly* awards for best female and male bartenders. Good for dancing too.

DOG & DUCK Irish
(Map p122; ☎875-9669; Kihei Kalama Village, 1913 S Kihei Rd) This cheery Irish pub attracts a younger crowd – yes, they have sports TV, but it's not blaring from every corner. Decent spuds and pub grub go along with the heady Guinness draft, and there's music most nights of the week.

OCEANS BEACH BAR & GRILL Beach Bar
(Map p122; ☎891-2414; Kukui Mall, 1819 S Kihei Rd) It's not on the beach, but it is open air, with surf videos and NFL games on the TV screens and dancing on the weekends.

FIVE PALMS Cocktails
(Map p122; ☎879-2607; www.fivepalmsrestaurant.com; 2960 S Kihei Rd) For sunset mai tais beside the beach, this is the place. Come early because the patio, on the ground floor of the Mana Kai Maui, fills quickly. Keawakapu Beach, a few steps away, is of the prettiest strands in South Maui.

ROADHOUSE Roadhouse
(☎874-1250; 95 E Lipoa St) Own a 4x4 pick-up? Then rumble in

The Best...
Bars

1 South Shore Tiki Lounge (p130)

2 Red Bar at Gannon's (p137)

3 Five Palms (p130)

4 Mulligan's on the Blue (p137)

5 Kiwi Roadhouse (p130)

and join friends at this rambunctious, freestanding roadhouse that's not at all close to the beach. Live music Wednesday to Sunday nights, from rock to blues to country.

LAVA JAVA Coffeeshop
(Map p122; www.lavajavamaui.com; Kihei Kalama Village, 1941 S Kihei Rd; ◷6am-8pm) Counter service can be slow in the morning but that might be due to the awesome 2-for-1 drink special (6am to 9am). The super-nice owner regularly serves free samples of iced mocha and can fill you in on everything you want to know about Hawaiian-grown coffee. Four computers with internet access (20¢ per minute) are in the back. Scaly gekko balls are in the middle.

DINA'S SANDWITCH Neighborhood Pub
(Map p126; ☎879-3262; 145 N Kihei Rd) Old salts and young salts – but very few hot peppers – keep this divey joint loud and convivial. Stop by for a shot of local flavor and walls that are covered with $1 bills – $17,000 worth they say.

Moose McGillycuddy's Beach Bar
(Map p122; www.moosemcgillycuddys.com; 2511 S Kihei Rd) Moose's open-air lanai is a fine place to head for a sunset drink. Tuesday night is $1 drink night with $5 cover.

 Shopping

PI'ILANI VILLAGE Shopping Center (Map p126; 225 Pi'ikea Ave) Kihei's largest shopping center has scores of stores perfect for stocking up on gifts – for others or yourself. Highlights include **Borders Express** (☎875-6607) for bestsellers, local travel and magazines; **Crazy Shirts** (☎875-6440) for quality Hawaiian-motif shirts; and **Hilo Hattie** (☎875-4545) for kitschy souvenirs.

KIHEI KALAMA VILLAGE Outdoor Market (Map p122; ☎879-6610; 1913 S Kihei Rd) More than 40 shops and stalls cluster under one roof at this shopping arcade. Ladies, for fashionable beachwear pop into **Mahina** (www.mahinamaui.com). Dudes can browse **808 Clothing Store** (www.the808clothingcompany.com) for T-shirts with original Maui designs.

❶ Information

Bank of Hawaii (☎879-5844; www.boh.com; Azeka Mauka, 1279 S Kihei Rd)

Kihei Police District Station (☎244-6400; Kihei Town Center, 1881 S Kihei Rd; ☺7:45am-4:30pm Mon-Fri)

Longs Drug (☎879-2259; 1215 S Kihei Rd; ☺7am-midnight) Kihei's largest pharmacy, with one aisle stocked totally with slippers (flip flops, yo').

Post Office (☎879-1987; 1254 S Kihei Rd)

Urgent Care Maui Physicians (☎879-7781; 1325 S Kihei Rd; ☺7am-9pm) This clinic accepts walk-in patients.

❶ Getting There & Around

To/From The Airport

Almost everyone rents a car at the airport in Kahului. Otherwise, expect to pay about $31 to $37 for a shuttle service or $35 to $62 for a taxi depending on your South Maui location.

Bicycle

Bike lanes run along both the Pi'ilani Hwy and S Kihei Rd, but cyclists need to be cautious of inattentive drivers making sudden turns across the lanes.

Po'olenalena Beach (p134)

GREG ELMS/LONELY PLANET IMAGES

South Maui Bicycles (☎ 874-0068; www. southmauibicycles.com; Island Surf Bldg, 1993 S Kihei Rd; per day $22-60, per week $99-250; ⏱10am-6pm Mon-Sat) Rents top-of-the-line Trek road bicycles and quality mountain bikes, as well as basic around-town bikes.

Bus

The **Maui Bus** (www.mauicounty.gov) serves Kihei with two routes. One route, the Kihei Islander 10, connects Kihei with Wailea and Ma'alaea; stops include Kama'ole Beach Park III, Pi'ilani Village shopping center, and Uwapo and S Kihei Rds. From Ma'alaea you can connect with buses bound for Lahaina and Kahului. The other route, the Kihei Villager 15, primarily serves the northern half of Kihei, with a half-dozen stops along S Kihei Rd and a stop in Ma'alaea. Both routes operate hourly from around 5:30am to 7:30pm and cost $1.

Car & Motorcycle

Kihei Rent A Car (☎ 879-7257, 800-251-5288; www.kiheirentalcar.com; 96 Kio Loop; per day/ week from $35/175) This family-owned company rents cars and jeeps to those aged 21 and over,

and includes free mileage. Provides Kahului Airport shuttle pickup for rentals over five days.

Hula Hogs (☎ 875-7433, 877-464-7433; www. hulahogs.com; 1279 S Kihei Rd; per day incl helmet from $120) These are the folks to see if you want to tour Maui on a Harley-Davidson Road King. In the store, look for the Harley Barbie, a hoot with her leather jacket and goth lipstick.

Wailea
POP 6600

With its tidy golf courses, protective privacy walls and discreet signage, Wailea looks like a members-only country club. And that's without mentioning the ubiquitous valets. Wailea is South Maui's most elite haunt, and it stands in sharp contrast to Kihei. Don't bother looking for a gas station or fast-food joint; this exclusive community is all about swank beachfront resorts and low-rise condo villas, with all the glitzy accessories.

One look at the beaches and it's easy to see why it's become such hot real estate. The golden-sand jewels sparkling along the Wailea coast are postcard material, offering phenomenal swimming, snorkeling and sunbathing. If you're not staying here, say a loud *mahalo* (thank you) for Hawaii's beach-access laws that allow you to visit anyway.

From Lahaina or Kahului, take the Pi'ilani Hwy (Hwy 31) to Wailea instead of S Kihei Rd, which is Kihei's stop-and-go main road. Once in Wailea, Wailea Alanui Dr turns into Makena Alanui Dr after Polo Beach and continues into Makena.

 Beaches

Wailea's fab beaches begin with the southern end of Keawakapu Beach in Kihei and continue south toward Makena. All of the beaches

Ulua Beach
PHOTOGRAPHER: LINDA CHING/LONELY PLANET IMAGES ©

Wailea

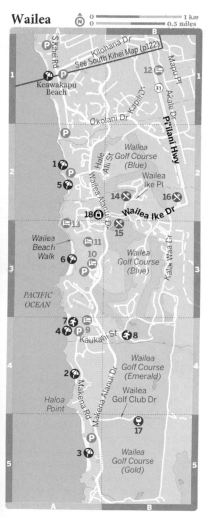

Wailea
N
0 ———————— 1 km
0 ———————— 0.5 miles

that are backed by resorts have public access, with free parking, showers and restrooms.

TOP CHOICE **ULUA & MOKAPU BEACHES**　　　Beach

You'll have to get up early to secure a parking space, but it's worth it. **Ulua Beach** offers Wailea's best easy-access snorkeling. Not only is it teeming with brilliant tropical fish, but it's also one of the best spots for hearing humpbacks sing as they pass offshore. Snorkelers should head straight for the coral at the rocky outcrop on the right side of Ulua Beach, which separates it from its twin to the north, **Mokapu Beach**. Snorkeling is best in the morning before the winds pick up and the crowds arrive. When the surf's up, forget snorkeling – go bodysurfing instead. Beach access is just north of the Wailea Beach Marriott Resort.

WAILEA BEACH　　　B

Wanna strut your stuff celebrity-st

Slip into your snazziest swimwea

Island Insights

Before setting out in their canoes for a day of fishing, Hawaiians would leave offerings, perhaps a shell or fishhooks, at a *ko'a* (fishing shrine). When they returned, the first catch of the day would be placed at the shrine to thank the gods for their favors. When ground was broken for construction of the Kihei library, an ancient stone fishing shrine, **Ko'a i Kama'ole (Map p122)**, was unearthed. The mound of rocks is marked by an interpretive plaque at the front of the library parking lot.

head to this sparkling strand, where most of Wailea's vacationers soak up the rays. The crescent-shaped beach, which fronts the Grand Wailea and Four Seasons, offers a full menu of water activities. The beach slopes gradually, making it a good swimming spot. When it's calm, there's decent snorkeling around the rocky point on the south end. Most afternoons there's a gentle shorebreak suitable for bodysurfing. Divers entering the water at Wailea Beach can follow an offshore reef that runs down to Polo Beach. The beach access road runs between the Grand Wailea and Four Seasons resorts.

PO'OLENALENA BEACH Beach
To avoid the resorts, drive south to this lovely long crescent favored by local families on weekends. Still, it's rarely crowded, and the shallow, sandy bottom and calm waters make for excellent swimming. There's good snorkeling off both the southern and northern lava points. The parking lot is on Makena Alanui Rd, a half-mile south of its intersection with Makena Rd.

POLO BEACH Beach
In front of the Fairmont Kea Lani, Polo Beach is seldom crowded. When there's wave action, boogie boarders and bodysurfers usually find good shorebreaks here. When calm, the rocks at the southern end of the beach provide good snorkeling. At low tide, the lava outcropping at the southern end holds tide pools teeming with spiny sea urchins and small fish. To find it, turn down Kaukahi St after

the Fairmont Kea Lani and look for the beach parking lot on the right.

PALAUEA BEACH Beach
This quiet sandy stretch to the south of Polo Beach attracts local surfers and boogie boarders. Kiawe trees block the view of the beach from the roadside, but you can find it easily by the line of cars parked along Makena Rd.

🏃 Activities

🚣 HAWAIIAN SAILING CANOE ADVENTURES Canoeing
(☎ 281-9301; www.mauisailingcanoe.com; adult/child 5-12 $99/79; ⏰ tours 8am & 10am) Learn about native traditions on two-hour sails aboard a Hawaiian-style outrigger canoe. With a max of six passengers, it's able to accommodate requests – including stopping to snorkel with turtles. Tours depart from Polo Beach.

WAILEA GOLF CLUB Golf
(☎ 875-7450; www.waileagolf.com; 100 Wailea Golf Club Dr; greens fee $135-179; ⏰ first tee around 7am) There are three championship courses in Wailea. The **Emerald course** is a tropical garden that consistently ranks at the top; the rugged **Gold course** takes advantage of volcanic landscapes; and the **Old Blue course** (120 Kaukahi St) is marked by an open fairway and challenging greens. For the cheapest fees, tee off after 1pm, when 'twilight' rates are in effect.

WAILEA BEACH WALK   Walking Trail

For the perfect sunset stroll, take the 1.3-mile shoreline path that connects Wailea's beaches and the resort hotels that front them. The undulating path winds above jagged lava points and back down to the sandy shore.

In winter this is one of the best places in all of Maui for spotting humpback whales. On a good day you may be able to see more than a dozen of them frolicking offshore. Forgot your binoculars? Just drop a coin in the telescope in front of the Wailea Beach Marriott Resort.

Some of the luxury hotels you'll pass along the walk are worth strolling through as well, most notably the Grand Wailea Resort, which is adorned with $30 million worth of artwork. In front of the Wailea Point condos you'll find the foundations of three Hawaiian house sites dating to AD 1300; this is also a fine spot to watch the sun drop into the sea.

Maui Ocean Activities   Watersports

(☏667-2001; www.mauiwatersports.com; Grand Wailea Resort Hotel & Spa, 3850 Wailea Alanui Dr; snorkel/boogie boards/kayak/stand up paddle board rental per hr $8/8/25/40) On the beach behind the Grand Wailea, Maui Ocean rents all you need for watery fun.

Mokapu Beach (p133), Wailea

Wailea Tennis Club   Tennis

(☏879-1958; www.waileatennis.com; 131 Wailea Ike Pl; per person $15; ☉8am-noon & 3-6pm Mon-Fri, 8am-3pm Sat & Sun) Nicknamed 'Wimbledon West,' this award-winning complex has 11 Plexi-pave courts and equipment rentals. One-hour lessons are also available (clinic/private $25/95).

 Festivals & Events

Maui Film Festival   Film Festival

(www.mauifilmfestival.com) Hollywood celebs swoop in for this five-day extravaganza in mid-June. Join the stars under the stars at various Wailea locations, including the open-air 'Celestial Theater' on a nearby golf course.

 Sleeping

TOP CHOICE **FOUR SEASONS MAUI AT WAILEA**   Resort Hotel $$$

(☏874-8000, 888-344-6284; www.four seasons.com/maui; 3900 Wailea Alanui Dr; r/ste from $465/945; P✳@☎☂♿) The Four Seasons is a dangerous crush. She'll embrace you with sophisticated style,

KARL LEHM

offer an orange blossom mint tea then whisper in your ear that she has no...resort fee. Oh, yes. We're hooked. Children are welcome – there are fun pools plus a Children for All Seasons program – but the resort feels more low-key than its neighbors. Standard rooms are midsized and furnished with understated tropical elegance, slightly more comfy than sophisticated. Marble-floored bathrooms have loads of counter space and a choice of piped-in music. For outlandish spa pampering, enjoy a Hawaiian hot stone massage with cocoa butter slathering in a seaside hale. Parking is $20 per day.

TOP CHOICE **PINEAPPLE INN MAUI**   Inn   **$$**
(☎ 298-4403, 877-212-6284; www.pineappleinnmaui.com; 3170 Akala Dr; r $139-149, cottages $215; P ❄ @ 🛜 🏊) For style with a personal touch, consider this inviting boutique inn overlooking Wailea, less than a mile from the beach. Rooms, which have ocean-view lanai and private entrances, are as nice as those at the exclusive resorts, but at a fraction of the cost. You can watch the sunset from the pool. Rooms have kitchenettes, and the two-bedroom cottage comes with a full kitchen.

GRAND WAILEA RESORT HOTEL & SPA   Resort Hotel   **$$$**
(☎ 875-1234, 800-888-6100; www.grandwailea.com; 3850 Wailea Alanui Dr; r from $725; ❄ 🏊 @ 🛜 🚹) We had planned to make this posh, fun-loving resort a top pick, but when Paris Hilton and Britney Spears have already given their tramp stamp of approval, why bother? We jest, but it's OK to tease an icon you love. The Grand Wailea's unbridled extravagance, from the million-dollar artwork in the lobby to the guest rooms decked out in Italian marble, is a wonder. But it's not all highbrow. The resort, part of the Hilton's Waldorf-Astoria line, boasts the most elaborate water-world wonders in Hawaii, an awesome series of nine interconnected pools with swim-through grottos and towering water slides. The $25 resort fee includes wi-fi.

WAILEA BEACH MARRIOTT RESORT & SPA   Resort Hotel   **$$$**
(☎ 879-1922, 888-236-2427; www.waileamarriott.com; 3700 Wailea Alanui Dr; r from $395; ❄ @ 🛜 🏊) Perched between two of Wailea's loveliest beaches, this is the smallest and most Hawaiian of the Wailea resorts. Instead of over-the-top flash,

Grand Wailea Resort Hotel & Spa

RON DAHLQUIST/GRAND WAILEA RESORT HOTEL & SPA

you'll find warm alohas, serene koi ponds and swaying palm trees. Rooms have a fresh and modern tropical flair. The daily resort fee is $25. Wi-fi is a separate $15 per day and available only in some common areas, including the lobby.

FAIRMONT KEA LANI
Resort Hotel **$$$**

(875-4100, 866-540-4456; www.fairmont.com/kealani; 4100 Wailea Alanui Dr; ste/oceanfront villa from $459/1500; ❄ @ ☎) The white exterior of this Moorish wonder looks a tad dingy and the alohas were not memorably warm on our visit, making us wonder if this seaside sultan has lost some abracadabra. Rooms are large and stylish, however, and views from upper levels are superb. Villas have private plunge pools. It's $20 per day for self-parking; wi-fi in the lobby only.

 Eating

 TOP CHOICE **PITA PARADISE** Mediterranean **$$**

(879-7177; www.pitaparadisehawaii.com; Wailea Gateway Center, 34 Wailea Gateway Pl; lunch $9-15, dinner $17-28; ⏱ 11am-9:30pm) So what if this Greek taverna anchors a cookie-cutter strip mall that lacks ocean views. The inviting patio, the eye-catching mural and the tiny white lights, not to mention the succulent Mediterranean chicken pita, will banish any locational regrets. And talk about fresh: owner John Arabatzis catches his own fish, which is served in everything from pita sandwiches to grilled dinners. This outpost of the popular Pita Paradise in Kihei (p129) opened in 2010.

FERRARO'S
Italian **$$$**

(874-8000; www.fourseasons.com/maui; Four Seasons, 3900 Wailea Alanui Dr; lunch $17-24, dinner $25-48; ⏱ 11:30am-9pm) No other place in Wailea comes close to this breezy restaurant for romantic seaside dining. Lunch strays into fun selections such as *kalua* pig quesadillas with mango poi and a Maine lobster sandwich with avocado spread. Dinner gets more serious, showcasing a rustic Italian menu.

JOE'S BAR & GRILL
Comfort Food **$$$**

(875-7767; www.bevgannonrestaurants.com/joes; 131 Wailea Ike Pl; mains $28-40; ⏱ dinner) A sister operation of the famed Hali'imaile General Store, Joe's is celebrated in its own right. Forget razzle-dazzle – the emphasis is on large portions and home-style simplicity. Think roast beef prime rib with whipped potatoes, chicken breast stuffed with herb cheese and pumpkin-seed-crusted fresh fish.

MATTEO'S
Italian **$$**

(874-1234; www.matteosmaui.com; 100 Wailea Ike Dr; pizzas $11-25; ⏱ 11:30am-9pm Mon-Fri, 5-9pm Sat & Sun) Grab a spot in line and order at the counter at this Italian eatery, an open-air pizzeria and trattoria on the Old Blue golf course near Shops at Wailea. The thin-crust pizzas are surprisingly good.

Waterfront Deli
Deli **$**

(891-2039; Shops at Wailea, 3750 Wailea Alanui Dr; mains under $12; ⏱ 7am-8pm) For a quick, inexpensive meal to-go, head to this deli inside the Whalers General Store at the back of Shops at Wailea.

 **Drinking & Entertainment**

All of the Wailea hotels have some sort of live music, most often jazz or Hawaiian, in the evening.

RED BAR AT GANNON'S
Cocktails

(www.gannonsrestaurant.com; 100 Wailea Golf Club Dr) Everyone looks sexier when they're swathed in a sultry red glow. Come to this chic spot at happy hour (3pm to 6pm) for impressive food and drink specials, as well as attentive bartenders and stellar sunsets. The bar is located inside Gannon's, Bev Gannon's new restaurant at the Gold and Emerald courses' clubhouse.

MULLIGAN'S ON THE BLUE

(874-1131; www.mulligansontheblue.co ... Kaukahi St) Rising above the golf cou ... Mulligan's offers entertainment r ... with anything from Irish folk mu ... pean jazz. It's also a good plac ...

ale while enjoying the distant ocean view, or catching a game on one of the 10 TVs.

Four Seasons Maui at Wailea Hawaiian (3900 Wailea Alanui) The lobby lounge has Hawaiian music and hula performances from 5:30pm to 7:30pm nightly, and jazz or slack key guitar later in the evening.

 Shopping

Shops at Wailea Mall
(www.shopsatwailea.com; 3750 Wailea Alanui Dr; ⏱9:30am-9pm) This outdoor mall has dozens of stores, most flashing designer labels such as Prada and Gucci, but there are some solid island choices, too, including:

Blue Ginger Boutique
(www.blueginger.com) Women's clothing in cheery colors and tropical motifs.

Honolua Surf Co Beachwear
(www.honoluasurf.com) Hip surfer-motif T-shirts, board shorts and aloha shirts.

Martin & MacArthur Hawaiian Crafts
(www.martinandmacarthur.com) Museum-quality Hawaiian-made woodwork and other crafts.

Maui Waterwear Swimwear
(www.mauiclothingcompany.com) Tropical swimwear you'll love to flaunt.

Aloha Shirt Museum & Boutique Hawaiian Clothing
(www.the-aloha-shirt-museum.com) Quality new and vintage aloha shirts. We like the 100% silk Elvis Aloha, aka the King's shirt, in blue ($95).

🛈 Information

Shops at Wailea (3750 Wailea Alanui Dr; ⏱9:30am-9pm) This outdoor mall has an ATM, as do many of the hotels.

Getting There & Around

Maui Bus (www.mauicounty.gov) operates ei Islander 10 between Wailea and Kahului ntil 8:30pm. The first bus leaves Shops at 6:30am and runs along S Kihei Rd before to the Pi'ilani Village shopping center From Ma'alaea you can connect to or Lahaina.

Makena

There's a resort here, with a well-manicured golf course, but Makena still feels wild, like a territorial outpost that hasn't quite been tamed. It's a perfect setting for aquatic adventurers who want to escape the crowds, offering primo snorkeling, kayaking and bodysurfing, plus pristine coral, reef sharks, dolphins and sea turtles galore.

The beaches are magnificent. The king of them all, Big Beach (Oneloa), is an immense sweep of glistening sand and a prime sunset-viewing locale. The secluded cove at neighboring Little Beach is Maui's most popular nude beach – you *will* see bare buns. Don't stare. Together these beaches form Makena State Park, but don't be misled by the term 'park,' as they remain in a natural state, with no facilities except for a couple of pit toilets and picnic tables. No one on Maui would have it otherwise.

 Beaches

TOP CHOICE **MALU'AKA BEACH** Beach
You wanna swim with sea turtles? Then make your way to this golden swath of sand (Map p139) in front of the Makena Beach & Golf Resort. Dubbed 'Turtle Beach,' it's popular with snorkelers and kayakers hoping to glimpse the surprisingly graceful sea turtles that feed along the coral here and often swim within a few feet of snorkelers. You'll find terrific coral about 100yd out, and the best action is at the south end of the beach. Come on a calm day – this one kicks up with even a little wind, and when it's choppy you won't see anything.

You'll find parking lots, restrooms and showers at both ends of the beach. At the north side, park at the lot opposite Keawala'i Congregational Church and then follow the road a short distance south. If the lot's full full, take the first right after Makena Beach & Golf Resort, where there's additional parking for about 60 cars.

MAKENA BAY Beach

There's no better place on Maui for kayaking and, when seas are calm, snorkeling is good along the rocks at the south side of **Makena Landing**, the boat launch that's the center of the action. Makena Bay (Map p139) is also a good place for shore dives; divers should head to the north side of the bay.

Kayak-rental companies deliver kayaks to Makena Landing – you can either head off on your own or join a tour. Although the norm is to make arrangements in advance (there are no shops here), if there's an extra kayak on the trailer, you might be able to arrange something on the spot. Paddle south along the lava coastline to **Malu'aka Beach**, where green sea turtles abound.

TOP CHOICE **BIG BEACH (ONELOA)** Beach

The crowning glory of Makena State Park, this untouched beach is arguably the finest on Maui. In Hawaiian it's called Oneloa, literally 'Long Sand.' And indeed the golden sands stretch for the better part of a mile and are as broad as they come. The waters are a beautiful

Makena to La Pérouse Bay

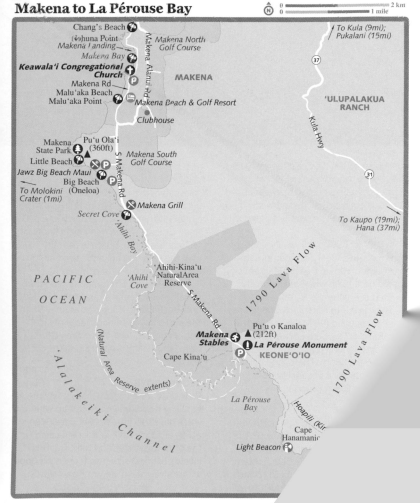

turquoise. When they're calm you'll find kids boogie boarding here, but at other times the breaks belong to experienced bodysurfers, who get tossed wildly in the transparent waves. There is a lifeguard station here.

In the late 1960s this was the site of an alternative-lifestyle encampment nicknamed 'Hippie Beach.' The tent city lasted until 1972, when police finally evicted everyone.

The turnoff to the main parking area a mile beyond the Makena Beach & ⸍ Resort. There's a port-o-john here. ᵔnd parking area lies a quarter of ᵔ the south. Thefts and broken ⸍ds are a possibility, so don't ᵔles in your car.

Beach

ᵔks walking north from ᵔ to Big Beach? The ᵔ and umbrellas? ᵔe Beach (Map ᵔu Ola'i Beach, ᵔaui's *au naturel*

beach. Mind you, nudity is officially illegal, though enforcement is at the political whim of the day. Hidden by a rocky outcrop that juts out from Pu'u Ola'i, the cinder hill that marks the north end of Big Beach, most visitors don't even know Little Beach is there. But take the short trail over the rock that links the two beaches and bam, there it is, bare buns city.

Little Beach fronts a sandy cove that usually has a gentle shorebreak ideal for bodysurfing and boogie boarding. When the surf's up, you'll find plenty of local surfers here as well. When the water's calm, snorkeling is good along the rocky point.

SECRET COVE   Beach
Well, once it was secret. Now a favorite for getaway weddings, it's a toss-up whether you'll have this little pocket cove (Map p139) all to yourself or it'll be packed to the brim with tuxes and tulle. But this lovely postcard-size beach of golden sand with a straight-on view of Kaho'olawe is certainly worth a peek. The cove is a

Left: Secret Cove; **Below:** Surfer and boogie boarders

PHOTOGRAPHER: (LEFT) GREG ELMS/LONELY PLANET IMAGES ©; (BELOW) ANDY JACKSON/ALAMY

quarter-mile after the southernmost Makena State Park parking lot. The entrance is through an opening in a lava-rock wall just south of house No 6900.

Festivals & Events

Xterra World Championship Triathlon (www.xterraplanet.com) Held in late October from the Makena Beach & Golf Resort, this race is a major off-road triathlon that begins with a 0.93-mile swim, followed by a 20-mile bike ride up – and back down – the slopes of Haleakalā then ends with a grueling 7-mile run over sand and lava fields.

Sleeping

MAKENA BEACH & GOLF RESORT Resort Hotel **$$$** (Map p139; ☎ 874-1111, 800-321-6284; www. makenaresortmaui.com; 5400 Makena Alanui Dr;

r from $289, ❄ @ ☎) Under new management following a foreclosure auction, this striking, fortress-like resort is revamping the decor in all rooms. Upgraded bathrooms will have granite countertops and two sinks. The resort is open during renovations, which should be completed by the end of 2011. At press time, management was in the midst of a hiring spree, picking up chefs as well as golf and tennis pros from nearby resorts. The property's 1800-acre perch beside Makena Beach is beautiful, not to mention a top launch pad for snorkelers and kayakers hoping to spy a sea turtle or two.

Eating

Vendors with cold coconuts, pineapples and other fruit are sometimes found along Makena Alanui Dr opposite Big Beach.

JAWZ FISH TACOS   Food Truck   **$**
(Makena State Park; snacks $5-10; ⊙10:30am-
5pm) Get your beach snacks – tacos, burri-
tos, shave ice – at this food truck beside
the northernmost Big Beach parking lot.

MAKENA GRILL   Roadside Grill   **$**
(www.makenagrill.com; Makena Alanui Dr; mains
$6-10; ⊙11am-4pm) This little roadside
smoke grill serves up fish tacos and
chicken kebabs. Hours can be irregular
but when it's open these are tasty grinds.
Take your goodies across the street to
Secret Cove and have a little picnic.

Beyond Makena

Makena Rd turns adventurous after
Makena State Park, continuing for three
narrow miles through the lava flows of
'Ahihi-Kina'u Natural Area Reserve before
dead-ending at La Pe'rouse Bay.

'Ahihi-Kina'u Natural Area Reserve

Chalk this one up to Maui's last lava flow,
which spilled down to the sea here in 1790
and shaped 'Ahihi Bay and Cape Kina'u.

The jagged lava coastline and the pristine
waters fringing it have been designated a
reserve (Map p139) because of its unique
marine habitat.

Thanks in part to the prohibition on
fishing here, the snorkeling is incredible.
Just about everyone heads to the little
roadside cove 100m south of the first
reserve sign – granted, it offers good
snorkeling, but there are better (and less-
crowded) options. Instead, drive 200m
past the cove and look for a large clearing
on the right. Park here and follow the
coastal footpath south for five minutes
to a black-sand beach with fantastic
coral, clear water and few visitors.
Enter the water from the left side of the
beach where access is easy; snorkel in a
northerly direction and you'll immediately
be over coral gardens teeming with an
amazing variety of fish. Huge rainbow
parrotfish abound here, and it's not
unusual to see turtles and the occasional
reef shark.

Large sections of the preserve are
closed to visitors until 2012, which
will allow the Department of Land and
Resource Management to protect the
fragile environment from tourist wear-
and-tear and to develop a long-term
protection plan. Visitation in the north is
still permitted between 5:30am and
7:30pm.

La Pérouse Bay

Earth and ocean merge at La
Pérouse Bay (Map p139)
with a raw desolate beauty
that's almost eerie. The
ancient Hawaiian village
of Keone'o'io flourished
here before the 1790
volcanic eruption. Its
remains – mainly house
and heiau platforms –
can be seen scattered
among the lava patches.
From the volcanic
shoreline look for pods
of spinner dolphins, which

'Ahihi-Kina'u Natural Area Reserve

Paniolo Roots

Sitting beneath the slopes of Upcountry's 'Ulupalakua Ranch, Makena was once a *paniolo* (cowboy) village, home to Hawaiian cowboys who corralled cattle at the landing and loaded them onto barges bound for Honolulu slaughterhouses. To catch a glimpse of Makena's roots, stop at the **Keawala'i Congregational Church**, just south of Makena Landing. One of Maui's earliest missionary churches, its 3ft-thick walls were constructed of burnt coral rock. In the seaside churchyard take a look at the old tombstones adorned with cameo photographs of the Hawaiian cowboys laid to rest a century ago.

commonly come into the bay during the early part of the day. The combination of strong offshore winds and rough waters rule out swimming, but it's an interesting place to explore on land.

History

In May 1786 the renowned French explorer Jean François de Galaup La Pérouse became the first Westerner to land on Maui. As he sailed into the bay that now bears his name, scores of Hawaiian canoes came out to greet him. Two years after leaving Hawaii, La Pérouse mysteriously disappeared in the Pacific. While no one knows his fate, some historians speculate that he and his crew were eaten by cannibals in the New Hebrides (now part of Vanuatu). A monument to the explorer is located at the end of the road at La Pérouse Bay.

 Activities

MAKENA STABLES   Horseback Riding
(Map p139; ☏879-0244; www.makenastables. com; 3hr trail rides $145-170; ☺8am-6pm) Located just before the road ends, this place offers morning and sunset horse-back rides across the lava flows and up the scenic slopes of 'Ulupalakua Ranch.

HOAPILI (KING'S HIGHWAY) TRAIL   Trail
(Map p139; https://hawaiitrails.ehawaii.gov) From La Pérouse Bay, this trail follows an ancient path along the coastline across jagged lava flows. Be prepared: wear hiking boots, bring plenty to drink, start early and tell someone where you're going. It's a dry area with no water and little vegetation, so it can get very hot. The first part of the trail is along the sandy beach at La Pérouse Bay. Right after the trail emerges onto the lava fields, it's possible to take a spur trail for three-quarters of a mile down to the light beacon at the tip of Cape Hanamanioa. Alternatively, walk inland to the Na Ala Hele sign and turn right onto the King's Hwy as it climbs through rough 'a'a lava inland for the next 2 miles before coming back to the coast to an older lava flow at Kanaio Beach. Although the trail continues, it becomes harder to follow and Kanaio Beach is the recommended turn around point. If you don't include the lighthouse spur, the roundtrip distance to Kanaio Beach is about 4 miles.

North Shore & Upcountry

Windsurfing capital of the world and the garden belt of Maui. Local as a ton of onions on a pickup truck, a rancher on horseback, a lone surfer beating across the waves.

The surf-sculpted North Shore coast stands in sharp contrast to the gently rolling pastures and bountiful gardens carpeting the Upcountry slopes. The towns – hip Pa'ia, artsy Makawao and mud-on-your-boots Keokea – boast as much weathered personality as their proud residents. Green and fragrant, the Upcountry simply begs a country drive. The scenery pulls at your soul; makes you want to hang around and browse the real-estate ads. So do. The possibilities for exploring are nothing short of breathtaking. Hike up a mountainside, zipline over deep gorges, paraglide down the hillsides or ride a horse through a lofty cloud forest.

North Shore & Upcountry Itineraries

One Day

1 **Makawao** (p158) Start off your day in this cowboy-centric town by popping into **Komoda Store & Bakery** for a cream puff. Now take a stroll – the art galleries and ranch shops beckon with quirky surprises.

2 **Olinda Rd** (p158) Next, head out of town on a scenic drive through a spicy eucalyptus forest.

3 **Waihou Springs Trail** (p159) Get out of the car and hike the shady paths of this cool trail.

4 **Ha'iku** (p163) Continue your countryside tour along the winding backroads to this surfing town. Grab a seat at **NorthShore Cafe** and join the locals over some home-style grinds.

5 **Ho'okipa Beach Park** (p148) In the afternoon, the winds will be on a tear.

Here you'll find the world's hottest pro windsurfers riding its gnarliest waves.

6 **HA Baldwin Beach Park** (p148) Grab your beach towel – it's time to catch some serious rays. If bodysurfing is your thing the center of this beach is your place. Otherwise walk down to the cove at the end of the beach and enjoy a swim.

7 **Pa'ia** (p148) By now the late afternoon light will be playing on the candy-colored plantation shacks that house Pa'ia's eclectic shops and eateries. Dinnertime brings a tough choice. If a wafting scent really grabs you, let it happen. Otherwise, check the nightly special at **Café des Amis**.

⊙ THIS LEG: 18 MILES

Two Days

1 **Surfing Goat Dairy** (p164) Start day two with a tour of this goat farm, the source of all that delicious chèvre and feta featured on the menus of Maui's top restaurants.

2 **Enchanting Floral Gardens** (p166) Next it's time to explore Kula's gardens, and this is the most wildly diverse of them all.

3 **La Provence** (p169) If you've worked up an appetite with your garden stroll, meander over to this French-inspired gem and order up a salad of fresh Kula greens and guess-who's goat cheese.

4 **Tedeschi Vineyards** (p173) Continue with an afternoon drive through rolling pastures that end at a winery tour.

5 **Grandma's Coffee House** (p172) After you've tipped your wine glass, go sip a cup of Upcountry's other favorite homegrown brew: folks here have been growing top-rate beans since grandma's days and they have the deckside coffee trees to prove it.

6 **Ali'i Kula Lavender** (p166) Soak up the fragrant scents on a stroll through this lavender garden at the foot of a dreamy cloud forest.

7 **Proflyght Paragliding** (p167) If you're feeling adventurous, take a 1000ft leap off a tall cliff and glide like an eagle.

8 **Polipoli Spring State Recreation Area** (p169) Alternatively, if the lavender has you all mellowed out, continue up the slopes to leisurely explore this cloud forest's misty trails.

9 **Hali'imaile General Store** (p158) End the day at this chef-driven restaurant where plantation era meets nouvelle Hawaii cuisine to create the Upcountry's finest dining experience.

➡ THIS LEG: 25 MILES

North Shore & Upcountry Highlights

1 **Best Beach: HA Baldwin Beach Park** (p148) This wide sandy strand is the North Shore's finest.

2 **Best Hiking: Polipoli Spring State Recreation Area** (p169) Lightly trodden trails in a unique cloud forest.

3 **Best Dining Scene: Pa'ia** (p172) Hip cafes and tasty treats abound.

4 **Best Garden: Ali'i Kula Lavender** (p166) Heady scents and sweeping views at this Upcountry favorite.

5 **Best Place to Toast: Tedeschi Vineyards** (p173) A fun vineyard on an eco-friendly ranch.

Fresh lavender, Ali'i Kula Lavender (p166)
PHOTOGRAPHER: GREG VAUGHN/ALAMY

Discover North Shore & Upcountry

Pa'ia

Home to an eclectic mix of surfers and soul seekers, Pa'ia (Map p154) is Maui's hippest burg. Once a thriving sugar town, a century ago Pa'ia boasted 10,000 residents living in plantation camps above the now-defunct sugar mill. During the 1950s there was an exodus to Kahului, shops were shuttered and Pa'ia began to collect cobwebs.

Attracted by low rents, hippies seeking paradise landed in Pa'ia in the 1970s.

A decade later, windsurfers discovered Ho'okipa Beach, and Pa'ia broke onto the map big-time. Its aging wooden storefronts, now splashed in sunshine yellows and sky blues, house a wild array of shops geared to visitors. And the dining scene? Any excuse to be here at mealtime will do.

Beaches

TOP CHOICE HO'OKIPA BEACH PARK   Beach

Ho'okipa (Map p150) is to daredevil windsurfers what Everest is to climbers. It reigns supreme as the world's premier windsurfing beach, with strong currents, dangerous shorebreaks and razor-sharp coral offering the ultimate challenge. Ho'okipa is also one of Maui's prime surfing spots. Winter sees the biggest waves for board surfers, and summer has the most consistent winds for windsurfers. To prevent intersport beefs, surfers typically hit the waves in the morning and the windsurfers take over during the afternoon.

The action in the water is suitable for pros only. But a **hilltop perch** overlooking the beach offers spectators a bird's-eye view of the world's top windsurfers doing their death-defying stuff. Ho'okipa is just before the 9-mile marker; to reach the lookout above the beach take the driveway at the east side of the park.

TOP CHOICE HA BALDWIN BEACH PARK   Beach

Bodyboarders and bodysurfers take to the waves at this palm-lined county park (Map p150) about a mile west of Pa'ia, at the 6-mile marker. The wide sandy beach drops off quickly, and when the shorebreak

Windsurfers, Ho'okipa Beach Park

is big, unsuspecting swimmers can get slammed soundly. Calmer waters, better suited for swimming, can be found at the east end of the beach where there's a little **cove** shaded by ironwood trees. Showers, restrooms, picnic tables, and a well-used baseball and soccer field round out the facilities. The park has a reputation for drunken nastiness after the sun sets, but it's fine in the daytime when there's a lifeguard on duty.

SPRECKELSVILLE BEACH · Beach
Extending west from HA Baldwin Beach, this 2-mile stretch of sand (Map p150) punctuated by lava outcrops is a good walking beach, but its near-shore lava shelf makes it less than ideal for swimming for adults. The rocks do, however, provide protection for young kids. If you walk toward the center of the beach, you'll soon come to a section dubbed '**baby beach**,' where local families take the little ones to splash. There are no facilities. To get there, turn toward the ocean on Nonohe Pl at the 5-mile marker, then turn left on Kealakai Pl just before the Maui Country Club.

TAVARES BEACH · Beach
This unmarked sandy beach (Map p150) is quiet during the week but livens up on weekends when local families come here toting picnics, guitars, dogs and kids. A submerged lava shelf runs parallel to the beach about 25ft from the shore and is shallow enough for swimmers to scrape over. Once you know it's there, however, the rocks are easy to avoid, so take a look before jumping in. The beach parking lot is at the first shoreline access sign on the Hana side of the 7-mile marker. There are no facilities.

 Sights

MAUI DHARMA CENTER · Buddhist Center
(http://mauidharma.org; 81 Baldwin Ave; ⏱6:30am-6:30pm) When the Dalai Lama came to Maui in 2007, he headed straight for Pa'ia to bless a new peace stupa. If

The Best...
Activities for Kids

1 Surfing Goat Dairy farm tour (p164)

2 Pony rides at Piiholo Ranch (p160)

3 Spreckelsville Beach (p149)

4 Hot Island Glass glassblowers (p162)

you want to share in the karma, the Maui Dharma Center invites visitors to join in morning meditation. Or just come by and seek a little enlightenment on your own by strolling clockwise around the stupa prayer wheel – it slows the day down nicely!

 Activities

Hana Hwy Surf · Surfing
(☎579-8999; www.hanahwysurf.com; 149 Hana Hwy; surfboards/boogie boards per day $25/10; ⏱9am-6pm Mon-Sat, 10am-5pm Sun) At Pa'ia's surfing headquarters the staff keep their finger on the pulse of the surf scene and provide a daily recorded surf report (☎871-6258).

Simmer · Windsurfing
(☎579-8484; www.simmerhawaii.com; 137 Hana Hwy; sailboards per day $50; ⏱9am-7pm) Simmer's all about windsurfing and handles everything from repairs to top-of-the-line gear rentals.

 Festivals & Events

High-Tech/Vans/Lopez Surfbash · Surf Meet
(www.mauisurfohana.org) This surf contest takes place at Ho'okipa Beach on the last weekend in November or the first weekend in December, with competing short-boarders, long-boarders and bodyboarders.

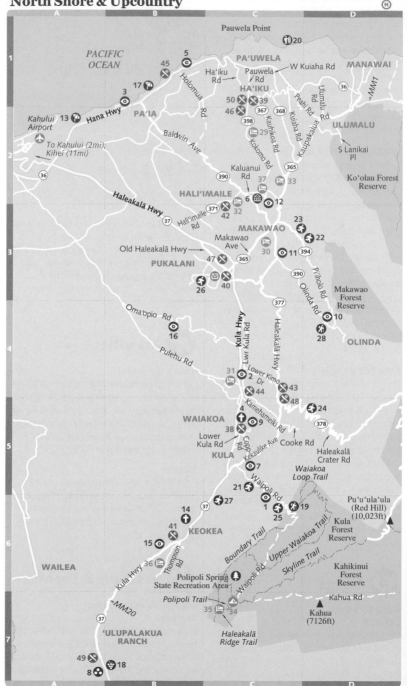

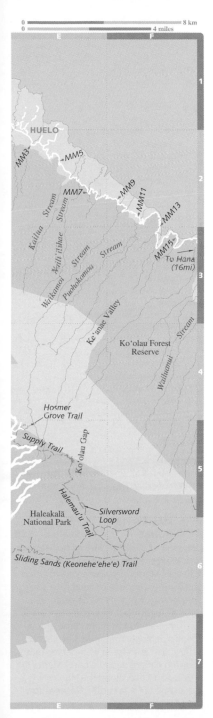

The map shows locations including:

HUELO

MM3, MM5, MM7, MM9, MM11, MM13, MM15

Kailua Stream
Waikamoi Stream
Nailiʻilihae Stream
Puohokamoa Stream
Ke'anae Valley
Waihumau Stream

To Hana (16mi)

Koʻolau Forest Reserve

Hosmer Grove Trail

Supply Trail

Koʻolau Gap

Halemauʻu Trail

Haleakalā National Park

Silversword Loop

Sliding Sands (Keoneheʻeheʻe) Trail

Sleeping

PAIA INN
TOP CHOICE   Inn **$$**

(☏579-6000; www.paiainn.com; 93 Hana Hwy; r incl breakfast $189-239; ✳@ 🛜) Take a classic century-old building, sound-proof the walls, spruce it up with bamboo floors, travertine bathrooms and original artwork, and you've got one classy place to lay your head. This friendly boutique inn, with seven appealing rooms, offers the ultimate Paʻia immersion. Step out the front and Paʻia's restaurants and shops are on the doorstep; step out the back and you're on a path to the beach.

BLUE TILE BEACH HOUSE
B&B **$$**

(☏579-6446; www.beachvacationmaui.com; 459 Hana Hwy; r $110-170, ste $250) Slide into your bathing suit, step out the door of this exclusive oceanfront estate and you're literally on Tavares Beach. Sleeping options range from a small straightforward room to a spacious honeymoon suite with wraparound ocean-view windows and a four-poster bed. All six rooms share a living room and a kitchen.

INN AT MAMA'S
Cottage **$$$**

(Map p150; ☏579-9764; www.mamasfishhouse.com; 799 Poho Pl; d $175-575; ✳🛜) Maui's most famous seafood restaurant has a cluster of pretty cottages, some with ocean views, others with garden settings. Think retro Hawaiian decor, rattan and bamboo, and an airy, clean simplicity that you'd expect at a high-end operation. One caveat: there's a lot of activity nearby and Mama's is not always the quietest of places.

RAINBOW SURF HOSTEL
Hostel **$**

(☏579-9057; www.mauirainbowsurfhostel.com; 221 Baldwin Ave; dm/r $27/75; @🛜) Within walking distance of Paʻia center, this small hostel in a tightly packed residential neighborhood offers simple clean rooms, a guest kitchen and a TV room. It attracts mostly a surfer crowd and is well suited for early risers – quiet-time rules are strictly enforced after 10pm.

North Shore & Upcountry

Eating

Most of Pa'ia's eateries are clustered around the intersection of Baldwin Ave and the Hana Hwy. Go poke your head in a few places and see what's cookin'. Nothing better awaits you in Hana, so grab your picnic supplies before heading onward.

TOP CHOICE **CAFÉ DES AMIS**   Cafe **$$**
(☎579-6323; 42 Baldwin Ave; mains $10-18; ☺8:30am-8:30pm) Grab a seat in the breezy courtyard to dine on the best cafe fare in Pa'ia. It's not always fast, but it's done right. The savory options include spicy Indian curry wraps with mango chutney, and mouth watering crepes. You'll also find vegetarian offerings, crea-tive breakfasts and a tempting array of drinks from fruit smoothies to fine wines. On Wednesday, Thursday and Saturday there's live music in the evenings.

TOP CHOICE **MAMA'S FISH HOUSE**   Seafood **$$$**
(Map p150; ☎579-8488; www.mamasfishhouse. com; 799 Poho Pl; mains $38-50; ☺11am-3pm & 4:30-9pm) Mama's is where you go when you want to propose or celebrate a big anniversary. Not only is the seafood as good as it gets, but when the beachside tiki torches are lit at dinnertime, the scene's achingly romantic. The island-caught fish is so fresh your server tells you who caught it, and where! Mama's is at Ku'au Cove, along the Hana Hwy, 2 miles east of Pa'ia center. Reservations are essential.

TOP CHOICE PA'IA FISH MARKET RESTAURANT
Seafood $$

(☎579-8030; www.paiafishmarket.com; 110 Hana Hwy; mains $10-16; ☺11am-9:30pm) It's all about the fish: fresh, local and affordable. The local favorite is *ono* fish and chips, but the menu includes plenty of other tempting fish preparations, from charbroiled mahi to Cajun-style snapper. And if you've yet to try Hawaii's signature fresh fish dish, order the blackened ahi sashimi as an appetizer. Little wonder the tables here are packed like sardines.

MOANA BAKERY & CAFÉ
Eclectic $$

(☎579-9999; www.moanacafe.com; 71 Baldwin Ave; mains $12-35; ☺8am-8pm) The best place in town to linger over a relaxing lunch in a jazzy setting. Locals love that the chef is agreeable to any special requests. Not that you won't find what you're looking for on the varied menu – perhaps the mahi steamed in banana leaves and served with green papaya salad, or the Hana Bay crab cakes with guava puree?

MANA FOODS
Takeout $

(www.manafoodsmaui.com; 49 Baldwin Ave; deli items $5-7; ☺8am-8:30pm; ☑) Dreadlocked, Birkenstocked or just needing to stock up – everyone rubs shoulders at Mana, a health food store, bakery and deli all wrapped into one. Don't miss the walnut cinnamon buns made fresh every morning. Then look out for the hot rosemary-grilled chicken and organic salad bar. It's gonna be such a g-o-o-d picnic!

CAFÉ MAMBO
Cafe $$

(www.cafemambomaui.com; 30 Baldwin Ave; mains $10-20; ☺8am-9pm) You can't walk by this upbeat, arty cafe without being pulled in by the aromatic scents wafting out the door. Choose from fragrant Moroccan stews, mouthwatering crispy duck fajitas and creative vegetarian fare. Mambo also packs box lunches in coolers for the road to Hana (per person $8.50).

The Ultimate Wave

When this monster rears its powerful head, it's big, fast and mean enough to crunch bones. What is it? **Jaws** (Map p150), Maui's famous big-wave surf spot. A few times a year, strong winter storms off the coast of Japan generate an abundance of energy that races unimpeded across the Pacific Ocean to Hawaii's shores, translating into the planet's biggest rideable waves.

News of the mammoth swells, which reach as high as a seven-story building, attracts gutsy surfers from all over the state and beyond. Unfortunately, there's no legitimate public access to the cliffs that look out toward Jaws, as getting to them requires crossing privately owned agricultural land.

When Jaws (also known locally as Pe'ahi) is up, it's impossible for surfers to paddle through the break to catch a ride. But where there's a thrill, there's a way. Tow-in surfers work in pairs, using small watercraft known as wave runners to get surfers and their boards beyond the break. When even a wave runner is outmatched, surfers get dropped into the ocean from a helicopter.

The equation of extreme sport says that thrill doesn't come without its share of danger. There are myriad opportunities for big-wave surfers to get hurt or killed. The insanely powerful waves can wash surfers into rocks, throw them into their wave runners, knock them against their surfboards or simply pummel them with the force of all that moving water. That said, these guys are pros and are very good at skirting the perils.

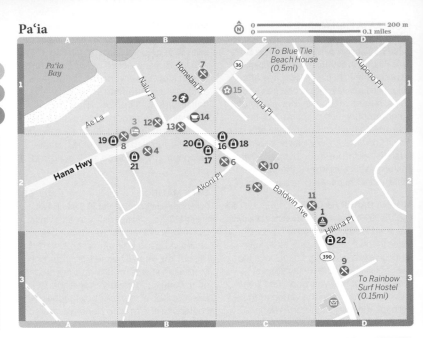

Pa'ia

◉ Sights
1 Maui Dharma Center D2

Activities, Courses & Tours
Hana Hwy Surf .... (see 7)
2 Simmer B1

🛏 Sleeping
3 Paia Inn B1

✖ Eating
4 Anthony's Coffee Company B2
5 Café des Amis C2
6 Café Mambo C2
7 Fiesta Time B1
8 Flatbread Company B2
9 Fresh Mint D3
10 Mana Foods C2
11 Moana Bakery & Café C2

12 Ono Gelato B1
13 Pa'ia Fish Market Restaurant B1
Penguini .... (see 3)

🍸 Drinking
14 Milagros B1

✪ Entertainment
15 Charley's C1

🛍 Shopping
16 Alice in Hulaland C2
17 Hemp House B2
18 Mandala C2
19 Maui Crafts Guild A2
20 Maui Girl B2
21 Maui Hands B2
22 Na Kani O Hula D3

FLATBREAD COMPANY Pizza **$$**
(☎579-8989; 89 Hana Hwy; pizzas $11-20; ⊙11:30am-10pm) Wood-fired pizzas made with organic sauces, nitrate-free pepperoni, Kula onions – you'll never stop at a chain pizza house again. Lots of fun combinations, from pure vegan to *kalua* pork with Surfing Goat chèvre (goat cheese). Eat even greener on Tuesday night when a cut of the profits goes to a local environmental cause.

ANTHONY'S COFFEE COMPANY Coffee Shop **$**
(☎579-8340; 90 Hana Hwy; mains $5-12; ⊙6am-2pm) The best cup of joe on this

side of the island. Fresh-ground organic coffee and a delish variety of goodies from pastries to lox Benedict. Staff even pack picnic boxes for the drive to Hana. You know everything's done right – you'll find the owner himself on the other side of the counter grinding away.

ONO GELATO
Dessert $

(www.onogelatocompany.com; 115 Hana Hwy; cones $5; ⏱11am-10pm) How cool is this? This little shop dishes up Maui-made organic gelato in island flavors such as guava, mango and Kula strawberry. For the ultimate treat, order the *liliko'i* quark, combining passion fruit and goat's cheese – it's awesome...really.

FRESH MINT
Vietnamese $$

(☎579-9144; 115 Baldwin Ave; mains $8-13; ⏱5-9pm; ✐) Authentic Vietnamese fare but totally veg, and the chef-owner of this place takes pride in her artistically presented dishes. Even meat eaters will be amazed at how soy takes on the flavors and texture of the foods it substitutes. In doubt? Just try the spicy ginger soy beef.

PENGUINI
Sandwiches $

(93 Hana Hwy; sandwiches $6; ⏱7:30am-5pm Mon-Fri) Come to this simple courtyard eatery at the side of the Paia Inn for healthy panini sandwiches at bargain prices. It also makes a tasty gelato using only Maui-grown fruit; you might want to give them a little taste comparison with Ono Gelato.

FIESTA TIME
Mexican $

(☎579-8269; 149 Hana Hwy; mains $5-13; ⏱7am-8pm) Surfers line up at this hole-in-the-wall for real-deal home-cooked Mexican food that's twice as good and half the price as nearby options. Quesadillas, tostadas, hot tamales – *muy delicioso!*

Drinking & Entertainment

CHARLEY'S
Bar

(www.charleysmaui.com; 142 Hana Hwy) Don't be surprised to find country-singer legend Willie Nelson at the next table. He's a part-time Pa'ia resident, and this cowboy-centric place is his favorite hang. Charley's has live music most nights – with a little luck it could even be Willie.

Milagros
Cafe

(3 Baldwin Ave) The spot for a late-afternoon beer. The sidewalk tables are perched perfectly for watching all the action on Pa'ia's busiest corner.

Shopping

This is a fun town for browsing, with owner-run shops and boutiques selling Maui-made goodies of all sorts.

Serving crepes, Café des Amis (p152)
PHOTOGRAPHER: GREG ELMS/LONELY PLANET IMAGES ©

TOP CHOICE MAUI CRAFTS GUILD   Crafts

(www.mauicraftsguild.com; 43 Hana Hwy) This longstanding collective of Maui artists and craftspeople sells everything from pottery and jewelry to handpainted silks and natural-fiber baskets at reasonable prices.

NA KANI O HULA   Hula Supplies

(www.nakaniohula.com; 115 Baldwin Ave) Hula *halau* (troupes) come here for *'uli'uli* (feather-decorated gourd rattles), bamboo nose flutes and other traditional dance and music crafts – any of which would make for a fascinating souvenir. Other quirky and perky places:

Maui Hands   Crafts
(www.mauihands.com; 84 Hana Hwy) Top-end koa bowls, pottery and Maui-themed paintings.

Hemp House   Hemp
(www.hemphousemaui.com; 16 Baldwin Ave) Sells all things hemp – well, almost all.

Mandala   Clothing
(29 Baldwin Ave) Lightweight cotton and silk clothing, Buddhas and Asian crafts.

Maui Girl   Swimwear
(www.maui-girl.com; 12 Baldwin Ave) Get your itty-bitty bikinis here.

Alice in Hulaland   Gifts
(www.aliceinhulaland.com; 19 Baldwin Ave) Kitschy but fun souvenirs.

ℹ Information

Bank of Hawaii (www.boh.com; 35 Baldwin Ave)

Haz Beanz Coffeehouse (📞268-0149; 115 Baldwin Ave; 🕐6am-2pm; 📶) Free wi-fi for the price of a cup of coffee.

Post office (www.usps.com; 120 Baldwin Ave)

ℹ Getting There & Around

BICYCLE Rent bicycles at **Maui Sunriders** (📞579-8970; www.mauibikeride.com; 71 Baldwin Ave; per day $30; 🕐9am-4:30pm). The price

Left: Hui No'eau Visual Arts Center (p158); **Below:** Hali'imaile General Store (p158)

PHOTOGRAPHERS: (LEFT) PHOTO RESOURCE HAWAII/ALAMY; (BELOW) ANN CECIL/LONELY PLANET IMAGES ©

includes a bike rack, so a travel companion could drop you off at the top of Haleakalā, or anywhere else, to cycle a one-way route.

BUS The Maui Bus operates between Kahului and Pa'ia ($1) every 90 minutes from 5:30am to 8:30pm.

CAR Parking is tight in Pa'ia; best bet is the parking lot on the west side of town before the gas station. Keep in mind Pa'ia is the last place to gas up your car before Hana.

Hali'imaile

The little pineapple town of Hali'imaile ('fragrant twining shrub') is named for the sweet-scented maile plants used in lei-making that covered the area before pineapple took over. The heart of town is the old general store (c 1918) that's been turned into Upcountry's best restaurant. Hali'imaile Rd runs through the town, connecting Baldwin Ave (Hwy 390) with the Haleakā Hwy (Hwy 37).

 **Sleeping**

PEACE OF MAUI Inn $
(Map p150; ☎572-5045; www.peaceofmaui. com; 1290 Hali'imaile Rd; r with shared bathroom $70, cottage $140; @ 🛜) This aptly named place in quiet Hali'imaile is Upcountry's top budget sleep. In the middle of nowhere yet within an hour's drive of nearly everywhere, it would make a good central base for exploring the whole island. Rooms, spotlessly clean, are small but comfortable, each with refrigerator and TV. There's a guest kitchen and a hot tub. If you need more space, there's a cottage that's large enough to sleep a family.

Eating

TOP CHOICE **HALI'IMAILE GENERAL STORE** Hawaii Regional **$$$**
(Map p150; ☎572-2666; www.bevgannon
restaurants.com; 900 Hali'imaile Rd; mains
$16-40; ☻11am-2:30pm Mon-Fri & 5:30-9:30pm
daily) Chef Bev Gannon was one of the
original forces behind the Hawaii Regional
Cuisine movement and a steady flow of
in-the-know diners beat a track to this
tiny village to feast on her inspired crea-
tions. You can tantalize the tastebuds
with fusion fare such as sashimi pizza and
Asian duck tostadas. The atmospheric
plantation-era decor sets the mood.

Makawao

Paint a picture of Makawao and what you
get is a mélange of art haven and cowboy
culture, with some chic boutiques and a
dash of New Age sensibility thrown in for
good measure.

Started as a ranching town in the
1800s, Makawao wears its *paniolo*
(cowboy) history in the Old West–style
wooden buildings lining Baldwin Ave. And
the cattle pastures surrounding town
remind you it's more than just history.

But that's only one side of Makawao.
Many of the old shops that once sold
saddles and stirrups now have artsy new
tenants who have turned Makawao into
the most happening art center on Maui.
Its galleries display the works of painters
and sculptors who have escaped frenzied
scenes elsewhere to set up shop in these
inspirational hills. If you enjoy browsing,
just about every storefront is worth
poking your head into.

Sights

FREE **HUI NO'EAU VISUAL ARTS CENTER** Art Gallery
(Map p150; www.huinoeau.com; 2841 Baldwin
Ave; ☻10am-4pm Mon-Sat) Occupying the
former estate of sugar magnates Harry
and Ethel Baldwin, Hui No'eau radiates
artistic creativity. The **plantation house**
with the main galleries was designed by

famed architect CW Dickey in 1917 and
showcases the Hawaiian Regional–style
architectural features he pioneered. The
prestigious arts club founded here in the
1930s still offers classes in printmaking,
pottery, woodcarving and other visual
arts. You're welcome to visit the **galleries**,
which exhibit the diverse works of island
artists, and walk around the grounds,
where you'll find stables converted into
art studios. The **gift shop** sells quality
ceramics, glassware and prints created
on-site. Pick up a walking-tour map at the
front desk. The center is just north of the
5-mile marker.

OLINDA RD Scenic Drive
For the ultimate country drive head into
the hills above Makawao along Olinda Rd
(Map p150), which picks up in town where
Baldwin Ave leaves off, drifting up past
the **Oskie Rice Arena**, where rodeos are
held, and the **Maui Polo Club**, which hosts
matches on Sunday afternoons in the fall.
From here the winding road is little more
than a path through the forest, with knotty
tree roots as high as your car caressing
the roadsides. The air is rich with the spicy
fragrance of eucalyptus trees and oc-
casionally there's a clearing with an ocean
vista. Four miles up from town, past the 11-
mile marker, is the **Maui Bird Conserva-
tion Center** (closed to the public), which
breeds nene (native Hawaiian goose) and
other endangered birds. To make a loop,
turn left onto Pi'iholo Rd near the top of
Olinda Rd and wind back down into town.

SACRED GARDEN OF MALIKO Labyrinth Walk
(Map p150; www.sacredgardenmaui.com; 460
Kaluanui Rd, Makawao; admission free; ☻10am-
5pm) Up for a meditative moment? The
Sacred Garden of Maliko, a self-described
healing sanctuary, has a pair of rock-
garden labyrinth walks guaranteed to
reset the harmony gauge. One's in an
orchid greenhouse facing a contemplative
Buddha statue; the other's in a *kukui* (can-
dlenut trees) grove beside Maliko Stream.
Take your time, feel each step on the
pebbles underfoot, listen to the trickling
stream, inhale the gentle scent of the gar-

den. S-o-o-o soul soothing. To get there, turn east off Baldwin Ave onto Kaluanui Rd. After 0.8 miles you'll cross a one-lane bridge; 0.2 miles further look for a low stone wall – the garden is on the right just before a sharp S-curve in the road.

Activities

PIIHOLO RANCH ZIPLINE Zipline
TOP CHOICE
(Map p150; ☎ 572-1717; www.piiholo zipline.com; Waiahiwi Rd; zip tours $140-190; ⊙ 8am-3pm Mon-Sat) Maui's newest zipline is a top-rate operation that takes great care to orient zip-riders before they actually take a jump. The first zip is over a gentle sloping meadow, so you can get the butterflies out of your stomach. It becomes progressively more interesting, with the last zip – Hawaii's longest – ripping an awesome 2800ft at an eagle's height of 600ft above the tree canopy. The cheaper tour bypasses the last zip, so for the ultimate rush go for it all. Dual lines let you zip side by side with a buddy. Another advantage with Piiholo – you can drive right up to the staging area for the first jump and the need to use ATVs to get between zips is minimal.

WAIHOU SPRINGS TRAIL Hiking
If you're ready for a quiet walk in the woods, take this peaceful trail (Map p150), which begins 4.75 miles up Olinda Rd from central Makawao. The forest is

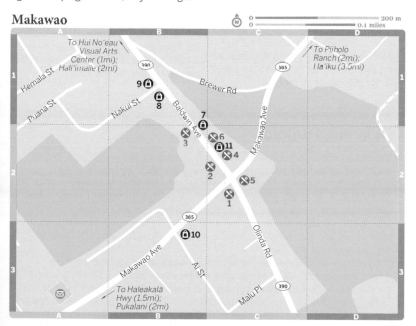

Makawao

0 ————————— 200 m
0 ————————— 0.1 miles

To Hui No'eau Visual Arts Center (1mi); Hali'imaile (2mi)

To Piiholo Ranch (2mi); Ha'iku (3.5mi)

Brewer Rd

Hemala St
Puana St
Nakui St
Baldwin Ave
Makawao Ave
Olinda Rd

To Haleakalā Hwy (1.5mi); Pukalani (2mi)

Ai St
Malu Pl

Makawao

⊗ Eating

	Casanova Deli	(see 1)
1	Casanova Restaurant	C2
2	Komoda Store & Bakery	C2
3	Makawao Farmers Market	B2
4	Makawao Garden Café	C2
5	Polli's	C2
6	Rodeo General Store	C2

⊕ Shopping

7	Aloha Cowboy	B1
8	Designing Wahine	B1
9	Hot Island Glass	B1
10	Randy Jay Braun Gallery	B3
11	Sherri Reeve Gallery	C2
	Viewpoints Gallery	(see 9)

amazingly varied, having been planted by the US Forest Service in an effort to determine which trees would produce the best quality lumber in Hawaii. Thankfully these magnificent specimens never met the woodman's ax. The trail, which begins on a soft carpet of pine needles, passes Monterey cypress and eucalyptus as well as orderly rows of pine trees. After 0.7 miles, you'll be rewarded with a view clear out to the ocean, and up to this point it's easy going. It's also possible to continue steeply downhill for another 0.25 miles to reach Waihou Springs, but that part of the trail can be a muddy mess.

PIIHOLO RANCH Horseback Rides
(Map p150; ☎ 357-5544; www.piiholo.com; Waiahiwi Rd; 2hr ride $120; ⊙9am-3:30pm Mon-Sat; ⓰) Ride with real *paniolo* across the open range of this cattle ranch that's been worked by the same family for six generations. Mountain, valley and pasture views galore. Families can also book pony rides for children as young as 3.

 ## Festivals & Events

Upcountry Fair Agricultural Fair
Traditional agricultural fair with a farmers market, arts and crafts, chili cookoff, *keiki* (children's) games and good ol' country music; held on the second weekend in June at the Eddie Tam Complex.

Makawao Rodeo Rodeo
Hundreds of *paniolo* show up at the Oskie Rice Arena on the weekend closest to Independence Day (July 4) for Hawaii's premier rodeo. Qualifying roping and riding events occur all day on Thursday and Friday to determine who gets to compete for the big prizes over the weekend. For thrills on Friday night, head up to the arena to see the bull-riding bash.

Paniolo Parade Parade
Held on the Saturday morning closest to July 4, this festive parade goes right through the heart of Makawao; park at the rodeo grounds and take the free shuttle to the town center.

Ride 'em, Paniolo!

The history of *paniolo* (Hawaiian cowboys) dates back at least 50 years before Wild West cowboys on the mainland climbed into their stirrups.

It started with Captain Vancouver, who introduced cattle to Hawaii in 1793. Kamehameha the Great placed a kapu (taboo) on their slaughter and the cattle, allowed to range freely, were soon running rampant. In 1832 Kamehameha III, determined to rein in the herds, invited cowboys from Spanish California to show Hawaiians the ropes. Indeed, the word *paniolo* is likely a corruption of *español*, meaning Spaniard.

Soon there were Hawaiian *paniolo* rounding up cattle and driving them down the mountainside to Makena, where they were loaded onto boats bound for Honolulu slaughterhouses. A *paniolo* culture developed and riders such as Ikua Purdy brought the *paniolo* lasting fame. In 1908 Purdy won the world championship for rodeo steer-roping in Cheyenne, Wyoming. His record of two steers in 56 seconds has never been bettered. For 25 years Purdy worked as the foreman of Upcountry's 'Ulupalakua Ranch, where he was buried in 1945. A handful of *paniolo* still follow in his footsteps on the national rodeo circuit, and in 1999 Purdy was inducted into the National Cowboy Hall of Fame.

If you want to know more, *Aloha Cowboy* by Virginia Cowan-Smith provides a captivating account of *paniolo* life. Or better yet, take a horseback ride with *paniolo* on a working cattle ranch, such as **Piiholo Ranch** on the outskirts of Makawao or **Mendes Ranch** in Waihe'e, and experience it yourself.

Rodeo, Piiholo Ranch

GREG ELMS/LONELY PLANET IMAGES ©

 ## Sleeping

TOP\ WILD GINGER
CHOICE FALLS   Cottage $$
(Map p150; ✆573-1173; www.wildgingerfalls.
com; 355 Kaluanui Rd; d $155; 🛜) Fun setting!
This stylish studio cottage overlooks a
stone gorge and streambed that spouts
a waterfall after it rains. Banana and cof-
fee trees dot the lush garden surround-
ing the cottage and you can soak up the
scenery from an outdoor hot tub. It's
owned by one of Hawaii's top contem-
porary ceramic artists, and the cottage
has an engaging retro 1940s Hawaiiana
decor.

HALE HO'OKIPA INN   B&B $$
(✆572-6698; www.maui-bed-and-breakfast.
com; 32 Pakani Pl; r incl breakfast $140-180; 🛜)
A short walk from the town center, this
Craftsman-style house built in 1924 offers
four sunny guest rooms furnished with
antiques. It's all very casual and homey
with country-style furnishings in the
rooms and organic fruit from the yard on
the breakfast table.

 ## Eating

TOP\ KOMODA STORE &
CHOICE BAKERY   Bakery $
(3674 Baldwin Ave; pastries $1-2; ⏰7am-5pm
Mon, Tue, Thu & Fri, to 2pm Sat) This homespun bakery, legendary for its mouth-
watering cream puffs and guava-filled
malasadas (Portuguese donut), is a must-
stop. It's been a Makawao landmark since
Tazeko Komoda first stoked up the oven
in 1916 and his offspring, using the same
time-honored recipes, have been at it ever
since. Best believe they've got it down
pat! Do arrive early though – it often sells
out by noon.

TOP\ CASANOVA
CHOICE RESTAURANT   Italian $$
(✆572-0220; www.cassanovamaui.com; 1188
Makawao Ave; mains $12-32; ⏰11:30am-2pm
Mon-Sat & 5:30-9pm daily) The one Maka-
wao restaurant that lures diners up the
mountain, Casanova offers reliably good
Italian fare. The crispy innovative pizzas
cooked in a kiawe-fired oven are as good
as they get. Juicy Maui-raised steaks and
classic Italian dishes shore up the rest of
the menu. Casanova also doubles as the

Upcountry's top entertainment venue, with a happening dance floor and live music several nights a week.

MAKAWAO GARDEN CAFÉ   Cafe $
(3669 Baldwin Ave; mains $7-10; ⏰11am-3pm Mon-Sat) On a sunny day there's no better place in town for lunch than this outdoor cafe tucked into a courtyard at the north end of Baldwin Ave. It's strictly sandwiches and salads, but everything's fresh, generous and made to order by the owner herself.

CASANOVA DELI   Deli $
(1188 Makawao Ave; mains $6-9; ⏰7am-5:30pm Mon-Sat, 8:30am-5:30pm Sun) Makawao's hippest haunt brews heady espressos and buzzes all day with folks munching on buttery croissants, thick Italian sandwiches and hearty Greek salads. Take it all out to the roadside deck for the town's best people-watching.

RODEO GENERAL STORE   Takeout $
(3661 Baldwin Ave; meals $5-8; ⏰6:30am-10pm) Stop here to grab a tasty takeout meal. The deli counter sells everything from fresh salads and Hawaiian *poke* (marinated raw fish) to hot teriyaki chicken and plate lunches ready to go. Everything is made from scratch.

POLLI'S   Mexican $$
(www.pollismexicanrestaurant.com; 1202 Makawao Ave; mains $8-22; ⏰11am-10pm) Locals and visitors alike flock to this old standby Tex-Mex restaurant to down a few *cervezas* (beers) while munching away on nachos, tacos and sizzling fajitas. The food's just average, but surf videos and plenty of spirited chatter keep the scene high energy.

Makawao Farmers Market   Produce $
(www.makawaofarmersmarket.com; 3654 Baldwin Ave; ⏰10am-5pm Wed) Upcountry gardeners gather to sell their homegrown veggies and fruit once a week at this small open-air market opposite Rodeo General Store.

Shopping

Start your exploration by wandering down Baldwin Ave, beginning at its intersection with Makawao Ave.

HOT ISLAND GLASS   Handblown Glass
(www.hotislandglass.com; 3620 Baldwin Ave) Head here to watch **glassblowers** spin their red-hot creations (from 10:30am to 4pm) at Maui's oldest handblown glass studio. Everything from paperweights with ocean themes to high-art decorative pieces.

Viewpoints Gallery   Art Gallery
(www.viewpointsgallery. com; 3620 Baldwin Ave) You'll feel like you're walking into a museum at this classy gallery, where a dozen of the island's finest artists hang their works.

Handblown glass, Hot Island Glass

Randy Jay Braun Gallery　Photo Gallery
(www.randyjaybraungallery.com; 1152 Makawao
Ave) Braun's sepia photographs of Hawaiian
cowboys and traditional hula dancers are among
the most recognized photo art in Hawaii today.

Aloha Cowboy　Souvenir Shop
(www.alohacowboy.net; 3643 Baldwin Ave) Get
your cowboy-themed retro lunch pails and
rhinestone-studded leather bags here.

Designing Wahine　Gift Shop
(www.designingwahine.com; 3640 Baldwin Ave)
Quality gifts, classic aloha shirts and hand-dyed
Ts with *paniolo* themes.

Sherri Reeve Gallery　Art Gallery
(www.sreeves.com; 3669 Baldwin Ave) Floral
watercolors in a pastel palette on everything
from T-shirts to full-size canvasses.

🛈 Information

Minit Stop (1100 Makawao Ave; ⏱5am-
11:30pm) There's no bank in town, but this gas
station has an ATM.

Post office (www.usps.com; 1075 Makawao Ave)

Haʻiku

In some ways this little town is what Paʻia
was like before the tourists arrived. Like
Paʻia, Haʻiku has its roots in sugarcane –
Maui's first 12 acres of the sweet stuff
were planted here in 1869, and the village
once had both a sugar mill and pineapple
canneries. Thanks to its affordability and
proximity to Hoʻokipa Beach, it's a haunt of
pro surfers who have rejuvenated the town.
Today the old cannery buildings are once
again the heart of the community, housing
a yoga studio, several surfboard shops and
the kind of eateries that make a detour fun.

🤸 Activities

STUDIO MAUI　Yoga
(Map p150; 📞575-9390; www.thestudiomaui.
com; Haʻiku Marketplace, 810 Haʻiku Rd; classes
$15-30; ⏱7:30am-10pm) Attracts a high-
energy, good-karma crowd with a full
schedule of yoga classes from Anusara
basics to power-flow yoga, as well as ec-
static dance, New Age concerts and more.

NAME: NATALIE O'BRIEN

OCCUPATION: STUDENT AT
MAUI COLLEGE CULINARY
ACADEMY

RESIDENCE: MAKAWAO

**If friends were visiting,
where would you take them?** I would
definitely go into the forest, to Waihou
Springs Trail (p164), up Olinda Rd. The trees
are really picturesque.

Where's the action on the North Shore?
Hoʻokipa (p148) is the number one
windsurfing destination – If the surf's going
off, drive by and check it out. Also, sometimes
turtles are right in the shorebreak when
there's big surf...go down toward the center
section, by the trees, to see them...they come
to ride the waves for fun too.

Do you swim at Hoʻokipa? I have, but it can
be rough. Baldwin (p148) is a better beach for
swimming. Down toward the right side there's
a little cove area with shade trees – that's
where I like to go.

What's your favorite Paʻia restaurant?
Café des Amis (p152). It has the most
amazing crepes. I love the tomato, mozzarella
and basil crepe and I always *have* to have the
nutella crepe. They drizzle it with chocolate
and put whipped cream on it and it's just
delicious. Also Mana Foods (p153) has a
really good salad bar for beach snacks. It's a
cool store.

How about Makawao? Coffee at
Casanova's Deli (p161). Dounuts at
Komoda's (p161) *for sure* in the morning.
Very old school. They've been there forever.

**Do you have other favorites in the
Upcountry?** Definitely. Grandma's (p172)
has an awesome breakfast, awesome view
and outdoor seating. Tedeschi Vineyards
(p173) is a picturesque place to go. It
makes a fromboise, a raspberry dessert
wine, that's delicious, really decadent.

🛏 Sleeping

PILIALOHA
TOP CHOICE   Cottage   **$$**

(Map p150; ☏572-1440; www.pilialoha. com; 2512 Kaupakalua Rd; d $145; 🛜) Pilialoha blends countryside charm with all the comforts of a home away from home. The sunny split-level cottage has one pretty setting, nestled in a eucalyptus grove. Everything inside is pretty, too. But it's the warm hospitality and attention to detail – from the fresh-cut roses on the table to the Hawaiian music collection and cozy quilts on the beds – that shine brightest. Breakfast goodies for your first morning and coffee for the entire stay are provided.

HAIKU CANNERY INN B&B   B&B   **$$**

(Map p150; ☏283-1274; www.haikucanneryinn. com; 1061 Kokomo Rd; r incl breakfast $105-125) Down a winding dirt road, surrounded by banana and breadfruit trees, this 1920s plantation house beams with character. High ceilings, hardwood floors and period decor reflect the place's century-old history. In addition to the rooms in the main house, there's a roomy two-bedroom detached cottage for $190.

🍴 Eating

NORTHSHORE CAFE
TOP CHOICE   Cafe   **$**

(Map p150; www.northshorecafe.net; 824 Kokomo Rd; meals $5-20; ⏰7am-2pm daily, 5-9pm Tue-Sat) It's got a funky little interior with chairs that look like they were hauled out of a 1950s attic but this homespun eatery dishes up unbeatable value. Breakfast, served until 2pm, tops out at $8.08 and includes a knockout eggs Benedict. Steaks, seafood and sushi kick in at dinner. The cafe is hidden behind the power station opposite Colleen's but you'll be glad you searched it out.

COLLEEN'S   American   **$$**

(Map p150; www.colleensinhaiku.com; Ha'iku Marketplace, 810 Ha'iku Rd; mains $8-20; ⏰6am-9pm) Surfers get their pre-sunrise espresso jolt here and return in the evening to cap things off with a pint of Big Swell Ale. Colleen's is pure locavore. The burgers and steaks are made with hormone-free Maui cattle, the salads with organic Kula greens and the beers Colleen pours are Hawaiian microbrews.

VEG OUT   Vegetarian   **$**

(Map p150; Ha'iku Town Center, 810 Kokomo Rd; mains $5-10; ⏰11:30am-7:30pm; 🍴) Tucked inside a former warehouse, this rasta-casual vegetarian eatery serves up a dynamite burrito loaded with beans, hot tofu and jalapenos. Also right on the mark are the taro cheeseburgers and pesto-chèvre pizza.

Pukalani & Around

True to its name, which means Heavenly Gate, Pukalani is the gateway to the lush Upcountry. Most visitors just drive past Pukalani on the way to Kula and Haleakalā, and unless you need to pick up supplies or gas up you won't miss much by sticking to the bypass road.

To reach the business part of town, get off Haleakalā Hwy (Hwy 37) at the Old Haleakalā Hwy exit, which becomes Pukalani's main street. There are a couple of gas stations along this street – the last gas before Haleakalā National Park.

👁 Sights & Activities

SURFING GOAT DAIRY
TOP CHOICE   Farm

(Map p150; ☏878-2870; www.surfing goatdairy.com; 3651 Oma'opio Rd; admission free; ⏰10am-5pm Mon-Sat, to 2pm Sun; 👶) 'Feta mo betta' is the motto at this 42-acre farm, the source of all that luscious chèvre adorning the menus of Maui's top restaurants. The shop here carries an amazing variety of creamy goat cheeses; for island flavor try the mango chutney. Not everything is geared to the connoisseur – your kids will love meeting the goat kids up close in a fun 20-minute dairy tour ($7). On some of the tours they can even try their hand at milking.

PUKALANI COUNTRY CLUB   Golf
(Map p150; ☎572-1314; www.pukalanigolf.com;
360 Pukalani St; green fees $87; ☺7am-dusk) A
mile west of Old Haleakala Hwy, this golf
course has 18 holes of smooth greens
with sweeping views. Here's a bargain:
come after 2:30pm and golf the rest of
the day for just $27 – cart included!

Eating

SERPICO'S   Italian $$
(Map p150; ☎572-8498; www.serpicosmaui.com;
cnr Aewa Pl & Old Haleakalā Hwy; mains $7-16;
☺11am-10pm; 👪) In the center of Pukalani,
opposite McDonald's, this casual Italian
eatery makes New York–style pizzas and
pasta dishes, and it makes them well. If
you're in a hurry, there are sandwiches
and inexpensive lunch specials, as well as
a $5 kids menu.

FOODLAND   Takeout $
(Map p150; Pukalani Terrace Center, cnr Old
Haleakalā Hwy & Pukalani St; ☺24hr) This
always-open supermarket is a convenient
stop for those heading up Haleakalā for

the sunrise or coming down for supplies.
There's also a Starbucks inside the store.

ℹ Information

Bank of Hawaii (www.boh.com; Pukalani Terrace
Center, cnr Old Haleakalā Hwy & Pukalani St) The
last bank and ATM before reaching Kula and
Haleakala National Park.

Post office (www.usps.com; Pukalani Terrace
Center, cnr Old Haleakalā Hwy & Pukalani St)

Kula

It's cooler in Kula – refreshingly so. Think
of this Upcountry heartland as one big
garden, and you won't be far off. The very
name Kula is synonymous with fresh
veggies on any Maui menu worth its salt.
So bountiful is Kula's soil, it produces
most of the onions, lettuce and strawberries grown in Hawaii and almost all of the
commercially grown proteas. The latest
addition, sweet-scented lavender, is finding its niche, too.

The magic is in the elevation. At
3000ft, Kula's cool nights and sunny days
are ideal for growing all sorts of crops.
Kula's farmers first gained fame during

Goats, Surfing Goat Dairy

ABBOT LOW MOFFAT III

the California gold rush of the 1850s, when they shipped so many potatoes to West Coast miners that Kula became known as 'Nu Kaleponi,' the Hawaiian pronunciation for New California. In the late 19th century Portuguese and Chinese immigrants who had worked off their contracts on the sugar plantations also moved up to Kula and started small farms, giving Kula the multicultural face that it still wears today.

◉ Sights

Stop and smell the roses...and the lavender and all those other sweet-scented blossoms. No two gardens in Kula are alike, and each has its own special charms.

TOP CHOICE ALI'I KULA LAVENDER Garden
(Map p150; ☎878-8090; www.aklmaui. com; 1100 Waipoli Rd; admission free; ◷9am-4pm) Immerse yourself in a sea of purple at Ali'i Kula Lavender. Start by strolling along the garden paths where dozens of varieties of these fragrant plants blanket the hillside. Take your time, breathe

deeply. Then sit for a spell on the lanai (veranda) with its sweeping views and enjoy a lavender scone and perhaps a cup of lavender tea. Browse through the gift shop, and sample the lavender-scented oils and lotions. If you want to really dig in, a variety of activities from garden-tea tours to wedding packages are available. To get to the parking area, drive pass the farm, go through the Kula Forest Reserve gates and follow the signs.

🌿 ENCHANTING FLORAL GARDENS Garden
(Map p150; ☎878-2531; www.flowersofmaui.com; 2505 Kula Hwy; adult/child 6-12 $7.50/1; ◷9am-5pm) A labor of love, this colorful garden showcases the green thumb of master horticulturist Kazuo Takeda. Kula has microclimates that change with elevation and this garden occupies a narrow zone where tropical, temperate and desert vegetation all thrive. The sheer variety is amazing. You'll find everything from flamboyant proteas and orchids to orange trees and kava – all of it identified with Latin and common names. Your garden stroll ends with a sampling of fruits grown here.

Holy Ghost Church

DISCOVER NORTH SHORE & UPCOUNTRY

KULA BOTANICAL GARDEN
Garden

(Map p150; ☎878-1715; www.kulabotanical garden.com; 638 Kekaulike Ave; adult/child 6-12 $10/3; ⊙9am-4pm) Pleasantly overgrown and shady, this mature garden has walking paths that wind through acres of theme plantings, including native Hawaiian specimens and a 'taboo garden' of poisonous plants. Because a stream runs through it, the garden supports water-thirsty plants that you won't find in other Kula gardens. When the rain gods have been generous the whole place is an explosion of color.

MAUI AGRICULTURAL RESEARCH CENTER
Garden

(Map p150; ☎878-1213; www.ctahr.hawaii.edu; 424 Mauna Pl; admission free; ⊙7:30am-3:30pm Mon-Thu) It was in this garden operated by the University of Hawai'i that the state's first proteas were planted in 1965. Today you can walk through row after row of their colorful descendants. Named for the Greek god Proteus, who was noted for his ability to change form, the varieties are amazingly diverse – some look like over-sized pincushions, others like spiny feathers. Nursery cuttings from the plants here are distributed to protea farms across Hawaii, which in turn supply florists as far away as Europe. To get here, take Copp Rd (between the 12- and 13-mile markers on Hwy 37) for half a mile and turn left on Mauna Pl.

HOLY GHOST CHURCH
Church

(Map p150; www.kulacatholiccommunity.org; 4300 Lower Kula Rd; ⊙8am-5pm) Waiakoa's hillside landmark, the octagonal Holy Ghost Church was built in 1895 by Portuguese immigrants. The church features a beautifully ornate interior that looks like it came right out of the Old World, and indeed much of it did. The gilded altar was carved by renowned Austrian wood-carver Ferdinand Stuflesser and shipped in pieces around the Cape of Good Hope. The church is on the National Register of Historic Places.

Activities

Pony Express and Skyline Eco-Adventures operate on land belonging to Haleakala Ranch, a working cattle ranch that sprawls across the slopes beneath Haleakala National Park. The businesses are adjacent to each other on Hwy 378, 2.5 miles up from Hwy 377.

PONY EXPRESS
Horseback Rides

(Map p150; ☎667-2200; www.ponyexpresstours. com; Haleakalā Crater Rd; trail rides $95-185; ⊙8am-5pm) A variety of horseback rides are offered, beginning with easy nose-to-tail walks across pastures and woods. But the real prize is the ride into the national park's Haleakalā crater that starts at the crater summit and leads down onto the floor of this lunar-like wonder.

SKYLINE ECO-ADVENTURES
Zipline

(Map p150; ☎878-8400; www.skylinehawaii.com; Haleakalā Crater Rd; zip $95; ⊙8:30am-4:30pm) Maui's first zipline scored a prime location on the slopes of Haleakalā. Even though the zips are relatively short compared with the new competition, there's plenty of adrenaline rush as you soar above the treetops over a series of five gulches. A half-mile hike and a suspension bridge are tossed in for good measure.

PROFLYGHT PARAGLIDING
Paragliding

(Map p150; ☎874-5433; www.paraglidehawaii. com; Waipoli Rd; paraglide $79; ⊙varies with weather) If the Skyline ziplines don't get you high enough, try surfing the sky. On this one, you strap into a tandem paraglider with a certified instructor and take a running leap off the cliffs beneath Polipoli Spring State Recreation Area for a 1000ft descent. The term 'bird's-eye view' will never be the same.

Tours

O'O FARM
Farm Tour

(Map p150; ☎667-4341; www.oofarm.com; Waipoli Rd; lunch tour $50; ⊙10:30am-1pm Wed & Thu) Whether you're a gardener or a gourmet, you're going to love a tour of famed Lahaina chef James McDonald's organic Upcountry farm. Where else can you help harvest your own meal, turn the goodies over to a gourmet chef and feast on the bounty? Bring your own wine.

 Festivals & Events

Holy Ghost Feast   Portuguese Festival (www.kulacatholiccommunity.org) Enjoy the aloha of Upcountry folks at this festival celebrating Kula's Portuguese heritage. Held at the Holy Ghost Church on the fourth Saturday and Sunday in May, it's a family event with games, craft booths, a farmers market and a free Hawaiian-Portuguese lunch on Sunday.

 Sleeping

KULA VIEW BED & BREAKFAST   B&B **$$**
(Map p150; ☎878-6736; www.kulaview.com; 600 Holopuni Rd; studio incl breakfast $115) With her *paniolo* roots, this host knows the Upcountry inside out. She provides everything you'll need for a good stay, including warm jackets for the Haleakalā sunrise. The studio unit sits atop her country home and offers sunset ocean views. Breakfast includes fruit from the backyard and homemade muffins.

KULA SANDALWOODS COTTAGES   Cottage **$$**
(Map p150; ☎878-3523; www.kulasandalwoods. com; 15427 Haleakalā Hwy; r $130; 🛜) A half-dozen freestanding cottages dot the hillside above Kula Sandalwoods Restaurant. Think rustic – you shouldn't expect too much in terms of creature comforts, but the sweeping view from the lanai is top rate and the price is a bargain for being on the doorstep of the national park.

 Eating

CAFÉ 808   Local Food **$**
(Map p150; ☎878-6874; 4566 Lower Kula Rd, Waiakoa; mains $6-10; ⏰6am-8:30pm) Its motto, 'The Big Kahuna of Island Grinds,' says it all. This unpretentious eatery, a quarter-mile south of the Holy Ghost Church, offers a wall-size chalkboard of all things local, from banana pancakes to gravy-laden plate lunches. Servings are hefty. Breakfast is served to 11am, making it a good choice for an inexpensive eat after sunrise on the mountain.

KULA SANDALWOODS RESTAURANT   Cafe **$**
(Map p150; ☎878-3523; www. kulasandalwoods.com; 15427 Haleakalā Hwy; mains $9-14; ⏰7am-3pm Mon-Fri, 7-11:30am Sat & Sun) The owner-chef earned her toque from the prestigious Culinary Institute of America. At breakfast the eggs Benedict is the favorite. Lunch features garden-fresh Kula salads and heaping chicken and

Ziplining, Skyline Eco-Adventures (p167)

beefsteak sandwiches on homemade onion rolls.

SUNRISE COUNTRY MARKET Takeout $
(Map p150; ☎878-1600; Haleakalā Crater Rd; simple eats $4-8; ⏰7am-3pm) Stop at this convenient shop, a quarter-mile up from the intersection of Hwys 378 and 377, to pick up post-sunrise java, breakfast burritos and sandwiches. Then take a stroll behind the shop to enjoy the protea garden.

LA PROVENCE Pastries, Restaurant $
(Map p150; ☎878-1313; www.laprovencekula.com; 3158 Lower Kula Rd, Waiakoa; pastries $3-4, mains $8-15; ⏰7am-2pm Wed-Sun) One of Kula's best-kept secrets, this little courtyard restaurant in the middle of nowhere is the domain of Maui's finest pastry chef. Even if you're not hungry now, do yourself a favor and swing by La Provence to pick up a ham-and-cheese croissant or some flaky chocolate-filled pastries for that picnic further down the road. If you're hungry now, well, grab a seat in the courtyard. The crepes are fabulous but just about anything for breakfast will do. At lunch the warm goat cheese and Kula greens salad is a locavore treat to savor. One caveat: the food would make a Parisian chef smile but the service is leisurely – if time is tight, get your goodies from the pastry counter.

La Provence is a little tricky to find: look for the low-key sign on the Kula Hwy as you approach Waiakoa. After the highway's 11-mile marker turn east onto Lower Kula Rd and continue 0.1 miles; the restaurant comes up on the left opposite a car repair shop.

Polipoli Spring State Recreation Area

Crisscrossed with lightly trodden hiking and mountain-biking trails, this misty cloud forest on the western slope of Haleakalā takes you deep off the beaten path. The shade from tall trees and the cool moist air add up to a refreshing walk in the woods. Layers of clouds drift in and out; when they lift, you'll get panoramic views across green rolling hills to the islands of Lana'i and Kaho'olawe. It's very

The Best…

Upcountry-Grown Treats

1 Lunch tour at O'o Farm (p167)

2 Mango chèvre at Surfing Goat Dairy (p164)

3 Elk burgers at 'Ulupalakua Ranch Store (p173)

4 Maui Splash wine at Tedeschi Vineyards (p173)

5 Lavender scones at Ali'i Kula Lavender (p166)

6 Maui-grown coffee at Grandma's Coffee House (p172)

Zen-like – apart from the symphony of bird calls, everything around you is still.

It's not always possible to get all the way to the park without a 4WD, but it's worth driving part of the way for the view. Access is via Waipoli Rd, off Hwy 377, just under 0.5 miles before its southern intersection with the Kula Hwy (Hwy 37). Waipoli Rd is a narrow, switchbacking, one-lane road through groves of eucalyptus and open rangeland.

The road has some soft shoulders, but the first 6 miles are paved. After the road enters the Kula Forest Reserve, it becomes dirt. When it's muddy, the next four grinding miles to the campground are not even worth trying without a 4WD vehicle.

 **Activities**

WAIAKOA LOOP TRAIL Hiking
The trailhead for the Waiakoa Loop Trail (Map p150) starts at the **hunter check station**, 5 miles up Waipoli Rd, which is all

paved to this point. Walk three-quarters of a mile down the grassy spur road on the left to a gate marking the trail. The hike, which starts out in pine trees, makes a 3-mile loop, passing through eucalyptus stands, pine forest, and scrub land scored with feral pig trails. This is a fairly gentle, easy hike, or good moderately strenuous fun on a mountain bike. You can also connect with the Upper Waiakoa Trail at a junction about a mile up the right side of the loop.

UPPER WAIAKOA TRAIL   Hiking
The Upper Waiakoa Trail (Map p150) is a strenuous 7-mile trail that begins off Waiakoa Loop at an elevation of 6000ft, climbs 1800ft, switchbacks and then drops back down 1400ft. It's stony terrain, but it's high and open, with good views. Bring plenty of water.

The trail ends on Waipoli Rd between the **hunter check station** and the campground. If you want to start at this end of the trail, keep an eye out for the

trail marker for Waohuli Trail, as the Upper Waiakoa Trail begins across the road.

BOUNDARY TRAIL   Hiking
This 4-mile trail (Map p150) begins about 200yd beyond the end of the paved road. Park to the right of the cattle grate that marks the boundary of the Kula Forest Reserve. It's a steep downhill walk that crosses gulches and drops deep into woods of eucalyptus, pine and cedar, as well as a bit of native forest. In the afternoon the fog generally rolls in and visibility fades.

SKYLINE TRAIL   Hiking
Also partially in this park is the rugged Skyline Trail (Map p150), which begins near the summit of Haleakalā National Park and drops more than 3000ft, passing cinder cones and craters, and offering clear-on views of West Maui and the islands of Hawai'i, Kaho'olawe and Lana'i before descending into the forest of Polipoli Spring State Recreation Area. For details on this hike, see p187.

Left: Enchanting Floral Gardens (p166); **Below:** Grandma's Coffee House (p172)

Sleeping

To stay in Polipoli is to rough it. Tent camping (Map p150) is free, but requires a permit from the state. Facilities are primitive, with toilets but no showers or drinking water. Fellow campers are likely to be pig hunters. Otherwise the place can be eerily deserted, and damp. Come prepared – this is cold country, with winter temperatures frequently dropping below freezing at night.

The park also has one housekeeping cabin (Map p150). Unlike other state park cabins, this one has gas lanterns and a wood-burning stove but no electricity or refrigerator. See p319 for details on camping and cabin permits, and reservations.

Keokea

Modest as it may be, Keokea is the last real town before Hana if you're swinging around the southern part of the island. The sum total of the town center consists of a coffee shop, an art gallery, a gas station and two small stores, the Ching Store and the Fong Store.

Sights & Activities

Drawn by rich soil, Hakka Chinese farmers migrated to this remote corner of Kula at the turn of the 20th century. Their influence is readily visible throughout the village. Keokea's landmark **St John's Episcopal Church**, c 1907 (Map p150) still bears its name in Chinese characters. For a time Sun Yat-sen, father of the Chinese nationalist movement, lived on the outskirts of Keokea. He's honored at **Sun Yat-sen Park** (Map p150), found along the Kula Hwy (Hwy 37), 1.7 miles beyond Grandma's Coffee House. The park has picnic tables and is a great place to soak up the broad vistas that stretch clear across to West Maui.

171

THOMPSON RANCH Horseback Rides
(Map p150; ☎878-1910; www.thompsonranch
maui.com; cnr Middle & Polipoli Rds; 2hr ride
$100; ⏰departs 9am) Join these folks for
horseback rides across ranch land in the
cool Upcountry bordering Polipoli Spring
State Recreation Area. At elevations of
4000ft to 6000ft, it's a memorable ride
for those who enjoy mountain scenery.

Sleeping

STAR LOOKOUT Cottage **$$**

TOP CHOICE (Map p150; ☎907-250-2364; www.star
lookout.com; 622 Thompson Rd; cottage $200;
📶) A fabulous ocean view, outdoor hot
tub and grounds so quiet you can hear the
flowers bloom. Half a mile up a one-lane
road from Keokea center, this two-bed-
room cottage with a loft could sleep four
people comfortably, six in a pinch. Nice,
but what makes it spectacular is the set-
ting, which overlooks 1000 acres of green
pastureland that's now owned by Oprah
Winfrey and set aside for preservation.

Eating

**GRANDMA'S COFFEE
HOUSE** Cafe **$**
(Map p150; www.grandmascoffee.com; 9232 Kula
Hwy; pastries $3-5, deli fare $6-10; ⏰7am-5pm)
If you thought Kona was the only place
with primo Hawaii-grown coffee, just
check out the brew at Grandma's. This
earthy cafe dishes up homemade pas-
tries, hearty sandwiches and deli salads.
Grandma's family has been growing cof-
fee in Keokea for generations. Take your
goodies out on the lanai and you can eat
right under the coffee trees.

'Ulupalakua Ranch

This sprawling 20,000-acre ranch (Map
p150) was established in the mid-19th
century by James Makee, a whaling
captain who jumped ship and befriended
Hawaiian royalty. King David Kalakaua,
the 'Merrie Monarch,' became a frequent
visitor who loved to indulge in late-night
rounds of poker and champagne. The
ranch is still worked by *paniolo*, Hawaiian
cowboys who have been herding cattle
here for generations. Some 6000 head
of cattle, as well as a small herd of Rocky
Mountain elk, dot the hillside pastures.

The ranch is active on environmental
fronts. It's staged to host Upcountry's
first wind farm and is restoring a
rare native dryland forest on the
upper slopes of ranch property.

Today most people come
to visit Tedeschi Vineyards,
which is on 'Ulupalakua
Ranch land 5.5 miles south
of Keokea. Hwy 37 winds
south through ranch
country, offering good
views of Kaho'olawe
and the little island of
Molokini.

After the vineyard, it's
another 25 dusty, bumpy
miles to Kipahulu along the
remote Pi'ilani Hwy.

Tedeschi Vineyards
PHOTOGRAPHER: TEDESCHI VINEYARDS

Island Insights

So tiny is the crescent volcanic crater of Molokini that King David Kalakaua once wagered it all in a game of poker at 'Ulupalakua Ranch. When he lost, he claimed that he had not bet Molokini, but rather *'omole kini* (a bottle of gin).

Sights

TEDESCHI VINEYARDS Winery
(Map p150; ☎878-6058; www.mauiwine. com; Kula Hwy; ☺10am-5pm, tours 10:30am & 1:30pm) Maui's sole winery offers free tours and tastings in the historic stone cottage where King David Kalakaua once slept. In the 1970s, while awaiting its first grape harvest, the winery decided to take advantage of Maui's prickly fruit. Today its biggest hit is the sweet Maui Splash, a light blend of pineapple and passion fruit. Other pineapple novelties worth a taste: the dry Maui Blanc and the sparkling Hula O'Maui. This is no Napa Valley, however, and the grape wines are less of a splash.

Don't miss the fascinating little exhibit at the side of the tasting room that features Kalakaua lore, ranch history and ecological goings-on. At the side of the cottage, tall shade trees and picnic tables invite a linger. Walking around the grounds you can easily see why a king would want to unwind here. Pick up a sandwich from the ranch store across the street and have a Kalakaua moment yourself. Note that groups of 10 or more wanting to join a tour must book in advance.

Opposite the winery, you can see the stack remains of the **Makee Sugar Mill** (Map p150), built in 1878.

Festivals & Events

TOP CHOICE **'ULUPALAKUA SUNDAY DRIVE EVENT** Festival
(www.ulupalakuaranch.com) Four times a year, 'Ulupalakua Ranch sponsors a fun bash on the lawn of Tedeschi Vineyards with live slack key guitar music, glassblowing demonstrations, cowboy-centric food and exhibits of ecological goings-on. The music's a highlight. Jeff Peterson, son of an 'Ulupalakua Ranch *paniolo* and a Grammy Award winner, performs at some of the events. The festival takes place on a Sunday in March, June, September and December.

Eating

'ULUPALAKUA RANCH STORE Deli $
(Map p150; www.ulupalakuaranch.com; burgers $9; ☺grill 11am-2:30pm, store 9:30am-5pm) Sidle up to the life-size wooden cowboys on the front porch and say howdy. Then pop inside and check out the cowboy hats and souvenir T-shirts. If it's lunchtime, mosey over to the grill and treat yourself to an organic ranch-raised elk burger. Can't beat that for local.

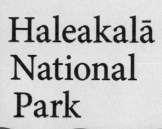

Haleakalā National Park

Omnipresent Haleakalā looms over you like a goddess, taking center stage while you sun on the beach in Kihei or wind down the road to Hana.

Whether you come for sunrise or come at the height of the day, by all means get yourself here. You haven't seen Maui – or at least, haven't looked into its soul – until you've made the trek to the top of this awe-inspiring mountain. Lookouts on the crater's rim provide breathtaking views of Haleakalā's moonscape surface. But there's a lot more to Haleakalā than just peering down from on high. With a pair of hiking boots you can walk down into the crater on crunchy trails that meander around cinder cones. Or saddle up and mosey down onto the crater floor on horseback. For the ultimate adventure, bring a sleeping bag and spend the night.

View of West Maui, Lana'i and Moloka'i from Haleakalā National Park

Haleakalā National Park Itineraries

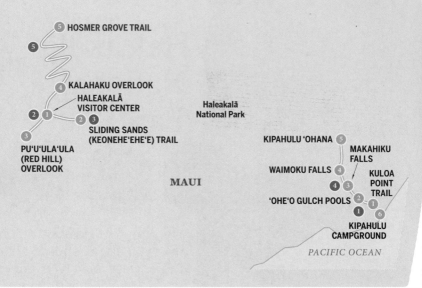

One Day

1 Haleakalā Visitor Center (p181) Haleakalā National Park has two distinct sections, and if you have just one day for the park, the summit is where you want to be. Whether you make a pre-dawn haul up the mountain to watch the sunrise, or mosey on up after breakfast, begin your explorations here. Not only is the visitor center the ideal perch for crater views, it's also a fine starting point for jaunts into the crater.

2 Sliding Sands (Keonehe'ehe'e) Trail (p184) Burn off the morning chill with an invigorating hike on the sun-warmed cinders of this unearthly trail.

3 Pu'u'ula'ula (Red Hill) Overlook (p182) Once you've completed your lunarlike crater hike, continue your road trip to Maui's highest point. By now you've probably

worked up an appetite, so break out your picnic goodies at the summit, admire the silversword garden and follow it with a ranger talk.

4 Kalahaku Overlook (p180) It's time to head back down the mountain. Make your way to this lookout, a crater rim hugger with an eye-poppingly wide-angle view of the cinder cones dotting the crater floor.

5 Hosmer Grove Trail (p188) You've seen the starkly barren side of Haleakalā. Now make acquaintance with its lush green face by taking a walk in this forest brimming with birdsong.

● ●

⊙ **THIS LEG: 17 MILES**

Two Days

1 **Kuloa Point Trail** (p195) If you have two days for Haleakalā National Park, give the second day over to the wet and wild Kipahulu section of the park. There's no food here, so bring a picnic basket and break it out at the trail's grassy knoll, savoring the ocean view.

2 **'Ohe'o Gulch pools** (p195) Now it's time to get your bathing suit wet. You won't believe your good fortune at the first sight of these enticing pools, which cascade one into the next as they step down the hillside. The only challenge is deciding which one to jump into first.

3 **Makahiku Falls** (p195) After you dry off, head upstream from the pools on the **Pipiwai Trail**. It's only 10 minutes to the 200ft Makahiku Falls.

4 **Waimoku Falls** (p195) Enjoy the majestic view at Makahiku but don't stop there; keep going, keep going. There's a magical **bamboo forest** to walk through and the prize at the end of the trail is the towering 400ft cascade of Waimoku Falls.

5 **Kipahulu 'Ohana** (p196) Dig deeper by joining Native Hawaiian taro farmers for an ethnobotanical tour to learn firsthand the deeply rooted traditions of this sacred Hawaiian place.

6 **Kipahulu campground** (p197) Now that you're in tune with the mana (spirit) of Kipahulu, pitch a tent at the site of an ancient Hawaiian settlement. Perched on the edge of a wild ocean, the surf will lullaby you to sleep. It's the perfect starlit finale to your Haleakalā experience.

➡ THIS LEG: 8 MILES

Haleakalā National Park Highlights

1 **Best Swimming Hole** 'Ohe'o Gulch pools (p195) Pick your favorite from two dozen terraced pools.

2 **Best View: Haleakalā Visitor Center** (p181) Watch the clouds spin at your feet around a kaleidoscope of cinder cones.

3 **Best Hike: Sliding Sands (Keonehe'ehe'e) Trail** (p184) There's nothing like a trek into the crater to experience this unique park up close.

4 **Best Waterfall: Makahiku Falls** (p195) A beaut at the end of a short trail.

5 **Best Wildlife: Nene at Park Headquarters Visitor Center** (p179) These guys love to visit the lawn here, making it a prime viewing spot.

'Ohe'o Gulch (p195)

Discover Haleakalā National Park

Summit Area

Haleakalā's astonishing volcanic landscape so resembles a lunar surface that astronauts practiced mock lunar walks here before landing on the moon.

Often referred to as the world's largest dormant volcano, the floor of Haleakalā is a colossal 7.5 miles wide, 2.5 miles long and 3000ft deep – large enough to swallow the island of Manhattan. In its prime, Haleakalā reached a height of 12,000ft before water erosion carved out two large river valleys that eventually eroded into each other to form Haleakalā crater. Technically, as geologists like to point out, it's not a true 'crater,' but to sightseers that's all nitpicking. Valley or crater, it's a phenomenal sight like no other in the US National Park system.

History

Haleakalā was not inhabited by the ancient Hawaiians, but they came up the mountain to worship and built heiau (temples) at some of the cinder cones. The primary goddess of Haleakalā, Lilinoe (also known as the mist goddess), was worshipped at a heiau near the summit. Unfortunately, any evidence of that sacred monument was destroyed during the construction of the Science City observatories.

Prince Jonah Kalanianaole, the man who could have been king if the Hawaiian monarchy hadn't been overthrown (but instead became Hawaii's first congressional delegate), proposed Haleakalā as a national park. When the bill was signed into law in 1916, Haleakalā became part of Hawai'i National Park, along with its Big Island siblings, Mauna Loa and Kilauea. In 1961 Haleakalā National Park became an independent entity and in 1969 it expanded its boundaries down into the Kipahulu Valley. In 1980 the park was designated an International Biosphere Reserve by Unesco.

◉ Sights

HOSMER GROVE   Grove
Hosmer Grove, off a side road just after the park's entrance booth, is primarily visited by campers and picnickers, but it's well

Pu'u'ula'ula (Red Hill) Overlook (p182)
PHOTOGRAPHER: GREG ELMS/LONELY PLANET IMAGES ©

worth a stop for its forested half-mile loop trail (p188) that begins at the edge of the campground. The whole area is sweetened with the scent of eucalyptus and alive with the red flashes and calls of native birds. Drive slowly on the road in, as this is one of the top places to spot nene (native Hawaiian goose).

WAIKAMOI PRESERVE
Nature Preserve

(☏ hike reservations 572-4459; 3hr tour free; ⏱ tour Mon & Thu 9am) This windswept native cloud forest supports one of the rarest ecosystems on earth. Managed by the Nature Conservancy, the 5230-acre preserve provides the last stronghold for 76 species of native plants and forest birds. You're apt to spot the *'i'iwi* and the *'apapane* (honeycreepers with bright red feathers) and the yellow-green *'amakihi* flying among the preserve's koa and ohia trees. You might also catch a glimpse of the yellow-green *'alauahio* (Maui creeper) or the *'akohekohe* (Maui parrotbill), both endangered species found nowhere else on earth.

The only way to see the preserve is to join a **guided hike**. The National Park Service offers three-hour, 3-mile guided hikes that enter the preserve from Hosmer Grove campground. It's best to make reservations, which you can do up to one week in advance. Expect wet conditions; bring rain gear. The hike is rated moderately strenuous. Occasionally on a Sunday afternoon, a longer five-hour, 5-mile hike is offered in the preserve.

PARK HEADQUARTERS VISITOR CENTER
Visitor Center

(☏ 572-4400; ⏱ 8am-4pm) Less than a mile beyond the entrance, this visitor center is the place to pick up brochures, buy nature books and get camping permits. It also has the skinny on ranger talks and other activities being offered in the park during your visit. And if you need to take care of earthly needs, this is a convenient stop for restrooms and one of only two places in the park where you'll find drinking fountains. If you're going hiking, you'll

The Best...
Haleakalā Hikes

1 Sliding Sands (Keonehe'ehe'e) Trail (p184)

2 Pipiwai Trail (p195)

3 Kuloa Point Trail (p195)

4 Halemau'u Trail (p185)

5 Hosmer Grove Trail (p188)

want to make sure your water bottles are filled before leaving here.

Keep an eye out for nene wandering around the grounds, as they're frequent visitors at this spot. Also note that these endangered birds are much too friendly for their own good; do not feed them, and be careful when driving in and out of the parking lot – most nene deaths in the park are the result of being hit by cars.

LELEIWI OVERLOOK
Overlook

A stop at Leleiwi Overlook (8840ft), midway between the Park Headquarters Visitor Center and the summit, offers your first look into the crater, and gives you a unique angle on the ever-changing clouds floating in and out. You can literally watch the weather form at your feet. From the parking lot, it's a five-minute walk across a gravel trail to the overlook. En route you'll get a fine view of the West Maui Mountains and the isthmus connecting the two sides of Maui. The trail has plaques identifying native plants, including the silver-leafed *hinahina,* found only at Haleakalā, and the *kukae-nene,* a member of the coffee family.

In the afternoon, if weather conditions are right, you might see the **Brocken specter**, an optical phenomenon that occurs at high elevations. Essentially, by standing between the sun and the

179

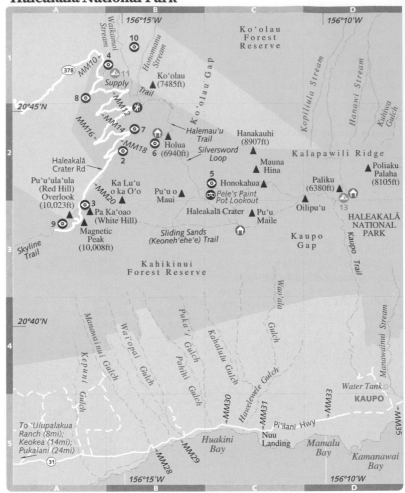

clouds, your image is magnified and projected onto the clouds. The light reflects off tiny droplets of water in the clouds, creating a circular rainbow around your shadow.

KALAHAKU OVERLOOK   Overlook
Whatever you do, don't miss this one. Kalahaku Overlook (9324ft), 0.8 miles beyond Leleiwi Overlook, offers a bird's-eye view of the crater floor and the ant-size hikers on the trails snaking around the cinder cones below. At the observation deck, plaques provide information on

each of the volcanic formations that punctuate the crater floor.

From the deck you'll also get a perfect angle for viewing both the Ko'olau Gap and the Kaupo Gap on Haleakalā's crater rim and on a clear day you'll be able to see the Big Island's Mauna Loa and Mauna Kea, Hawaii's highest mountaintops. It all adds up to one heck of a view.

Between May and October the *'ua'u* (Hawaiian dark-rumped petrel) nests in burrows in the cliff face at the left side of

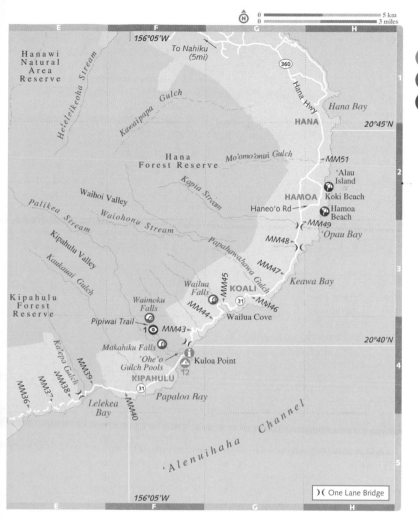

the observation deck. Even if you don't spot the birds, you can often hear the parents and chicks making their unique clucking sounds. Of the fewer than 2000 'ua'u remaining today, most nest right here at Haleakalā, where they lay just one egg a year. These seabirds were thought to be extinct until sighted in the crater during the 1970s.

A short **trail** below the parking lot leads to a field of native silversword, ranging from seedlings to mature plants.

HALEAKALĀ VISITOR CENTER
Visitor Center

(🕐 sunrise-3pm) Perched on the rim of the crater, the visitor center at a 9745ft elevation is the park's main viewing spot. And what a magical sight awaits. The ever-changing interplay of sun, shadow and clouds reflecting on the crater floor creates a mesmerizing dance of light and color.

The center has displays on Haleakalā's volcanic origins and details on what you're seeing on the crater floor 3000ft

Haleakalā National Park

below. Nature talks are given, books on Hawaiian culture and the environment are for sale, and there are drinking fountains and restrooms here.

By dawn the parking lot fills with people coming to see the sunrise show (see boxed text, p189), and it pretty much stays packed all day. Leave the crowds behind by taking the 10-minute hike up **Pa Ka'oao** (White Hill), which begins at the east side of the visitor center and provides stunning crater views.

PU'U'ULA'ULA (RED HILL) OVERLOOK
Lookout

Congratulations! The 37-mile drive from sea level to the 10,023ft summit of Haleakalā you've just completed is the highest elevation gain in the shortest distance anywhere in the world. As a matter of fact, it's so high that you need to be cautious if you've come up in the late afternoon in winter, as a sudden rainstorm at this elevation can result in ice-coated roads.

Sitting atop Pu'u'ula'ula, Maui's highest point, the **summit building** provides a top-of-the-world panorama from its wraparound windows. On a clear day you can see the Big Island, Lana'i, Moloka'i and even O'ahu. When the light's right, the colors of the crater from the summit are nothing short of spectacular, with an array of grays, greens, reds and browns. Brief natural and cultural history talks are given at the summit several times a day.

A **silversword garden** has been planted at the overlook, making this the best place to see these luminous, endangered silver-leafed plants in various stages of growth.

MAGNETIC PEAK
Hill

The iron-rich cinders in this flat-top hill, which lies immediately southeast of the summit building, in the direction of the Big Island, pack enough magnetism to play havoc with your compass. Modest looking as it is, it's also – at 10,008ft – the second-highest point on the island of Maui.

SCIENCE CITY
Observatories

On the Big Island's Mauna Kea, scientists study the night sky. Here at Haleakalā, appropriately enough, they study the sun. Science City, just beyond the summit, is off-limits to visitors. It's under the jurisdiction of the University of Hawai'i, which owns some of the domes and leases other land for a variety of private and government research projects.

Department of Defense–related projects here include laser technology associated with the 'Star Wars' project, satellite tracking and identification, and a deep-space surveillance system. The Air Force's Maui Space Surveillance System (MSSS), an electro-optical state-of-the-art facility used for satellite tracking, is the largest telescope anywhere in use by the Department of Defense. The system is capable of identifying a basketball-size object in space 22,000 miles away.

The Faulkes Telescope, a joint University of Hawai'i and UK operation, is dedicated to raising students' interest in astronomy, with a fully robotic telescope that can be controlled in real time via the internet from classrooms in both Britain and Hawaii.

 **Activities**

For information on other activities that occur on the slopes beneath Haleakalā National Park, including ziplines and paragliding, see the North Shore & Upcountry chapter.

Ranger Programs

Be sure to stop at the Park Headquarters Visitor Center to see what's happening. All park programs offered by the National Park Service are free. **Ranger talks** on Haleakalā's unique natural history and Hawaiian culture are given at the Haleakalā Visitor Center and the Pu'u'ula'ula (Red Hill) Overlook; the schedule varies, but the talks typically take place between 7am and 1pm and there's usually half a dozen to choose from each day.

Ranger-led **walks** through Waikamoi Preserve are held throughout the year.

Hiking

Strap on a pair of hiking boots and you can climb into the very heart of this other-worldly place. There's something for everyone, from short nature walks ideal for families to hardy treks that take a couple of days. Those who hike the crater will discover a completely different angle on Haleakalā's lunar landscape. Instead of peering down from the rim, you'll be craning your neck skyward at the walls and towering cinder cones. It's a world away from any place else. The crater is remarkably still. Cinders crunching underfoot are often the only sound, except for the occasional bark of a *pueo* (Hawaiian owl) or honking of a friendly nene. No matter what trail you take, give yourself plenty of time just to absorb the wonder of it all.

To protect Haleakalā's fragile environment, keep to established trails and don't be tempted off them, even for well-trodden shortcuts through switchbacks.

Be prepared. Hikers without proper clothing risk hypothermia. Remember the

Silversword Comeback

Goats ate them by the thousands. Souvenir collectors pulled them up by their roots. They were even used to decorate parade floats, for cryin' out loud. It's a miracle any of Haleakalā's famed silverswords are left at all.

It took a concerted effort to bring them back from the brink of extinction, but Haleakalā visitors can once again see this luminous relative of the sunflower in numerous places around the park.

The silversword (*'ahinahina*) takes its name from its elegant silver spiked leaves, which glow with dew collected from the clouds. The plant lives for up to 50 years before blooming for its first and last time. In its final year it shoots up a flowering stalk that can reach as high as 9ft. During summer the stalk flowers gloriously with hundreds of maroon and yellow blossoms. When the flowers go to seed in late fall, the plant makes its last gasp and dies.

Today the silversword survives solely because its fragile natural environment has been protected. After years of effort, the National Park Service has finished fencing the entire park with a 32-mile-long fence to keep out feral goats and pigs. You can do your part by not walking on cinders close to the plant, which damages the silversword's shallow roots that radiate out several feet just inches below the surface.

climate changes radically as you cross the crater floor. In the 4 miles between Kapalaoa and Paliku cabins, rainfall varies from an annual average of 12in to 300in! Take warm clothing in layers, sunscreen, rain gear, a first-aid kit and lots of water.

Here are our recommendations for day hikes, depending on the time you have:

○ **Ten hours** If you're planning a full-day outing, and you're in good physical shape, the 11.2-mile hike that starts down Sliding Sands Trail and returns via Halemau'u Trail is the prize. It crosses the crater floor, taking in both a cinder desert and a cloud forest, showcasing the park's amazing diversity. Get an early start. As for getting back to your starting point, hitchhiking is allowed in the park and there's a designated place to hitch on Haleakalā Crater Rd opposite the Halemau'u trailhead.

○ **Three hours** For a half-day experience that offers a hearty serving of crater sights, follow Sliding Sands Trail down to the Ka Lu'u o ka O'o cinder cone and back. The easy bit: it takes one hour to get down.

However, on the way back, you've got yourself a 1500ft elevation rise, making the return a strenuous two-hour climb.

○ **One hour** Take to the forest on the Hosmer Grove Trail and see the green side of Haleakalā National Park.

TOP CHOICE SLIDING SANDS (KEONEHE'EHE'E) TRAIL

Hiking Sliding Sands (Keonehe'ehe'e) Trail starts at the south side of the Haleakalā Visitor Center at 9740ft and winds down to the crater floor. If you take this hike after catching the sunrise, you'll walk directly into a gentle warmish wind and the rays of the sunshine.

The first thing you'll notice is how quiet everything is. The only sound is the crunching of volcanic cinders beneath your feet. The path descends gently into an unearthly world of stark lava sights and ever-changing clouds.

Even if you're just coming to the summit for a peek at the incredible view, consider taking a short hike down Sliding

Sands Trail. Just walking down 20 to 30 minutes will reward you with an into-the-crater experience and fab photo opportunities; but keep in mind that the climb out takes nearly twice as long as the walk down.

The full trail leads 9.2 miles to the Paliku cabin and campground, passing the Kapalaoa cabin at 5.6 miles after roughly four hours.

The first 6 miles of the trail follow the south wall. There are great views on the way down, but virtually no vegetation. About 2 miles down, a steep spur trail leads past silversword plants to **Ka Lu'u o ka O'o** cinder cone, about 0.5 miles north. Four miles down, after an elevation drop of 2500ft, Sliding Sands Trail intersects with a spur trail that leads north into the cinder desert; that spur connects with the Halemau'u Trail after 1.5 miles.

Continuing on Sliding Sands, as you head across the crater floor for 2 miles to Kapalaoa, verdant ridges rise on your right, giving way to ropy *pahoehoe*

(smooth-flowing lava). From Kapalaoa cabin to Paliku, the descent is gentle and the vegetation gradually increases. Paliku (6380ft) is beneath a sheer cliff at the eastern end of the crater. In contrast to the crater's barren western end, this area receives heavy rainfall, with ohia forests climbing the slopes.

HALEMAU'U TRAIL
Hiking

Hiking the Halemau'u Trail down to the Holua campground and back – 7.4 miles return – can make a memorable day hike. Just be sure to start early before the afternoon clouds roll in and visibility vanishes. The first mile of this trail is fairly level and offers a fine view of the crater with Ko'olau Gap to the east. It then descends 1400ft along 2 miles of switchbacks to the crater floor and on to the Holua campground.

At 6940ft, **Holua** is one of the lowest areas along this hike, and you'll see impressive views of the crater walls rising a few thousand feet to the west. A few large **lava tubes** here are worth exploring: one is up a short, steep cliff behind the cabin and the other is a 15-minute detour further along the trail. According to local legend, the latter tube was a spiritual place where mothers brought the *piko* (umbilical cords) of their newborns to gather mana (spiritual essence) for the child.

If you have the energy, push on just another mile to reach colorful cinder cones, being sure to make a short detour onto the **Silversword Loop**, where you'll see these unique plants in various stages of growth. If you're here during the summer, you should be able to see the plants in flower, their tall stalks ablaze with hundreds of maroon and yellow blossoms. But be careful – half of all silverswords today are trampled to death as seedlings, mostly by careless hikers who wander off trails and inadvertently crush the plants' shallow, laterally growing roots. The trail continues another 6.3 miles to the Paliku cabin.

The trailhead to Halemau'u is 3.5 miles above the Park Headquarters Visitor Center and about 6 miles below the Haleakalā Visitor Center. There's a fair chance you'll see nene in the parking lot.

If you're camping at Hosmer Grove, you can take a shortcut over to the crater rim via the little-known, and less exciting, **Supply Trail** that follows the old mule path used to get supplies down to the cabins on the crater floor. The trail starts on the campground turnoff road and after 1.5 miles opens up to broad vistas of the volcano's rainforest slopes and out to sea. After one more mile, the Supply Trail intersects with the Halemau'u Trail down into the crater.

CINDER DESERT   Hiking

Almost all hiking trails lead to the belly of the beast. There's no way to see this amazing area without backtracking. Three spur trails connect Sliding Sands Trail, from near Kapalaoa cabin, with the Halemau'u Trail between Paliku and Holua cabins. As the trails are not very long, if you're camping you may have time to do them all.

The spur trail furthest west takes in many of the crater's most kaleidoscopic cones, and the viewing angle changes with every step. If you prefer stark, black and barren, both of the other spur trails take you through *'a'a* (rough, jagged lava) and *pahoehoe* lava fields, with the one furthest east splattered with rust-red cinders.

All three trails end up on the north side of the cinder desert near **Kawilinau**, also known as the Bottomless Pit. Legend says the pit leads down to the sea, though the National Park Service says it's just 65ft deep. Truth be told, there's not much to see, as you can't really get a good look down

Mamane blossom, Skyline Trail

the narrow shaft. The real prize is the nearby short loop trail, where you can sit for a while in the saddle of **Pele's Paint Pot Lookout**, the crater's most brilliant vantage point.

KAUPO TRAIL
Hiking

The most extreme of Haleakalā's hikes is the Kaupo Trail, which starts at the Paliku campground and leads down to Kaupo on the southern coast. Be prepared for ankle-twisting conditions, blistered feet, intense tropical sun and torrential showers. Your knees will take a pounding as you descend more than 6100ft over 8.6 miles.

The first 3.7 miles of the trail drop 2500ft in elevation before reaching the park boundary. It's a steep rocky trail through rough lava and brushland, with short switchbacks alternating with level stretches. From here you'll be rewarded with spectacular ocean views.

The last 4.9 miles pass through Kaupo Ranch property on a rough jeep trail as it descends to the bottom of Kaupo Gap, exiting into a forest where feral pigs snuffle about. Here trail markings become vague, but once you reach the dirt road, it's another 1.5 miles to the end at the east side of the Kaupo Store.

The 'village' of Kaupo is a long way from anywhere, with light traffic. Still, what traffic there is – sightseers braving the circle-island road and locals in pickup trucks – moves slowly enough along Kaupo's rough road to start conversation, so you'll probably manage a lift. If you have to walk the final stretch, it's 8 miles to the 'Ohe'o Gulch campground.

Because this is such a strenuous and remote trail, it's not advisable to hike it alone. No camping is allowed on Kaupo Ranch property, so most hikers spend the night at the Paliku campground and then get an early start.

SKYLINE TRAIL
Hiking

This otherworldly trail, which rides the precipitous crater-dotted spine of Haleakalā, begins just beyond Haleakalā's summit at a lofty elevation of 9750ft and leads down to the campground at Polipoli

Spring State Recreation Area (p169) at 6200ft. It covers a distance of 8.5 miles and takes about four hours to walk. Get an early start to enjoy the views before clouds take over.

To get to the trailhead, go past Pu'u'ula'ula (Red Hill) Overlook and take the road to the left just before Science City. The road, which passes over a cattle grate, is signposted not for public use, but continue and you'll soon find a Na Ala Hele sign marking the trailhead.

The Skyline Trail starts in barren open terrain of volcanic cinder, a moon walk that passes more than a dozen cinder cones and craters. The first mile is rough lava rock. After three crunchy miles, it reaches the tree line (8500ft) and enters native *mamane* forest. In winter *mamane* is heavy with flowers that look like yellow sweet-pea blossoms. There's solitude on this walk. If the clouds treat you kindly, you'll have broad views all the way between the barren summit and the dense cloud forest. Eventually the trail meets the Polipoli access road, where you can either walk to the paved road in about 4 miles, or continue via the **Haleakalā Ridge Trail** and **Polipoli Trail**

to the campground. If you prefer treads to hiking boots, the Skyline Trail is also an exhilarating adventure on a mountain bike.

TOP CHOICE **HOSMER GROVE TRAIL**   Hiking
Anyone who is looking for a little greenery after hiking the crater will love this shaded woodland walk, and birders wing it here as well.

The half-mile loop trail starts at Hosmer Grove campground, three-quarters of a mile south of the Park Headquarters Visitor Center, in a forest of lofty trees. The exotics in Hosmer Grove were introduced in 1910 in an effort to develop a lumber industry in Hawaii. Species include fragrant incense cedar, Norway spruce, Douglas fir, eucalyptus and various pines. Although the trees adapted well enough to grow, they didn't grow fast enough at these elevations to make tree harvesting practical. Thanks to this failure, today there's a park here instead.

After the forest, the trail moves into native shrubland, with 'akala (Hawaiian raspberry), *mamane, pilo, kilau* ferns and sandalwood. The 'ohelo, a berry sacred

Horseback riders, Haleakalā crater

The Sunrise Experience

Since ancient times people have been making the pilgrimage up to Haleakalā to watch the sunrise. It's an experience that borders on the mystical. Mark Twain called it the 'sublimest spectacle' he'd ever seen.

Plan to arrive at the summit an hour before the sunrise. Around that point the night sky begins to lighten and turn purple-blue, and the stars fade away. Ethereal silhouettes of the mountain ridges appear. The undersides of the clouds lighten first, accenting the night sky with pale silvery slivers and streaks of pink.

About 20 minutes before sunrise, the light intensifies on the horizon in bright oranges and reds. Turn around for a look at Science City, whose domes turn a blazing pink. For the grand finale, when the the sun appears, all of Haleakalā takes on a fiery glow. It feels like you're watching the earth awaken.

Come prepared – it's going to be c-o-l-d! However many layers of clothes you can muster, it won't be too many.

The best photo opportunities occur before the sun rises. Every morning is different, but once the sun is up, the silvery lines and the subtleties disappear.

One caveat: a rained-out sunrise is an anticlimactic event after tearing yourself out of bed in the middle of the night to drive up a pitch-dark mountain. So check the weather report (☎866-944-5025) the night before to calculate your odds of having clear skies.

If you just can't get up that early, sunsets at Haleakalā have inspired poets as well.

to the volcano goddess Pele, and the *pukiawe,* which has red and white berries and evergreen leaves, are favored by nene.

Listen for the calls of the native *'i'iwi* and *'apapane;* both are fairly common here. The *'i'iwi* has a very loud squeaking call, orange legs and a curved salmon-colored bill. The *'apapane,* a fast-moving bird with a black bill, black legs and a white undertail, feeds on the nectar of bright red ohia flowers, and its wings make a distinctive whirring sound.

Horseback Riding

PONY EXPRESS   Horeseback Riding
(☎667-2200; www.ponyexpresstours.com; Haleakalā Crater Rd; trail ride $185; ⏰8am-5pm) This outfit can get you in the stirrups for the ride of your life on a half-day horse-back journey deep into Haleakalā crater. It starts at the crater summit and follows Sliding Sands Trail, offering jaw-dropping scenery the entire way. If you're not hiking down to the crater this is the only other way to get eye to eye with this geological marvel. Book early, as there's a maximum of nine riders taken. The Pony Express office is on Hwy 378, 2.5 miles up from Hwy 377.

Cycling

One-way downhill group cycle tours are no longer allowed to cycle within the park (see the boxed text, p194), though they do offer tours that begin pedaling just below park boundaries. A better bet is to forgo cycling with a pack and instead rent a bicycle and head here on your own. Individual cyclists are allowed to pedal their way up and down the mountain without restriction. Up is a real quad buster. If you prefer to do it just downhill, most bicycle rental companies listed in this book can rent you a bicycle rack for your car.

GREG ELMS/LONELY PLANET IMAGES ©

Mountain Biking

For experienced mountain bikers Haleakalā's **Skyline Trail** is the island's ultimate wild ride, plunging some 3000ft in the first 6 miles with a breathtaking 10% grade. The trail starts out looking like the moon and ends up in a cloud forest of redwood and cypress trees that resembles California's northern coast. The route follows a rough 4WD road that's used to maintain Polipoli Spring State Recreation Area. For cripes sake, equip yourself with full pads, use a proper downhill bike and watch that you don't run any hikers down.

Crater Cycles Hawaii Mountain Biking (🕿893-2020; www.cratercycleshawaii.com; 96 Amala Pl, Kahului; downhill bikes per day $85; ⏲9am-5pm Mon-Thu, 10am-5pm Sat) Rents quality full-suspension downhill bikes, complete with helmet, pads and a roof rack for transporting the bike.

Stargazing

On clear nights, stargazing is phenomenal on the mountain. You can see celestial objects up to the 7th magnitude, free of light interference, making Haleakalā one of the best places on the planet for a sky view.

STARGAZING PROGRAMS Stargazing (🕿for schedule 572-4400; program free; ⏲7pm Fri & Sat May-Sep) Hour-long evening programs are offered between May and September at Hosmer Grove. These talks, which are free and ranger-led, are occasionally held in the winter as well; call for the schedule. If you've got a pair of binoculars, bring them along.

If your visit doesn't coincide with a program, pick up a free **star map** of the night sky for the current month at the Park Headquarters Visitor Center and have your own cosmic experience.

 Sleeping

Maui's best campgrounds are right in Haleakalā National Park. To spend the night at Haleakalā is to commune with nature. All of the camping options are primitive; none has electricity or showers. Backcountry campgrounds have pit toilets and limited nonpotable water supplies that are shared with the crater cabins. Water needs to be filtered or chemically treated before drinking; conserve it, as water tanks occasionally run dry. Fires are allowed only in grills and in times of drought are prohibited entirely. You must pack in all your food and supplies and pack out all your trash. Also be aware that during periods of drought, you'll be required to carry in your own water.

Keep in mind that sleeping at an elevation of 7000ft is not like camping on the beach. You need to be well equipped – without a waterproof tent and a winter-rated sleeping bag, forget it.

HOSMER GROVE CAMPGROUND

Camping

(camping free) Wake up to the sound of birdsong at Hosmer Grove, the only drive-up campground in the mountainous section of Haleakalā National Park. Surrounded by lofty trees and adjacent to one of Maui's best birding trails, this campground at an elevation of 6800ft tends to be a bit cloudy, but a covered picnic pavilion offers shelter if it starts to rain. Campers will also find grills, toilets and running water.

Camping is free on a first-come, first-served basis. No permit is required, though there's a three-day camping limit per month. It's busier in summer than in winter and is often full on holiday weekends. The campground is just after the park entrance booth. And here's a bonus: you're close to the summit, so it's a cinch getting up for the sunrise.

BACKCOUNTRY CAMPING

Camping

(permits at Park Headquarters Visitor Cente; camping free) For hikers, two backcountry campgrounds lie in the belly of Haleakalā Crater. The easiest to reach is at **Holua**, 3.7 miles down the Halemau'u Trail. The other is at **Paliku**, below a rainforest ridge at the end of Halemau'u Trail. Weather can be unpredictable at both. Holua at 6940ft is typically dry after sunrise, until clouds roll back in the late afternoon. Paliku at 6380ft is in a grassy meadow, with skies overhead alternating between stormy and sunny. Wasps are present at both campsites, so take precautions if you're allergic to stings.

Unlike at Hosmer Grove, permits are required for backcountry camping in the crater. They are free and issued at the Park Headquarters Visitor Center on a first-come, first-served basis between 8am and 3pm on the day of the hike. Camping is limited to three nights in the crater each month, with no more than two consecutive nights at either campground. Because only 25 campers are allowed at each site, permits can go quickly when larger parties show up, a situation more likely to occur in summer.

Ka Lu'u o ka O'o cinder cone (p185)

HALEAKALĀ WILDERNESS CABINS
Cabins

(📞 572-4400; https://fhnp.org/wcr; cabin 1-12 people per night $75) Three rustic cabins, which date from the 1930s, lie along trails on the crater floor at Holua, Kapalaoa and Paliku. Each has a wood-burning stove, two propane burners, cooking utensils, 12 bunks with sleeping pads (but no bedding), pit toilets and a limited supply of water and firewood.

Hiking distances to the cabins from the crater rim range from 4 miles to 9 miles. The driest conditions are at Kapalaoa in the middle of the cinder desert off the Sliding Sands Trail. Those craving lush rainforest will find Paliku serene. Holua has unparalleled sunrise views. There's a three-day limit per month, with no more than two consecutive nights in any cabin. Each cabin is rented to only one group at a time.

The cabins can be reserved up to 90 days in advance. You'll need to use a credit card to make reservations; you can do this online or by calling between 1pm and 3pm Monday to Friday.

Even those without reservations have a shot, as cancellations sometimes occur at the last minute. You can check for vacancies in person at the Park Headquarters Visitor Center between 8am and 3pm. As an added boon, if you get a vacancy within three weeks of your camping date, the cabin fee drops to $60 a night.

ℹ️ Information

- The nonprofit **Friends of Haleakalā National Park** (www.fhnp.org) helps preserve the park's habitats and wildlife. Its Adopt-a-Nene program, which costs $30, funds the protection of nene from predators such as mongoose and feral cats. The organization also coordinates volunteer projects in the park so if you'd like to donate a day's work pulling up invasive plants, check out its website.

- Pack plenty of snacks, especially if you're going up for the sunrise. No food or bottled water is sold anywhere in the park. You don't want a growling stomach to send you back down the mountain before you've had a chance to explore the sights.

- Check out the current weather conditions at the summit by logging on to the crater webcam at **Haleakalā Crater Live Camera** (http://koa.ifa.hawaii.edu/crater).

- Bring extra layers of clothing. The temperature can drop dramatically at any point in the day.

Entrance Fees & Passes

Haleakalā National Park (📞 572-4400; www.nps.gov/hale; 3-day entry pass per car $10, per person on foot, bicycle or motorcycle $5) never closes, and the pay booth at the park entrance opens before dawn to welcome the sunrise crowd. If you're planning several trips, or are going on to the Big Island, consider buying an annual pass ($25), which covers all of Hawaii's national parks.

Nene (native goose)

Nene Watch

The native nene, Hawaii's state bird, is a long-lost cousin of the Canada goose. By the 1950s, hunting, habitat loss and predators had reduced its population to just 30. Thanks to captive breeding and release programs, it has been brought back from the verge of extinction and the Haleakalā National Park's nene population is now holding steady at about 250.

Nene nest in high cliffs from 6000ft to 8000ft, surrounded by rugged lava flows with sparse vegetation. Their feet have gradually adapted by losing most of their webbing. The birds are extremely friendly and love to hang out where people do, anywhere from cabins on the crater floor to the Park Headquarters Visitor Center.

Their curiosity and fearlessness have contributed to their undoing. Nene don't fare well in an asphalt habitat and many have been run over by cars. Others have been tamed by too much human contact, so no matter how much they beg for your peanut butter sandwich, do not feed the nene. It only interferes with their successful return to the wild.

Maps

National Geographic's *Haleakala National Park Trails Illustrated Map* makes the perfect companion for hikers, showing elevations and other useful features on the routes. It's waterproof and can be purchased at Haleakalā Visitor Center for $12.

Dangers & Annoyances

The weather at Haleakalā can change suddenly from dry, hot conditions to cold, windswept rain. Although the general rule is sunny in the morning and cloudy in the afternoon, fog and clouds can blow in at any time, and the windchill can quickly drop below freezing. Dress in layers and bring extra clothing; don't even think of coming up without a jacket.

At 10,000ft the air is relatively thin, so expect to tire more quickly, particularly if you're hiking. The higher elevation also means that sunburn is more likely.

Visitors rarely experience altitude sickness at Haleakalā summit. An exception is those who have been scuba diving in the past 24 hours, so plan your Haleakalā trip accordingly. Children, pregnant women and those in generally poor health are also susceptible. If you experience difficulty breathing, sudden headaches and dizziness, or more serious symptoms such as confusion and lack of motor coordination, descend immediately. Sometimes driving down the crater road just a few hundred feet will alleviate the problem. Panicking or hyperventilating only makes things worse.

ℹ Getting There & Around

Getting to Haleakalā is half the fun. Snaking up the mountain it's sometimes hard to tell if you're in an airplane or a car – all of Maui opens up below you, with sugarcane and pineapple fields creating a patchwork of green on the valley floor. The highway ribbons back and forth, and in some places as many as four or five switchbacks are in view all at once.

Haleakala Crater Rd (Hwy 378) twists and turns for 11 miles from Hwy 377 near Kula up to the park entrance, then another 10 miles to Haleakalā summit. It's a good paved road all the way, but it's steep and winding. You don't want to rush it, especially when it's dark or foggy. Watch out for cattle wandering freely across the road.

The drive to the summit takes about 1½ hours from Pa'ia or Kahului, two hours from Kihei and a bit longer from Lahaina. If you need gas, fill up the night before, as there are no services on Haleakalā Crater Rd.

On your way back downhill, be sure to put your car in low gear to avoid burning out your brakes.

Going Downhill

For years downhill bike tours were heavily promoted. A van ride to Haleakalā summit for the sunrise was followed by a bicycle cruise 38 miles down the 10,000ft mountain, snaking along winding roads clear to the coast. What a rush. And no need to be in shape, since there's no pedaling involved.

But it became *too* popular. Some mornings as many as 1000 cyclists huddled at the crater overlooks jostling for space to watch the sun rise. Then, group by group, they'd mount their bikes and take off.

Residents who needed to use Upcountry roads for more mundane reasons, like getting to work, were forced to slow to a crawl, waiting for a gaggle of cyclists and their support van to pull over to let them pass. The narrow roads have few shoulders, so the wait was often a long one.

Then there were the accidents. They often involved people who hadn't been on a bicycle in years. Sometimes the weather was bad, with fog cutting visibility to near zero. Ambulance calls for injured cyclists became weekly occurrences. After two cyclist fatalities in 2007, Haleakalā National Park suspended all bicycle tour operations. A compromise now lets the van tours come up for the sunrise then drive back down to the park's boundary, where the trailers are unpacked and riders begin their cycle to the coast.

However, another fatality in 2010 has spurred the county to consider restrictions of its own. For downhill bike tours, the road ahead remains a bumpy one.

Kipahulu Area ('Ohe'o Gulch)

There's more to Haleakalā National Park than the cindery summit. The park extends down the southeast face of the volcano all the way to the sea. The crowning glory of the Kipahulu section of the park is 'Ohe'o Gulch, with its magnificent waterfalls and wide pools, each one tumbling into the next one below. When the sun shines, these cool glistening pools make the most inviting swimming holes on Maui.

Back in the 1970s 'Ohe'o Gulch was dubbed the 'Seven Sacred Pools' as part of a tourism promotion and the term still floats around freely, much to the chagrin of park officials. It's a complete misnomer since there are 24 pools in all, extending from the ocean to Waimoku Falls, and they were never sacred – but they certainly are divine.

The waters once supported a sizable Hawaiian settlement of farmers who cultivated sweet potatoes and taro in terraced gardens beside the stream. Archaeologists have identified the stone remains of more than 700 ancient structures at 'Ohe'o.

One of the expressed intentions of Haleakalā National Park is to manage its Kipahulu area 'to perpetuate traditional Hawaiian farming and *ho'onanea*' – a Hawaiian word meaning to pass the time in ease, peace and pleasure. So kick back and have some fun!

Because there's no access between the Kipahulu section of the park and the main Haleakalā summit area, you'll be visiting the two sections of the park on different days. So hold on to your ticket – it's good for both sections of the park.

◎ Sights & Activities

Rangers at the **Kipahulu Visitor Center** offer cultural history talks and demonstrations on the lives and activities of the early Hawaiians who lived in the area that's now within park boundaries. Short guided hikes can also make it onto the agenda, but keep in mind the schedule varies with the day and the availability of rangers.

LOWER POOLS   Freshwater Pools

Even if you're tight on time, you've got to take this 20-minute stroll! The **Kuloa Point Trail**, a half-mile loop, runs from the visitor center down to the lower pools and back. At the junction with Pipiwai Trail go right. A few minutes down, you'll come to a broad grassy knoll with a gorgeous view of the Hana coast. On a clear day you can see the Big Island, 30 miles away across 'Alenuihaha Channel. This is a fine place to stop and unpack your lunch.

The large freshwater pools along the trail are terraced one atop the other and connected by gentle cascades. They're usually calm and great for swimming, and their cool waters refreshingly brisk. The second big pool below the bridge is a favorite swimming hole.

However, be aware: conditions can change in a heartbeat. Heavy rains falling far away on the upper slopes can bring a sudden torrent through the pools at any time. If the water starts to rise, get out immediately. Several people have been swept out to sea from these pools by flash floods. Slippery rocks and unseen submerged ledges are other potential hazards, so check carefully before jumping in. Heed all park warning signs, including temporary ones posted based on weather conditions.

TOP CHOICE **WATERFALL TRAILS**   Walking Trail

The **Pipiwai Trail** runs up the 'Ohe'o streambed, rewarding hikers with picture-perfect views of waterfalls. The trail starts on the *mauka* (inland) side of the visitor center and leads up to Makahiku Falls (0.5 miles) and Waimoku Falls (2 miles). Or take a little shortcut by picking up the trail from the pedestrian crossing at the highway. To see both falls, allow about two hours return. The upper section is muddy, but boardwalks cover some of the worst bits.

Along the path, you'll pass large mango trees and patches of guava before coming to an overlook after about 10 minutes. **Makahiku Falls**, a long bridal-veil waterfall

Walkers, Kuloa Point Trail

GREG ELMS/LONELY PLANET IMAGES ©

GREG ELMS/LONELY PLANET IMAGES ©

that drops into a deep gorge, is just off to the right. Thick green ferns cover the sides of 200ft basalt cliffs where the water cascades – a very rewarding scene for such a short walk.

Continuing along the main trail, you'll walk beneath old banyan trees, cross Palikea Stream (killer mosquitoes thrive here) and enter the wonderland of the **Bamboo Forest**, where thick groves of bamboo bang together musically in the wind. Beyond them is **Waimoku Falls**, a thin, lacy 400ft waterfall dropping down a sheer rock face. When you come out of the first grove, you'll see the waterfall in the distance. Forget swimming under Waimoku Falls – its pool is shallow and there's a danger of falling rocks.

If you want to take a dip, you'll find better pools along the way. About 100yd before Waimoku Falls, you'll cross a little stream. If you go left and work your way upstream for 10 minutes, you'll come to an attractive waterfall and a little pool about neck deep. There's also an inviting pool in the stream about halfway between Makahiku and Waimoku Falls.

 Tours

KIPAHULU 'OHANA   Cultural Tour
(☎ 248-8558; www.kipahulu.org; 2/3½hr tour $49/79) Kipahulu was once a breadbasket, or more accurately a poi bowl, for the entire region. For fascinating insights into the area's past, join one of the ethnobotanical tours led by Kipahulu 'Ohana, a collective of Native Hawaiian farmers who have restored ancient taro patches within the national park. Some of these are in the most incredible places, including high bluffs overlooking waterfalls. The tours include a sampling of Hawaiian foods and intriguing details on the native plants and ancient ruins along the way. The two-hour outing includes about 2 miles of hiking, leaves at 10am and concentrates on the farm activities. The 3½-hour tour leaves at 12:30pm, covers 4.5 miles and adds on a hike to Waimoku Falls. Both tours leave from the Kipahulu Visitor Center; advance reservations are advised. This could well be a highlight of your trip.

 **Sleeping**

KIPAHULU CAMPGROUND Camping
(camping free) If you've got a tent, you're going to love this campground, which has an incredible setting on oceanside cliffs amid the stone ruins of an ancient Hawaiian village. Good mana here! This is a primitive campground. Facilities include pit toilets, picnic tables and grills, but there's no water so bring your own. Permits aren't required. Camping is free but limited to three nights within a 30-day period. In winter you'll usually have the place to yourself, and even in summer there's typically enough space to handle everyone who shows up. Bring mosquito repellent and gear suitable for rainy conditions. The campground is a quarter of a mile southeast of the Kipahulu Visitor Center.

 **Information**

Kipahulu Visitor Center (248-7375; www.nps.gov/hale; 3-day entry pass per car $10, per person on foot, bicycle or motorcycle $5; park 24hr, visitor center 8:30am-5pm) Staffed by rangers who can give you an orientation to the park.

Getting There & Around

Note that there's no access between the summit section of Haleakalā National Park and the Kipahulu section; the two sections must be visited separately. The Kipahulu section of Haleakalā National Park is on Hwy 31, 10 scenic miles south of Hana. For more information on the spectacular drive between Hana and Kipahulu, see p220.

The Road to Hana

You're about to experience the most ravishingly beautiful drive in Hawaii. The serpentine Hana Hwy delivers one jaw-dropping view after the other as it winds between jungly valleys and towering cliffs. Along the way, 54 one-lane bridges mark nearly as many waterfalls, some tranquil and inviting, others so sheer they kiss you with spray as you drive past.

But there's a lot more to this beauty than the drive. When you're ready to get out and stretch your legs the real adventure begins: hiking trails climb into cool forests, short paths lead to Eden-like swimming holes, side roads wind down to sleepy seaside villages. If you've never tried smoked breadfruit, taken a dip in a spring-fed cave or gazed upon an ancient Hawaiian temple, set the alarm early – you've got a big day coming up.

Hana Hwy

Road to Hana Itineraries

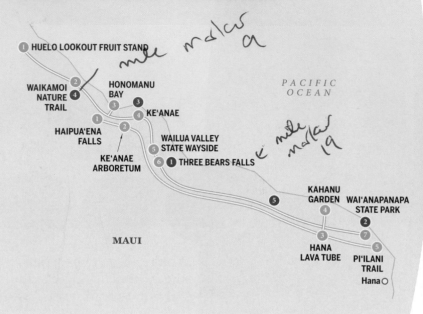

One Day

① Huelo Lookout Fruit Stand (p203)
Start with a stop at this organic fruit stand for a mango crêpe and a jolting java to kick off your road trip.

② Waikamoi Nature Trail (p203) Slip into your hiking shoes for a 30-minute loop through fragrant trees full of birdsong; along the way you'll be rewarded with ridge-top views of the dramatic road ahead.

③ Honomanu Bay (p206) You'll start getting glimpses as the Hana Hwy begins to wind down to the coast, but don't settle for just a glimpse – find the unmarked road into the bay and see a slice of untamed Hawaiian coast up close.

④ Ke'anae (p206) To really get a sense of the timeless nature of life in these parts you need to stop and unwind – and this friendly village is just the place.

⑤ Wailua Valley State Wayside (p209)
Next, climb the steps here and – bam – a 360-degree view unfolds from the mountains clear down to the sea.

⑥ Three Bears Falls (p210) Continue on to find the prom queen among Road to Hana waterfalls, the first in a magnificent run of roadside cascades that pop up between the 19 and 25 mile markers. Have a camera ready!

⑦ Wai'anapanapa State Park (p213) Your final stop harbors a beautiful black-sand beach, cool caves, a sea arch and a blowhole all within strolling distance of each other.

⊙ THIS LEG: 33 MILES

Two Days

1 **Haipua'ena Falls** (p205) If you've got two days for the Road to Hana, plan to take in the sights above and add the following to your itinerary. To begin, break out a beach towel and make your way to this Eden-like pool just begging a dip.

2 **Ke'anae Arboretum** (p206) Take a streamside walk through this arboretum for a microcosm of the heady sights and scents you see along the Hana Hwy – painted eucalyptus trees, brilliant tropical flowers and patches of Hawaiian taro, to name just a few.

3 **Hana Lava Tube** (p213) Easily the quirkiest site along the route, this place flips all the splendor above ground on its head, taking you into the bowels of the earth – a world of dripping stalactites and stalagmites. It's large enough to drive a train through, but it'll be just you and a flashlight on this one.

4 **Kahanu Garden** (p212) Continuing past the Hana Lava Tube toward the coast brings you a preserved corner of ancient Hawaii that's home to the most incredible collection of Polynesian gardens and the largest heiau (temple) in Hawaii.

5 **Pi'ilani Trail** (p214) Follow with a walk in the footsteps of the early Hawaiians on this ancient coastal footpath that offers a fascinating mix of historic ruins and wild coastal vistas. Do the whole hike roundtrip for a 6-mile outing or take advantage of the way it packs the top sights into the first leg and make it an easy 2-mile jaunt.

● ●

➡ THIS LEG: 27 MILES

Road to Hana Highlights

1 **Best Waterfall: Three Bears Falls** (p210) This triple-whammy beaut is the most picturesque waterfall on the entire drive.

2 **Best Beach: Pa'iloa Beach** (p213) Maui's finest black-sand strand.

3 **Best Village: Ke'anae** (p206) Come here for stunning ocean views in a welcoming setting.

4 **Best Hike: Waikamoi Nature Trail** (p203) Highlights on this meditative walk include towering trees and fine views.

5 **Best Lunch Stop: Nahiku** (p212) Choose between homecooked Hawaiian, Thai and vegetarian treats.

Three Bears Falls (p210)
PHOTOGRAPHER: KARL LEHMANN/LONELY PLANET IMAGES ©

Discover
the Road to Hana

Twin Falls

Heading south from Pa'ia, houses give way to fields of sugarcane and the scenery gets more dramatic with each mile. After the 16-mile marker on Hwy 36 the Hana Hwy changes numbers to Hwy 360 and the mile markers begin again at zero. Just after the 2-mile marker a wide parking area with a fruit stand marks the start of the trail to **Twin Falls** (Map p204). Local kids and tourists flock to the pool beneath the lower falls,

about a 10-minute walk in. Twin Falls gets a lot of attention as being the 'first waterfall on the road to Hana.' Truth be told, unless you're interested in taking a dip in muddy waters, this one's not worth the time. You'll find more idyllic options en route to Hana.

Huelo

With its abundant rain and fertile soil Huelo (Map p204) once supported more than 50,000 Hawaiians, but today it's a sleepy, scattered community of farms and enviable cliffside homes.

The double row of mailboxes and green bus shelter that come up after a blind curve 0.5 miles past the 3-mile marker marks the start of the narrow road that leads into the village. The only sight, Kaulanapueo Church, is a half-mile down.

It's tempting to continue driving past the church, but not rewarding, as the road shortly turns to dirt and dead-ends at gated homes. There's no public beach access.

 Sights

KAULANAPUEO CHURCH Historic Church
(Map p204) Constructed in 1853 of coral blocks and surrounded by a manicured green lawn, this tidy church remains the heart of the village. It has been built in early Hawaiian missionary style, with a spare interior and a tin roof topped with a green steeple. Swaying palm trees add a tropical backdrop. There are no formal opening hours, but the church is typically unlocked during the day.

Twin Falls
PHOTOGRAPHER: GREG ELMS/LONELY PLANET IMAGES ©

Sleeping & Eating

TEA HOUSE Cottage **$$**
(Map p204; ☏ 572-5610; www.mauitea
house.com; Hoolawa Rd; s/d $135/150) Built
with walls recycled from a Zen temple,
this one-of-a-kind cottage is so secluded
it's off the grid and uses its own solar
power to stoke up the lights. Yet it has
everything you'll need, including a kitchen
with gas burners and an open-air shower
in a redwood gazebo. The grounds also
contain a Tibetan-style stupa with a spec-
tacular cliff-top ocean view and a second
cottage that rents by the week ($500).

TOP **HUELO LOOKOUT FRUIT**
CHOICE **STAND** Fruit Stand **$**
(Map p204; www.huelolookout.coconut
protectors.com; 7600 Hana Hwy; snacks $5;
◷7:30am-5:30pm) The fruit stand itself
is tempting enough: drinking coconuts,
smoothies, French crèpes. And every-
thing's organic from its own 12-acre farm.
But it doesn't stop there: take your good-
ies down the steps, where there's a table
with a panorama out to the coast.

Ko'olau Forest Reserve

This is where it starts to get wild! As the
highway snakes along the edge of the
Ko'olau Forest Reserve (Map p204), the
jungle takes over and one-lane bridges
appear around every other bend. Ko'olau
means 'windward,' and the upper slopes
of these mountains squeeze a mighty
200in to 300in of rain from passing
clouds annually. No surprise – that makes
for awesome waterfalls as the rainwater
rushes down the reserve's abundant
gulches and streams.

Kailua

After the 5-mile marker you'll pass
through the village of Kailua (Map p204).
This little community of tin-roofed houses
is the home base for the employees of
the East Maui Irrigation (EMI) Com-
pany. These EMI workers maintain the
extensive irrigation system that carries
water from the rainforest to the thirsty
sugarcane fields in central Maui.

Hana Trip Tips

- Beat the crowd – get a sunrise start.

- Fill up the tank in Pa'ia; the next
gas station isn't until Hana.

- Bring snacks and plenty to drink.

- Wear a bathing suit under
your clothes so you're ready for
impromptu swims.

- Pull over to let local drivers pass –
they're moving at a different pace.

After leaving the village, just past
the 6-mile marker, you'll be treated to
a splash of color as you pass planted
groves of **painted eucalyptus** with
brilliant rainbow-colored bark. Roll
down the windows and inhale the sweet
scent given off by these majestic trees
introduced from Australia.

Ko'olau Ditch

For more than a century the Ko'olau Ditch
(Map p204) has been carrying up to 450
million gallons of water a day through 75
miles of flumes and tunnels from Maui's
rainy interior to the dry central plains. You
can get a close-up look by stopping at the
small pull-off just before the bridge that
comes up immediately after the 8-mile
marker. Just 30ft above the road you'll
see water flowing through a hand-hewn,
stone-block section of the ditch before
tunneling into the mountain.

Waikamoi Nature Trail & Waterfalls

Sights & Activities

TOP **WAIKAMOI NATURE TRAIL** Hiking
CHOICE Put on your walking shoes and rel-
ish the majestic sights and spicy scents
along this 30-minute nature trail (Map
p204). A covered table at the top offers
one pretty spot to break out that picnic

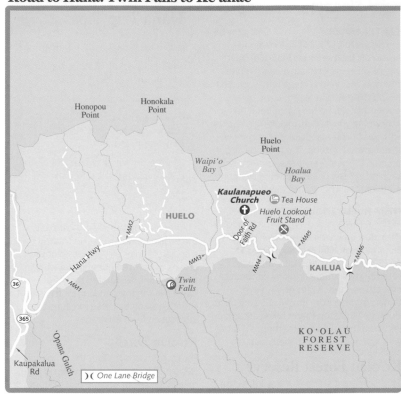

Honopou
Point

Honokala
Point

Huelo
Point

Waipi'o
Bay

Hoalua
Bay

**Kaulanapueo
Church** 🕆 Tea House

HUELO

Huelo Lookout
Fruit Stand ✕

Door of
Faith Rd

Hana Hwy

MM2

MM3

MM4

MM5

MM6

KAILUA

36

MM1

Twin
Falls

365

KO'OLAU
FOREST
RESERVE

'Opana Gulch

Kaupakalua
Rd   )(One Lane Bridge

lunch. Look for the signposted trailhead 0.5 miles past the 9-mile marker, where there's a wide dirt pull-off with space for several cars to park.

At the start of this 0.8-mile trail you're welcomed by a sign that reads 'Quiet. Trees at Work' and a strand of grand reddish *Eucalyptus robusta,* one of several types of towering eucalyptus trees that grow along the path. Once you reach the ridge at the top of the loop, you'll be treated to fine views of the winding Hana Hwy.

WAIKAMOI FALLS   Waterfall
There is space for just a few cars before the bridge at the 10-mile marker, but unless it's been raining recently don't worry about missing this one. The East Maui Irrigation Company diverts water from the stream, and as a result the falls are usually just a trickle. After you drive

past the bridge, bamboo grows almost horizontally out from the cliffs, creating a green canopy over the road.

GARDEN OF EDEN
ARBORETUM   Botanical Garden
(www.mauigardenofeden.com; 10600 Hana Hwy; admission $10; ◷8am-3pm) So why pay a steep $10 per person – not per carload, mind you – to visit an arboretum when the entire road to Hana is a garden? Well, it does offer a tamer version of paradise. The winding paths are neatly maintained, the flowers are identified and the hilltop picnic tables sport gorgeous views, including ones of Puohokamoa Falls and Keopuka Rock, which was featured in the opening shot of *Jurassic Park*. The arboretum is 0.5 miles past the 10-mile marker.

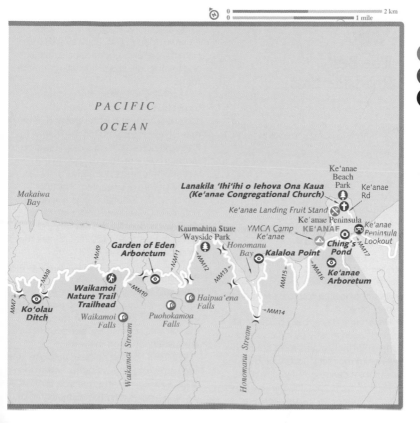

PUOHOKAMOA FALLS — Waterfall

Immediately after the 11-mile marker you'll pass Puohokamoa Falls. This waterfall no longer has public access, but you can get a glimpse of it from the bridge, or a bird's-eye view of the falls from the Garden of Eden Arboretum.

HAIPUA'ENA FALLS — Waterfall

If you're ready for a dip, Haipua'ena Falls, 0.5 miles past the 11-mile marker, provides a gentle waterfall (Map p204) with a Zen-like pool deep enough for swimming. Since you can't see the pool from the road, few people know it's here. Actually, it's not a bad choice if you forget your bathing suit. There's space for just a couple of cars on the Hana side of the bridge.

To reach the falls, walk 100yd upstream. Wild ginger grows along the path, and ferns hang from the rock wall behind the waterfall, making an idyllic setting. Be aware of slippery rocks and flash floods.

Kaumahina State Wayside Park

Clean restrooms, much appreciated right about now, and a grassy lawn with picnic tables make this roadside park a family-friendly stop. The park comes up 0.2 miles after the 12-mile marker. Be sure to take the short walk up the hill past the restrooms for an eye-popping view of the coastal scenery that awaits to the south.

For the next several miles, the scenery is absolutely stunning, opening up to a new vista as you turn round each bend. If it's been raining recently, you can expect to see waterfalls galore crashing down the mountains.

The Best...
Roadside Eats

1 Huelo Lookout Fruit Stand (p203)

2 Ke'anae Landing Fruit Stand (p208)

3 Up in Smoke (p212)

4 Jen's Thai Food (p212)

Honomanu Bay

You'll get your first view of this striking stream-fed bay (Map p204) from the 13-mile marker, where there's a roadside pull-off that invites you to pause and take in the scene.

Honomanu Bay's rocky black-sand beach is used mostly by local surfers and fishers. Surfable waves form during big swells, but the rocky bottom and strong rips make it dangerous if you're not familiar with the spot. Honomanu Stream, which empties into the bay, forms a little pool just inland from the beach that's good for splashing around, and on weekends local families take the young 'uns here to wade in its shallow water.

Just after the 14-mile marker, an inconspicuous road plunges straight down to Honomanu Bay. But the road can be shockingly bad – if you're not in a high-clearance vehicle, send a scout before driving down.

KALALOA POINT Lookout
For a fascinating view of the coast stop at the wide pull-off on the ocean side of the highway 0.4 miles past the 14-mile marker. From the point (Map p204) you can look clear across Honomanu Bay and watch ant-size cars snaking down the mountain cliffs on the other side. If there's no place to park, there's another pull-off with the same view 0.2 miles further.

Ke'anae

Congratulations – you've made it to Ke'anae (Map p204), halfway to Hana. Here's your reward: dramatic landscapes and the friendliest seaside village on the route.

According to legend, the god Kane thrust his spear into Ke'anae Valley's solid rock walls and water gushed out to nourish the forest and farms. Thanks to Kane's generosity, to this day, Hawaiian farmers continue to grow taro in the wetland patches on Ke'anae Peninsula.

The views are sweeping. Starting way up at the Ko'olau Gap in the rim of Haleakalā Crater and stretching clear down to the coast, Ke'anae Valley radiates green, thanks to the 150in of rainfall that drenches it each year.

At the foot of the valley lies Ke'anae Peninsula, created by a late eruption of Haleakalā that sent lava gushing all the way down Ke'anae Valley and into the ocean. Unlike its rugged surroundings, the volcanic peninsula is perfectly flat, like a leaf floating on the water.

You'll want to see Ke'anae up close. But keep an eye peeled, as sights come up in quick succession. After passing the YMCA Camp 0.5 miles past the 16-mile marker, the arboretum pops up on the right and the road to Ke'anae Peninsula heads off to the left around the next bend.

◉ Sights

KE'ANAE ARBORETUM Trails
Up for an easy walk? Ke'anae Arboretum (Map p204), 0.6 miles past the 16-mile marker, follows the Pi'ina'au Stream past an array of shady trees. Most eye-catching are the painted eucalyptus trees and the golden-stemmed bamboo; its green stripes look like the strokes of a Japanese *shodo* (calligraphy) artist. The arboretum is divided into two sections, with exotic timber and ornamental trees in one area and Hawaiian food and medicinal plants in the upper section.

The 0.6-mile path, which starts on a paved road and then turns to dirt, takes about 30 minutes to walk. It passes ginger and other fragrant plants before ending at irrigated patches with dozens of varieties of taro. Do expect some mosquitoes on the way.

TOP CHOICE **KE'ANAE PENINSULA** Village
A coastline pounded by relentless waves embraces a village (Map p204) so quiet you can hear the grass grow. This rare slice of 'Old Hawaii' is reached by taking the unmarked Ke'anae Rd on the *makai* (seaward) side of the highway just beyond Ke'anae Arboretum. Here, families who have had roots to the land for generations still tend stream-fed taro patches.

Marking the heart of the village is **Lanakila 'Ihi'ihi o Iehova Ona Kaua** (Ke'anae Congregational Church), built in 1860. The church is made of lava rocks and coral mortar that hasn't had its exterior covered over with layers of whitewash. It's a welcoming place with open doors and a guest book to sign. You can get a feel for the community by strolling the church cemetery, where the gravestones have cameo portraits and fresh-cut flowers.

Just past the church is **Ke'anae Beach Park**, with a scenic coastline of jagged black rock and hypnotic white-capped waves. Forget swimming: not only is the water rough, but this is all sharp lava and no beach. You could drive for a couple of minutes more, but it becomes private and the scenery is no better, so be a good neighbor and stop at the park.

The rock islets you see off the coast – **Mokuhala** and **Mokumana** – are seabird sanctuaries.

CHING'S POND Waterfall Pool
Back up on the Hana Hwy, the stream that feeds Ke'anae Peninsula pauses to create a couple of swimming holes (Map p204) just below the bridge, 0.9 miles after the 16-mile marker. You won't see anything driving by, but there's a good-sized pull-off immediately before the bridge where you can park. Just walk over to the bridge and behold: a deep crystal-clear pool and a little waterfall. You'll often

see locals swimming here, but note the 'No Trespassing' signs. Enjoy the sight, but take your dip elsewhere.

KE'ANAE PENINSULA LOOKOUT
Lookout

You'll get a superb bird's-eye view of the lowland peninsula and village by stopping at the paved pull-off (Map p204) just past the 17-mile marker on the *makai* side of the road. There's no sign, but it's easy to find if you look for the yellow tsunami speaker. From here you can see how Ke'anae Peninsula was formed late in the geological game – outlined in a jet-black lava coast, it still wears its volcanic ...thmark around the edges. The views ...oconut palms and patchwork taro ... Ke'anae Stream make one tasty ...f it's been raining lately, look to ...t to spot a series of cascading

Sleeping & Eating

YMCA CAMP KE'ANAE Cabins $
(Map p204; ☎248-8355; www.mauiymca.org; 13375 Hana Hwy; campsite & dm $18, cottages $150) When they're not rented by groups, the Y's cabins, on a knoll overlooking the coast, are available to individuals as hostel-style dorms. You'll need your own sleeping bag, and cooking facilities are limited to simple outdoor grills. Another option is to pitch your tent on the grounds. The Y also has two cottages, each with full facilities, two bedrooms and a lanai (veranda) with spectacular ocean views. The camp is between the 16- and 17-mile markers.

TOP CHOICE **KE'ANAE LANDING FRUIT STAND** Fruit Stand $
(Map p204; Ke'anae Peninsula; banana bread $5; ⏰8:30am-3pm) 'Da best' banana bread on the entire road to Hana is baked fresh every morning, and is so good you'll find as many locals as tourists pulling up here.

You can also get fresh fruit and drinks at this stand in the village center just before Ke'anae Beach Park.

Wailua

A quarter-mile after the 18-mile marker, the unmarked Wailua Rd leads to the left into the village of Wailua.

There's little to see but you will pass **Our Lady of Fatima Shrine** (Map p210). Also known as the Coral Miracle Church, this blue-and-white chapel was built in 1860 using coral from a freak storm that deposited the material onto a nearby beach. After the church was completed, another rogue storm hit the beach and swept all the leftover piles of coral back into the sea...or so the story goes. Since the chapel has just half a dozen little pews, the congregation long outgrew it and now uses the newer church out front.

From Wailua Rd you can also get a peek of the long cascade of **Waikani Falls** (Map p210) if you look back up toward the Hana Hwy. Wailua Rd dead-ends a half-mile down, though you won't want to go that far as blocked-off driveways prevent cars from turning around.

Waysides & Waterfalls

WAILUA VALLEY STATE WAYSIDE   Lookout

Back on the Hana Hwy, just before the 19-mile marker, Wailua Valley State Wayside (Map p210) lookout comes up on the right, providing a broad view into verdant Ke'anae Valley, which appears to be 100 shades of green. You can see a couple of waterfalls, and on a clear day you can steal a view of Ko'olau Gap, the break in the rim of Haleakalā Crater. If you climb up the steps to the right, you'll find a good view of Wailua Peninsula as well. Now, how's that for a package? A word of caution: the wayside is signposted but it comes up quickly after turning round a bend, so be on the lookout.

WAILUA PENINSULA LOOKOUT
Lookout

For the most spectacular view of Wailua Peninsula, stop at the large paved pull-off on the ocean side of the road 0.25 miles past the 19-mile marker. There's no sign but it's not hard to find, as two concrete picnic tables mark the spot. Grab a seat, break out your snack pack and ogle the taro fields and jungly vistas unfolding below.

THREE BEARS FALLS
TOP CHOICE
Waterfall

A real beauty, Three Bears, 0.5 miles past the 19-mile marker, takes its name from the triple cascade that flows down a steep rockface on the inland side of the road. Catch it after a rainstorm and the cascades come together and roar as one mighty waterfall. There's a small turnout with parking for a few cars right before crossing the bridge.You can scramble down to the falls via a steep ill-defined path that begins on the Hana side of the bridge. The stones are moss-covered and slippery, so either proceed with caution or simply enjoy the view from the road.

PUA'A KA'A STATE WAYSIDE PARK
Swimming Hole

A delightful park with an odd name, Pua'a Ka'a (Rolling Pig) rolls along both sides of the highway 0.5 miles after the 22-mile marker. Some unlucky passersby see just the restrooms on the ocean side of the road and miss the rest. But you brought your beach towel, didn't you? Cross the highway and head inland to find a pair of delicious waterfalls cascading into pools. The best for swimming is the upper pool, which is visible just beyond the picnic tables. To reach it, you'll need to cross the stream, skipping across a few rocks. (Also

Road to Hana: Wailua to Wai'anapanapa State Park

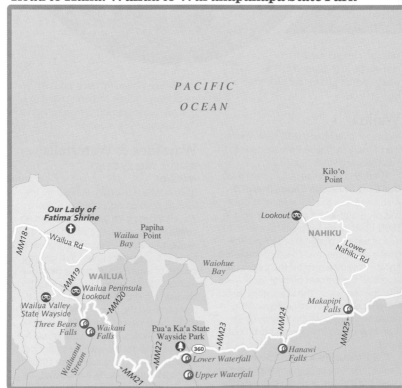

be aware of the possibility of falling rocks beneath the waterfall and of flash floods.) To get to the lower falls, which drop into a shallow pool, walk back to the south side of the bridge and then follow the trail upstream. And while you're at it, be sure to catch the scene from the bridge. Just don't hog the view.

HANAWI FALLS   Waterfall
Another waterfall with a split personality, Hanawi Falls sometimes flows gently into a quiet pool and sometimes gushes wildly across a broad rockface. No matter the mood it always invites popping out the camera and snapping a pic. The falls are 0.1 miles after the 24-mile marker. There are small pull-offs before and after the bridge.

MAKAPIPI FALLS   Waterfall
Most waterfall views look up at the cascades, but this one offers a rare chance to experience an explosive waterfall from the top. Makapipi Falls makes its sheer plunge right beneath your feet as you stand on the ocean side of the Makapipi Bridge. You don't see anything from your car so if you didn't know about it, you'd never even imagine this waterfall was here.

It's 0.1 miles after the 25-mile marker; you'll find pull-offs before and after the bridge.

Nahiku
While the rural village of Nahiku is down on the coast, its tiny 'commercial' center – such as it is – is right on the Hana Hwy, just before the 29-mile marker. Here you'll find the Nahiku

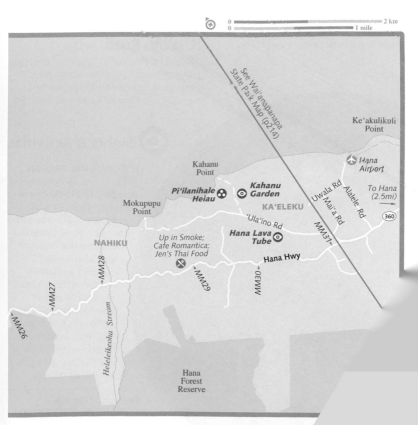

0   2 km
0   1 mile

See Wai'anapanapa
State Park Map (p214)

Ke'akulikuli Point

Kahanu Point

Hana Airport

Pi'ilanihale Heiau

Kahanu Garden

KA'ELEKU

Mokupupu Point

Uwala Rd
Mai'a Rd
Alalele Rd

To Hana (2.5mi) →
360

'Ula'ino Rd

Hana Lava Tube

NAHIKU

MM31

Up in Smoke; Cafe Romantica; Jen's Thai Food

Hana Hwy

MM28
MM29
MM30

MM27

Heleleikeoha Stream

MM26

Hana Forest Reserve

The Best...
Views

1 Ke'anae Peninsula Lookout (p208)

2 Wailua Valley State Wayside (p209)

3 Wai'anapanapa State Park (p213)

4 Honomanu Bay (p206)

5 Three Bears Falls (p210)

Marketplace, home to a little coffee shop, fruit stand and several small eateries clustered together.

If you're hungry, you will want to stop. The food's tempting and this is the last place to eat between here and Hana.

Eating

TOP CHOICE **UP IN SMOKE** Hawaiian **$**
(Map p210; Nahiku Marketplace, Hana Hwy; snacks $3-6; ⊙10am-5pm Sun-Thu) Hawaiian food never tasted so good. This bustling barbecue stand is *the* place to try kiawe-smoked breadfruit and *kalua* pig tacos.

JEN'S THAI FOOD Thai **$**
(Map p210; Nahiku Marketplace, Hana Hwy; mains $8-10; ⊙11am-4pm) A new addition to the mix, Jen uses only fresh-caught Hana fish in her savory curries. The green papaya salad and pad Thai get raves too.

CAFE ROMANTICA Vegetarian **$**
(Map p210; Nahiku Marketplace, Hana Hwy; mains $5-10; ⊙noon-5pm; 🌿) At this class act, a skilled chef whips up gourmet vegetarian dishes out of a vintage food truck, complete with a lighted awning and bar stools.

'Ula'ino Road

'Ula'ino Rd (Map p210) begins at the Hana Hwy just south of the 31-mile marker. Hana Lava Tube is half a mile from the highway and Kahanu Garden a mile more.

Sights & Activities

TOP CHOICE **KAHANU GARDEN** Historical Site
(Map p210; 📞248-8912; www.ntbg.org; 'Ula'ino Rd; adult/child under 12 $10/free, guided tour $25; ⊙self-guided tour 10am-2pm Mon-Fri; guided tour 10am-noon Sat) This one-of-a-kind place delivers a double blast of mana (spiritual essence). Hawaii's largest temple and one of its most important ethnobotanical gardens share the 294-acre site. The National Tropical

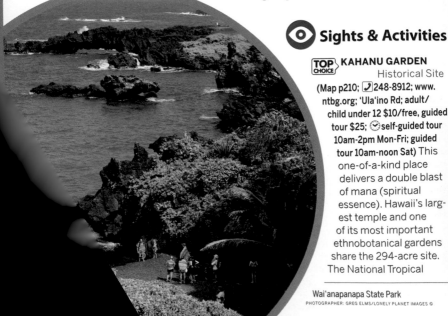

Wai'anapanapa State Park
PHOTOGRAPHER: GREG ELMS/LONELY PLANET IMAGES ©

Botanical Garden, which is dedicated to the conservation of rare and medicinal plants from the tropical Pacific, maintains Kahanu. Most interesting is the **canoe garden**, landscaped with taro and other plants brought to Hawaii by early Polynesian settlers. The scope is amazing, as the garden holds the world's largest breadfruit tree collection and a remarkable variety of coconut palms.

The garden paths also skirt **Pi'ilanihale Heiau**, an immense lava-stone platform reaching 450ft in length. The history of this astounding heiau (temple) is shrouded in mystery, but there's no doubt that it was an important religious site for Hawaiians. Archaeologists believe construction began as early as AD 1200 and the heiau was built in sequences. The final grand scale was the work of Pi'ilani (the heiau's name means House of Pi'ilani), the 14th-century Maui chief who is also credited with the construction of many of the coastal fishponds in the Hana area. It's a memorable place to bring the entire family.

Since visiting Kahanu Garden takes a couple of hours, few day-trippers come this way and you may well have the place to yourself. The site, on Kalahu Point, is 1.5 miles down 'Ula'ino Rd from the Hana Hwy. The road is crossed by a streambed immediately before reaching the gardens; if it's dry you should be able to drive over it OK, but if it's been raining heavily don't even try.

HANA LAVA TUBE   Caves
(Map p210; www.mauicave.com; 'Ula'ino Rd; admission $12; ☉10:30am-4pm) One of the odder sights on this otherwise lushly green drive are these mammoth caves formed by ancient lava flows. The big kahuna of lava tubes, these caves are so formidable that they once served as a slaughterhouse – 17,000lb of cow bones had to be removed before they were opened to visitors! Winding your way through the extensive underground lava tubes, which reach heights of up to 40ft, you'll find a unique ecosystem of dripping stalactites and stalagmites. You'll need about an hour to explore the caves. The admission includes flashlights and hard hats. Bring a sweater – it's cool down under.

Wai'anapanapa State Park

Swim in a cave, sun on a black-sand beach, explore ancient Hawaiian sites – this is one cool park. A sunny coastal trail and a seaside campground make it a tempting place to dig in for awhile. Honokalani Rd, which leads into Wai'anapanapa State Park (Map p214), is just after the 32-mile marker. The road ends overlooking the park's centerpiece, the jet-black sands at Pa'iloa Bay.

 Beaches

TOP CHOICE **PA'ILOA BEACH**   Beach
The beach (Map p214) here is a stunner – hands down the prettiest black-sand beach on Maui. Walk on down, sunbathe, enjoy. But if you're thinking of jumping in, be cautious. It's open ocean with a bottom that drops quickly and water conditions that are challenging, even for strong swimmers. Powerful rips are the norm (Pa'iloa means 'always splashing') and there have been several drownings here.

Island Insights

On certain nights of the year, the waters in Wai'anapanapa State Park's lava-tube caves take on a red hue. Legend says it's the blood of a princess and her lover who were killed in a fit of rage by the princess's jealous husband after he f[...] them hiding together he[...] Less romantic types at[...] the phenomenon to [...] tiny bright-red shr[...] *'opaeula,* which [...] emerge from s[...] cracks in the [...]

Sights & Activities

ROAD TO HANA

LAVA CAVES   Caves
A 10-minute loop path north from
the beach parking lot leads to a pair
of impressive lava-tube caves. Their
garden-like exteriors are draped with
ferns and colorful impatiens, while their
interiors harbor deep spring-fed pools.
Wai'anapanapa means 'glistening waters'

and the pools' crystal-clear mineral waters reputedly rejuvenate the skin. They
certainly will invigorate – these sunless
pools are refreshingly brisk!

PI'ILANI TRAIL   Hiking
This gem of a coastal trail leads 3 miles
south from the park to Kainalimu Bay, just
north of Hana Bay, offering splendid views
along the way. It's one of those trails that
packs a lot up front, so even if you just

Wai'anapanapa State Park

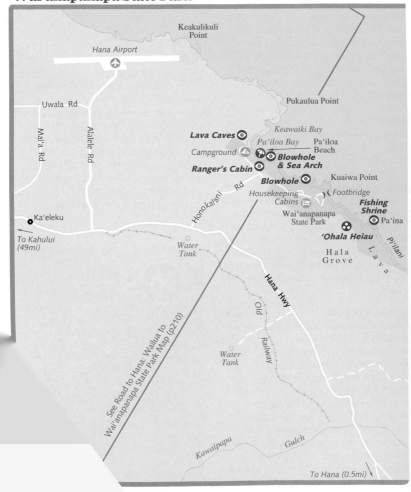

have time to do the first mile, you won't regret it. If you plan to hike the whole trail be sure to bring water, as it's unshaded the entire way, and good hiking shoes, as it gets rougher as you go along.

The route follows an ancient footpath known as the King's Highway that was the main land route between Hana and villages to the north. Some of the worn stepping stones along the path date from the time of Pi'ilani, the king who ruled Maui in the 14th century. The trail begins along the coast just below the camping area and parallels the ocean along lava sea cliffs. Just a few minutes along you'll pass a burial ground, a natural **sea arch** and a **blowhole** that roars to life whenever there's pounding surf. This is also the area where you're most likely to see endangered Hawaiian monk seals basking onshore.

Perched above the sea at 0.7 miles are the remains of **'Ohala Heiau**, a place of worship to the harvest god Lono. A **fishing shrine** ahead on the left affords a good view south of basalt cliffs lined up all the way to Hana. Hala and ironwood encroaches the shoreline past the heiau. Round stones continue to mark the way across lava and a grassy clearing, fading briefly on the way over a rugged sea cliff. A dirt road comes in from the right as the trail arrives at **Luahaloa**, a ledge with a small **fishing shack**. Inland stands of ironwood heighten the beauty of the scenic last mile of cliff-top walking to **Kainalimu Bay**. Stepping stones hasten the approach to the bay ahead, as the trail dips down a shrubby ravine to a quiet, black-cobble beach. Dirt roads lead another mile from here south to Hana.

 ## Sleeping

Fall asleep to the lullaby of the surf in the park's **campground** (site per night $18) on a shady lawn near the beach. It's a great place to camp but there is one caveat – this is the rainy side of the island, so it can get wet at any time. Plan accordingly.

The park also has a dozen housekeeping **cabins** (per night $90) that are extremely popular and usually book up months in advance. Contact the **Division of State Parks** (☎984-8109; www.hawaiistateparks.org; 54 S High St, Wailuku; ⏰8:30am-3:30pm Mon-Fri) for information on permits, fees and reservations.

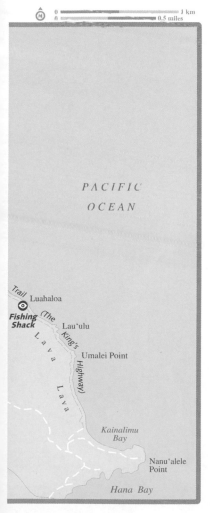

Ⓝ 0 _____ 1 km
0 _____ 0.5 miles

PACIFIC
OCEAN

Trail — Luahaloa
Fishing Shack — (The — Lau'ulu
King's — Lava — Umalei Point
Highway) — Lava

Kainalimu
Bay

Nanu'alele
Point

Hana Bay

Hana & East Maui

Where do Mauians go when they want to get away? To raw and rugged East Maui, the most isolated side of the island.

Instead of golf courses and beach resorts, you'll see a face that's barely changed a speck for tourism. The awesome road to Hana is so special we've dedicated an entire chapter to it (see p199). This chapter starts with time-honored Hana, where you'll relearn the meaning of s-l-o-w and talk story with people who actually take the time. Beyond Hana lies Wailua Falls, the most stunning roadside waterfall on the entire island, and the cool forested trails of 'Ohe'o Gulch. In sleepy Kipahulu, discover the gravesite of famed aviator Charles Lindbergh and savor organic snacks at off-the-grid farms. A fitting finale to it all is the adventurous romp along the Pi'ilani Hwy and through the cowboy village of Kaupo.

Wailua Falls (p228)
PHOTOGRAPHER: DOUGLAS PEEBLES/PHOTOLIBRARY

Hana & East Maui Itineraries

One Day

1 **Hana Town Center** (p221) If you've got one day it's all about slowing down to experience Hana's aloha. Wander around town, taking in the generations-old **Hasegawa General Store** and the 19th-century **Wananalua Congregational Church**, then stop by the **Hana Coast Gallery** to peruse the museum-quality artwork.

2 **Hana Cultural Center** (p221) Head across town to this community museum, which harbors worthy sights within its walls and the historic grounds.

3 **Kaihalulu (Red Sand) Beach** (p220) It's time for a dip, so grab a towel (bathing suit optional) and sneak off to Hana's hidden red-sand strand.

4 **Pranee's Thai Food** (p226) Hungry after that swim? Join the locals over an aromatic home-cooked lunch at this tasty Thai eatery.

5 **Hana Beach Park** (p220) Go see what's happening at the town's favorite hangout. When ex-Beatle George Harrison lived in Hana, he'd occasionally be seen at the beach park in the evening strumming a tune with Hana folk. Come see who's here today.

6 **Lyon's Hill** (p221) End your day with a hike through green pastures and past grazing cattle to the top of Hana's highest hill to watch the sun set over this timeless town.

●●●●●●●●●●●●●●●●●●●●●●●●●●●●●●●●●●●●●●

➡ THIS LEG: 3 MILES

Two Days

1 Hamoa Beach (p231) On day two, head south from Hana to this beach and see for yourself why the legendary author James Michener called Hamoa the only beach in the North Pacific that actually looked as if it belonged in the South Pacific.

2 Wailua Falls (p228) As you continue south the scenery gets lusher and greener, with the lofty cascades of Wailua Falls plunging by the roadside just begging a picture.

3 'Ohe'o Gulch (p229) Continue on to more watery delights at 'Ohe'o Gulch, where you can dip into heavenly pools, hike to towering waterfalls and take a look at ancient Hawaiian sites.

4 Kipahulu (p229) Quiet Kipahulu holds hidden treasures, including **Charles Lindbergh's grave**, where you can soak up the solitude that brought the great aviator to this remote village. For a *paniolo* (Hawaiian cowboy) experience, take the reins at nearby **Maui Stables** and trot off into the wilderness on a horseback ride. Next stop: stretch your legs pedaling your own organic fruit smoothie at the off-the-grid **Laulima Farms**.

5 Pi'ilani Hwy (p230) Now it's time to continue your journey on the most remote road in all of Hawaii: the Pi'ilani Hwy around the southern flank of Haleakalā. In cowboy-centric Kaupō, step up to the counter at the **Kaupo Store** and take in the vintage scene. As you continue your adventure on the lonesome highway, enjoy the dramatic untouched coastal scenery, sea arches and lava flows along the way.

⮕ THIS LEG: 38 MILES

Hana & East Maui Highlights

1 Best Beach: Hamoa Beach (p230) The region's favorite sun and surf haunt.

2 Best View: Wailua Falls (p228) The most dramatic cascade on a drive full of drama.

3 Best Activity: Maui Stables (p229) A real-deal horseback ride led by *paniolo* (Hawaiian cowboys).

4 Best Swimming Hole: 'Ohe'o Gulch (p229) Pick your own pool from a terraced collection.

5 Best Festival: East Maui Taro Festival (p223) You'd never imagine taro could have so many incarnations.

Hamoa Beach (p230)
PHOTOGRAPHER: ANN CECIL/LONELY PLANET IMAGES ©

Discover
Hana & East Maui

Hana

After the spectacular drive to get here, some visitors are surprised to find the town is a bit of a sleeper – Hana (population 1855) doesn't hit you with a bam. Cows graze lazily in green pastures stretching up the hillsides. Neighbors chat over plate lunches at the beach. Even at Hana's legendary hotel, the emphasis is on relaxation.

Isolated as it is by that long and winding road, Hana stands as one of the most Hawaiian communities in the state. Folks share a strong sense of *'ohana* (family), and if you listen closely you'll hear the words 'auntie' and 'uncle' a lot. There's a timeless rural character, and though 'Old Hawaii' is an oft-used cliché elsewhere, it's hard not to think of Hana in such terms. What Hana has to offer is best appreciated by those who stop and unwind.

History

It's hard to imagine little Hana as the epicenter of Maui, but this village produced many of ancient Hawaii's most influential *ali'i* (chiefs). Hana's great 14th-century chief Pi'ilani marched from here to conquer rivals in Wailuku and Lahaina, and become the first leader of unified Maui.

The landscape changed dramatically in 1849 when ex-whaler George Wilfong bought 60 acres of land to plant sugarcane. Hana went on to become a booming plantation town, complete with a narrow-gauge railroad connecting the fields to the Hana Mill. In the 1940s Hana could no longer compete with larger sugar operations in Central Maui and the mill went bust.

Enter San Francisco businessman Paul Fagan, who purchased 14,000 acres in Hana in 1943. Starting with 300 Herefords, Fagan converted the cane fields to ranch land. A few years later he opened a six-room hotel as a getaway resort for well-to-do friends and brought his minor-league baseball team, the San Francisco Seals, to Hana for spring training. That's when visiting sports journalists gave the town its moniker, 'Heavenly Hana.' Hana Ranch remains the backbone of Hana's economy and its hillside pastures graze some 2000 head of cattle worked by *paniolo* (Hawaiian cowboys).

Hana Beach Park

Beaches

TOP CHOICE **HANA BEACH PARK**   Beach
Some towns have a central plaza. Hana's pulse beats from this bayside park. Families come here to take the kids for a splash, to picnic on the black-sand beach and to strum their ukuleles with friends.

When water conditions are very calm, snorkeling and diving are good out in the direction of the light beacon. Currents can be strong, and snorkelers shouldn't venture beyond the beacon. Surfers head to **Waikoloa Beach** at the northern end of the bay.

KAIHALULU (RED SAND) BEACH   Beach

A favored haunt of nude sunbathers, this hidden cove on the south side of Ka'uiki Head is a beauty in contrasts, with rich red sand set against brilliant turquoise waters. The cove is partly protected by a lava outcrop, but currents can be powerful when the surf's up (Kaihalulu means 'roaring sea'). Water drains through a break on the left side, which should be avoided. Conditions are unpredictable, so swimmers should use caution at all times; your best chance of finding calm waters is in the morning.

The path to the beach starts across the lawn at the lower side of **Hana Community Center**, and continues as a steep 10-minute trail down to the cove. The route is narrow with a mix of crumbly volcanic cinders and slippery clay that can be treacherous, particularly when wet; wear appropriate shoes. En route you'll pass an overgrown Japanese cemetery, a remnant of the sugarcane days.

Sights

HANA CULTURAL CENTER   Museum
([☎] 248-8622; www.hanaculturalcenter. org; 4974 Uakea Rd; adult/child under 12 $3/free; [🕑] 10am-4pm Mon-Thu; [👪]) Soak up a little local history at this down-home museum displaying Hawaiian artifacts, wood carvings and hand-stitched quilts.

Local Knowledge

NAME: GEORGE KAHUMOKU JR
OCCUPATION: GRAMMY-WINNING SLACK KEY GUITARIST, TARO FARMER
RESIDENCE: MAUI NUI

What are your favorite experiences in East Maui? MauiFest Hawaii (p223). It's all Hawaiian stuff. It's home grown. It gets the public involved, shows movies and short clips made by local guys, and then there's music. It serves local food. If you just happen to be there in Hana you're going to experience all the locals there coming out, all the families and grandparents coming, they come out of Kipahulu and everything.

What's the East Maui Taro Festival like? It's also a big 'ohana (family) event. Everybody comes. It's not just music. It's a big taro event too. One year we tasted about 60 varieties. There's all different kinds of taro. Some taro is better as poi, some is better eating straight, some is better for frying up, making taro chips.

Other must-do's for travelers in this area? You also have to visit the 'ulu (breadfruit) botanical garden at Kahanu Garden (p212) north of town on the Hana Hwy. If you go to Hana you got to see that.

Any other tips for delving deeper into Hawaiian culture? If you're going to be in Hana awhile, there's Ala Kukui (p223). It's a real resource. It has workshops all year round, all sorts of things – music, meditation, Hawaiian plants. I've done some workshops with them, taught ukulele, guitar, songwriting.

The museum grounds harbor still more cultural gems, including four authentically reconstructed thatched *hale* (houses), which can be admired even outside opening hours. Here, too, is a three-bench, c 1871 **courthouse**. Although it looks like a museum piece, this tiny court is still used on the first Tuesday of each month when a judge shows up to hear

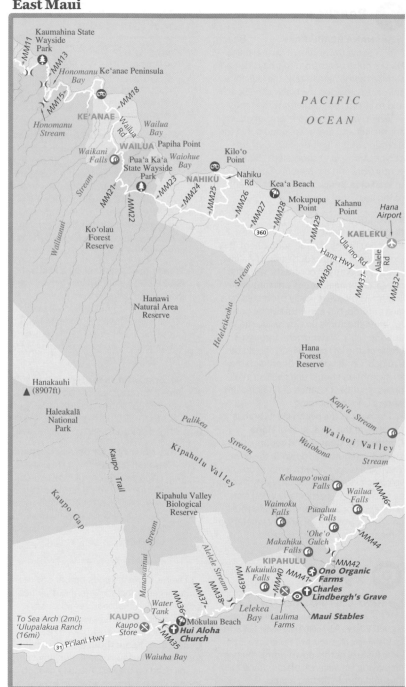

PACIFIC OCEAN

Kaumahina State Wayside Park

MM11

MM13

Honomanu Bay

Ke'anae Peninsula

MM15

KE'ANAE

Honomanu Stream

MM18

Wailua Rd

WAILUA

Wailua Bay

Waikani Falls

Pua'a Ka'a State Wayside Park

Waiohue Bay

Papiha Point

Kilo'o Point

NAHIKU

Nahiku Rd

Kea'a Beach

Mokupupu Point

Kahanu Point

Hana Airport

KAELEKU

MM21

MM22

MM23

MM24

MM25

MM26

MM27

MM28

MM29

MM30

MM31

MM32

360

Hana Hwy

'Ula'ino Rd

Alalele Rd

Waituanui

Ko'olau Forest Reserve

Hanawi Natural Area Reserve

Heleleikeoha Stream

Hana Forest Reserve

Haleakalā National Park

Hanakauhi ▲ (8907ft)

Kaupo Trail

Kaupo Gap

Palikea Stream

Kipahulu Valley

Kipahulu Valley Biological Reserve

Kapi'a Stream

Waihoi Valley

Waiohona Stream

Kekuapo'owai Falls

Wailua Falls

MM46

Waimoku Falls

Puaaluu Falls

'Ohe'o Gulch

Makahiku Falls

MM44

KIPAHULU

Kukuiula Falls

MM40

MM42

MM47

Ono Organic Farms

Charles Lindbergh's Grave

Maui Stables

Manawainui Stream

Alelele Stream

MM39

MM38

MM37

MM36

MM35

Lelekea Bay

Laulima Farms

KAUPO

Water Tank

Mokulau Beach

Hui Aloha Church

Kaupo Store

To Sea Arch (2mi); 'Ulupalakua Ranch (16mi)

31 Pi'ilani Hwy

Waiuha Bay

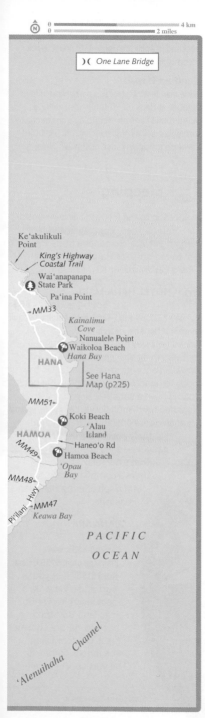

minor cases, sparing Hana residents with traffic tickets the need to drive all the way to Wailuku.

WANANALUA CONGREGATIONAL CHURCH
Historic Church

(cnr Hana Hwy & Hau'oli St) On the National Register of Historic Places, this church (c 1838) has such hefty walls it resembles an ancient Norman church. Also noteworthy is the little **cemetery** at the side, where the graves are randomly laid out rather than lined up in rows.

Hana Coast Gallery
Gallery

(☎248-8638; 5031 Hana Hwy; ⊙9am-5pm) Even if you're not shopping, visit this gallery at the north side of Hotel Hana-Maui to browse the museum quality wooden bowls, paintings and Hawaiian featherwork.

 Activities

Hotel Hana-Maui organizes activities, including kayaking, for its guests.

LYON'S HILL
Hiking

Former Hana Ranch owner Paul Fagan often ended his day with a walk up Lyon's Hill – and if you've got time you might want to follow in his footsteps. The big cross topping the hill, a memorial to Fagan, is Hana's most dominant landmark. The 15-minute trail up Lyon's Hill starts opposite Hotel Hana-Maui.

HANG GLIDING MAUI
Ultralight Flight

(☎572-6557; www.hangglidingmaui.com; Hana Airport; 30/60min flight $150/250; ⊙by appointment) For the ultimate bird's-eye view hop aboard a tandem ultralight aircraft. Flight suits are provided; all you need is a little daring! You actually get to fly this cool craft that looks like a motorcycle with wings – dual controls allow the passenger to take the reins once it's airborne.

HANA RANCH STABLES
Horseback Riding

(☎270-5258; Mill Rd; 1hr ride $60) These stables, which book through Hotel Hana-Maui, give horseback riders the option to either trot along Hana's black-lava coastline or to head for the hills into green cattle pasture.

ALA KUKUI Retreat Center
(248-7841; www.alakuki.com) Classes in ukulele, slack key guitar, meditation, yoga and Hawaiian medicinal plants are held at this 12-acre retreat center at the north side of town.

Honua Spa Spa
(270-5290; Hotel Hana-Maui, 5031 Hana Hwy; treatments $120-290) If the long drive to Hana has tightened you up, this posh spa can work off the kinks with *lomilomi* (traditional Hawaiian massage).

Luana Spa Retreat Spa
(248-8855; 5050 Uakea Rd; treatments $40-150) Offers massages and body treatments in a Hawaiian-style open-air setting.

Festivals & Events

TOP CHOICE **East Maui Taro Festival** Festival
(www.tarofestival.org) Maui's most Hawaiian town throws its most Hawaiian party. If it's native, it's here – outrigger canoe races, a taro pancake breakfast, poi making,

hula dancing and a big jamfest of top ukulele and slack key guitarists. Held on the last weekend in April, it's Hana at its finest. Book accommodations well in advance.

MauiFest Hawaii Festival
(www.mauifest.net) Held on a weekend in October at Hana Bay, this big bash includes island-made films on everything from music to surfing, as well as hula dancing and big-time Hawaiian musicians such as Brother Noland.

Sleeping

In addition to the following accommodation options, there are cabins and tent camping at Wai'anapanapa State Park, just to the north of Hana, and camping at 'Ohe'o Gulch, about 10 miles south.

TOP CHOICE **HOTEL HANA-MAUI**
Boutique Hotel $$$
(248-8211, 800-321-4262; www.hotelhanamaui.com; 5031 Hana Hwy; r from $325; @) This famed getaway hotel breathes tranquility. Everything's airy and open, rich with Hawaiian accents, from island art in the lobby to hand-stitched quilts on the beds. Rooms have a subdued elegance with bleached hardwood floors, ceiling fans and French doors opening to trellised patios. Delightfully absent are electronic gadgets – sans even alarm clocks! If that's not relaxing enough, there's complimentary yoga and a spa offering Hawaiian massage.

LUANA SPA RETREAT Yurt $$
(248-8855; www.luanaspa.com; 5050 Uakea Rd; d $150) Just you, a yurt and a view. On a secluded hill overlooking Hana Bay, this back-to-nature charmer fuses outdoor living with indoor comforts. The yurt sports a well-

Yurt, Luana Spa Retreat
PHOTOGRAPHER: GREG ELMS/LONELY PLANET IMAGES ©

Hana

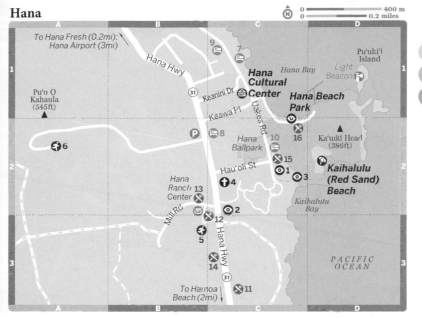

Hana

equipped kitchenette and a stereo with Hawaiian music. Shower outdoors in a bamboo enclosure, enjoy spectacular stargazing over the bay – this is pure romance, Hana-style. Stays of more than two nights cut the rate to $135 a night, a real bargain for Hana.

HANA KAI-MAUI Condo **$$**
(☎248-8426, 800-346-2772; www.hanakai. com; 1533 Uakea Rd; studios/1br from $185/210) Hana's only condo complex is just a stone's throw from Hana's hottest surfing beach. The units are nicely fitted and although the walls are thin, the sound of the surf drowns out neighboring chatter. For primo ocean views request a top-floor

corner unit. Unlike most condo rentals on Maui, Hana Kai-Maui has no minimum stay, offering an easy option for turning your Hana drive into a two-day event.

HANA'S TRADEWINDS COTTAGE
Cottage **$$**

(☎ 248-8980; www.hanamauirentals.com; 135 Alalele Pl; d $175) In the midst of a 5-acre tropical flower farm, this cozy cottage has enough space to accommodate a small family, though there's a $25 charge for each person beyond two. It's only a 10-minute drive to town but quiet enough to feel like you're in the boonies. Best of all, if you've been hiking all day you can come home and soak in your own private hot tub.

JOE'S PLACE
Budget Hotel **$**

(☎ 248-7033; www.joesrentals.com; 4870 Uakea Rd; r with shared/private bathroom $50/60) Hana's only nod to the budget traveler offers a dozen basic rooms. The linoleum's worn, the decor dates back to the '60s, but there's a fresh coat of paint on the walls and the place is kept sparkling clean. The shared facilities – a barbecue, den and kitchen – provide homey opportunities to exchange tips with fellow travelers after a day of sightseeing.

Eating

Hana has just a couple of stores with limited grocery selections, so if you're staying awhile stock up in Kahului before heading down.

TOP CHOICE BRUDDAH HUTT'S BBQ
Barbecue **$**

(Hana Hwy; meals $8-14; ⏱10am-4pm) It's a bit like a neighborhood barbecue, with diners sitting on folding chairs under a canvas awning and an extended family cooking away over gas grills. Favorites are the barbecued chicken and the fish tacos. Expect a crowd at noon, and don't take the closing time too seriously as it shuts down when the food runs out.

TOP CHOICE PRANEE'S THAI FOOD
Thai $

(☎ 248-8855; 5050 Uakea Rd; meals $8-10; ⊙11am-3pm Sun-Wed) Only a few lucky travelers stumble upon this hidden gem set back from the road opposite Hana Ballpark. It's just a simple outdoor cafe, but chef Pranee is famous in these parts for her fiery curries and fresh stir-fried dishes.

HANA FRESH
Farm Stand $

(www.hanafresh.org; 4590 Hana Hwy; lunch $6; ⊙8am-5:30pm Mon-Sat, to 2pm Sun) This roadside stand in front of Hana Health sells organic produce grown right on site and healthy takeout plates featuring locally caught fish. If you happen to come by at lunch time, it's the best deal in Hana.

HANA RANCH RESTAURANT TAKEOUT
Burger Joint $

(☎ 248-8255; Hana Ranch Center, Mill Rd; meals $9-12; ⊙11am-4pm) It's just a takeout window but this is the busiest lunch spot in town. Everybody comes for the juicy burgers made of free-range Hana beef. The ocean view from the adjacent picnic tables goes down well too.

Tutu's
Snack Bar $

(☎ 248-8224; Hana Beach Park; snacks $5-10; ⊙8:30am-4pm; ☺) Hana Beach Park's fast-food grill serves the expected menu of shave ice, burgers and plate lunches. Grab a table on the beach and you've got yourself a picnic.

Ono Farmers Market
Farmers Market $

(Hana Hwy; ⊙10am-6pm Sun-Thu) This is the place to pick up Kipahulu-grown coffee, jams and the most incredible array of fruit, from papaya to rambutan.

Hana Ranch Store
Grocery

(☎ 248-8261; Hana Ranch Center; ⊙7am-7:30pm) Sells groceries and liquor.

Drinking & Entertainment

PANIOLO BAR Bar
(☎248-8211; Hotel Hana-Maui, 5031 Hana Hwy;
⊘11am-9pm) A classy place to enjoy a drink,
this open-air bar at Hotel Hana-Maui has
live Hawaiian music some evenings.

Shopping

**HASEGAWA GENERAL
STORE** General Store
(☎248-8231; 5165 Hana Hwy; ⊘7am-7pm Mon-
Sat, 8am-6pm Sun) For a century, this family-
run, tin-roofed store has been Hana's
sole general store, its narrow, jam-packed
aisles selling everything from fishing gear
and machetes to soda pop and bags of
poi (mashed taro). This icon of mom-and-
pop shops is always crowded with locals
picking up supplies, travelers stopping for
snacks and sightseers buying 'I Survived
the Hana Highway' T-shirts.

 Information

Hana Ranch Center (Mill Rd) is the commercial
center of town.

Bank of Hawaii (☎248-8015; Hana Ranch
Center; ⊘3-4:30pm Mon-Thu, to 6pm Fri) No
ATM.

Hana Health (☎248-8294; 4590 Hana Hwy;
⊘8:30am-5pm) At the north side of town.
Hasegawa General Store (☎248-8231; 5165
Hana Hwy; ⊘7am-7pm Mon-Sat, 8am-6pm Sun)
Has an ATM.

Post office (Hana Ranch Center; ⊘8am-4:30pm
Mon-Fri)

 Getting There & Around

There are two ways to get to Hana: a drive down
the winding Hana Hwy or a prop-plane flight into
Hana Airport. **Dollar Rent-A-Car** (☎248-8237)
has a booth at the Hana Airport that's staffed
when flights come in. The Maui Bus doesn't serve
East Maui.

Hana closes up early. The sole gas station in
all of East Maui is **Hana Gas** (☎248-7671; cnr
Mill Rd & Hana Hwy; ⊘7am-8:30pm), so plan
accordingly.

Hana to Kipahulu

South from Hana, the road winds down
to Kipahulu, passing 'Ohe'o Gulch, the
southern end of Haleakalā National
Park. This lush stretch brims with
raw natural beauty. Between
its twists and turns, one-lane
bridges and drivers trying to
take in all the sights, it's a
slow-moving 10 miles, so
allow yourself an hour
just to reach Kipahulu.

 Sights

WAILUA FALLS
Waterfalls
As you continue south,
you'll see waterfalls
cascading down the cliffs,
orchids growing out of

'Ohe'o Gulch
PHOTOGRAPHER: KARL LEHMANN/LONELY PLANET IMAGES ©

the rocks, and jungles of breadfruit and coconut trees. Hands-down the most spectacular sight along the way is Wailua Falls, which plunges a mighty 100ft just beyond the road. It appears 0.3 miles after the 45-mile marker but you won't need anyone to point this one out, as folks are always lined up along the roadside snapping photos.

'OHE'O GULCH Swimming Hole
Fantastic falls, cool pools, paths galore. The indisputable highlight of the drive past Hana is 'Ohe'o Gulch, aka the Kipahulu section of Haleakalā National Park. See the Haleakalā National Park chapter for details on all the things to see and do, as well as entry fees and camping options.

Kipahulu

Less than a mile south of 'Ohe'o Gulch lies the little village of Kipahulu. It's hard to imagine, but this sedate community was once a bustling sugar-plantation town. After the mill shut down in 1922, most people left for jobs elsewhere. Today mixed among modest homes, organic farms and back-to-the-landers living off the grid are a scattering of exclusive estates, including the former home of famed aviator Charles Lindbergh.

◉ Sights & Activities

CHARLES LINDBERGH'S GRAVE Gravesite
Charles Lindbergh moved to remote Kipahulu in 1968. Although he relished the privacy he found here, he did occasionally emerge as a spokesperson for conservation issues. When he learned he had terminal cancer, he decided to forgo treatment on the mainland and came home to Maui to live out his final days.

Following his death in 1974, Lindbergh was buried in the graveyard of **Palapala Ho'omau Congregational Church.** The church (c 1864) is also notable for its window painting of a Polynesian Christ draped in the red-and-yellow feather capes that were reserved for Hawaii's highest chiefs.

The Best…
Locavore

1 Laulima Farms (p230)

2 Ono Organic Farms (p229)

3 Hana Fresh (p226)

4 Bruddah Hutt's BBQ (p226)

Lindbergh's desire to be out of the public eye may still be at play; many visitors fail to find his grave, getting the location mixed up with St Paul's Church, which sits on the highway three-quarters of a mile south of 'Ohe'o Gulch. Palapala Ho'omau church is half a mile beyond that.

Charles Lindbergh's grave, a simple granite slate laid upon lava stones, is in the yard behind the church. The inscription reads simply, '...If I take the wings of the morning, and dwell in the uttermost parts of the sea...C.A.L.'

Walk a minute or two past the graveyard to reach a hilltop vantage point with a fine view of the jagged Kipahulu coast – one look and you'll understand why Lindbergh was so taken by this area.

To get to Palapala Ho'omau, turn left at the sign for Maui Stables, which is 0.2 miles south of the 41-mile marker and then veer left after the stables. The church is 0.2 miles further.

TOP CHOICE **MAUI STABLES** Horseback Riding
(☏248-7799; www.mauistables.com; 3hr ride $150; ⏰rides 10am) Ride off into the wilderness on horseback trips that mix breathtaking views with Hawaiian storytelling and chanting – a real cultural immersion experience led by Native Hawaiian cowboys. Among the sights along the way are the thundering waterfalls in the national park. The stable is between the 40- and 41-mile markers.

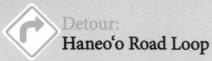

Detour:
Haneo'o Road Loop

Author James Michener was so taken by the coastal sights along this 1.5-mile loop drive that he compared them to the South Pacific. To see what tickled him, take the turnoff onto Haneo'o Rd just before the 50-mile marker.

At the base of a red cinder hill less than a half-mile from the start of the loop, the chocolate-brown sands of **Koki Beach** attract local surfers. The offshore isle topped by a few coconut palms is **'Alau Island**, a seabird sanctuary. Incidentally, those trees are a green refreshment stand of sorts, planted by Hana residents to provide themselves with drinking coconuts while fishing from the island.

A little further is **Hamoa Beach**, whose lovely gray sands are maintained by Hotel Hana-Maui but are open to all. When the surf's up, surfers and boogie boarders flock here, though be aware of rip currents. When seas are calm, swimming is good in the cove. Public access is down the steps just north of the hotel's bus-stop sign. Facilities include showers and restrooms.

TOP CHOICE **ONO ORGANIC FARMS** Farm Tour
(☏248-7779; www.onofarms.com; 90min tours adult/child under 10 $35/free; ⏰1:30pm Mon-Fri) It's hard to imagine a farm as wildly exotic as Ono. The variety is amazing – scores of tropical fruits, the likes of which you've never seen, spices, cocoa and coffee; all of it top rate and grown organically. The tour ends with a generous spread of seasonal tastings. Advance reservations required. The farm is on the inland side of the road just south of the national park.

🍴 Eating

TOP CHOICE **LAULIMA FARMS** Farm Stand **$**
(snacks $3-7; ⏰10:30am-5pm) Pedal power takes on new meaning at this off-the-grid fruit stand (between the 40- and 41-mile markers), where customers take the seat on a stationary bike and rev up enough power to run the blender, juicing their own fruit smoothies. The rest of the operation is powered by solar panels and a generator using recycled vegetable oil. Everything sold here, from the hand-picked organic coffee to the GMO-free veggies, is homegrown. Refreshing in ~y way.

Pi'ilani Highway

The untamed Pi'ilani Hwy (Hwy 31) travels 25 ruggedly scenic miles between Kipahulu and 'Ulupalakua Ranch as it skirts along the southern flank of Haleakalā.

Diehards will love this road, while the more timid may wonder what they've gotten themselves into in these lonesome boonies. Signs such as 'Motorists assume risk of damage due to presence of cattle' and 'Safe speed 10mph' give clues that this is not your typical highway.

The road winds like a drunken cowboy but most of it is paved. The trickiest section is around Kaupo, where the road is rutted. Depending on when it was last graded, you can usually make it in a regular car, though it may rattle your bones a bit. But after hard rains, streams flow over the road, making passage difficult, if not dangerous.

Flash floods occasionally wash away portions of the road, closing down the highway until it's repaired. The **Kipahulu Visitor Center** (☏248-7375) at 'Ohe'o Gulch can tell you whether or not the road is open.

The best way to approach the drive is with an early-morning start, when the road is so quiet you'll feel like the last soul on earth. Pack something to eat and plenty to drink, and check your oil and spare tire before setting out. It's a long haul to civilization if you break down – gas stations and other services are nonexistent between Hana and the Upcountry.

KAUPO

Near the 35-mile marker you'll reach Kaupo, a scattered community of *paniolo*, many of them fourth-generation ranch hands working at Kaupo Ranch. As the only lowlands on this section of coast, Kaupo was once heavily settled and is home to several ancient heiau (temples) and two 19th-century churches. However, don't expect a developed village in any sense of the word. The sole commercial venture on the entire road is **Kaupo Store** (☎ 248-8054; ⏰ 10am-5pm Mon-Sat), which sells snacks and drinks and is worth popping inside just to see the vintage displays lining the shelves – it's like stepping back to your grandmother's days.

Kaupo's prettiest site, the whitewashed **Hui Aloha Church** (1859), sits above the black-sand **Mokulau Beach**, an ancient surfing site.

KAUPO TO 'ULUPALAKUA RANCH

Past Kaupo village, you'll be rewarded with striking views of **Kaupo Gap**, the southern opening in the rim of majestic Haleakalā. Near the 31-mile marker a short 4WD road runs down to **Nu'u Bay**, favored by locals for fishing and swimming. If you're tempted to hit the water, stay close to shore, as riptides inhabit the open ocean beyond.

Just east of the 30-mile marker you'll see two gateposts that mark the path to dramatic **Huakini Bay**. Park at the side of the highway and walk down the rutted dirt

drive. It takes just a couple of minutes to reach this rock-strewn beach whipped by violent surf. After the 29-mile marker, keep an eye out for a natural lava **sea arch** that's visible from the road.

At the 19-mile marker the road crosses a vast **lava flow** dating from 1790, Haleakalā's last-gasp eruption. This flow, part of the Kanaio Natural Area Reserve, is the same one that covers the La Pérouse Bay area. It's still black and barren all the way down to the sea.

Just offshore is Kaho'olawe and on a clear day you can even see the Big Island popping its head up above the clouds. It's such a wide-angle view that the ocean horizon is noticeably curved. You'll wonder how anyone could ever have thought the world was flat!

As you approach 'Ulupalakua Ranch, groves of fragrant eucalyptus trees replace the drier, scrubbier terrain and you find yourself back in civilization at Tedeschi Vineyards. Cheers!

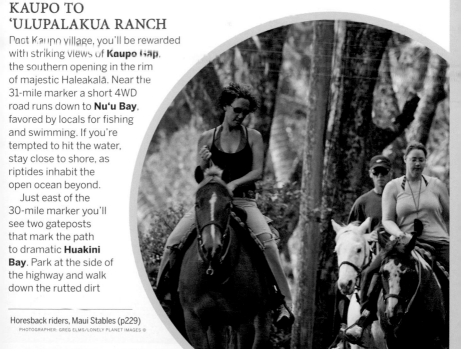

Horseback riders, Maui Stables (p229)
PHOTOGRAPHER: GREG ELMS/LONELY PLANET IMAGES ©

Side Trips: Lanaʻi & Molokaʻi

Itching to get off the beaten track? Just a skip across the channel, Maui's sister islands of Lanaʻi and Molokaʻi beg exploration.

Both have deep roots in farming, but each has taken a different route towards tourism. Lanaʻi has plowed under its pineapple fields and sprouted two of the most pampering resorts in Hawaii. Molokaʻi, on the other hand, is damn proud of its success at keeping would-be developers at bay. It's barely changed a wink in decades – indeed, its leading tourist attraction remains a mule ride.

But on both of these slow-paced islands you'll find people with time to talk story, wild untouched landscapes and miles of deserted beaches. Arriving in the towns of Lanaʻi City and Kaunakakai is like being transported to another era, free of traffic lights and chain restaurants. Just across the channel from Maui, yes – but a world apart.

Sun setting over Lanaʻi (p236)

233

Lana'i & Moloka'i Itineraries

PAPOHAKU BEACH PARK ⑤

PALA'AU STATE PARK

HO'OLEHUA

⑤

① ⑦ KALAUPAPA PENINSULA

④ ③ ② ② ③

KUALAPU'U KALA'E

KALA'E

MOLOKA'I Halawa ○ Valley

EAST MOLOKA'I

⑧

HULA SHORES ⑥

Kalohi Channel

Pailolo Channel

Maui

GARDEN OF THE GODS ④

KOLOIKI RIDGE TRAIL

③

② ⑤ ④

LANA'I LANA'I CITY

'Au'au Channel

PACIFIC OCEAN

HULOPO'E BEACH ① ①

Two Days

① Hulopo'e Beach (p241) If you have two days for Lana'i, start your first day on the island's most stunning beach. Don a snorkel to fully appreciate the pristine waters with their vibrant coral gardens and colorful tropical fish. Dry off by taking a stroll out to **Pu'u Pehe** to ogle at this rock of legends. If you've got kids, don't miss the cool creatures in the tide pools along the way.

② Lana'i City (p236) In the afternoon, take a stroll around this classic plantation town. Watch the sun set over the majestic pines at Dole Park and then join the friendly islanders dining on local grinds at **Blue Ginger Café**.

③ Koloiki Ridge Trail (p238) Start day two with a hill country walk on this scenic 5-mile trail perched above the Four Seasons Resort Lana'i, The Lodge at Koele, for panoramic views galore.

④ Garden of the Gods (p245) When you're done hiking take a drive or a mountain-bike ride out to these unusual rock formations, which glow eerily in the late afternoon light. On the way back, stroll through **Kanepu'u Preserve**, the last native dryland forest in Hawaii.

⑤ Lana'i City Grille (p239) Grab a seat by the fireplace in this classic century-old dining room and order the best Lana'i fresh fish you'll ever taste.

⊙ THIS LEG: 30 MILES

Four Days

1. **Pala'au State Park** (p257) If you have two days for each island, plan the first two as per the first itinerary. Then fly to Moloka'i and start day three by driving to the end of Hwy 470 to relish the stunning cliff-top view of **Kalaupapa Peninsula** from the lookout. Follow with a sneak peek at Moloka'i's famed phallic rock.

2. **Kala'e** (p256) On the way back get the buzz on Moloka'i's agricultural roots at the **Moloka'i Museum & Cultural Center** in Kala'e.

3. **Kualapu'u** (p256) At lunchtime there's no better place to be than **Kualapu'u Cookhouse**, an old roadhouse serving the island's best food.

4. **Ho'olehua** (p256) Next see what's happening in the homegrown farm biz with a stop at **Purdy's Macadamia Nut Farm** in Ho'olehua.

5. **Papohaku Beach Park** (p260) For a long, solitary walk on a glorious windswept beach make your way to this unfrequented gem on Moloka'i's West End.

6. **Hula Shores** (p250) Cap off the day by toasting the magnificent sunset view with a frosty drink at this oceanfront bar at Hotel Moloka'i. Lucky you if it's a Friday, when the ukuleles come out and hula dancers take to the stage.

7. **Kalaupapa Peninsula** (p257) You've seen the peninsula from the overlook – now it's time to see it up close. On day four hike the switchback trail or take the **Molokai Mule Ride** down to one of the most unusual places in the national park system.

8. **East Moloka'i** (p251) The prettiest darn road in Moloka'i begs a drive in the afternoon. A glimpse of paradisical Halawa Valley is your reward at the end.

● ●

➡ **THIS LEG: 70 MILES**

Lana'i & Moloka'i Highlights

1. **Best Beach: Hulopo'e Beach** (p241) This one's such a beaut that sailboats from Maui bring daytrippers here.

2. **Best View: Kalaupapa Overlook** (p257) Come to this cliffside perch for the most captivating vista in Hawaii.

3. **Best Activity: Molokai Mule Ride** (p260) Trust your life to a mule on a breathtaking switchback trail.

4. **Best Plantation Town: Lana'i City** (p236) Get lost in time in this welcoming 1930s village.

5. **Best Homegrown Farm: Purdy's Macadamia Nut Farm** (p256) Crack open some fun at this sweetly natural family-run operation.

Hulopo'e Beach (p241)
KARL LEHMANN/LONELY PLANET IMAGES ©

Discover Side Trips:
Lana'i & Moloka'i

LANA'I

Once the world's largest pineapple plantation, Lana'i has replaced its pineapples with a crop of wealthy vacationers. Almost all of the island's residents still live in Lana'i City, the old plantation town built during the pineapple heyday. Lana'i's top attraction is gorgeous Hulopo'e Beach at the southern side of the island. Explorers who venture past town will find scores of red-dirt roads, oddball geology, deserted archaeological sites, and acres and acres of solitude.

● Getting There & Around

BOAT

Expeditions (📞661-3756, 800-695-2624; www.go-lanai.com; adult/child one way $30/20) This small ferry, which runs several times a day, is an unbeatable way to island hop between Maui and Lana'i. The boats leave from Lahaina and take an hour to reach Manele Bay. You've got a good chance of seeing dolphins en route.

CAR

Lana'i City Service (📞565-7227, 800-533-7808; 1036 Lana'i Ave, Lana'i City; 🕐7am-7pm) This affiliate of Dollar is the only car-rental company on the island. Expect to pay $140 a day for a 4WD. And you'll need a 4WD to do any serious exploring, since there are only three paved roads outside of Lana'i City.

SHUTTLE

Four Seasons runs a frequent shuttle between its Manele Bay resort, Lana'i City and its Lodge at Koele. Nonhotel guests pay between $5 and $10, depending on the length of trip.

Lana'i City

Don't be fooled by the name of this little place – the nearest real city is an island away! Lana'i City glows with small-town charm: its tin-roofed houses and shops have scarcely changed since the plantation days. It's easy to feel like you've stepped back in time. Walk around, soak up the flavor, catch a crimson sunset over the lofty pine trees...there's something truly special here.

Hulopo'e Beach (p241)

PHOTOGRAPHER: KARL LEHMANN/LONELY PLANET IMAGES ©

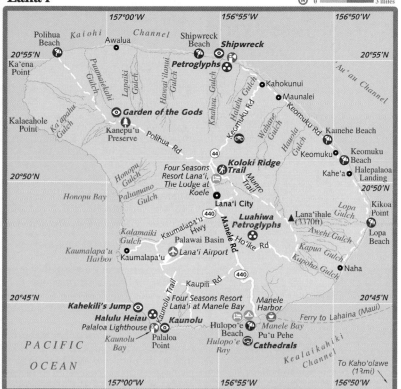

 Sights

'Sights' are pretty light on the ground, but then again the whole town is a sight in itself and fun to stroll around. Start your wanderings at Dole Park, Lana'i City's central green space lined with tall Norfolk Island pines. If you're here on Sunday morning, swing by the **Hawaiian church (cnr Houston & 5th Sts)** to be serenaded with choir music.

TOP CHOICE **LANA'I CULTURE & HERITAGE CENTER** Museum

(www.lanaichc.org; 111 Lana'i Ave; admission free; ☺8:30am-3:30pm Mon-Fri, 9am-1pm Sat) Beautifully revamped, this engaging little museum offers a peek into Lana'i's plantation past. Damn hard work in those pineapple fields!

LUAHIWA PETROGLYPHS Petroglyphs

Lana'i's highest concentration of ancient petroglyphs (stone carvings) are carved into three dozen boulders spread over three dusty acres on a remote slope overlooking the Palawai Basin.

To get to this seldom-visited site, head south from Lana'i City along tree-lined Manele Rd. After 2 miles, look for a cluster of six trees on the left and turn on to the wide dirt road. Stay on this road for 1.2 miles. When you see a house and gate, take a very sharp turn left onto a grass and dirt track for 0.3 miles. The large boulders will be on your right up the hill and there will be a turnout and small stone marker.

Many of the rock carvings are quite weathered, but you can still make out linear and triangular human figures, dogs and a canoe. Other than gusts of wind, the place is eerily quiet. You can almost

Lana'i City

offers sweeping views of remote valleys, Maui and Moloka'i.

The trail begins at the rear of the Lodge at Koele on the paved path that leads to the golf clubhouse. From here, follow the signposted path uphill past Norfolk Island pines until you reach a hilltop bench with a plaque bearing the poem *If* by Rudyard Kipling. Enjoy the view and then continue through the trees until you reach a chain-link fence. Go around the right side of the fence and continue up the hillside toward the power lines. At the top of the pass, follow the trail down through a thicket of guava trees until you reach an abandoned dirt service road, which you'll turn left on to. You'll soon intersect with the Munro Trail; turn right on it and after a few minutes you'll pass Kukui Gulch, named for the candlenut trees that grow here. Continue along the trail until you reach a thicket of tall sisal plants; after about 50yd bear right to reach Koloiki Ridge, where you'll be rewarded with panoramas.

STABLES AT KOELE   Horseback Riding
(☎ 565-4424; rides from $125; ⏱ 7am-5pm) The mainstay is a 1½-hour trail ride with scenic views of Maui and Lana'i. If the *keiki* (children) are ready to cowboy down too, pony rides are available for $25. To get here, turn left on to the dirt road just north of the Four Seasons Resort Lana'i, The Lodge at Koele.

feel the presence of the ancients here – honor their spirits and don't touch the fragile carvings.

Activities

EXPERIENCE AT KOELE   Golf
(☎ 565-4653; www.golfonlanai.com; fees $210-225; ⏱ 8am-6:30pm) Curving around the Four Seasons Resort Lana'i, The Lodge at Koele, this Greg Norman–branded course offers world-class golfing with knockout vistas. The front nine meanders through parklike settings; the signature 17th hole drops 200ft to a tree-shrouded gorge.

KOLOIKI RIDGE TRAIL   Hiking
This 5-mile return hike leads up to one of the most scenic parts of the Munro Trail. It takes about three hours' return and

Festivals & Events

Pineapple Festival   Festival
(www.visitlanai.net) Lana'i's main bash is held on the first weekend in July to celebrate the island's pineapple past with local grinds (food), games and live music at Dole Park.

 Sleeping

TOP **HOTEL LANA'I**   Hotel   **$$**
CHOICE (565-7211; www.hotellanai.com; 828 Lana'i Ave; r $100-160, cottage $190) From 1923 to 1990, the Hotel Lana'i was the only hotel on the island. Little has changed at the hotel over the decades. The 10 immaculately renovated rooms have hardwood floors, antiques, pedestal sinks, patchwork quilts and other period pieces. Go for a room with – appropriately – a lanai (veranda) for viewing town.

FOUR SEASONS RESORT LANA'I, THE LODGE AT KOELE   Resort   **$$$**
(Map p237; 565-3800, 800-321-4666; www. fourseasons.com/koele; 1 Keomuku Rd; r from $200; ✻ @ 🛜 🛋) Set on a rise above town, this pampering lodge affects the aristocratic demeanor of an English country estate, complete with afternoon tea, lawn bowling and croquet. The 'great hall' lobby brims with antiques and boasts Hawaii's two largest stone fireplaces.

DREAMS COME TRUE   B&B   **$$**
(565-6961, 800-566-6961; www.dreams cometruelanai.com; 1168 Lana'i Ave; r incl breakfast $130; @ 🛜) This spruced-up plantation house fuses antiques-laden charm with cozy comforts such as whirlpool baths. Guests have access to a well-equipped kitchen and the yard abounds with fruit just waiting to be picked. The owners can help you arrange activities and car rentals.

 Eating

TOP **LANA'I CITY GRILLE**   Fusion   **$$$**
CHOICE (565-7211; www.hotellanai.com; Hotel Lana'i, 828 Lana'i Ave; mains $28-40; ⏱5-9pm Wed-Sun) With a menu created by famed Maui chef Bev Gannon, you'll find Lana'i's finest fare at this century-old hotel. Sturdy 1930s schoolhouse furnishings

Lana'i City Grille

HOTEL LANAI

give the fireplaced dining room a vintage air, while the dishes feature fresh local seafood and organic meats in ways both familiar and surprising. The bar pours a fine highball and on Friday night live Hawaiian music draws a crowd.

TOP CHOICE **BLUE GINGER CAFÉ**   Cafe   **$**
(www.bluegingercafelanai.com; 409 7th St; breakfast & lunch $5-8, dinner $8-15; ⏱6am-8pm) If you need to quiet a growling stomach, or are just looking for a tasty pastry, this friendly bakery-cafe will fill the bill. Don't be put off by the cement floors and plastic chairs – the food here is first-rate. For the local favorite, order the panko-crusted chicken.

PELE'S OTHER GARDEN   Italian   **$$**
(cnr 8th & Houston Sts; lunch $5-9, dinner $10-20; ⏱11am-3pm & 5-8pm Mon-Sat) The talented kitchen leans Italian and serves up crispy thin-crust pizza, first-rate pesto and salads made with Lana'i-grown organic greens. There's a fine beer list, although last call in the tiny bar area is 8pm. Grab one of the tables out on the front lanai and watch the traffic trickle by.

CANOES LANA'I   Hawaiian   **$**
(419 7th St; meals $5-12; ⏱6:30am-1pm Thu, Sun-Tue, 6.30am-8pm Fri & Sat) Breakfast is always on the menu at this old-time Hawaiian cafe that is little changed since pineapple pickers filled the tables. The banana pancakes are sublime and best enjoyed at the counter. The best-seller? *Loco moco* (rice, fried egg and hamburger topped with gravy). Teriyaki figures prominently on the new dinner menu.

 **Shopping**

Shops and galleries encircle Dole Park, so stroll around and see what catches your fancy.

Mike Carroll Gallery   Art
(www.mikecarrollgallery.com; cnr 7th & Ko'ele Sts) Art lovers love this gallery, where you can find the eponymous owner either creating a new masterpiece or displaying the work of other artists.

ⓘ Information

Bank of Hawaii (460 8th St) Has a 24-hour ATM.

Lana'i Community Hospital (☏565-6411; 628 7th St) Offers 24-hour emergency medical services.

Post office (620 Jacaranda St)

Manele Bay & Hulopo'e Beach

To snorkel, dive or just spend a day at the beach, head straight to these adjacent bays, 8 miles south of Lana'i City. Crescent-shaped Manele Harbor provides a protected anchorage for sailboats and other small craft. From the harbor, it's just a 10-minute walk to Hulopo'e Beach.

Hulopo'e Beach
PHOTOGRAPHER: KARL LEHMANN/LONELY PLANET IMAGES ©

Lana'i Surf Beaches & Breaks *Jake Howard*

When it comes to surfing, Lana'i doesn't enjoy quite the bounty of waves as some of the other islands. Because rain clouds get trapped in the high peaks of Maui and Moloka'i there's very little rain on Lana'i, and thus far fewer reef passes have been carved out by runoff.

On the south shore the most consistent surf comes in around the **Manele Point** area, where the main break peels off the tip of Manele and into Hulopo'e Bay. Shallow reef and submerged rocks make this a dangerous spot at low tide or in smaller surf conditions; it's probably ideal on a double overhead swell. Not too far away from here, located in front of a deserted old Hawaiian settlement, is a spot called **Naha** (also known as Stone Shack). It offers a fun two-way peak, but does close out when it gets bigger.

Across the island, the north shore's wide-open **Polihua Beach** is the longest and widest sandy beach on Lana'i. Be careful of the current here, affectionately dubbed 'the Tahitian Express.' The water flowing between Moloka'i and Lana'i in the Kalohi Channel has driven many a ship into the reef, and it could easily take you on a trip to Tahiti if you're not careful.

Manele and Hulopo'e Bays are part of a marine-life conservation district that prohibits the removal of coral and restricts many fishing activities, all of which makes for great snorkeling and diving.

 Beaches

TOP CHOICE **HULOPO'E BEACH** Beach

Lana'i may have only one easy-access beach, but what a beauty it is. This gently curving white-sand beach is long, broad and protected by a rocky point to the south. Everybody loves it – locals taking the kids for a swim, tourists on daytrips from Maui and the spinner dolphins who frequent the bay during the early morning hours.

For the best **snorkeling**, head to the left side of the bay, where there's an abundance of coral, large parrotfish and other colorful tropicals. To the left just beyond the sandy beach, you'll find a low lava shelf with **tide pools** worth exploring. Here, too, is a protected shoreline **splash pool** ideal for children, with cement steps leading down to it. The park has full facilities, including picnic tables, solar-heated showers and restrooms.

 **Sights & Activities**

PU'U PEHE Natural Feature

From Hulopo'e Beach, a short path leads south to the end of the point that separates Hulopo'e and Manele Bays. The point is actually a volcanic cinder cone that's sharply eroded, exposing rich rust-red colors with swirls of gray and black. Its texture is bubbly and brittle – so brittle that huge chunks of the point have broken off and fallen onto the coastal shelf below.

Pu'u Pehe is the name of the cove left of the point as well as the rocky islet just offshore. This islet, also called Sweetheart's Rock, has a tomb-like formation on top that figures into Hawaiian legend.

It's said that an island girl named Pehe was so beautiful that her lover decided to make their home in a secluded coastal cave, lest any other young men in the village set eyes on her. One day when he was up in the mountains fetching water, a storm suddenly blew in. By the time he

241

rushed back down, powerful waves had swept into the cave, drowning Pehe. The lover carried Pehe's body to the top of Pu'u Pehe, where he erected a tomb and laid her to rest. Immersed in grief, he then jumped into the surging waters below and was thrown back onto the rock, joining his lover in death.

MANELE HARBOR Harbor

This is the jumping-off point for tourists coming from Maui on the ferry or a snorkeling cruise. All the real thrills here are beneath the surface. Coral is abundant near the cliff sides, where the bottom quickly slopes off to about 40ft. Beyond the bay's western edge is **Cathedrals**, the island's most spectacular dive site with arches and grottos galore.

Challenge at Manele Golf

(☎565-2222; Four Seasons Resort Lana'i at Manele Bay, Manele Bay Rd; guests/nonguests $210/225; ⏰7am-6:30pm) This Jack Nicklaus–branded course offers spectacular play along seaside cliffs. The 12th hole challenges golfers to hit across a fairway that is really the ocean's surf.

 Sleeping

FOUR SEASONS RESORT LANA'I AT MANELE BAY Resort **$$$**

(☎565-2000; www.fourseasons.com/manele bay; 1 Manele Bay Rd; r from $400; ❄️ 📶 🏊 👪) Of the two island resorts on offer, this one screams – well, stage-whispers – 'Hawaii vacation!' Although the decor's slightly overstuffed and frumpy, the views of the azure waters, the surrounds of the vast pool and the Asian-themed soaring lobbies are entrancing.

HULOPO'E BEACH CAMPING Camping **$**

(☎565-3319; Castle & Cooke, 111 Lana'i Ave, Lana'i City; per night $10) Camping is allowed on the lawn above Hulopo'e Beach. Call to reserve one of the eight spots and make arrangements to pick up a permit. There's typically a three-night maximum stay.

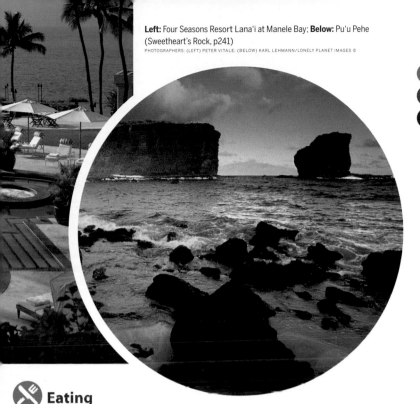

Eating

HULOPO'E COURT　　American **$$$**
(Four Seasons Resort Lana'i at Manele Bay,
Manele Bay Rd; mains $28-40; ⏰7-11am &
6-9;30pm) Overlooking the ocean, this
restaurant offers a bountiful breakfast
buffet but not quite as lavish as the $32
price implies. Dinner, the more interest-
ing choice, emphasizes fresh seafood.

Keomuku Road

The best drive on Lana'i is the stretch of
Keomuku Rd (Hwy 44) that heads north
from Lana'i City into cool upland hills
where fog drifts above grassy pastures.
As the road gently slopes down to the
coast, the scenery is punctuated by
peculiar rock formations sitting atop the
eroded red earth, similar to those at Gar-
den of the Gods (p245). Further along, a
shipwreck comes into view. After 8 miles,
the paved road ends near the coast.

Shipwreck Beach

This windswept stretch of sand extends
9 miles along Lana'i's northeast shore.
The beach takes its name from the many
ships that its tricky reef has snared.
You'll find lots of sun-bleached driftwood,
some pieces still bearing witness to their
past – hulls, side planks, perhaps even a
gangplank with a little imagination.

Take the dirt road north from the end
of Hwy 44, park about half a mile in and
then walk down to the beach. It's likely
to be just you and the driftwood. After
walking north for about a mile, you'll
reach a lava-rock point where you'll
see the cement foundation of a former
lighthouse. From here you'll get a good
view of a rusting **WWII liberty cargo
ship** that's wrecked on the reef. From the
lighthouse foundation, a trail leads inland
about 100yd to a cluster of **petroglyphs**.
The simple figures are etched into large
boulders on the right side of the path.

The lighthouse site is the turn-around point for most people but it's possible to walk another 6 miles all the way to **Awalua**, if you enjoy desolate walks without another person in sight. The hike is windy, hot and dry (bring water!).

South to Naha

This stretch of Keomuku Rd, a bumpy 4WD-only dirt road that heads southward from the end of Hwy 44 to Naha, is best suited for true diehards seeking an adventure. It's a barren stretch with a few marginal historical sites, scattered groves of coconuts and lots of kiawe trees. Keomuku Rd is likely to be either dusty or muddy, but if you catch it after it's been graded, it's drivable. Going the full 12 miles to Naha, at the end of the road, can take as long as two hours one way when the road is rough.

About 5.5 miles down is **Keomuku**, the former site of a short-lived sugarcane plantation. There's little left to see other than an old Hawaiian church and a century-old locomotive abandoned when the sugarcane company went broke in 1901.

Halepalaoa Landing, 2 miles south of Keomuku, was the site of a wharf used to ship the sugarcane to Maui. Another 4 miles brings you to **Naha**, which is the end of the road. With the wind whistling in your ears, it's an otherworldly place that seems utterly incongruous, given the view of developed Maui just across the waters.

Polihua Road

Polihua Rd starts near the stables at the Four Seasons Resort Lana'i, The Lodge at Koele. The stretch as far as the Garden of the Gods is a fairly good route that takes about 20 minutes from town. To travel onward to Polihua Beach is another matter, however; the road to the beach is rocky and suitable only for a 4WD. Depending on road conditions the trip could take anywhere from 20 minutes to an hour.

  Sights

KANEPU'U PRESERVE   Preserve
The 590-acre Kanepu'u Preserve, overseen by the Nature Conservancy, is the last native dryland forest of its kind in Hawaii. Five miles northwest of Lana'i City, the forest is home to 49 species of rare native plants, including endangered Hawaiian sandalwood. You'll get a close-up look at many of them on the short, self-guided interpretive trail.

GARDEN OF THE GODS
Natural Feature
Think rocks, not green gardens. Instead of flowers you'll find a barren landscape of strange wind-sculpted rocks in ocher, pink and sienna. Many have strange shapes that stand out against the seemingly martian landscape and you may expect the little Mars Explorer probe to come buzzing past.

Garden of the Gods
PHOTOGRAPHER: ANN CECIL/LONELY PLANET IMAGES ©

It's utterly silent up here and you can see up to four other islands across the white-capped waters. The colors change with the light – pastel in the early morning, rich hues in the late afternoon. How godly the garden appears depends on your perspective. Some people just see rocks, while others find the formations hauntingly beautiful.

POLIHUA BEACH   Beach
Polihua means 'eggs in the bosom' and this broad, 1.5-mile-long white-sand beach at the northwestern tip of the island takes its name from the green sea turtles that nest here. Although the beach itself is gorgeous, strong winds kicking up the sand often make it uncomfortable, and water conditions can be treacherous.

Munro Trail

This 12-mile adventure through verdant forest can be hiked, mountain biked or negotiated in a 4WD. For the best views, get an early start. Those hiking or biking should be prepared for steep grades and allow a whole day. If you're driving and the dirt road has been graded recently, give yourself two to three hours. However, be aware that rains turn the dirt into a red colored swamp that claims many a 4WD. Watch out for sheer drop-offs.

To start, head north on Hwy 44. About a mile past the Four Seasons Resort Lana'i, The Lodge at Koele, turn right onto the paved road that ends in half a mile at the island's **cemetery**. The Munro Trail starts left of the cemetery, passing through eucalyptus groves and climbing the ridge where the path is studded with Norfolk Island pines. These trees, a species that draws moisture from the afternoon clouds and fog, were planted in the 1920s as a watershed by naturalist George Munro, after whom the trail is named.

The trail looks down on deep ravines cutting across the east flank of the mountain, and passes **Lana'ihale** (3370ft), Lana'i's highest point. On a clear day, you can see all the inhabited Hawai'i Islands (except for distant Kaua'i and Ni'ihau) along the route. Stay on the main trail, descending 6 miles to the central

plateau. Keep the hills to your left and turn right at the big fork in the road. The trail ends back on Manele Rd (Hwy 440) between Lana'i City and Manele Bay.

Kaumalapa'u Highway

Kaumalapa'u Hwy (Hwy 440) connects Lana'i City to the airport before ending at Kaumalapa'u Harbor.

 Sights

KAUNOLU   Ancient Village
Perched on a majestic bluff at the southwestern tip of the island, the ancient fishing village of Kaunolu thrived until its abandonment in the mid-19th century. Now overgrown and all but forgotten, Kaunolu boasts the largest concentration of stone ruins on Lana'i, including **Halulu Heiau**. Northwest of the heiau (temple), a natural stone wall runs along the sea cliff. Look for a break in the wall at the cliff's edge, where there's a sheer 80ft drop known as **Kahekili's Jump**. In days past, Kamehameha the Great would test the courage of upstart warriors by having them make a death-defying leap from this spot.

To get to Kaunolu, follow Kaumalapa'u Hwy (Hwy 440) 0.6 miles past the airport, turning left onto a partial gravel and dirt

The Best...
Hawaiian Eats

1 Lana'i City Grille (p239)

2 Kualapu'u Cookhouse (p256)

3 Mana'e Goods & Grindz (p254)

4 Aunty Ruby's Cafe (p250)

5 Blue Ginger Café (p240)

road that runs south through abandoned pineapple fields for 2.2 miles. A carved stone marks the turn onto a much rougher but still 4WD-capable road down to the sea. After 2.5 miles you'll see a sign for a short **interpretive trail**, which has well-weathered signs explaining the history of Kaunolu. Another 0.3 mile brings you to a parking area amid the ruins.

MOLOKA'I

According to ancient chants, Moloka'i is a child of Hina, goddess of the moon. Sparsely populated, mostly by Native Hawaiians, Moloka'i is untouched by packaged tourism. People here are proud of their agricultural roots and their steadfast resistance to off-island developers who'd like to turn oceanside ranchland into million-dollar homes. This is a place to get in touch with the basics. In the morning you can sit on the edge of an 800-year-old fishpond and watch the sun rise over Haleakalā on distant Maui. In the evening you can watch the sun set behind the silhouette of Moloka'i's royal coconut grove.

Getting There & Around

AIR

Moloka'i (Ho'olehua) Airport (MKK) The island's main airport.

Pacific Wings (☎888-575-4546; www.pacificwings.com) These prop planes typically provide the cheapest flights between Maui and Moloka'i and can cost less than the ferry.

CAR

Renting a car is essential if you intend to fully explore the island. All of Moloka'i's highways and primary routes are good, paved roads, but some of the out-of-the-way sites, such as Kamakou Preserve, will require a 4WD. Keep in mind that rental cars can be in short supply, so book in advance.

Alamo Rental Car (☎800-462-5266; www.alamo.com) The sole operator at the airport.

Island Kine Auto Rental (☎553-5242; www.molokai-car-rental.com) A local outfit, offering a full range of vehicles at good rates. Pick-ups can be arranged from the ferry dock and airport.

Kapua'iwa Coconut Grove

SEA

Moloka'i Ferry (866-307-6524; www.molokaiferry.com; adult/child 4-12 $59/30) Runs a morning and late-afternoon ferry between Lahaina on Maui and Moloka'i's Kaunakakai Wharf. The 90-minute crossing through the Pailolo Channel can get choppy. Buy tickets online, by phone or on the *Moloka'i Princess* a half-hour before departure.

 Information

Exploring unmarked roads on Moloka'i is not advisable. Folks aren't too keen on strangers cruising around on their private turf and can get churlish. On the other hand, if there's a fishpond you want to see, and someone's house is between the road and the water, it's usually easy to strike up a conversation and get permission to cross. If you're lucky they might even share a little local lore and history with you, particularly the old-timers.

For the latest scoop on island happenings, check the website of **Molokai Dispatch** (www.themolokaidispatch.com), the island's weekly newspaper.

Kaunakakai

View a photo of Moloka'i's main town from 50 years ago and the main drag won't look much different than it does today. Worn wood-fronted buildings with tin roofs that roar in the rain seem like refugees from a Clint Eastwood western. But there's no artifice to Kaunakakai – it's the real deal. It's pure local – no chain restaurants, no stoplights and more pickup trucks than cars. As a popular T-shirt reads 'Moloka'i traffic jam: Two drivers stopped in the middle of the road talking story.'

⊙ Sights

KAUNAKAKAI WHARF   Wharf
The days when pineapples were loaded here are gone, but the harbor still hums. Kaunakakai has no swimmable beach, but a roped-off area with a floating dock provides a swim area. On the west side of the wharf, near the canoe shed, are the overgrown stone foundations of **King Kamehameha V's summer house**.

The Best... Moloka'i Views

KAPUA'IWA COCONUT GROVE   Grove
Standing tall about a mile west of downtown is this 10-acre grove planted by King Kamehameha V. Be careful where you park when you visit, because coconuts frequently plunge silently to the ground, landing with a deadly thump.

CHURCH ROW   Churches
Across from the coconut grove is Church Row, where churches are lined up like ducks in a row. Any denomination that attracts a handful of members receives its own little tract of land here.

🏃 Activities

The downtown **softball** and **baseball** fields are perhaps the most active spots on the island. For some local flavor, go down and cheer on the Moloka'i Farmers as they compete against their high-school rivals, the Lana'i Pinelads.

Moloka'i Fish & Dive   Watersports
(553-5926; www.molokaifishanddive.com; 61 Ala Malama Ave; ⏰8am-6pm Mon-Sat, to 2pm Sun) For activities on Moloka'i, these are the folks to see. It can arrange kayaking trips ($70) and scuba diving ($140) and rents all sorts of gear.

Molokai Bicycle   Cycling
(553-3931; www.molokaibicycle.com; 80 Mohala St; bike per day from $20; ⏰3-6pm Wed, 9am-2pm Sat, or by appointment) The place to rent mountain bikes and road bikes.

Moloka'i

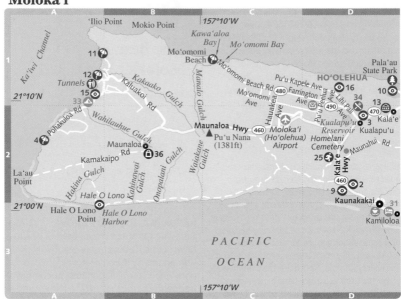

 Festivals & Events

Ka Moloka'i Makahiki — Festival
(www.visitmolokai.com) Moloka'i's biggest annual event is the celebration of the ancient *makahiki* festival (a big winter harvest festival dedicated to the agricultural god Lono). It takes place in January with Olympics-esque competitions of ancient Hawaiian sports, crafts and activities.

Moloka'i Ka Hula Piko — Hula Festival
(www.molokaievents.com/kahulapiko) Moloka'i's hula festival takes place in May with hula performances, food and crafts.

 Sleeping

HOTEL MOLOKA'I — Hotel $$
(553-5347, 800-535-0085; www.hotelmolokai. com; Kamehameha V Hwy; r $140-250;) Moloka'i's only hotel has a certain veteran feel about it, although some would say it is shell-shocked. It's not especially

alluring given the quirky rooms with a faux-native design that gives them tunnel-like qualities. Upstairs rooms are slightly larger and brighter.

MOLOKA'I SHORES — Condo $$
(553-5954, 800-535-0085; www.castle resorts.com; Kamehameha V Hwy; 1br $125-200;) This 1970s condo development has units ranging from atrocious to charming, depending on the whims of the individual owners. If you decide to stay here, choose your unit carefully.

KA HALE MALA — B&B $
(553-9009; www.molokai-bnb.com; apt incl breakfast $100;) Enjoy the spaciousness of a 900-sq-ft, one-bedroom apartment amid lush plantings, including trees laden with low-hanging fruit. The owners add to the bounty with organic vegetables and healthy breakfasts. It's about 5 miles east of Kaunakakai.

DISCOVER SIDE TRIPS: LANA'I & MOLOKA'I MOLOKA'I

248

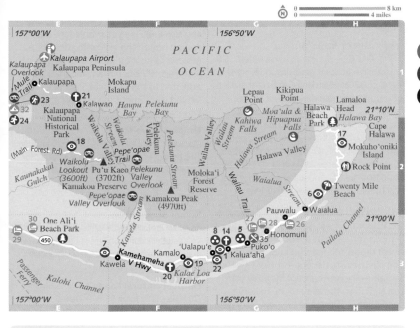

Moloka'i

◎ Sights

Activities, Courses & Tours

🏠 Sleeping

⊗ Eating

Drinking

🛍 Shopping

Eating

AUNTY RUBY'S CAFE
TOP CHOICE   Hawaiian $$

(www.auntyrubys.com; Ala Malama Ave; mains $8-14; ⏰6:30am-9pm Mon-Sat) Bright smiles light up the simple dining area at this family-run place. Think Hawai'i classics such as *loco moco* (dish of rice, fried egg and hamburger patty), roast pork, and hamburger steak as well as treats with influences as diverse as Asia and Portugal. Soup and salad specials are mighty fine and breakfast will do you 'til dinner.

KANEMITSU BAKERY   Bakery $
(Ala Malama Ave; ⏰5:30am-6:30pm Wed-Mon) Famous throughout the islands for its sweet bread and macnut lavosh crackers. The pastries are decent too. Here's a local secret: every night except Monday you can slip down the alley to the bakery's back door at 10pm and buy loaves of hot bread fresh from the oven.

MAKA'S KORNER   Cafe $
(cnr Mohala St & Alohi St; meals $5-8; ⏰7am-4pm Mon-Sat) Fine yet simple fare that is served hot off the grill onto your plate. Moloka'i's best burgers come with excellent fries, although many locals are simply addicted to the teri-beef. Pancakes are served throughout the day. Sit at the counter or at a picnic table outside.

Molokai Drive-Inn   Fast Food $
(Kamehameha V Hwy; meals $4-7; ⏰6am-10pm) This timeless fast-food counter is popular for classic plate lunches and simple local pleasures such as teri-beef sandwiches, omelettes with Spam and fried saimin noodles.

Kamoi Snack-N-Go   Ice Cream $
(Moloka'i Professional Bldg, Kamoi St; cones $3; ⏰10am-9pm Mon-Sun) This shop sells Hawaii-made ice cream in tropical flavors including banana fudge and mango.

Outpost Natural Foods   Market $
(70 Makaena Pl; lunch $5-8; ⏰9am-6pm Mon-Thu, to 4pm Fri, 10am-5pm Sun; 🍴) Not only a health food store, but a lunchtime deli with vegetarian burritos, salads and smoothies.

Friendly Market   Grocery
(Ala Malama Ave; ⏰8:30am-8:30pm Mon-Fri, to 6:30pm Sat) Moloka'i's best supermarket.

🍷 Drinking & Entertainment

HULA SHORES
TOP CHOICE   Open-air Bar

(Map p248; Hotel Moloka'i, Kamehameha V Hwy) Hands down the best place to have a sunset drink is the oceanfront bar at the Hotel Moloka'i. It's also the most likely spot to find someone strumming a ukulele or guitar after dark. Local *kapuna* (elders) gather around a table to play

Cocktail, Hotel Moloka'i (p248)

Kaunakakai

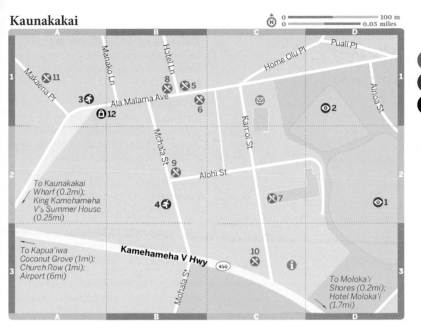

Kaunakakai

Hawaiian music on 'Aloha Fridays' from 4pm to 6pm – don't miss it.

 **Shopping**

MOLOKA'I ART FROM
THE HEART   Gallery
(64 Ala Malama Ave; ⏱9:30am-5pm Mon-Fri, 9am-2:30pm Sat) Run by local artists, this small shop is packed with works in all mediums, ranging from the earnest to the superb. The T-shirts with local sayings are the real sleepers in the souvenir department.

ⓘ Information

Bank of Hawaii (Ala Malama Ave) One of many locations with ATMs.

Moloka'i General Hospital (280 Puali St; ⏱24hr) Emergency services.

Moloka'i Mini Mart (Mohala St; internet per min 8¢; ⏱6am-11pm; @) Convenience store with internet access.

Moloka'i Visitors Association (MVA; ☎553-3876, 800-800-6367; www.gohawaii.com/molokai; 2 Kamoi St; ⏱9am-noon Mon-Fri) Stop here for tourist information.

Driving Distances & Times

Average driving times and distances from Kaunakakai are listed below.

DESTINATION	MILES	TIME
Halawa Valley	27	1¼ hours
Hoʻolehua Airport	6.5	10 minutes
Kalaupapa Trailhead	10	20 minutes
Maunaloa	17	30 minutes
Papohaku Beach	21.5	45 minutes
Pukoʻo	16	20 minutes
Twenty Mile Beach	20	40 minutes

Post office (Ala Malama Ave) Molokaʻi's main post office.

ⓘ Getting There & Around

Kaunakakai is a walking town.

Rawlin's Chevron (cnr Hwy 460 & Ala Malama Ave; ⏲ 6:30am-8:30pm Mon-Sat, 7am-6pm Sun) Has credit card–operated pumps, making it the only round-the-clock gas station on the island.

East Molokaʻi

The 27-mile road from Kaunakakai to Halawa Valley edges alongside the ocean for much of the drive, with the mountains of east Molokaʻi rising up to the north. It's all achingly pastoral, with small homes tucked into the valleys, horses grazing at the side of the road and silver waterfalls dropping down the mountainsides. There's no gas after Kaunakakai, so check your gauge before setting out.

Kawela to Kaluaʻaha
⊙ Sights

KAKAHAIA BEACH PARK   Beach
In Kawela you'll pass this beach park, a grassy strip wedged between the road and sea, shortly before the 6-mile marker. The park is the only part of the **Kakahaia National Wildlife Refuge** (www.fws.gov/kakahaia) open to the public. Most of the refuge is marshland inland from the road.

ST JOSEPH'S CHURCH   Church
Kamalo, a small roadside village 10 miles east of Kaunakakai, is home to St Joseph's Church. Built by Father Damien in 1876, this simple, one-room wooden church has some of its original wavy glass panes. A lei-draped **statue of Father Damien** and a little cemetery are beside the church.

SMITH-BRONTE LANDING   Historic Site
Three-quarters of a mile past the 11-mile marker, look for a small sign on the *makai* (seaward) side of the road pointing out this spot. A little memorial plaque set among the kiawe trees commemorates the first civilian flight from the US mainland to Hawaii. The two pilots were aiming for Oʻahu, but safely crash-landed on Molokaʻi in 1927.

ʻUALAPUʻE FISHPOND   Fishpond
A half-mile past the 13-mile marker, this impressive fishpond lies on the *makai* side of the road. The fishpond has been restored and restocked with mullet and milkfish, two species that were raised here in ancient times. After this, look to your left for the classic, but long closed, c 1930s **Ah Ping Store** and its old gas pump at the roadside.

KALUAʻAHA   Historic Sites
The ruins of Molokaʻi's first church are next at Kaluaʻaha, off the road and inland but (barely) visible. A quarter of a mile later is **Our Lady of Seven Sorrows Church**, a 1966 reconstruction of an 1874 church built by Father Damien.

ʻIliʻiliʻopae Heiau to Halawa
⊙ Sights & Activities

ʻILIʻILIʻOPAE HEIAU   Ancient Temple
This is Molokaʻi's biggest ancient stone temple and is thought to be the oldest as well. Once used for human sacrifices, its

stones still seem to emanate vibrations of the past. Visiting this heiau is a little tricky, since it's on private property; check with the **Moloka'i Visitors Association** (☏553-3876) for advice on getting permission.

The nearby sleepy backwater of **Puko'o** was once the seat of local government – complete with a courthouse, jail, wharf and post office – until the plantation folks shifted everything to Kaunakakai.

KAHINAPOHAKU FISHPOND Fishpond
This well-tended fishpond is a half-mile past the 19-mile marker. If you want beach over this way, look no further than the 20-mile marker, from where a stretch of white sand called **Twenty Mile Beach** pops up right along the thin roadside. Protected by a reef, the curve of fine sand fronts a large lagoon great for **snorkeling**. Near shore the waters can be very shallow, but work your way out and you'll be rewarded with schools of fish and more.

ROCK POINT Natural Feature
The pointy clutch of rocks sticking out, as the road swings left before the 21-mile marker, is called, appropriately enough,

Rock Point. This popular **surf spot** is the site of local competitions and it's the place to go if you're looking for east-end swells.

After the 21-mile marker, the road starts to wind upwards. It's a good paved road – the problem is there's not always enough of it. In places, including some cliff-hugging curves, this road is wide enough for only one car, so expect to go slow. The road levels out just before the 24-mile marker, where there's a fine view of the islet of **Mokuho'oniki**, a seabird sanctuary.

Pu'u O Hoku Ranch Horseback Riding
(☏558-8109; www.puuohoku.com) One mile from Rock Point brings you to Pu'u O Hoku Ranch. Stop by the ranch store for organic produce or to ask about horseback rides.

 Sleeping

TOP CHOICE **HALE LEI LANI** House **$$$**
(☏415-218-3037, 558-0808; www.tranquilmolokai.com; off Kamehameha V Hwy; from $250; 🛜❄) Perched on a hill near the 16-mile marker, this contemporary home has sweeping ocean views. Two large

Kahinapohaku Fishpond

bedrooms open off a great room and a kitchen that will inspire you to cook. There's a walled pool outside the door and fruit trees drop their bounty in the gardens.

DUNBAR BEACHFRONT COTTAGES
Cottage **$$**

(☎558-8153, 800-673-0520; www.molokai -beachfront-cottages.com; 2br cottage $180) The layout and furnishings are tidy and functional at these two cottages near the 18-mile marker. Each is fitted with a full kitchen, ceiling fans, laundry and a lanai, and sleeps up to four people. The Pu'unana cottage sits on stilts and has delicious sea views.

HILLTOP COTTAGE
Cottage **$$**

(☎558-8161, 336-2076; www.molokaihilltop cottage.com; Kamehameha V Hwy; cottage from $145; @) The wraparound lanai is almost as big as the living space and you can savor the views of the neighbor islands by day or millions of stars by night. There's one nicely furnished bedroom, a full kitchen, laundry facilities and a two-night minimum stay.

 Eating

TOP CHOICE **MANA'E GOODS & GRINDZ**
Hawaiian **$**

(16-mile marker, Kamehameha V Hwy; meals $5-10; ⊙8am-5pm) Even if it wasn't your only option, you'd still want to stop here. The plate lunches are something of a local legend: tender yet crispy chicken katsu, specials such as pork and peas, and standards such as excellent teriyaki burgers. The attached market is small but well stocked.

Halawa Valley

After passing the 25-mile marker, the jungle begins to close in, and the scent of eucalyptus fills the air. There are lots of beep-as-you-go hairpin bends. A quarter of a mile after the 26-mile marker there's a turnoff with a **panoramic view** of Halawa Valley and Moa'ula and Hipuapua Falls.

At the end of the road, **Halawa Beach Park** was a favored surfing spot for Moloka'i chiefs. The beach has double coves separated by a rocky outcrop. When the water is calm, there's good swimming, but both coves are subject to dangerous rip currents, especially in high surf or when Halawa Stream, which empties into the north cove, is flowing heavily.

Halawa Bay

Moloka'i Surf Beaches & Breaks *Jake Howard*

What Moloka'i possesses in beauty (it's one of the most breathtaking islands in Hawaii if not the entire pacific) it lacks in waves. Unfortunately, due to shadowing from the other Islands, there just isn't much in the way of consistent surf. Yet when the surf's up, keep in mind that the Friendly Isle encompasses the ideals of 'old Hawaii' in which family remains the priority, so remember to smile a lot and let the locals have the set waves.

On the western end of Moloka'i, winter swells bring surf anywhere between 2ft and 10ft (and, very rarely, 15ft). The break known as **Hale O Lono** is one such exposed area. It comprises several fun peaks and is the starting point for the annual Moloka'i-to-O'ahu outrigger and paddleboard races. On central Moloka'i's north shore, there are decent waves to be had at **Mo'omomi Bay**. Being an archaeological site, entry into the area is dependent on approval from the Department of Hawaiian Home Lands. For information ask at the airport when you arrive. **Tunnels**, south of Kepuhi Beach to the west, is a popular break for bodysurfing and boogie boarding, and is also the only sand-bottom spot on the island.

Central Moloka'i

Central Moloka'i takes in Mo'omomi Beach, the former plantation town of Kualapu'u and the forested interiors of Kamakou Preserve. On the remote north end of it all is Kalaupapa Peninsula, Hawaii's infamous leprosy colony.

The most trodden route in central Moloka'i is the drive up Hwy 470, past the coffee plantation, restored sugar-mill museum, mule stables and the trailhead down to Kalaupapa Peninsula. The road ends at Pala'au State Park.

Kamakou Area

The mountains that form the spine of Mokola'i's east side reach up to Kamakou, the island's highest peak (4970ft). Few visitors make it up this way. If you're lucky enough to be one of them, you'll be rewarded with stunning views of the island's impenetrable north coast and an opportunity to explore a near-pristine rainforest.

Kamakou is a treasure but not an easily reached one. It's accessed via a narrow rutted dirt road (Maunahui Rd) and you'll need a 4WD. The turnoff for Kamakou begins between the 3- and 4-mile markers on Hwy 460, immediately east of the Manawainui Bridge. The road is marked with a sign for Homelani Cemetery.

 Sights

MOLOKA'I FOREST RESERVE Reserve
The 10-mile drive up to Waikolu Lookout takes about 45 minutes, depending on road conditions. A mile before the lookout you'll find the 19th-century **Sandalwood Pit**, a grassy depression on the left. The pit was dug to the exact measurements of a ship's hold. After being filled with fragrant sandalwood logs, the wood was strapped to the backs of laborers, who hauled it down to the harbor for shipment to China.

Waikolu Lookout (3600ft), just before Kamakou Preserve entrance, offers a breathtaking view of remote Waikolu Valley. If it's been raining recently, waterfalls stream down the sheer cliff sides. Morning is the best time for views, as afternoon trade winds commonly bring clouds.

KAMAKOU PRESERVE Preserve
Hiking back through three million years of evolution on the **Pepe'opae Trail** is

255

Kamakou's star attraction. Crossed by a boardwalk, this undisturbed Hawaiian montane bog is a miniature primeval forest of stunted trees, dwarfed plants and lichens that make it feel like it's the dawn of time. From the trail's end at **Pelekunu Valley Overlook**, you'll be rewarded with a fantastic view of majestic cliffs, and if it's not too cloudy, you'll see the ocean beyond.

To reach the Pepeʻopae Trail from Waikolu Lookout, follow Kamakou's main 4WD road 2.5 miles to the marked trailhead; this makes a nice hour-long forest walk in itself.

A great way to see Kamakou is by joining one of the guided hikes led by the **Nature Conservancy** (📞553-5236; www.nature.org/hawaii; 23 Pueo Pl, Kualapuʻu; tour $25) on the first or second Saturday of every month. Transportation is provided to and from the preserve.

Kualapuʻu

Molokaʻi's second town, Kualapuʻu is a small, spread-out farming community with a pint-sized town center.

Kualapuʻu was a pineapple-plantation town until Del Monte pulled out of Molokaʻi in 1982. In 1991 coffee saplings were planted on the fallow pineapple fields, and now cover some 600 acres beneath the town center.

 Activities

Coffees of Hawaii
Coffee Tastings & Tours (www.coffeesofhawaii.com; cnr Hwys 470 & 490; ⏰7am-5pm Sun-Fri, 8am-8pm Sat) Stop by for samples of its Kualapuʻu-grown coffees or to inquire about tours.

 Eating

TOP CHOICE **KUALAPUʻU COOKHOUSE** Hawaiian $$
(Hwy 490; meals $5-20; ⏰7am-8pm) This old roadhouse serves the island's best food. Breakfasts are huge and feature perfect omelettes. Panko-crusted Monte Cristo sandwiches join the plate-lunch brigade, while at dinner inventive fare such as ahi in lime cilantro sauce or lusciously juicy prime rib star. Beer and wine can be purchased at the grocery across the street.

Hoʻolehua

Hoʻolehua, the dry central plains that separate eastern and western Molokaʻi, is home to a community of Native Hawaiian homesteaders operating small farms.

 Sights

TOP CHOICE **PURDY'S MACADAMIA NUT FARM**
Organic Farm
(www.molokai-aloha.com/macnuts; admission free; ⏰9:30am-3:30pm Mon-Fri, 10am-2pm Sat) The Purdy family runs the best little macadamia nut farm tour in all of Hawaii. Unlike tours on the Big Island that focus on processing,

Post-a-Nut, Hoʻolehua Post Office
PHOTOGRAPHER: NED FRIARY

Post-a-Nut

Why settle for a mundane postcard, or worse an emailed photo of you looking like a tan-lined git, when it comes to taunting folks in the cold climes you've left behind? Instead, send a coconut. Gary, the world-class postmaster of the **Ho'olehua Post Office** (Pu'u Peelua Ave; ⊙8:30am-4pm Mon-Fri), has baskets of them for free. Choose from the oodles of markers and write the address right on the husk. Add a cartoon or two. Imagine the joy when a loved one waits in a long line for a parcel and is handed a coconut! All you pay is the postage – depending on the size of your nut, that'll cost $8 to $13.

Tuddie Purdy takes you into his orchard and personally explains how the nuts grow.

Everything is done in quaint Moloka'i style: you can crack open macadamia nuts on a stone with a hammer and sample macadamia-blossom honey scooped up with slices of fresh coconut. Macadamia nuts (superb!) and honey are for sale.

To get to the farm, turn onto Hwy 490 from Hwy 470. After 1 mile, take a right onto Lihi Pali Ave, just before the high school. The farm is a third of a mile up, on the right.

Mo'omomi Beach

Windswept Mo'omomi Beach, on the western edge of the Ho'olehua Plains, is ecologically unique: it's home to several endangered native plant species and nesting grounds for green sea turtles. Mo'omomi is not lushly beautiful, but windswept, lonely and wild – and that's the appeal. A red-dirt road starts at the end of Farrington Hwy and leads 2.5 miles to the beach.

Mo'omomi Bay, a small sandy beach that is part of Hawaiian Home Lands, is marked by a picnic pavilion. The broad, white-sand beach that people call Mo'omomi is at **Kawa'aloa Bay**, a windy 20-minute walk to the west. Because of the fragile ecology of the dunes, visitors should stay along the beach and on trails only.

 Tours

Nature Conservancy   Guided Hikes
(☎553-5236; www.nature.org/hawaii; 23 Pueo Pl, Kualapu'u; tour $25) Leads guided hikes of Mo'omomi; transportation is provided to and from the preserve. Reservations are required.

Kala'e

⊙ **Sights**

MOLOKA'I MUSEUM & CULTURAL CENTER   Museum
(☎567-6436; adult/child $3.50/2; ⊙10am-2pm Mon-Sat) Four miles northeast of Hwy 460 is the sugar mill built by Rudolph W Meyer, an entrepreneurial German immigrant. Meyer was en route to the California gold rush when he stopped off on the islands, married a member of Hawaiian royalty and landed a tidy bit of property in the process. In 1876 Meyer turned his lands over to sugar and built a mill. Now on the National Register of Historic Places, this restored mill is the last of its kind. The museum includes the sugar mill and intriguing displays of Moloka'i's history.

Pala'au State Park

⊙ **Sights**

KALAUPAPA OVERLOOK   Lookout
Perched on the edge of a 1600ft cliff, this overlook is the highlight of this woodsy park, at the end of Hwy 470. Kalaupapa means 'flat leaf' and the view of the peninsula below is stunning – almost like seeing it from an airplane.

257

KAULEONANAHOA Natural Feature

A five-minute walk in the opposite direction leads to Kauleonanahoa ('the penis of Nanahoa'). Hawaii's premier phallic stone pokes up in a little clearing inside an ironwood grove. Nature has endowed it well, but it's obviously been touched up by human hands. Women who wish to become pregnant leave offerings underneath, and it is said that those who stay overnight return home pregnant.

 Sleeping

Camping is allowed in a grassy field near the park entrance, but keep in mind this is one of the wetter parts of the island. See p318 for permit information.

Kalaupapa National Historical Park

Wildly beautiful and strikingly isolated, Kalaupapa Peninsula is fronted by tumultuous waters and backed by the world's highest sea cliffs. Because of this remoteness, people suffering from leprosy (Hansen's disease) were forced into isolation here. Although the isolation policies were abandoned in 1969, a handful of elderly patients still remain. The remote peninsula is a national historical park that's jointly managed by the Hawaii Department of Health and the **National Park Service** (www.nps.gov/kala).

The mule trail down the *pali* (cliffs) is the only land route to the peninsula. You can hike the 3 miles down the trail but start early to avoid fresh mule dung. The mules start to descend at 8:30am.

History

In 1835 doctors diagnosed Hawaii's first case of leprosy, one of many diseases introduced by foreigners. Alarmed by the spread of the disease, King Kamehameha V signed a law banishing people with leprosy to Kalaupapa Peninsula.

Hawaiians call leprosy *mai ho'oka'awale,* which means 'separating sickness,' a disease all the more dreaded

because it tore families apart. Some patients arrived at the peninsula in boats, whose captains were so terrified of the disease they dropped patients overboard. Those who could, swam to shore; those who couldn't, drowned

Once the afflicted arrived on Kalaupapa Peninsula, there was no way out, not even in a casket. Early conditions were unspeakably horrible and lifespans short.

Father Damien (Joseph de Veuster), a Belgian priest, arrived at Kalaupapa in 1873. He wasn't the first missionary to come, but he was the first to stay. A talented carpenter, he built 300 simple houses, nursed the sick and buried the dead. On average, he buried one person a day. Damien's work inspired others, including Mother Marianne Cope, who stayed 30 years and came to be known as the mother of the hospice movement. Damien died of Hansen's disease in 1889 at the age of 49. In 2009 he became Hawaii's (and America's) first Catholic saint.

Sights

The village looks nearly deserted; the sights you'll see on a tour are mainly cemeteries, churches and memorials. Visitors are not permitted to photograph the residents. But as your guide will tell you, residents are happy to have visitors come to Kalaupapa because it keeps their story from being forgotten.

The park **visitors center** displays period photos of the settlement. On the east side of the peninsula, in Kalawao, is the beautifully set **St Philomena Church**, built in 1872. You can still see where Damien cut open holes in the floor so that the sick, who needed to spit, could attend church without shame. The amazing view from Kalawao offers views of the world's highest **sea cliffs**, towering 3300ft and folding out in successive verdant ripples.

Tours

Molokai Mule Ride Mule Ride
(☎567-6088, 800-567-7550; www.muleride.com; ride $200; ⊘Mon-Sat) This is one of the best-known outings in Hawaii. While the mules move none too quickly, there's a certain thrill in trusting your life to these sure-footed beasts as they descend 1600 feet on the narrowest of switchbacks. Make reservations well in advance. Lunch and the land tour with Damien Tours are included in the rate.

Damien Tours Settlement Tours
(☎567-6171; tours $50; ⊘Mon-Sat) Everyone who comes to Kalaupapa must visit the settlement with this outfit. Make reservations in advance. Tours last 3½ hours; bring your own lunch.

West End

Maunaloa Hwy (Hwy 460) heads west from Kaunakakai, passes Moloka'i Airport and climbs into the high, grassy rangeland of Moloka'i's arid western side.

Maunaloa

If something begins to look a bit contrived here, it is. In the 1990s, Moloka'i Ranch bulldozed the atmospheric old plantation town of Maunaloa, leveling all but a few buildings. New buildings mimicking old, plantation-style homes were erected. This drove up rent and forced out some small businesses, provoking the ire of island residents.

Ironically, the new development is now all but closed. Shuttered are a boutique hotel, luxury beach campsites, a cinema and even the local outlet of KFC.

🔒 Shopping

TOP CHOICE **Big Wind Kite Factory & Plantation Gallery** Gallery
(www.bigwindkites.com; 120 Maunaloa Hwy; ⊘8:30am-5pm Mon-Sat, 10am-2pm Sun) This homespun shop, which makes and sells custom-made kites of all shapes and size, is reason enough to come to Maunaloa. Lessons are available.

West End Beaches

Off Hwy 460 at the 15-mile marker, a road leads down to Moloka'i's best beaches. The beaches are located one after another along the coastal Kaluakoi Rd.

Beaches

TOP CHOICE **PAPOHAKU BEACH PARK** Beach
A beach to die for. The 2.5-mile-long Papohaku Beach could hold the entire population of Moloka'i without getting crowded, although that would be an unlikely scenario. You're more likely to be here all by yourself. So where is everybody? Well, for one, it can be windy, with gusts of sand. But the main drawback is the water itself, which is usu-

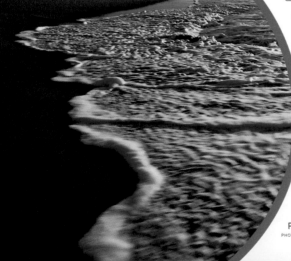

Papohaku Beach Park
PHOTOGRAPHER: JAMES MARSHALL/LONELY PLANET IMAGES ©

Kaho'olawe

Seven miles southwest of Maui, the uninhabited island of Kaho'olawe (also called Kanaloa) has long been central to the Hawaiian-rights movement. Many consider the island a living spiritual entity, *pu'uhonua* (refuge) and *wahi pana* (sacred place).

Yet for nearly 50 years, from WWII to 1990, the US military used Kaho'olawe as a bombing range. Beginning in the 1970s, liberating the island from the military became a rallying point for a resurgence of Native Hawaiian pride. Today, the bombing has stopped, the navy is gone and healing the island is considered both a symbolic act and a concrete expression of Native Hawaiian sovereignty.

Kaho'olawe is 11 miles long and 6 miles wide, with its highest point the 1482ft Luamakika. The island and its surrounding waters are now a reserve that is off-limits to the general public because of the wealth of unexploded ordnance that remains on land and in the sea.

Working with KIRC as official stewards of Kaho'olawe, **Protect Kaho'olawe 'Ohana** (PKO; www.kahoolawe.org) conducts monthly visits to the island to pull weeds, plant native foliage, clean up historic sites and honor the spirits of the land. It welcomes respectful volunteers who are ready to work (not just sightsee). Visits last four days during or near the full moon; volunteers pay a $125 fee, which covers food and transportation to the island. You'll need your own sleeping bag, tent and personal supplies. PKO's website lists details, schedules and contact information.

ally too treacherous for swimming. It is, however, fantastic for long walks.

The beach park is a choice site for **camping** – beautiful and quiet, with the surf lulling you to sleep and the birds waking you up. Full facilities as well. Permits are available through the **Department of Parks & Recreation** (☏553-3204; Mitchell Pauole Center, Kaunakakai; ⏰8am-4pm Mon-Fri).

DIXIE MARU BEACH
Beach

This beach at the end of the road is the most protected cove on the west shore, and the most popular swimming area in Moloka'i. Consequently there are usually a fair number of island families here, especially on weekends. The waters are generally calm, except when the surf is high enough to break over the mouth of the bay.

KAWAKIU BEACH
Beach

The northernmost of the West End beaches is reached by walking north along the coastal golf greens and up over a rocky point. Kawakiu Beach is a white-sand crescent with bright turquoise waters and good swimming when seas are calm, most often in summer.

KEPUHI BEACH
Beach

This white-sand beach in front of the defunct Kaluakoi Hotel is OK for sunbathing but swimming conditions are usually dangerous. Not only can there be a tough shorebreak but strong currents can be present even on calm days. Experienced surfers take to the northern end of the beach.

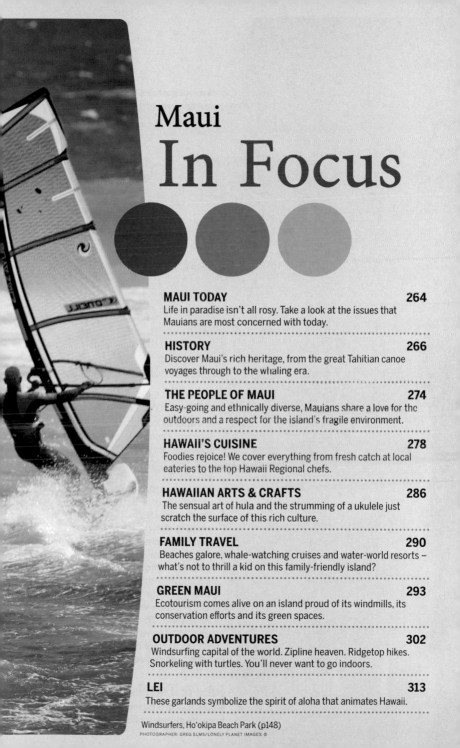

Maui
In Focus

Windsurfers, Ho'okipa Beach Park (p148)
PHOTOGRAPHER: GREG ELMS/LONELY PLANET IMAGES ©

Maui
Today

Volunteer working on Ko'ie'ie Fishpond (p121).

> *Few topics raise more debate on Maui than development issues*

ethnicity
(% of population)

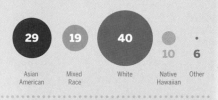

29	**19**	**40**	**10**	**6**
Asian American	Mixed Race	White	Native Hawaiian	Other

if Maui were 100 people

29 would be 0-24 years old
29 would be 25-44 years old
28 would be 45-64 years old
14 would be 65+ years old

population per sq mile

♦ ≈ 40 people

Maui Big Island O'hau

New Government

On Maui all local government is adminis-tered on a county level. In 2011 Alan Arakawa took over the reins as Maui's new mayor and there's optimism in the air. Voters were fed up with the former administration's policies and the red tape involved in obtain-ing permits of all sorts. One consequence affecting travelers was that some B&Bs were forced to close for upwards of a year. Others simply ceased operations altogether and the loss of vacation rentals on the North Shore, which has no hotels, was so great that some surfing competitions left Maui. Haiku, a town catering to surfers, saw several restaurants go under. Arakawa vows to streamline permits on several fronts. Things are improving. Although there are still fewer B&Bs than in the past, many places have reopened and we have sev-eral good recommendations in this book.

Jobs & Tourism

Maui's tourism-based economy has taken a hit from the global economic slump. Unemploy-

wash down the slopes, flooding low-lying communities and muddying the coral reefs. Just about everyone on Maui takes the issue seriously. Even big-wave surfer Laird Hamilton attributes climate change as a source of the 100ft surf he rides off Maui's North Shore. In a move to decrease their own carbon emissions, Mauians have supported a broad spectrum of green initiatives, including the erection of windmills on Maui's slopes. On the stop-greenhouse-gases front, islanders' outrage scuttled a plan by Maui Electric to import palm oil fuel from Indonesian plantations that leveled rainforests.

Bulldozing Paradise

Few topics raise more debate on Maui than development issues. The latest target of corporate bulldozers is the starkly beautiful and largely untouched village of Makena. The area is home to some of Maui's finest unspoiled beaches. If developers have their way, dry coastal scrubland will be turned into green golf links and condos geared to wealthy visitors. With Maui's increasing exposure to droughts, siphoning off water to feed resorts has become a hot political topic. As farmers here say, 'no can eat golf balls.' Others argue that Maui's resources should be used to provide affordable homes for islanders, not second homes for mainlanders. The cost of buying a modest home on Maui is head spinning, even by Hawaii standards. That's forcing a new generation of Maui-born people to move to places like Seattle, where living is more affordable. No surprise then that 'Save Makena' has become the most popular bumper sticker on Maui.

While the majority sentiment is against developing Makena, some people do welcome the jobs that resort development creates.

ment, statistically negligible before the crisis, has shot up to around 8%. The recession has hit Maui in other ways as well: corporate sponsors for the island's signature cultural event, the International Festival of Canoes in Lahaina, have pulled their support, leading to the cancellation of the two-week festival.

Other events are facing the chopping block too, including high-profile world tour competitions. The Billabong Pro Maui in Honolua, the coveted final event in the Women's Triple Crown of Surfing, got axed in 2010 when it lost its sponsor. That's not just bad news for athletes – it has a ripple effect on businesses of all stripes.

Climate Change

Mauians know intimately the consequences of global warming. Extended periods of drought have become commonplace in the past decade. Some years the droughts end with record-setting bursts of torrential rains that

History

Launching canoes, Lahaina

KARL LEHMANN/LONELY PLANET IMAG

The first Polynesian voyagers to discover this slice of paradise were so enamored by the sight that they journeyed back across 2400 miles of open ocean to tell their friends. So began the perilous Pacific voyages, the Western colonization and the kingdom intrigue, all of which make this island's history so compelling. Today Maui is one of the most ethnically diverse places in the USA.

The Great Canoe Voyages

The earliest Polynesian settlers of Hawaii came ashore around AD 500. Archaeologists disagree on exactly where these explorers came from, but artifacts indicate the first to arrive were from the Marquesas Islands. The next wave of settlers were from Tahiti and arrived around AD 1000. Unlike the Marquesans, who sparsely settled the tiny islands at the northwest end of the Hawaiian Islands, the Tahitians arrived in great numbers and

900,000 years ago
The volcanoes that formed Maui rise from the sea; the buildup continues until 400,000 BC.

settled each of the major islands in the Hawaiian chain. Although no one knows what set them on course for Hawaii, when they arrived in their great double-hulled canoes they were prepared to colonize a new land, bringing with them pigs, dogs, taro roots and other crop plants.

Their discovery of Hawaii may have been an accident, but subsequent journeys were not. These Tahitians were highly skilled seafarers, using only the wind, stars and wave patterns to guide them. Yet, incredibly, they memorized their route over 2400 miles of open Pacific and repeated the journeys between Hawaii and Tahiti for centuries.

And what a story they must have brought back with them, because vast waves of Tahitians followed to pursue a new life in Hawaii. So great were the number of Tahitian migrations that Hawaii's population probably reached a peak of approximately 250,000 by the year 1450. The voyages back and forth continued until around 1500, when all contact between Tahiti and Hawaii appears to have stopped.

European Explorers

On January 18, 1778, an event occurred on the islands that would change the life of Hawaiians in ways inconceivable at the time. On that day British explorer Captain James Cook sighted Hawaii while en route to the Pacific Northwest in search of a possible 'northwest passage' between the Pacific and Atlantic oceans.

Cook's appearance was not only the first Western contact, it also marked the end of Hawaii's 300 years of complete isolation that followed the end of the Tahiti voyages. Cook anchored on the Big Island, across the channel from Maui, and stayed long enough to refresh his food supplies before continuing his journey north.

Cook sighted Maui but never set foot on the island. The first Westerner to land on Maui was French explorer Jean François de Galaup La Pérouse, who sailed into Keoneʻoʻio Bay (now called La Pérouse Bay) on Maui's southern shore in 1786, traded with the Hawaiians and left after two days of peaceful contact.

Royal Power Struggles

From the early days of Polynesian settlement, Maui was divided into separate kingdoms, with rival chiefs occasionally rising up to battle for control of the island.

In the 16th century Piʻilani, the king of the Hana region, marched north to conquer Lele (now Lahaina) and Wailuku, uniting Maui for the first time under a single royal rule.

During the 1780s Maui's king Kahekili became the most powerful chief in all Hawaii, bringing both Oʻahu and Molokaʻi under Maui's rule.

AD 500
Polynesian colonists traveling thousands of miles across open seas in double-hulled canoes arrive in Hawaii.

1500
The migration voyages between the South Pacific and Hawaii end.

1778
British Captain James Cook becomes the first-known Westerner to sight Maui.

The Best... Native Hawaiian Sites

In 1790, while Kahekili was in O'ahu, Kamehameha the Great launched a bold naval attack on Maui. Using foreign-acquired cannons and two foreign seamen, Isaac Davis and John Young, Kamehameha defeated Maui's warriors in a fierce battle at 'Iao Valley that was so bloody that the waters of 'Iao Stream ran red for days.

An attack on his own homeland by a Big Island rival forced Kamehameha to withdraw from Maui, but the battle continued over the years. When the aging Kahekili died in 1794, his kingdom was divided among two quarreling heirs, which left a rift that Kamehameha quickly took advantage of.

In 1795 Kamehameha invaded Maui again, with a force of 6000 canoes. This time he conquered the entire island and brought it under his permanent rule. Later that year Kamehameha went on to conquer O'ahu and unite the Hawaiian Islands under his reign.

In 1810 Kamehameha became the first *mo'i* (king) of the Kingdom of Hawaii. He established Lahaina as his royal court, where he built a royal residence made of brick, the first Western-style building in Hawaii. Lahaina remained the capital of the kingdom until 1845, when King Kamehameha III moved the capital to Honolulu on O'ahu.

Here Come the Westerners

After Captain Cook's ships returned to England, news of his discovery quickly spread throughout Europe and America, opening the floodgates to a foreign invasion of explorers, traders, missionaries and fortune hunters.

By the 1820s Hawaii was becoming a critical link in the growing trade route between China and the USA. British, American, French and Russian traders all used Hawaii as a mid-Pacific station to provision their ships and to buy Hawaiian sandalwood, which was a highly lucrative commodity in China.

Whalers

The first whaling ship to stop in Maui was the *Balena,* which anchored at Lahaina in 1819. The crew was mostly New England Yankees with a sprinkling of Gay Head Indians and former slaves. As more ships arrived, men of all nationalities roamed Lahaina's streets. Most were in their teens or 20s, and ripe for adventure. Lahaina became a bustling port of call with shopkeepers catering to the whalers. Saloons, brothels and hotels boomed.

1786
French explorer La Pérouse becomes the first Westerner to land on Maui.

1790
Kamehameha the Great invades Maui, decimating island warriors in a bloody battle at 'Iao Valley.

1810
Kamehameha the Great moves to Maui, declaring Lahaina the royal seat of the Hawaiian kingdom.

A Bloody Confrontation

In January 1790, the American ship *Eleanora* arrived on Maui, eager to trade Western goods for food supplies and sandalwood. Late one night a party of Hawaiian men stole the ship's skiff. In retaliation, Captain Simon Metcalf lured a large group of Hawaiians to his ship under the pretense of trading with them. Instead he ordered his men to fire every cannon and gun aboard the ship at the Hawaiians, murdering over 100 men, women and children. This tragic event, one of the first contacts between Westerners and Maui islanders, is remembered as the Olowalu Massacre.

A convenient way station for whalers of both the Arctic and Japanese whaling grounds, by the 1840s Hawaii was the whaling center of the Pacific. In Lahaina the whalers could transfer their catch to trade ships bound for America. This allowed whalers to stay in the Pacific for longer periods of time without having to return home with their payload, resulting in higher profits. At the peak of the whaling era, more than 500 whaling ships were pulling into Lahaina each year.

Whaling brought big money to Maui and the dollars spread beyond Lahaina. Many Maui farmers got their start supplying the whaling ships with potatoes. Hawaiians themselves made good whalers, and sea captains gladly paid a $200 bond to the Hawaiian government for each Hawaiian sailor allowed to join their crew. Kamehameha IV even set up his own fleet of whaling ships that sailed under the Hawaiian flag.

Whaling in the Pacific peaked in the mid-19th century and quickly began to burn itself out. In a few short years all but the most distant whaling grounds were being depleted and whalers were forced to go further afield to make their kills.

The last straw for the Pacific whaling industry came in 1871, when an early storm in the Arctic caught more than 30 ships by surprise, trapping them in ice floes above the Bering Strait. Although more than 1000 seamen were rescued, half of them Hawaiian, the fleet itself was lost.

Soul Savers

Shortly after the first missionaries arrived on Maui they made inroads with Hawaiian leaders. By a twist of fate, they arrived at a fortuitous time, when Hawaiian society was in great upheaval after the death of Kamehameha the Great. It made the missionaries' efforts to save the souls of the 'heathen' Hawaiians much easier. The *ali'i* (royalty), in particular, were keen on the reading lessons offered by the

1819
Kamehameha the Great dies and the Hawaiian religious system is cast aside.

1819
The first whaling ship anchors in Maui at Lahaina.

The Best… Missionary-era Sites

1 Baldwin Home (p37)

....

2 Hale Pa'i (p39)

....

3 Bailey House Museum (p104)

....

4 David Malo's Church (p120)

....

missionaries in the Hawaiian language, which had never before been put into written form. Indeed, by the middle of the 1850s, Hawaii had a higher literacy rate than the USA.

Lahaina became a center of activity. In 1831 Lahainaluna Seminary (now Lahainaluna High School), in the hills above Lahaina, became the first secondary school to be established west of the Rocky Mountains. Lahaina was also home to the first newspaper, *Ka Lama Hawaii,* printed west of the Rocky Mountains.

But the New England missionaries also helped to destroy traditional Hawaiian culture. They prohibited the dancing of the hula because of its lewd and suggestive movements and they denounced the traditional Hawaiian chants and songs that paid homage to the Hawaiian gods. In the late 19th century they even managed to prohibit the speaking of the Hawaiian language in schools as another means of turning Hawaiians away from their 'hedonistic' cultural roots – a major turnaround from the early missionary days when all students were taught in Hawaiian.

Sugar & Immigration

In the 1840s, sugar growing began to emerge as an economic force. Maui's role in sugar production had begun in 1839, when King Kamehameha III issued small parcels of land to individual growers who were required to have their crop processed at a mill built by the king in Wailuku. Half of the crop went to the king. Of the remaining half, one-fifth was taken as a tax to support the government and the remainder went to the grower.

In the heyday of sugar, there were as many as 10 plantations on Maui, cultivating thousands of acres of land throughout the island. In 1876 the Hamakua Ditch began transporting water from the rainy mountains to the dry plains, allowing sugar plantations to spread. One of the most prominent mills, the Pioneer Mill in Lahaina, was founded in 1863 by American entrepreneurs. In 1890 the first train to run in West Maui was opened to bring freshly cut sugarcane to the mill.

As sugar production grew, sugar barons were worried about the shortage of field laborers, who were mostly Hawaiian. There had been a severe decline in the Native Hawaiian population due to introduced diseases, such as typhoid, influenza and smallpox, for which the Hawaiians had no immunities. To expand their operations, plantation owners began to look overseas for a cheap labor supply. First they recruited laborers from China. In 1868 recruiters went to Japan, and in the 1870s they brought in Portuguese workers from Madeira and the Azores Islands.

1820
Christian missionaries arrive, filling the gap left by the abandonment of Hawaii's traditional religion.

1831
Lahainaluna Seminary, the first secondary school west of the Rocky Mountains, is built in Lahaina.

1848
Under the influence of Westerners, the first system of private land ownership is introduced.

The labor contracts typically lasted for two to three years, with wages as low as $1 per week. Workers lived in ethnically divided 'camps' set up by the plantations that included modest housing, a company store, a social hall and other recreational amenities. At the end of their contracts, some returned to their homelands, but most remained on the islands, integrating into the multicultural mainstream.

After Hawaii's 1898 annexation, US laws, including racially biased prohibitions against Chinese immigration, were enforced in Hawaii. Because of these new restrictions, plantation owners turned their recruiting efforts to Puerto Rico and Korea. Filipinos were the last group of immigrants brought to Hawaii to work in the fields and mills between 1906 and 1946.

The Great Land Grab

Throughout the monarchy period, the ruling sovereigns of Hawaii fought off continual efforts on the part of European and American settlers to gain control of the kingdom.

In 1848, under pressure from foreigners who wanted to own land, a sweeping land reform act known as the Great Mahele was instituted. This act allowed, for the first time, the ownership of land, which had previously been held exclusively by monarchs

Alexander & Baldwin Sugar Museum (p110)

PHOTOGRAPHER: GREG ELMS/LONELY PLANET IMAGES ©

1868
Thousands of Japanese laborers arrive on Maui to work newly planted sugarcane fields.

1893
While attempting to restore Native Hawaiian rights, Queen Lili'uokalani is overthrown by American businessmen.

1898
Hawaii is annexed by the USA and becomes a US territory.

and chiefs. The chiefs had not owned the land in the Western sense but were caretakers of the land, and the commoners who lived on the land worked it, giving a portion of their harvest in return for the right to stay.

The reforms of the Great Mahele had far-reaching implications. For foreigners, who had money to buy land, it meant greater economic and political power. For Hawaiians, who had little or no money, it meant a loss of land-based self-sufficiency and forced entry into the low-wage labor market, primarily run by Westerners.

When King David Kalakaua came to power in 1874, American businessmen had wrested substantial control over the economy and were bent on gaining control over the political scene as well. Kalakaua was an impassioned Hawaiian revivalist, known as the 'Merrie Monarch.' He brought back the hula, reversing decades of missionary repression against the 'heathen dance,' and he composed the national anthem *Hawaii Ponoi,* which is now the state song. Kalakaua also tried to ensure a degree of self-rule for Native Hawaiians, who had become a minority in their own land.

Overthrow of the Monarchy

When King Kalakaua died in 1891, his sister ascended the throne. Queen Lili'uokalani was a staunch supporter of her brother's efforts to maintain Hawaiian independence.

In January 1893, Queen Lili'uokalani was preparing to proclaim a new Constitution to restore royal powers when a group of armed US businessmen occupied the Supreme Court and declared the monarchy overthrown. They announced a provisional government, led by Sanford Dole, son of a pioneer missionary family.

After the overthrow of the monarchy, the new government leaders pushed hard for annexation, believing that it would bring greater stability to the islands, and more profits to Caucasian-run businesses. Although US law required that any entity petitioning for annexation must have the backing of the majority of its citizens through a public vote, no such vote was held in Hawaii.

Nonetheless on July 7, 1898, President William McKinley signed a joint congressional resolution approving annexation. Some historians feel that Hawaii would not have been annexed if it had not been for the outbreak of the Spanish–American War in April 1898, which sent thousands of US troops to the Philippines, making Hawaii a crucial Pacific staging point for the war.

World War II

On December 7, 1941, when Japanese warplanes appeared above the Pearl Harbor area, most residents thought they were mock aircraft being used in US Army and Navy practice maneuvers. Even the loud anti-aircraft gunfire didn't raise much concern. Of course it was the real thing, and by the day's end hundreds of ships and airplanes had been destroyed, more than 1000 Americans had been killed and the war in the Pacific had begun. The impact on Hawaii was dramatic. The army took control of the islands, martial law was declared and civil rights were suspended. Unlike on the mainland,

1901
The Pioneer Inn, Maui's first hotel, is built on the waterfront in Lahaina.

1927
Convict road gangs complete the construction of the Hana Hwy.

1941
Japanese warplanes attack Pearl Harbor, turning Hawaii into a war zone under martial law.

Japanese–Americans in Hawaii were not sent to internment camps because they made up most of the labor force in the cane fields in Hawaii's sugar-dependent economy.

The Japanese–Americans' loyalty to the USA was still questioned and they were not allowed to join the armed forces until 1943. When the US government reversed its decision and approved the formation of an all-Japanese combat unit, called the 100th Infantry Battalion, more than 10,000 men answered the recruitment call. The 442nd Regimental Combat Team of the battalion, made up largely of Hawaii's Japanese–American population, eventually saw fierce action in Europe and fought so bravely that they became the most decorated fighting unit in US history.

Statehood

Throughout the 20th century numerous statehood bills were introduced in Congress, only to be shot down. One reason for this lack of support was racial prejudice against Hawaii's multi-ethnic population. US congressmen from a still-segregated South were vocal in their belief that making Hawaii a state would open the doors to Asian immigration and the so-called 'Yellow Peril' threat that was so rampant at the time. Others believed Hawaii's labor unions were hotbeds of communism.

The fame of the 442nd Regimental Combat Team in WWII went a long way toward reducing anti-Japanese sentiments on the mainland and increasing support for statehood. In March 1959 Congress voted again, this time admitting Hawaii into the Union. On August 21, President Eisenhower signed the admission bill that officially deemed Hawaii the 50th state.

Statehood had an immediate economic impact on the islands, most notably in the boosting of the tourism industry. Coupled with the advent of jet airplanes, which could transport thousands of people per week to the islands, tourism exploded, creating a hotel-building boom previously unmatched in the USA. Tourism went on to become the largest industry on Maui.

The Best...
Immigrant
Influences

IN FOCUS HISTORY

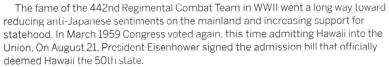

1959
On August 21, Hawaii becomes the 50th state of the USA.

1962
Hawaii's first resort destination outside of Waikiki is built at Ka'anapali Beach.

GREG ELMS/LONELY PLANET IMAGES ©

The People
of Maui

ABBOT LOW MOFFA

The bond that unites all Mauians is a sense of aloha ʻaina – a love of the land. Add to this strong family ties, an appreciation for chitchat and a culture that embraces generosity and hospitality, and you've got a style of community rarely seen anymore on the hard-charging, rootless mainland.

Island Identity

Nobody sweats the small stuff in Maui. It's all good. No worries. No problem. And if somebody is noticeably wound-up? They're from the mainland, guaranteed. Folks on Maui tend to have sunny dispositions, and they're more laid-back than their mainland cousins, dressing more casually and spending more time outside. On weekends everybody can be found hanging on the beach stripped down to T-shirts and bikinis, and wearing those ubiquitous flip-flops known in Hawaii as *slippahs*.

Located 2500 miles from the nearest continent, the Hawaiian Islands are practically another country. On Maui, streets all have Hawaiian names, mixed-race people are the norm and school kids participate in hula contests. Here you'll find no daylight savings time and no significant change of seasons.

The geographical distance puts local, rather than national, news on the front page. Even California can seem like a foreign land. Just consider the nickname for over-developed Kihei in South Maui. It's been dubbed 'Haole-wood' by the locals. Haole? It's the Hawaiian term for Caucasian.

People on Maui never walk by anybody they know without partaking in a little talk story, stopping to ask how someone is doing (and mean it) and to share a little conversation. Islanders prefer to avoid heated arguments and generally don't jump into a controversial topic just to argue a point. Politically, most residents are middle-of-the-road Democrats and tend to vote along party, racial, ethnic, seniority, and local and nonlocal lines.

To locals, it is best to avoid embarrassing confrontations and to 'save face' by keeping quiet. At community meetings or activist rallies, the most vocal, liberal and passionate will probably be mainland transplants. Of course, as more and more mainlanders settle in Hawaii, the traditional stereotypes are fading.

Mauians tend to be self-assured without being cocky. Though Honolulu residents may think other Hawaiian Islands are 'da boonies,' they generally give a different nod to Maui. In the greater scheme of Hawaiian places, Maui is considered the more sophisticated sister, with a more polished scene than the Big Island or Kaua'i.

Lifestyle

Take a Sunday afternoon drive along the West Maui coast and you'll see the same scene repeated at the different beach parks: overflowing picnic tables, smoking grills and multi-generational groups enjoying the sun and surf. On Maui, the *'ohana* (family) is central to island lifestyles. *'Ohana* includes all relatives, as well as close family friends. Growing up, 'auntie' and 'uncle' are used to refer to those who are dear to you, whether by blood or friendship. Weekends are typically set aside for family outings, and it's not uncommon for as many as 50 people to gather for a family picnic.

People are early risers, often taking a run along the beach or hitting the waves before heading to the office. Most work a 40-hour week – overtime and the workaholic routine common elsewhere in the USA are the exceptions here.

Who's Who

Haole White person, Caucasian. Often further defined as 'mainland haole' or 'local haole.'

Hapa Person of mixed ancestry, most commonly referring to *hapa haole* who are part white and part Asian.

Hawaiian Person of Native Hawaiian ancestry. It's a faux pas to call a non-native Hawaii resident 'Hawaiian.'

Kama'aina Person who is a resident of Hawaii, literally defined as 'child of the land.'

Local Person who grew up in Hawaii. Locals who move away retain their local 'cred,' at least in part. But longtime transplants never become local. To call a transplant 'almost local' is a compliment.

Neighbor Islander Person who lives on any Hawaiian Island other than O'ahu.

Transplant Person who moves to the islands as an adult.

In many ways, contemporary culture in Maui resembles contemporary culture in the rest of the USA. Mauians listen to the same pop music and watch the same TV shows. The island has rock bands and classical musicians, junk food and nouvelle cuisine. The wonderful thing about Maui, however, is that the mainland influences largely stand beside, rather than engulf, the culture of the island.

Not only is traditional Hawaiian culture an integral part of the social fabric, but so are the customs of the ethnically diverse immigrants who have settled here. Maui is more than a meeting place of East and West; it's a place where the cultures merge, typically in a manner that brings out the best of both worlds.

Recent decades have seen a refreshing cultural renaissance in all things Hawaiian. Hawaiian-language classes are thriving, local artists and craftspeople are returning to traditional mediums and themes, and hula classes are concentrating more on the nuances behind hand movements and facial expressions than on the stereotypical hip-shaking.

Visitors will still encounter packaged Hawaiiana that seems almost a parody of island culture, from plastic lei to theme-park luau. But fortunately, the growing interest in traditional Hawaiian culture is having a positive impact on the tourist industry, and authentic performances by hula students and Hawaiian musicians are now the norm.

Folks on Maui are quite accepting of other people, which helps explain the harmonious hodgepodge of races and cultures here. Sexual orientation is generally not an issue and gays and lesbians tend to be accepted without prejudice.

Most locals strive for the conventional 'American dream': kids, home ownership, stable work and ample free time. Generally, those with less-standard lifestyles (eg B&B owners, artists, unmarrieds and world travelers) are mainland transplants.

Although the median price of a home in Maui has dropped during the recession, from $700,000 to about $500,000, this price is still $350,000 higher than the national median. Half a million is a steep purchase price when the median annual income for a household hovers between $64,000 and $68,000. For working-class people, it generally takes two incomes just to make ends meet. Considering that food, gasoline and energy costs are about 20% higher than on the mainland, it can be a tough go in paradise. Yet most agree that nothing compares to living on Maui and would leave only if absolutely necessary.

Multiculturalism

Maui is one of the most ethnically diverse places in the USA. Need proof? Just look at its signature dish: the plate lunch. This platter, with its meat, macaroni salad and two scoops of rice, merges the culinary habits of Native Hawaiians with those of a global array of immigrants – Portuguese, Japanese, Korean Filipino – to create one heaping plate of goodness. A metaphor never tasted so good.

But the diversity is both eclectic and narrow at once. That's because Hawaii's unique blend of races, ethnicities and cultures is quite isolated from the rest of the world. On one hand, Hawaii is far removed from any middle-American, white-bread city. On the other, it lacks major exposure to certain races and ethnicities, particularly blacks and Mexican Hispanics, that are prevalent in the mainland US population.

Any discussion regarding multiculturalism must address whether we are talking about locals (insiders) or nonlocals (outsiders). Among locals, social interaction has hinged on old plantation stereotypes and hierarchies since statehood. During plantation days, whites were the wealthy plantation owners. For years afterward, minorities would joke about their being the 'bosses' or about their privileges due to race. As the Japanese rose to power economically and politically, they tended to capitalize on their 'minority' status, emphasizing their insider status as former

Shaka Sign

Islanders greet each other with the *shaka* sign, made by folding down the three middle fingers to the palm and extending the thumb and little finger. The hand is then shaken back and forth in greeting. On Maui, it's as common as waving.

plantation laborers. But the traditional distinctions and alliances are fading as the plantation generation dies away.

Of course, any tension among local groups are quite benign compared with racial strife on the mainland USA. Locals seem slightly perplexed at the emphasis on 'political correctness.' Among themselves, locals good-naturedly joke about island stereotypes: talkative Portuguese, stingy Chinese, goody-goody Japanese and know-it-all haole.

When nonlocals enter the picture, the balance shifts. Generally, locals feel bonded with other locals. While tourists and transplants are welcomed, they must earn the trust and respect of the locals. It is unacceptable for an outsider to assume an air of superiority and to try to 'fix' local ways. Such people will inevitably fall into the category of 'loudmouth haole.'

That said, prejudice against haole is minimal. If you're called a haole, don't worry. It's generally not an insult or threat (if it is, you'll know). Essentially, locals are warm and gracious to those who appreciate island ways.

Island Etiquette

Dial it down a notch when you get to Maui. Big city aggression and type-A maneuvering won't get you far. As the bumper sticker says, 'Live Aloha.'

When driving on narrow roads like the Road to Hana and the Kahekili Hwy, the driver who reaches a one-way bridge first has the right of way, if the bridge is otherwise empty. If facing a steady stream of cars, yield to the entire queue.

Remember the simple protocol when visiting sacred places: don't place rocks at the site as a gesture of thanks; better to use words instead. It is also considered disrespectful to stack rocks or build rock towers. Finally don't remove rocks from national parks.

When surfing there's a pecking order, and tourists are at the bottom. The person furthest outside has the right of way. When somebody is up and riding, don't take off on the wave in front of them. Wait your turn, be generous and surf with a smile.

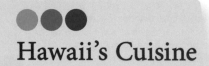

Hawaii's Cuisine

Hawaii's cuisine has a sense of inclusive fun. Yes, there are the official culinary distinctions that fascinate gourmands: Local Food, Hawaii Regional Cuisine and Native Hawaiian. But that's not why we love it. We love it for its tasty insouciance and its no-worries embrace of foreign flavors. The plate lunch. Loco moco. Even Spam musubi has a sassy — if salty — charm. Sample the unknown, take another bite. Maui isn't the place to diet. It's the broke-da-mout reward.

Staples & Specialties

Sticky white rice is more than a side dish in Hawaii; it's a culinary building block, an integral partner in everyday meals. Without rice, Spam *musubi* would be a slice of canned meat. *Loco moco* would be nothing more than an egg-covered hamburger. And without two-scoop rice, the plate lunch would be a ho-hum conversation between meat and macaroni rather than a multicultural party.

And by the way, sticky white rice means sticky white rice. While you might find couscous or mashed potatoes at fancy restaurants, day-to-day meals are served with sticky white rice. Not flaky rice. Not wild rice. Not flavored rice. And *definitely* not Uncle Ben's. Locals can devour mounds of the stuff and it typically comes as two scoops. The top condiment is soy sauce, known by its Japanese name *shōyu*, which combines well with sharp Asian flavors such as ginger, green onion and garlic.

Meat, chicken or fish are often key components of a meal, too. For quick, cheap eating, locals devour anything tasty, from Portuguese sausage to hamburger steak to corned beef. But the dinner-table highlight is always seafood, especially freshly caught fish.

One word of caution: Maui's attempts at nonlocal classics such as pizza, bagels, croissants and southern BBQ are typically disappointing. Stick with *local* local food.

Local Food

Day-to-day eats reflect the state's multicultural heritage, with Asian, Portuguese and native Hawaiian influences the most immediately evident. Cheap, fattening and tasty, local food is also the stuff of cravings and comfort.

The classic example of local food is the ubiquitous plate lunch. Picture this: chunky layers of tender *kalua* pork, a dollop of smooth, creamy macaroni and two hearty scoops of white rice. Yum, right? The pork can be swapped for other proteins like fried mahimahi or teriyaki chicken. Served almost like street food, the plate lunch is often served on disposable plates and eaten using chopsticks. A favorite breakfast combo includes fried egg and spicy Portuguese sausage (or bacon, ham, Spam etc) and, always, two scoops of rice.

Pupu is the local term used for all kinds of munchies or 'grazing' foods. Much more than just cheese and crackers, *pupu* represent the ethnic diversity of the islands and might include boiled peanuts in the shell, *edamame* (boiled fresh soybeans in the pod) and universal items such as fried shrimp.

Not to be missed is *poke* (raw fish marinated in *shōyu*, oil, chili peppers, green onions and seaweed). It comes in many varieties – sesame ahi (yellowfin tuna) is particularly delicious and goes well with beer.

Another local 'delicacy' is Spam *musubi* (a rice ball topped with sautéed Spam and wrapped with dried seaweed). Locals of all stripes enjoy this only-in-Hawaii creation.

And, finally, there's shave ice. Ignore those joyless cynics who'll tell you that shave ice is nothing more than a snow cone. Shave ice is *not* just a snow cone. It's a tropical 21-gun salute – the most spectacular snow cone on earth. The specifics? The ice is shaved as fine as powdery snow, packed into a paper cone and drenched with sweet fruit-flavored syrups in dazzling hues. For added decadence, add Kauai cream, azuki beans and ice cream.

Spam a Lot

Spam was introduced to Hawaii during WWII, when fresh meat imports were replaced by this standard GI ration. By the war's end, Hawaiians had developed a taste for the fatty canned stuff. Today, locals consume about 5 million pounds of Spam annually!

Spam looks and tastes different in Hawaii. It's eaten cooked (typically sautéed to a light crispiness in sweetened *shōyu*), not straight from the can, and served as a tasty meat dish.

The popular Spam *musubi* is a rice ball with a slice of fried Spam on top, or in the middle, wrapped with a strip of sushi nori (dried seaweed). It's commonly seen at grocers and convenience stores.

Native Hawaiian

Kalua pig (which is traditionally baked in an underground oven) and poi are the 'meat and potatoes' of native Hawaiian food. Poi is served as the main side dish with every Hawaiian-style meal. The purple paste is pounded from cooked taro roots, with water added to make it pudding-like. It's nutritious and easily digested, but for many non-locals it is also an acquired taste, largely because of its pasty consistency.

A common main dish is *laulau* (a bundle of pork or chicken and salted butterfish wrapped in a taro leaf that's steamed until it has a soft spinach-like texture). Other Hawaiian foods include baked *'ulu* (breadfruit), which has a texture similar to a potato and *haupia* (a delicious pudding made of coconut cream thickened with cornstarch or arrowroot). *Haupia* ice cream made on Maui offers a nice cross between traditional and modern cuisine.

Hawaii Regional Cuisine

Twenty years ago, Hawaii was a culinary backwater. Sure, you could slum it on local grinds (food) and get by on the slew of midrange Asian eateries, but fine dining was typically a European-style meal that ignored locally grown fare and the unique flavors of the islands.

In the 1990s a handful of island chefs smashed this tired mold and created a new cuisine, borrowing liberally from Hawaii's various ethnic influences. They partnered with local farmers, ranchers and fishers to highlight fresh local fare and transform their childhood favorites into grown-up, gourmet masterpieces. The movement was dubbed 'Hawaii Regional Cuisine' and the pioneering chefs became celebrities. A trio with Maui connections are Roy Yamaguchi (Roy's Kahana Bar & Grill in Kahana), Beverly Gannon (Hali'imaile General Store) and Mark Ellman (Mala Ocean Tavern and Penne Pasta Café in Lahaina).

The *real* catchwords for Hawaii Regional Cuisine are fresh, organic and locally grown. Think Upcountry greens, Maui chèvre (goat cheese), Kula onions, free-range Hana beef and locally caught fish. The spread of the movement has been a boon to small-scale farmers. Some Maui chefs, like James McDonald (O'o Farm in Kula), have even started their own organic farms. And it's all contributing to a greening of Maui's gardens and menus.

Drinks

Hawaii is the only US state that grows coffee commercially. Both Maui and Moloka'i have coffee farms, and their final products are certainly worth a try. However, the only Hawaiian coffee with gourmet cachet is the world-renowned Kona coffee, grown on the Big Island. Aficionados rave about Kona coffee's mellow flavor that has no bitter aftertaste.

Fruit drinks are everywhere on Maui, but inexpensive canned drinks are usually not pure juice. One native Hawaiian juice tonic is *noni* (mulberry), which grows with wild abandon alongside roads. Proponents claim that *noni* reduces inflammation, boosts energy and helps cure everything from arthritis to cancer. *Noni* is pungent, if not repulsive, in smell and taste, so it's typically mixed with other juices.

Nineteenth-century whalers introduced Hawaiians to alcohol, even teaching them to make their own, *'okolehao* (alcohol distilled from the *ti* root). Instead of alcohol, Hawaiians used *'awa* (kava) as a mild intoxicant. Today, Wow-Wee Maui's Kava Bar & Grill in Kahului serves this bitter, mouth-numbing drink. The lactones in *'awa* are believed to relieve anxiety and fatigue, while fostering restful sleep and vivid dreams. The effect is mildly narcotic, but not mind-altering. *'Awa* is not recommended for pregnant women or for daily use.

Beer is cheap and widely available. Maui has its own microbrewery, Maui Brewing Company, which brews a range of beers that can be found in convenience stores and restaurants across the island.

At Tedeschi Vineyards you can sample Maui-made wines, including its popular pineapple wine.

And, of course, at every beachside bar you can order a colorful tropical drink topped with a fruit garnish and a tiny umbrella. Three favorites are piña colada, made with rum, pineapple juice and cream of coconut; mai tai, a mix of rum, grenadine, and lemon and pineapple juices; and Blue Hawaii, a vodka drink colored with blue curaçao.

It's Perfectly Clear

What starts a mile under the waves, costs $35 a bottle and gives a head-spinning high?

It's Ocean, a distilled-on-Maui vodka made with desalinated water drawn from the depths of the ocean. It's become the hottest spirit in Maui bars and fine restaurants. Passion fruit screwdriver, anyone?

Celebrations

The traditional Hawaiian feast marking special events is the luau. Local luau are still commonplace in modern Hawaii for christenings, anniversaries and other celebrations. These gatherings, typically big, include extended family, co-workers and friends.

The main dish at any luau is *kalua* pig, which is roasted in an earthen oven called an *imu*. The imu is readied for cooking by building a fire and heating rocks in the pit. When the rocks are glowing red, layers of moisture-laden banana trunks and green *ti* leaves are placed over the stones. A pig that has been slit open is filled with the hot rocks and laid on top of the bed. Other foods wrapped in *ti* and banana leaves are placed around it. It's all covered with more *ti* leaves and a layer of coconut-frond mats, then topped with dirt to seal in the heat. This bakes and steams the food. The process takes about four to eight hours depending on the size of the pig and the amount of other food added. Anything cooked in this style is called *kalua*.

Food plays center stage in many other Hawaiian celebrations and festivities. On Sundays the beach parks are packed full of large family gatherings, picnic tables covered with a massive spread of potluck dishes. On standard American holidays, mainstream foods like Super Bowl beer and Thanksgiving turkey appear along with nontraditional local fare such as rice, sweet-potato tempura and hibachi-grilled teriyaki beef.

Maui food festivals such as the East Maui Taro Festival and the Maui Onion Festival showcase home-style island crops. At the Kapalua Wine & Food Festival, top Maui chefs whip up island foods with gourmet flair.

Where To Eat & Drink

In this guide, budget eateries offer menu items under $12 and include bakeries, breakfast joints, and sandwich and taco shops. Midrange restaurants, serving Chinese, Thai, pizza, gourmet sandwiches, plate lunches and no-frills seafood, cost between $12 and $30. Top-end dining establishments are typically found on prime oceanfront perches as well as in resorts and golf course clubhouses. Meals start at $30 per person. To sample top cuisine at a good price, visit during happy hour when prices on appetizers are often reduced.

For quick takeout, plate-lunch eateries are great choices. They pack things tidily so you can carry your meal to a nearby beach for an impromptu picnic lunch. One tip: a lunchtime, decide what you want before reaching the register. Lines typically move quickly and the indecisive can muck up the system. Lunch vans, known as *kaukau* (food) wagons, aren't that common on Maui but you can occasionally find one at the beach.

Maui has a happening cafe scene, and these are the best places to relax over a good lunch in an engaging setting and at a fair price. If the setting isn't important, there are plenty of diner-style Asian restaurants with formica tables and vinyl chairs, no view and no decor. They generally offer quick service and often have surprisingly good food at decent prices.

Maui's top-end restaurants are outright impressive and include some of the most highly rated chef-driven places in Hawaii. Most are set on the beach and forgo the pompous fastidiousness common to upscale urban restaurants on the mainland.

For groceries, head to farmers markets and locally owned supermarkets. Note that in Hawaii, 80% of groceries are imported from the mainland, including milk and eggs (unless labeled 'Island Fresh'), chicken, pork, produce and most beef. If absolute freshness matters to you, choose locally raised beef, island-caught fish and Maui-grown produce.

Habits & Customs

Locals eat meals early and on the dot: typically 6am for breakfast, noon for lunch and 6pm for dinner. Restaurants are jammed packed around the habitual mealtimes, but they clear out an hour or two later, as locals are not lingerers. If you dine at 8:30pm you might not have to wait at all. But bear in mind that restaurants also close early and night owls must hunt for places to eat.

Locals tend to consider quantity as important as quality – and the portion sizes are telling, especially at plate-lunch places. If you're a light eater, feel free to split a meal or take home the leftovers.

Home entertainment for local folks always revolves around food, which is usually served 'potluck style' with all the guests adding to the anything-goes smorgasbord. Locals rarely serve dinner in one-at-a-time courses. Rather, meals are served 'family style,' where diners help themselves. Throwaway paper plates and wooden chopsticks make for an easy cleanup, and the rule is 'all you can eat' (and they definitely mean it!).

If you're invited to someone's home, show up on time and bring a dish – preferably homemade, but a bakery cake or Sam Sato's *manju* are always a certain hit. Remove your shoes at the door. And don't be surprised if you're forced to take home a plate of leftovers.

Vegetarians & Vegans

While most locals are omnivores, vegetarians and vegans can feast on Maui, too. That said, vegetarians aren't the target market: a plate lunch without meat or fish is not quite a plate lunch, and high-end restaurants tend to focus on seafood, though some feature at least one vegetarian main dish nightly. Greens and veggies grow so prolifi-

The Best... Food Experiences

1 Hawaii Regional Cuisine: Hali'imaile General Store (p158)

2 Shave Ice: Tom's Mini-Mart (p106)

3 Plate Lunch: Da Kitchen Express (p126)

4 Farm Tour: O'o Farm (p167)

5 Waterfront Breakfast: Gazebo (p77)

6 Make-Your-Own Smoothie: Laulima Farms (p230)

cally in the Upcountry that salads have a leading role on menus and the smarter cafes will invariably have meal-sized vegetarian salads.

The Asian influence guarantees lots of vegetable and tofu options – walk into any Thai or Vietnamese restaurant and you'll find a extensive listing of vegetarian dishes. If you want to be in a totally meat-free space, there are vegetarian-only restaurants in Ha'iku and Pa'ia.

Eating With Children

Maui's family-oriented, casual atmosphere means *keiki* (children) are welcome almost everywhere. Sit-down restaurants are quick to accommodate kids with high chairs and booster seats.

During the day, eat outdoors. The balmy weather allows for impromptu plate lunches at the beach or fresh fruit at roadside stands. To really act local, buy a straw mat at a convenience shop, pack a picnic and head to the nearest park.

Locals share a big sweet tooth, so finding treats is easy. Premium ice cream, shave ice, home-style cookies and chocolate-covered macadamias are omnipresent temptations. As for main dishes, the local palate is kid friendly, tending toward the sweet and straightforward, without too much garlic, bitter greens, pungent cheeses or strong spices.

You might assume that all fancy restaurants frown on parties that include kids, but many actually cater to them with special menus. In restaurants with an exhibition-kitchen (a large open area with a loud dining room) kids' chatter will blend into the overall din. At hotel luau, kids receive a discount and most will enjoy the show.

Sampling coconut jui

FOOD GLOSSARY

Island food, with its blend of Pacific influences, is unique enough to require a little translation. In addition to the following food glossary, we offer a free downloadable Hawaiian Language & Glossary at www.lonelyplanet.com/hawaiian-language, which provides more Hawaiian and pidgin terms as well as pronunciation tips.

adobo – Filipino chicken or pork cooked in vinegar, *shōyu,* garlic and spices

'awa – kava; a native plant used to make an intoxicating drink

bento – Japanese-style box lunch

broke da mout – delicious; literally 'broke the mouth'

crack seed – Chinese-style preserved fruit; a salty, sweet or sour snack

donburi – meal-sized bowl of rice and main dish

grind – to eat

grinds – food; *'ono kine grinds* is good food

guava – fruit with green or yellow rind, moist pink flesh and lots of edible seeds

gyoza – grilled dumpling usually containing minced pork or shrimp

haupia – coconut pudding

hulihuli chicken – rotisserie-cooked chicken

imu – underground earthen oven used to cook *kalua* pig and other luau food

kalo – Hawaiian word for taro

kalua – Hawaiian method of cooking pork and other luau food in an *imu*

kamaboko – steamed fish cakes; used to garnish Japanese dishes

katsu – deep-fried fillets, usually chicken; also see *tonkatsu*

kaukau – food

laulau – bundle of pork or chicken and salted butterfish wrapped in taro and *ti* leaves and steamed

li hing mui – sweet, salty preserved plum; type of crack seed; also refers to the flavor powder

liliko'i – passion fruit

loco moco – dish of rice, fried egg and hamburger patty topped with gravy or other condiments

lomilomi salmon – minced and salted salmon, diced tomato and green onion

luau – Hawaiian feast

mai tai – 'tiki bar' drink typically containing rum, grenadine, and lemon and pineapple juices

malasada – Portuguese fried doughnut, sugar-coated

manapua – Chinese steamed or baked bun filled with *char siu*

manju – Japanese bun filled with sweet bean paste

mochi – Japanese sticky-rice dumpling

noni – type of mulberry with smelly yellow fruit; used medicinally

nori – Japanese seaweed, usually dried

ono – delicious

pho – Vietnamese soup, typically beef broth, noodles and fresh herbs

pipikaula – Hawaiian beef jerky

poi – staple Hawaiian starch made of steamed, mashed taro

poke – cubed, marinated raw fish

ponzu – Japanese citrus sauce

pupu – snacks or appetizers

saimin – local-style noodle soup

shave ice – cup of finely shaved ice sweetened with colorful syrups

shōyu – soy sauce

soba – buckwheat noodles

star fruit – translucent green-yellow fruit with five ribs like the points of a star and sweet, juicy pulp

taro – plant with edible corm used to make poi and with edible leaves eaten in *laulau; kalo* in Hawaiian

teppanyaki – Japanese style of cooking with an iron grill

tonkatsu – Japanese breaded and fried pork cutlets; also prepared as chicken *katsu*

tsukemono – Japanese pickled vegetables

ume – Japanese pickled plum

Name that Fish

In Hawaii, most fish go by Hawaiian names (see the Hawai'i Seafood Buyers' Guide at www.hawaii-seafood. org). The fish in the following list are good sustainable choices – if they are caught in Hawaiian waters. Ask before ordering, as some fish are imported.

ahi – yellowfin or bigeye tuna with red flesh; excellent raw or rare

aku – red-fleshed skipjack tuna; strong flavor; *katsuo* in Japanese

kajiki – Pacific blue marlin; *a'u* in Hawaiian

mahimahi – dolphin fish or dorado; pink flesh, popular cooked

nairagi – striped marlin; *a'u* in Hawaiian

ono – white-fleshed wahoo

opah – moonfish; firm and rich

'opakapaka – pink snapper; delicate flavor, premium quality

'opelu – pan-sized mackerel scad; delicious fried

shutome – swordfish; succulent and meaty

tako – octopus

The Best... Hawaiian Cookbooks

○ **Roy's Feasts From Hawaii** Roy Yamaguchi
○ **Hali'imaile General Store Cookbook** Beverly Gannon
○ **Maui Tacos Cookbook** Mark Ellman
○ **Tastes and Flavors of Maui** Various editors
○ **What Hawaii Likes to Eat** Muriel Miura and Betty Shimabukuro
○ **Hawaii Cooks With Taro** Marcia Zina Mager and Muriel Miura

IN FOCUS HAWAII'S CUISINE

Hawaiian Arts & Crafts

Tiki statue, Maui Stables (p229)

GREG ELMS/LONELY PLANET IMAG

'Hula is the language of the heart, and therefore the heartbeat of the Hawaiian people,' said King Kalakaua, the 19th-century ruler who resurrected hula and other native art forms after years of suppression by zealous missionaries. Today that heartbeat is strong, especially in Maui where traditional hula shows as well as slack key guitar festivals and stone-carving workshops embrace the island's heritage.

Music

The guitar was introduced to the Hawaiian Islands by Spanish cowboys in the 1830s. Hawaiians made it uniquely their own, however. In 1889, Joseph Kekuku, a Native Hawaiian, designed the steel guitar, one of only two major musical instruments invented in what is now the USA. (The other is the banjo.) The Hawaiian steel guitar is usually played with slack key tunings. For the slack key method the six strings are slacked from their standard tuning to facilitate a full sound on a single guitar. The thumb plays the bass and rhythm chords, while the fingers play the melody and improvisations, in a picked style.

The most influential slack key artist was Gabby Pahinui (1921–80), who launched the modern slack key era with his first recording in 1946. Other pioneering slack key masters were Sonny Chillingworth and Atta Isaacs. Today the tradition lives on in Dennis Kamakahi, Keola Beamer, Led Ka'apana and Cyril Pahinui.

Universally beloved is the ukulele, derived from the *braguinha* (a Portuguese instrument introduced to Hawai'i in the late 19th century). Ukulele means 'jumping flea' in Hawaiian, referring to the way players' deft fingers swiftly 'jump' around the strings. Hawaii's ukulele masters include Eddie Kamae, Herb Ohta and contemporary uke whirlwind Jake Shimabukuro.

The ukulele and the steel guitar were essential to the lighthearted, romantic music popularized in Hawai'i between the 1930s and 1950s, during which time 'My Little Grass Shack' and 'Lovely Hula Hands' became classics.

In the 1970s Hawaiian music enjoyed a rebirth, and artists such as Cecilio & Kapono and the Beamer Brothers remain icons in Hawaii. The Hawaiian sound spurred offshoots like reggae-inspired 'Jawaiian,' but the traditional style lives on in gifted contemporary voices, such as Keali'i Reichel (also a hula master), and Raiatea Helm, who has been scooping up Hawaii's top music awards. Still, the most famous island musician is the late Israel Kamakawiwo'ole, whose album *Facing Future* is Hawaii's all-time bestseller. A Grammy Award for Best Hawaiian Music Album was established in 2005. In that year the award went to a slack key collection featuring Maui's own Jeff Peterson and Keoki Kahumoku.

To learn more about slack key guitar, visit George Winston's Dancing Cat Records (www.dancingcat.com). For guitar and ukulele information, visit www.taropatch.net.

Hula

In ancient Hawai'i, hula was not entertainment but a type of religious expression. Dancers used hand gestures, facial expression and rhythmic movement to illustrate historical events, legendary tales and the accomplishments of the great *ali'i* (royalty). Rhythmic chants and drum beatings accompanied performances, serving to connect with the spirit world. Dancers wore *kapa* (bark cloth), never the stereotypical grass skirts.

There are many hula troupes active on Maui. Some practice in public places, such as in school grounds and at parks, where visitors are welcome to watch. Although many of the *halau* (schools) rely on tuition fees, others receive sponsorship from hotels or shopping centers and give weekly public performances in return. Two places presenting authentic hula are the Old Lahaina Luau and the Lahaina Cannery Mall, both in Lahaina. If in Maui at the time, don't miss the Hula O Na Keiki competition in Ka'anapali.

Local Arts & Craftwork

Woodworking is an ancient skill that remains popular and commercially viable. In old Hawai'i, the best artisans used giant logs to build canoes. Today, the most common creations are hand-turned wooden bowls and furniture – impossibly smooth and polished – made from a variety of hardwood. Traditionally koa was the wood of choice but, for variety, other gorgeous island woods are also used. Don't be fooled by cheap monkeypod bowls made in the Philippines.

Lei-making is a more transitory art form. Although the lei most visitors wear are made of fragrant flowers such as plumeria and tuberose, traditional lei of *mokihana* berries and maile leaves were more commonly worn in old Hawai'i. Both types are still made and sold today.

Lauhala weaving is another traditional craft. Weaving the *lau* (leaves) of the *hala* (pandanus) tree is the fun part, while preparing the leaves, which have razor-sharp spines, is difficult, messy work. Traditionally *lauhala* served as mats and floor coverings, but today smaller items such as hats, placemats and baskets are most commonly made.

Literature

'I went to Maui to stay a week and remained five,' wrote Mark Twain in *Letters from the Sandwich Islands*. 'I never spent so pleasant a month before or bade a place good-bye so regretfully.' Twain's 1860s observations, along with those of 19th-century British adventurer Isabella Bird, began a long tradition of Hawaii literature dominated by nonlocal Western writers observing the state's exoticism.

Novels of this type include *Hawaii,* James Michener's ambitious saga of Hawaii's history, and *Hotel Honolulu,* Paul Theroux's novel about a washed-up writer who becomes the manager of a rundown hotel.

Today, a growing body of local writers is redefining Hawaii literature. Stories don't consciously highlight Hawaii as an exotic setting but instead focus on the lives of universal characters. Bamboo Ridge Press (www.bambooridge.com) publishes contemporary local fiction and poetry in a biannual journal and has launched many local writers' careers. Some have hit the national scene, such as Nora Okja Keller, whose first novel, *Comfort Woman,* won the 1998 American Book Award, and Lois-Ann Yamanaka, who introduced pidgin to literary circles with *Saturday Night at the Pahala Theatre* – winner of the 1993 Pushcart Prize for poetry – and critically acclaimed novels such as *Behold the Many*.

Much locally written literature features pidgin English, especially in dialogue. The book *Growing Up Local: An Anthology of Poetry and Prose from Hawaii* (Bamboo Ridge Press) is a good introduction. Also highly amusing are the pidgin writings by Lee Tonouchi, author of *Living Pidgin: Contemplations on Pidgin Culture* (essays) and *Da Kine Dictionary* (pictorial dictionary).

Cinema & TV

Book 'em, Danno. In 2010 a revamped *Hawaii-5-0* hit the primetime line-up. For *Lost* fans mourning the loss of Hawaiian scenery from their TV screens, this slick reboot came none too soon.

Best Hawaiian Sounds

Familiarize yourself with the dynamic panoply of Hawaiian music:

- **Genoa Keawe** (www.genoakeawe.com) No one epitomizes Hawaii like 'Aunty Genoa,' whose extraordinary signature falsetto sets the standard.
- **Israel Kamakawiwoʻole** A discussion of Hawaiian music isn't complete without honoring the late 'Braddah Iz,' whose album *Facing Future* is Hawaii's all-time bestseller.
- **Jake Shimabukuro** (www.jakeshimabukuro.com) A ukulele virtuoso and exhilarating performer, Shimabukuro is known for lightning-fast fingers and a talent for playing any musical genre on the ukulele.
- **Kealiʻi Reichel** (www.kealiireichel.com) Charismatic vocalist Reichel is also a *kumu hula* (hula teacher) and the founder of a Hawaiian-language immersion school on Maui.

Hawaiian Quilting

Christian missionaries introduced the concept of patchwork quilting, but the Hawaiians didn't have a surplus of cloth scraps. Cutting up new lengths of fabric simply to sew them back together in small squares seemed absurd.

Instead, Hawaiian women created designs using larger cloth pieces, typically with stylized tropical flora on a contrasting background. The story goes that when the first group of Hawaiian quilters spread their white cloth on the ground, a breadfruit leaf cast its shadow onto the cloth. The outline of the leaf was traced to produce the first native design.

Maui Quilt Shop (www.mauiquiltshop.com) in Kihei sells Hawaiian quilting materials.

Hollywood's love affair with Hawaii began in 1913 and bloomed in the 1930s, when the islands captured the public's imagination as a sultry, care-free paradise. In film classics such as *Waikiki Wedding* (featuring Bing Crosby's Oscar-winning song, 'Sweet Leilani'), *Blue Hawaii* (an Elvis favorite) and a spate of WWII dramas, including the 1953 classic *From Here to Eternity,* viewers saw Hawaii through foreigners' eyes.

Hundreds of feature films have been filmed in Hawaii, including *Pirates of the Caribbean: On Stranger Tides; Raiders of the Lost Ark, Godzilla, Pearl Harbor,* and *Jurassic Park* and its two sequels. Unless homegrown films are produced, expect to see the same themes and stereotypes in Hollywood movies. Essentially, Hawaii is often just a colorful backdrop for mainland characters. Viewers might not even realize they're seeing Hawaii, as the islands often serve as stand-ins for Costa Rica, Africa, Vietnam and similar settings.

Maui is rarely the island seen in these productions. Kaua'i is the celluloid darling, while O'ahu (*Magnum PI, Lost* and the *Hawaii 5-0's*) draws directors with its more advanced facilities. Movies filmed in part on Maui include *The Hulk* (2003), *Jurassic Park III* (2001) and the James Bond film *Die Another Day* (2002). MTV shot two reality series (*Island Fever,* about young folk, and *Living Lahaina,* about adventurous surf instructors) on Maui in 2006.

For an insider's look at surf culture, don't miss Stacy Peralta's *Riding Giants,* which features three titans in big-wave surfing – Greg Noll, Jeff Clark and Laird Hamilton – hitting the waves on Maui. For more information, see the Hawaii Film Office (www.hawaiifilmoffice.com) website.

Family Travel

Surfing Goat Dairy (p164)

COURTESY OF SURFING GOAT DAIRY, PHOTO BY CHRISI HEINEN-S

Children are welcome everywhere on Maui. Hawaiians love kids – large families are common and keiki (children) are an integral part of the scenery. Maui has everything a child on vacation could dream of: sandy beaches, splashy hotel pools, all sorts of yummy food and tons of outdoor activities. Maui also offers plenty of cool cross-cultural opportunities, from hula lessons to outrigger canoe rides.

Sights & Activities

Brimming with glorious beaches and abundant resort activities, South Maui and West Maui are the two top destinations for families.

Both have excellent opportunities for swimming, snorkeling, boogie boarding, catamaran sails and whale-watching – that alone could keep the whole family in splashy fun for a week! Older kids will gravitate toward the more challenging water activities such as kayaking and paddle boarding.

In Lahaina, kids can climb America's largest banyan tree. The dangling aerial roots invite at least one Tarzan-style swing. Little tots will want to ride the Sugar Cane Train. And the rest of the clan can take the plunge with a surfing lesson on Lahaina's gentle waves.

Speaking of Tarzan, Maui is zipline heaven. For thrills galore, opt for Piiholo

Ranch Zipline or the Kapalua Adventures zipline; both have dual lines that allow family members to zip along side by side.

Some activities (such as horseback riding, ziplines and watersports lessons) require that children be of a certain age, height or weight to participate. Inquire beforehand as to what restrictions apply. Ziplines, for instance, require participants to be at least 10 years old and weigh 75lbs

Be sure to take a day for Haleakalā National Park. Every kid loves playing astronaut on a crunchy walk into the wildly lunar-like crater.

Hotel luau offer up flashy dances, fire tricks and a large buffet where kids can pick and choose their own meal – what's not to love? Children get a discount, usually half-price, and are often invited to come on stage and enjoy the fun.

Keep an eye out for festivals, even small local events. They're invariably family oriented with plenty of *keiki*-geared activities tied in.

Eating With Kids

Maui's family-oriented, casual atmosphere means children will feel at home almost everywhere. Sit-down restaurants are quick to accommodate kids with high chairs and booster seats.

You might assume that all fancy restaurants frown on parties that include children, but many actually cater to them with special kids' menus. The trend toward exhibition-kitchen restaurants – one large open area with a loud dining room – means that kid chatter will blend into the overall din.

As for restaurant food, the local palate tends toward the sweet and straightforward, which typically agrees with kid tastes, without too much garlic or pungent flavors.

Kids love a picnic and impromptu picnicking on Maui is a cinch – you can scarcely go a mile without finding a park with picnic tables. Many restaurants pack food for takeout, and grocery stores invariably have extensive deli sections with grab-and-go meals.

When you're traveling around the island, stop at roadside fruit stands to let everyone pick their own healthful snack. It's fun watching a coconut being cracked open with a machete and then slurping up the coconut water through a straw.

Practicalities

Restaurants, hotels and sights that especially cater to families, and have good facilities for children, are marked with a family icon (👪) throughout this book.

Children are welcome at hotels throughout Maui and those under 17 typically stay free when sharing a room with their parents and using existing bedding.

Many sights and activities offer discounted childrens rates, sometimes as cheap as half price.

Car-hire companies on Maui lease child-safety seats, but they don't always have enough on hand so don't wait until the last minute to book your car.

If you're traveling with infants and forget to pack some of your gear, go online to www.akamaimothers.com to rent cribs, strollers and other baby items.

The Best…
Activities for Kids

1 Whale-watching cruise (p43)

2 Haleakalā crater walk (p183)

3 Maui Ocean Center (p111)

4 Zipline tour (p159)

5 Snorkeling at Molokini (p303)

6 Surfing Goat Dairy tour (p164)

Need to Know

- **Changing facilities** Found in shopping malls and resorts
- **Cots** Request in advance when booking a room
- **Highchairs** Available at most restaurants
- **Kids' menus** Family-oriented restaurants have them
- **Nappies** (diapers) Grocery and convenience stores sell them
- **Strollers** Bring your own or rent in Maui
- **Car safety seats** Reserve in advance with your car rental

For an evening out alone, the easiest and most reliable way to find a babysitter is through the hotel concierge.

Maui is an open-minded place, and although public breast feeding is not commonplace it's unlikely to elicit unwanted attention.

Children's Programs

○ Many Maui beach resorts have *keiki* day programs where kids can do fun things while you head off for the spa.

○ Visitors to Haleakalā National Park should take advantage of the free junior ranger program geared for ages 7 to 12.

○ The Pacific Whale Foundation provides a free Junior Marine Naturalist handbook that introduces kids to Hawaii marine life through quizzes, anagrams and the like. Pick one up on board a whale watch or at Ulua Beach in Wailea.

Green Maui

Bio-Beetle (p331), powered by recycled vegetable oil

GREG ELMS/LONELY PLANET IMAGES ©

Green is a way of thinking and living in Maui. People spend most of their waking hours outdoors, communing with each other and with nature. Environmental stewardship is an integral part of the experience. As a visitor, it won't take long to feel the 'aloha 'aina (love for the land), too. Best part? With scores of environmental groups and programs, Maui makes it ridiculously easy to get involved.

MAUI GOES GREEN

Maui has a long history of protecting its environment. Islanders of all backgrounds are activists – from Native Hawaiians volunteering to restore an ancient fishpond to scientists fighting invasive plants. The island has no polluting heavy industry and not a single roadside billboard to blight the natural vistas.

Today, Maui and its residents are leaders in eco-activism. Maui was the first island in Hawaii to approve a ban on single-use plastic bags. Businesses and restaurants that violate the ordinance, which went into effect on January 11, 2011, will incur a $500 daily fine. A powerful incentive!

Parks, forest reserves and watersheds cover nearly half of the island. The crowning glory is Haleakalā National Park, which, thanks to the collaborative work of environmental groups, now extends from its original perch in the center of Maui clear down to the south coast. On the first and third Sunday of every month, volunteers can visit the park to work and help rid Hosmer Grove of invasive pine trees.

As for renewable energy, some 20% of Maui's electricity comes from wind power and from the burning of bagasse, the byproduct of sugar production. Twenty wind turbines on the slopes above wind-whipped Ma'alaea produce enough emission-free energy to light 10% of the homes on Maui. Fourteen additional wind turbines should be added to the slopes by the end of 2012.

Sustainable Maui

As you plan your trip, consider your impact on the island. There are numerous ways to lighten your tourist footprint.

Transportation

On a short trip, consider ditching the car. The Maui Bus (www.mauicounty.gov) loops past convenient stops in Lahaina, Ka'anapali, Kihei, Kahului and Wailuku. It also runs several 'islander' routes between major towns and resorts. In Ka'anapali and Kapalua, free resort shuttles swing past major hotels and beaches.

For longer stays, rent a smaller, less gas-guzzling vehicle. Not only will that be gentler on Maui's environment, but the island's narrow roads will be easier to negotiate. Consider renting a Bio-Beetle (p331), which runs on recycled cooking oil.

Treading Lightly

Before arriving on Maui, clean your shoes and wipe off your luggage so you don't inadvertently bring seeds or insects, introducing yet another invasive species. When hiking, stay on trails; when snorkeling, stay off the coral.

Don't disturb cultural sites, and respect the 'Kapu – No Trespassing' signs that you'll see around the island.

Eating Locally

Every food product not grown or raised on Maui is shipped to the island by boat or plane. Considering the great distances and the amount of fuel used, that makes the 'locavore' or 'eat local' movement particularly relevant.

See p295 for a list of farmers markets and restaurants showcasing local fare.

Sustainable Icon

It seems like everyone's going 'green' these days, but how can you know which Maui businesses are genuinely eco-friendly and which are simply jumping on the sustainable bandwagon? Throughout the book, this Sustainable icon indicates listings that we are highlighting because they demonstrate an active sustainable-tourism policy. Some are involved in conservation or environmental education, while others maintain and preserve Hawaiian identity and culture, and many are owned and operated by local and indigenous operators.

Recycling

Many beach parks have a bin for recycling aluminum cans, and you can often find eco-friendly businesses with bins for plastic and glass as well. Ask at your hotel how they recycle: should you keep your cans and bottles separate? If they're not committed recyclers, asking helps raise the consciousness level.

Tap water on Maui is perfectly fine for drinking, so resist those California spring-water imports. At the very least, refill your plastic bottle.

On the Ground & in the Sea

There are environmentally friendly organizations across the island that offer ways to be active and adventurous with less environmental impact.

Instead of a boat dive, try a shore dive (no diesel fuel, no dropped anchors) with a company that specializes in them, such as Maui Dreams Dive Company in Kihei. Opt for a sailboat cruise over a motorboat cruise. Riding with the wind is more eco-friendly, and sailboats get closer to whales and dolphins, which are repelled by motorboat noise. Consider companies such as Trilogy Excursions that fly a green flag, indicating that the boat adheres to strict environmental practices and doesn't discharge waste into the ocean.

To really go local, take an outrigger canoe trip with the Kihei Canoe Club or Hawaiian Sailing Canoe Adventures.

Local farms sell fruits and vegetables at farmers markets in Kihei and Honokowai, and at the Maui Swap Meet in Kahului. More and more restaurants are showcasing locally caught seafood, Maui-raised beef and Maui-grown produce. The range is wide, from the deli at Mana Foods in Pa'ia to the gourmet food at I'O in Lahaina. One buy-local restaurant, Flatbread Company in Pa'ia, gives a cut of the night's profits to local environmental groups that show up to rap with customers every Tuesday night. At Laulima Farms in Kipahulu, the faster you pedal the stationary bike, the faster you'll get your self-powered smoothie.

Buying Maui-made products supports the local economy and often helps sustain the environment as well. Ali'i Kula Lavender in Kula produces organic lavender blossoms that are used by two dozen home-based businesses to make lavender jams, vinegars and salad dressings sold at the farm. For picnics, buy cheese from Surfing Goat Dairy and wine from Tedeschi Vineyards. Shops selling Maui-made artwork are listed online at www.madeinmaui.com.

Helpful Organizations

Groups committed to a green and sustainable Maui include:

Hawai'i 2050 (www.hawaii2050.org) Public, private and community groups are formulating a long-term sustainability plan.

Kahea (www.kahea.org) Activist organization tackling Hawaiian cultural rights and environmental issues.

The Best... Sites for Agritourism

1 Ali'i Kula Lavender (p166)

2 Surfing Goat Dairy (p164)

3 O'o Farm lunch tour (p167)

4 Tedeschi Vineyards (p173)

5 Enchanting Floral Gardens (p166)

6 Ono Organic Farms (p230)

IN FOCUS GREEN MAUI

The Best... Places to Honor the Sun

1 Haleakalā Crater for sunrise (p178)

2 Wai'anapanapa State Park for sunrise (p213)

3 Big Beach (Oneloa) for sunset (p139)

4 Papawai Point for sunset (p65)

5 Lahaina for sunset (p34)

Kauahea (www.kauahea.org) Connected to the Maui Arts & Cultural Center, it promotes Hawaiian culture.

Maui County Green Book (www.mauicountygreenbook.com) List of Maui businesses offering sustainable goods and services, plus farmers markets and volunteer opportunities.

Malama Hawai'i (www.malamahawaii.org) Coordinates over 70 cultural and environmental organizations.

Maui Coastal Land Trust (www.mauicoastallandtrust.org) Protects Maui's shorelines.

Maui Tomorrow (www.maui-tomorrow.org) Promotes sustainable development policies and preservation of open space.

Na Ala Hele (www.hawaiitrails.org) Maintains and preserves hiking trails.

Sierra Club, Maui Chapter (www.hi.sierraclub.org/maui) Everything from political activism to weekend outings eradicating invasive plants from forests.

Surfrider Foundation, Maui Chapter (www.surfrider.org/maui) Surfer organization protecting Maui's ocean and beaches.

Environmental Issues

Because it's one of the most geographically isolated places on earth (2500 miles from the nearest continent), Hawaii's environment constitutes a rare living textbook of Darwinian evolution – so fragile that some of it is vanishing before our eyes. The havoc began the moment humans stepped into this unique landscape of plants and wildlife that had evolved without people, land mammals or agricultural crops. Today Hawaii accounts for approximately 75% of all documented plant and animal extinctions in the USA, and it is the undisputed 'endangered species capital of the world.'

There have been notable turn-arounds. Haleakalā National Park recently completed a decade-long project to fence in the park and eradicate wild cats and pigs. Thanks to that effort, both the endangered native silversword (see the boxed text, p183) and the nene (see the boxed text, p193) have come back from the brink of extinction.

The waters around Maui and the other Hawaiian Islands are home to 84% of the coral found in the USA. The most significant threats to these reefs are created by people – from overfishing, and from land-based pollution from agriculture and golf courses. Two Maui tour companies were fined by the state for damaging coral reefs: one of the companies destroyed 1200 coral colonies near Molokini in 2006 when one of its charter boats, operated by a new captain, sank. The company was fined nearly $400,000.

You can help by eating sustainable fish (see www.seafoodwatch.org) and practicing responsible diving.

The effects of global warming are another concern. Some scientists believe droughts that have hit the island in recent years are at least in part the consequence of climate change.

Many of Maui's environmental issues revolve around development, especially in water-thirsty south Maui, which relies upon precious water from Upcountry farms and central Maui to run its taps and turn desert into lawns.

ENVIRONMENT

Breaching whales, flowery tropical blooms and fascinating underwater sights that exist nowhere else on the planet – Maui's environmental wonders are in a class by themselves.

The Land

Maui is the second-largest Hawaiian island, with a land area of 728 sq miles. Set atop a 'hot spot' on the Pacific Plate, Maui rose from the ocean floor as two separate volcanoes. Lava flows and soil erosion eventually built up a valleylike isthmus between the volcanic masses, linking them in their present form. This flat region provides a fertile setting for sugarcane fields and is home to Maui's largest urban center, the twin towns of Kahului and Wailuku.

The eastern side of Maui, the larger and younger of the two volcanic masses, is dominated by the lofty Haleakalā (10,023ft). This dormant volcano, whose crater-like floor is dotted with cinder cones, last erupted in 1790. The second, more ancient volcano formed the craggy West Maui Mountains, which top out at the Pu'u Kukui (5778ft). Both mountains are high enough to trap the moisture-laden clouds carried by the northeast tradewinds, bringing abundant rain to their windward eastern sides. Consequently, the lushest jungles and gushiest waterfalls are found along the Hana Hwy, which runs along Haleakalā's eastern slopes, while the driest, sunniest beaches are on the western coasts.

Wildlife

All living things that reached Maui were carried across the sea on wing, wind or wave – seeds clinging to a bird's feather, or insects in a piece of driftwood. Scientists estimate that successful species arrived once every 70,000 years – and they included no amphibians and only two mammals: a bat and a seal.

However, the flora and fauna that made it to Maui occupied an unusually rich and diverse land. In a prime example of 'adaptive radiation,' the 250 flowering plants that arrived evolved into 1800 native species. Lacking predators, new species dropped defensive protections – thorns, poisons and strong odors disappeared, which explains why they fare so poorly against modern invaders.

The Polynesians brought pigs, chickens, coconuts and about two dozen other species, not to mention people. The pace of change exploded after Western contact in

Green Beer

Okay, so the beer at Maui Brewing Company isn't *green,* but the folks who brew it are committed to eco-minded business practices. For example, used vegetable oil from the brewpub is converted to diesel fuel, which powers the cars of owners Garrett and Melanie Marrero as well as the delivery truck. Spent grain is given to local ranchers for composting, and the brewery's retail beers are sold in recyclable cans. Cans over glass? Yep, cans aren't breakable, so they're less of a threat on the beach. Cans are also lighter than glass, leaving a smaller footprint. At press time, the brewery's rooftop solar panels were on order. For a sudsy and sustainable toast, visit its Kahana brewpub. Cheers for green beers!

Maui's Top Protected Areas

- **'Ahihi-Kina'u Natural Area Reserve** A pristine bay, lava flows and ancient sites; good for hiking and snorkeling.
- **Haleakalā National Park** (Summit Section) With towering waterfalls, cascading pools and ancient sites; good for hiking, swimming and camping.
- **Haleakalā National Park** (Kipahulu Section) A large, dormant volcano; good for hiking, camping and horseback riding.
- **'Iao Valley State Park** Features streams, cliffs and swimming holes; good for hiking and photography.
- **Kahanu Garden & Pi'ilanihale Heiau** A national botanic garden and ancient site; good for walking.
- **Kealia Pond National Wildlife Refuge** Bird sanctuary; good for birdwatching.
- **Molokini Crater** A submerged volcanic crater; ideal for snorkeling and diving.
- **Polipoli Spring State Recreation Area** With cloud forest and uncrowded trails; good for hiking, camping and mountain biking.
- **Wai'anapanapa State Park** Lava tubes and trail over rugged sea cliffs to Hana; good for hiking and camping.

the late 18th century. Cattle and goats were introduced and set wild, with devastating consequences. Even today, sitting on a Kihei beach looking out at Kaho'olawe in the late afternoon, you'll notice a red tinge from the dust whipping off the island, a consequence of defoliation by wild goats released there a century ago.

But there is progress. On Kaho'olawe the goats are gone and native reforestation has begun; Haleakalā National Park has made great strides in reintroducing and protecting native species; and the first public garden totally dedicated to endemic Hawaiian species, Maui Nui Botanical Gardens, has opened at the site of a former exotic zoo.

If you see a wild animal in distress, report it to the state **Division of Conservation & Resource Enforcement** (DOCARE; ☎ 984-8110).

Animals

Most of Maui's wildlife attractions are found in the water or on the wing. Hawaii has no native land mammals.

Marine Life

Of the almost 700 fish species living in Hawaiian waters, nearly one-third are found nowhere else in the world. Maui's nearshore waters are a true rainbow of color: turquoise parrotfish, bright yellow tangs and polka-dotted pufferfish, to name a few.

Green sea turtles (*honu*) abound in Maui's waters. To the thrill of snorkelers and divers, *honu* can often be seen feeding in shallow coves and bays. Adults can grow to more than 3ft – an awesome sight when one swims past you in the water. Much less common is the hawksbill turtle, which occasionally nests on Maui's western shores.

The sheltered waters between Maui, Lana'i and Moloka'i are the wintering tination for thousands of North Pacific humpback whales. The majestic creatures he fifth-largest of the great whales, reaching lengths of 45ft and weighing up to

45 tons. Humpback whales are coast-huggers and are visible from the beach in winter along Maui's west and southwest coasts.

Maui is also home to a number of dolphins. The spinner dolphin (named for its acrobatic leaps) comes into calm bays during the day to rest.

With luck you might see the Hawaiian monk seal, which lives primarily in the remote Northwestern Hawaiian Islands, but occasionally hauls out on Maui beaches. It was nearly wiped out last century, but conservation efforts have edged the species back from the brink of extinction.

Don't touch, approach or disturb marine mammals; most are protected, making it illegal to do so. Watch dolphins, whales, seals and sea turtles from a respectful distance.

Birds

Many of Hawaii's birds have evolved from a single species in a spectacular display of adaptive radiation. For example, all 57 species of Hawaiian honeycreepers likely evolved from a single finch ancestor. Left vulnerable to new predatory species and infectious avian diseases after Europeans arrived, half of Hawaii's native bird species are already extinct, and more than 30 of those remaining are still under threat.

The endangered nene, Hawaii's state bird, is a long-lost cousin of the Canada goose. Nene nest in high cliffs on the slopes of Haleakalā and their feet have adapted to the rugged volcanic environment by losing most of their webbing. Nene have black heads, light-yellow cheeks, a white underbelly and dark gray feathers.

At least six birds native to Maui are found nowhere else in the world and all are endangered, including the Maui parrotbill, which exists solely in the Kipahulu section of Haleakalā National Park, and the cinnamon-colored po'ouli, which was last seen in 2004 and may already be extinct. Alas, it's unlikely you'll see any of those birds. But other native forest birds, including the 'apapane, a vivid red honeycreeper, can be sighted in Hosmer Grove in Haleakalā National Park.

Maui's two waterbird preserves, the Kanaha Pond Bird Sanctuary and Kealia Pond National Wildlife Refuge are nesting sites for the ae'o (Hawaiian black-necked stilt), a wading bird with a white underbelly and long orange legs.

Plants

Maui seems suitable for just about anything with roots. On a mile-for-mile basis, Hawaii has the highest concentration of climatic and ecological zones anywhere on earth. They vary from lowland deserts along the coast to lush tropical rainforests in the

Volunteering on Vacation? Easy!

In 2007 the Pacific Whale Foundation and the Hawaii Tourism Authority began the **'Volunteering on Vacation' program** (☎ 808-249-8811 ext 1; www. volunteersonvacation.org) to organize voluntourism opportunities across Maui. All projects are free, and they all sound cool, from removing invasive plants at Haleakalā National Park (entrance fee is covered) to helping at an organic to maintaining a coastal trail. The list goes on. Projects require one-day's (two for Haleakala) and last about three hours. Since the program's inc has attracted 3000 volunteers who have provided 10,000 houses of se the website for a current list of projects.

mountains. And the diversity within a small region can be amazing. In the Upcountry there are so many microclimate zones that hillside farms, such as Enchanting Floral Gardens in Kula, can grow tropical fruit trees just a few sloping acres from where temperate roses thrive. Another mile up, don't even bother looking for tropical fruit trees as you're now in the zone where cool-weather crops grow.

Many native species have adapted to very narrow geographic ecosystems, such as Maui's endangered silversword, which grows at the summit of Haleakalā.

Flowering Plants & Ferns

For travelers, the flower most closely identified with Hawaii is the hibiscus, whose generous blossoms are worn by women tucked behind their ears. Thousands of varieties of hibiscus bushes grow in Hawaii; on most, the flowers bloom early in the day and drop before sunset. The variety most frequently seen is the introduced red *Hibiscus rosa-sinensis,* which is used as a landscape hedge throughout Maui. Much rarer is the *koki'o ke'oke'o,* a native white hibiscus tree that grows up to 40ft high; it can be seen at Maui Nui Botanical Gardens in Kahului.

Two native plants at the beach are pohuehue, a beach morning glory with pink flowers that's found just above the wrack line; and beach naupaka, a shrub with oval leaves and a small white five-petal flower that looks as if it's been torn in half.

Throughout the Upcountry you'll find gardens filled with protea, a flashy flower inally from South Africa that takes many forms. Named after the Greek god us (who could change shape at will), blossoms range from small pincushiony tall stalklike flowers with petals that look like feathers. You'll also see plenty of wy exotic flowers throughout Maui, including the brilliantly orange-and-blue adise and various heliconias with bright orange and red bracts.

about 200 varieties of Hawaiian ferns and fern allies (such as mosses) rests and colonizing lava flows.

Yellow hibiscus

Trees & Shrubs

The most revered of the native Hawaiian forest trees is koa, found at higher elevations on Maui. Growing up to 100ft high, this rich hardwood is traditionally used to make canoes, surfboards and even ukuleles.

Brought by early Polynesian settlers, the *kukui* tree has chestnutlike oily nuts that the Hawaiians used for candles, hence its common name, candlenut tree. It's recognizable in the forest by its light silver-tinged foliage.

Two coastal trees that were well utilized in old Hawaii are *hala,* also called pandanus or screw pine, whose spiny leaves were used for thatching and weaving; and the coconut palm *(niu),* which loves coral sands and yields about 75 coconuts a year

Kiawe, a non-native tree, thrives in dry coastal areas. A member of the mesquite family, kiawe is useful for making charcoal but is a nuisance for beachgoers as its sharp thorns easily pierce soft sandals. Also plentiful along the beach are stands of ironwood, a conifer with drooping needles that act as natural windbreaks and prevent beach erosion.

Other trees that will catch your eye include the African tulip tree, a rainforest tree abloom with brilliant orange flowers that grows profusely along the road to Hana; plumeria, a favored landscaping tree whose fragrant pink-and-white blossoms are used in lei making; and majestic banyan trees, which have a canopy of hanging aerial roots with trunks large enough to swallow small children.

National, State & County Parks

Haleakalā National Park accounts for nearly 10% of Maui's land area. The park not only offers superb hiking and other recreational activities but also protects Hawaiian cultural sites and the habitat of several endangered species. Maui's numerous state and county parks also play an important role in preserving undeveloped forest areas and much of Maui's coastline. The parks are well used by Maui residents – from surfers to pig hunters – as well as by tourists.

The state's **Department of Land & Natural Resources** (DLNR; ☎984-8100; www.state. hi.us/dlnr; 54 S High St, Wailuku) has useful online information about hiking, history and aquatic safety. The DLNR oversees the **Division of State Parks** (☎984-8109; www. hawaiistateparks.org), which issues camping permits on Maui and **Na Ala Hele** (p295), which coordinates public access to hiking trails.

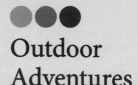

Outdoor Adventures

Surfers, Ho'okipa Beach Park (p148)

JOHN ELK III/LONELY PLANET IMAGES

After climbing Haleakalā in 1866, Mark Twain wrote that the sunrise there was 'the sublimest spectacle I ever witnessed.' Today, outdoor adventurers might pay the same compliment to the whole of Maui. Just look around. Kiteboarders skip across swells. Surfers rip monster waves. Snorkelers float beside green turtles. Hikers climb misty mountains while zipliners swoop across the slopes. Sea, land and sometimes the air between — it is a spectacle sublime.

AT SEA

The Pacific Ocean is Maui's ultimate playground. Here are the best ways to enjoy it.

Bodysurfing & Boogie Boarding

If you want to catch your waves lying down, bodysurfing and boogie boarding are suitable water activities for anybody.

There are good beginner to intermediate shorebreaks at the Kama'ole Beach Parks and Charley Young Beach in Kihei, and at Ulua Beach and Wailea Beach in Wailea. Experienced bodysurfers should head to DT Fleming Beach Park and Slaughterhouse Beach in Kapalua; Big Beach in Makena; and HA Baldwin Beach Park near Pa'ia.

Special bodysurfing flippers, which are smaller than snorkel fins, will help you paddle out. Boogie boards rent for around $10 per day.

Diving

Excellent visibility. Warm water temperatures. Hundreds of rare fish species. Maui is a diving mecca for a reason. Here you can often see spinner dolphins, green sea turtles, manta rays and moray eels. With luck you might even hear humpback whales singing underwater – you'll never forget it.

Most dive operations on Maui offer a full range of dives as well as refresher and advanced certification courses. Introductory dives for beginners get you beneath the surface in just a couple of hours. Experienced divers needn't bring anything other than a swimsuit and certification card. Don't monkey around with activity desks – book directly with the dive operators.

On Maui, the granddaddy of dives is crescent-shaped Molokini. The other prime destination is untouched Cathedrals on the south side of Lana'i, which takes its name from the amazing underwater caverns, arches and connecting passages.

Lonely Planet's *Diving & Snorkeling Hawaii* includes color photos of sites and fish.

Molokini Crater

No underwater site draws more visitors than Molokini, the fascinating volcanic crater that lies midway between the islands of Maui and Kaho'olawe. Half of the crater rim has eroded away, leaving a crescent-moon shape that rises 160ft above the ocean surface, with a mere 18 acres of rocky land high and dry. But it's what's beneath the surface that draws the crowds. Snorkelers and divers will be thrilled by steep walls, ledges, white-tipped reef sharks, manta rays, turtles and abundant fish.

The legends about Molokini are myriad. One says Molokini was a beautiful woman who was turned to stone by jealous Pele, goddess of fire and volcanoes. Another claims one of Pele's lovers angered her by secretly marrying a mo'o (shape-shifting water lizard). Pele chopped the sacred lizard in half, leaving Molokini as its tail and Pu'u 'Olai in Makena as its head. Yet another tale alleges that Molokini, which means 'many ties' in Hawaiian, is the umbilical cord left over from the birth of Kaho'olawe.

The coral reef that extends outward from Molokini is awesome, though it's lost some of its variety over the years. Most of the black coral that was once prolific in Molokini's deeper waters made its way into Lahaina jewelry stores before the island was declared a marine conservation district in 1977. During WWII the US Navy shelled Molokini for target practice, and live bombs are still occasionally spotted on the crater floor. In 2006 a tour boat with an inexperienced captain sank at Molokini. No one was injured, but after an inept salvage job, 1200 coral colonies had been destroyed. The company is paying a $396,000 state-imposed fine.

There are a few things to consider when planning a Molokini excursion. The water is calmest and clearest in the morning, so don't fall for discounted afternoon tours – go out early for the smoothest sailing and best conditions. For snorkelers, there's simply not much to see when the water's choppy. The main departure points for Molokini trips are Ma'alaea and Lahaina harbors. You'll get out there quicker if you hop a boat from Ma'alaea, which is closer to Molokini. Going from Lahaina adds on more sail time, but if it's winter it'll also increase the possibilities for spotting whales along the way, so it's sometimes worth an extra hour out of your day.

Parks & Beaches

Details about county parks and beaches in Maui, including contact information and lifeguard availability, can be found on the Maui County government website (www.co.maui.hi.us).

Responsible Diving

The popularity of diving is placing immense pressure on many sites. Please consider the following tips to help preserve the ecology and beauty of reefs.

o Avoid touching living marine organisms with your body or dragging equipment across the reef. Polyps can be damaged by even the gentlest contact. Never stand on coral. If you must hold on to the reef, touch only exposed rock or dead coral.

o Be conscious of your fins. Even without contact, the surge from heavy fin strokes near the reef can damage delicate organisms. When treading water in shallow reef areas, take care not to kick up clouds of sand. Settling sand can easily smother the delicate organisms of the reef.

o Do not use reef anchors and take care not to ground boats on coral.

o Minimize your disturbance of marine animals. It is illegal to approach endangered marine species too closely; these include whales, dolphins, sea turtles and the Hawaiian monk seal. In particular, do not ride on the backs of turtles!

o Practice and maintain proper buoyancy control. Major damage can be done by divers descending too fast and colliding with the reef. Make sure you are correctly weighted and that your weight belt is positioned so that you stay horizontal.

o Resist the temptation to feed marine animals. You may disturb their normal eating habits, encourage aggressive behavior or feed them food that is detrimental to their health.

o Spend as little time in underwater caves as possible, as your air bubbles may be caught within the roof and leave previously submerged organisms high and dry.

Don't leave any rubbish, and remove any litter you find. Plastics in particular are a ⁻ious threat to marine life. Turtles can mistake plastic for jellyfish and eat it.

⁻n't collect (or buy) coral or shells. Aside from the ecological damage, taking home ⁻e souvenirs depletes the beauty of a site and spoils the enjoyment of others.

Kayakers, Makena Landing (p139)
PHOTOGRAPHER: GREG ELMS/LONELY PLANET IMAGES ©

○ Divers Alert Network **(DAN; ☎919-684-9111, 800-446-2671; www.diversalertnetwork.org)** gives advice on diving emergencies, insurance, decompression services, illness and injury

Diving & Snorkeling Outfitters

○ **Lahaina Divers** (p39) Boat dives and snorkeling, departs from Lahaina.

○ **Maui Dive Shop** (p121) Boat dives and snorkeling, departs from Lahaina.

○ **Maui Dreams Dive Company** (p121) Shore dives and boat dives, departs from Kihei and Ma'alaea

○ **Pacific Whale Foundation** (p43) Snorkeling, departs from Ma'alaea

Fishing

Deep-sea sportfishing charters set out from Maui for such legendary game as *ahi* (yellowfin tuna) and, most famous of all, Pacific blue marlin, which can reach 1000lb. Licenses aren't required, and charter boats are available on the pier in Lahaina Harbor and Ma'alaea. Sharing a boat costs around $139 to $210 per person, depending on how many hours you book. Many boats let you keep only a small fillet from your catch; see **Maui Fishing** (www.mauifishing.com) for reasons why...and more.

Kayaking

There's a lot to see underwater just off the coast, so most outfitters offer snorkel-kayak combos. The top spot is Makena, an area rich with marine life, including sea turtles, dolphins and wintering humpback whales. In the calmer summer months, another excellent destination is Honolua–Mokule'ia Bay Marine Life Conservation District at Slaughterhouse Beach and Honolua Bay north of Kapalua, where there are turtles aplenty and dolphin sightings. Water conditions on Maui are usually clearest and calmest early in the morning, so that's an ideal time to go.

The top island outfitter for kayak rentals and tours is South Pacific Kayaks (p121).

Kitesurfing

Kitesurfing is a bit like strapping on a snowboard, grabbing a huge kite and riding with the wind across the water. It looks damn hard and certainly takes stamina, but if you already know how to ride a board, there's a good chance you'll master it quickly. According to surf legend Robby Naish, who pioneered kitesurfing, it's the most accessible of all extreme sports.

There's no better place to learn than on Maui's Kite Beach, at the western end of Kanaha Beach Park. Visiting kitesurfers need to check with locals to clarify the no-fly zones. Get the lowdown from the **Maui Kiteboarding Association** (www.mauikiteboardingassociation.com) and **Maui Kitesurfing Community** (www.mauikitesurf.org).

The Best... Beaches for Children

1 Kalepolepo Beach Park (p118)

2 Spreckelsville Beach (p149)

3 Launiupoko Beach Park (p60)

4 Kapalua Beach (p80)

5 Wailea Beach (p132)

The Best... Snorkel Spots

1 Malu'aka Beach (p138)

2 Ulua Beach (p132)

3 'Ahihi-Kina'u Natural Area Reserve (p142)

4 Molokini Crater (p303)

5 Pu'u Keka'a (Black Rock; p65)

6 Honolua Bay (p80)

Outrigger Canoeing

Polynesians were Hawaii's first settlers, paddling outrigger canoes across 2000 miles of open ocean – so you could say canoeing was Hawaii's earliest sport. The first Europeans to arrive were awestruck at the skill Hawaiians displayed, timing launches and landings perfectly, and paddling among the waves like dolphins.

Today canoe clubs keep the outrigger tradition alive. The Kihei Canoe Club (p121) invites visitors to dip a paddle with them – a great way to experience the sport if you're going to be on Maui a while. Hawaiian Sailing Canoe Adventures in Wailea (p143) offers guided outrigger canoe tours. Both share cultural insights as you paddle along the coast.

Parasailing

Soaring 200ft above the ocean tethered to a speedboat towline is a quick seven-minute thrill, available from the beach huts at Ka'anapali Beach. Because parasailing upsets humpback whales, the activity is banned in Maui during the winter season. But from mid-May to mid-December, the rush is on. Expect to pay around $65 per trip.

Sailing

Breezy Lahaina is the jump-off point for most sails. If you're in the mood to just unwind, hop on a sunset sail. For an exciting daylong journey consider a sail to Lana'i.

Snorkeling

The waters around Maui are a kaleidoscope of coral, colorful fish and super-big sea turtles. Best of all, you don't need special skills to view them. If you can float, you can snorkel – it's a cinch to learn. If you're a newbie, fess up at the dive shop or beach hut where you rent your snorkel gear – mask, snorkel and fins – and they'll show you everything you need to know. And it's cheap: most snorkel sets rent for under $10 per day.

Snorkelers should get an early start. Not only does the first half of the morning offer the calmest water, but at some of the popular places crowds begin to show by 10am.

The hottest spots for snorkeling cruises are the largely submerged volcanic crater of Molokini (p303), off Maui's southwest coast, and Lana'i's Hulopo'e Beach. Both brim with untouched coral and an amazing variety of sealife.

Stand Up Paddle Surfing

The stand up paddle surf invasion has begun. For proof, drive from Papawai Point northwest to Lahaina and look seaward. Platoons of paddle-wielding surfers, standing on 9ft to 11ft boards, are plying the waves just off the coast at seemingly every beachside park.

Abbreviated SUP, and known in Hawaii as Ku Hoe He'e Nalu, this quickly emerging sport is great for less limber adventurers since you don't need to pop up into a stance. It takes coordination to learn but isn't harder than regular surfing – although you should be a strong swimmer. Consider a class with paddle-surf champ Maria Souza in Kihei, or with the instructors at Maui Wave Riders in Lahaina.

Surfing

Maui lies smack in the path of all the major swells that race across the Pacific, creating legendary peaks for surfing. The island's north shore sees the biggest waves, which roll in from November to March, though some places, like famed Ho'okipa Beach, have good wave action year-round.

Newbies should head directly to Lahaina, which has beginner friendly waves and instructors that can get you up on a board in just one lesson. You won't be tearing across mammoth curls, but riding a board is easier than it looks and there's no better place to get started. Two primo owner-operated surf schools that have the perfect blend of patience and persistence are Goofy Foot Surf School and Nancy Emerson's School of Surfing.

A great place to rent quality surfboards is Hana Hwy Surf, which also maintains a surf report **hotline** (📞871-6258) that's updated daily. You can also get a surf report online at **OMaui** (www.omaui.com).

Surf Beaches & Breaks

While there are hippie holdouts from the 1960s who believe the spirit of Jimi Hendrix roams the Valley Isle's mountains, today Maui's beaches are where most of the island's action is found. On the north shore, near the town of Ha'iku, is the infamous big-wave spot known as **Pe'ahi**, or Jaws. Determined pro surfers, such as Laird Hamilton, Dave Kalama and Derrick Doerner, have helped put the planet's largest, most perfect wave on the international map, appearing in everything from American Express commercials to mutual fund ads. Jaws' waves are so high that surfers must be towed into them by wave runners.

Not into risking your life on your vacation? No worries, there are plenty of other waves to ride. Maui's west side, especially around Lahaina, offers a wider variety of surf. The **Lahaina Breakwall** and **Harbor's** fun reef breaks cater to both beginner and intermediate surfers. To the south is **Ma'alaea Pipeline**, a fickle right-hand reef break that is often considered one of the fastest waves in the world. On the island's northwest corner is majestic **Honolua Bay**. This right point break works best on winter swells and is considered one of the premier points not just in Hawaii, but around the world.

Gentler shorebreaks good for bodysurfing can be found around **Pa'ia**, **Kapalua** and the beaches between **Kihei** and **Makena**.

The Original Boardriders

Hawaii is the birthplace of surfing. Researchers have traced chants mentioning *he'e nalu* (surfing) and petroglyphs depicting surfers back to at least 1500 AD.

When the first missionaries arrived in Hawaii in the 1820s they promptly started stamping out the 'hedonistic' act of surfing and, save a few holdouts, by 1890 surfing was all but extinct.

Then in the early 1900s modern surfing's first icon, Duke Kahanamoku, stepped off the beach and into history. Kahanamoku grew up on the sands of Waikiki, where he rode the reefs on traditional *olo*-style boards. After winning Olympic gold in swimming at Stockholm in 1912, Duke began to travel the world demonstrating the Hawaiian 'Sport of Kings.'

The Best...
Beaches

1 Honolua Bay (p80)
Surfing in winter,
snorkeling in summer.

2 DT Fleming Beach
(p79) A beauty that'll
make you wonder if
you've reached the
South Pacific.

3 Ka'anapali Beach
(p65) A happening
resort beach with all
the expected facilities.

4 Keawakapu Beach
(p118) The perfect
beach for a sunset
swim.

5 Malu'aka Beach
(p138) The best place
to snorkel with turtles.

6 Big Beach (p138)
For long beach strolls,
boogie boarding and
bodysurfing.

Swimming

Whoever coined the phrase 'Maui *no ka 'oi*' (Maui is the best) was surely thinking of Maui's beaches, which are arguably the best in the Hawaiian Islands.

The northwest coast from Ka'anapali to Kapalua and the southwest coast from Kihei to Makena harbor scores of sandy beaches with good year-round swimming conditions. The windward northern and eastern coasts are generally rough for swimming in winter but quieten down in summer, when they can become as calm as a swimming pool.

Whale Watching

With their tail-slaps, head lunges and spy hops, humpback whales sure know how to impress a crowd. Each winter, about 10,000 of these graceful leviathans – two-thirds of the entire North Pacific humpback whale population – come to the shallow coastal waters off the Hawaiian Islands to breed and give birth. And like other discerning visitors to Hawaii, these intelligent creatures favor Maui. The western coastline of the island is their chief birthing and nursing ground. Luckily for whale watchers, humpbacks are coast-huggers, preferring shallow waters to protect their newborn calves.

Much of Hawaii's ocean waters are protected as the **Hawaiian Islands Humpback Whale National Marine Sanctuary** (www.hawaiihumpbackwhale.noaa.gov), whose Kihei headquarters is abuzz with cool whale happenings. Along the coast there's great whale watching at many places, including Papawai Point, and along beach walks in Kihei and Wailea.

If you want to get within splashing distance of 40-ton leviathans acrobatically jumping out of the water, take a whale-watching cruise. No one does them better than **Pacific Whale Foundation** (www.pacificwhale.org), a conservation group that takes pride in its green, naturalist-led whale watch trips. Maui's peak whale-watching season is from January through March, although whales are usually around for a month or so on either side of those dates.

Windsurfing

This sport reaches its peak on Maui. Ho'okipa Beach, near Pa'ia, hosts top international windsurfing competitions. The wind and waves combine at Ho'okipa in such a way that makes gravity seem arbitrary. Ho'okipa is for experts only, as hazards include razor-sharp coral and dangerous shorebreaks. For kick-ass wind without risking life and limb, the place to launch is Kanaha Beach in Kahului, but avoid the busy weekends when the water becomes a sea of sails.

Overall, Maui is known for its consistent winds. Windsurfers can find action in any onth, but as a general rule the best wind is from June to September and the flattest lls are from December to February.

At Ma'alaea, where the winds are usually strong and blow offshore toward Kaho'olawe, conditions are ripe for advanced speed sailing. In winter, on those rare occasions when *kona* (leeward) winds blow, the Ma'alaea–Kihei area can be the only place windy enough to sail. Get the inside scoop on the windsurfing scene at **Maui Windsurfing** (www.mauiwindsurfing.net).

Most windsurfing shops are based in Kahului and handle rentals, give lessons, sell windsurfing gear and even book package tours that include gear, accommodations and car.

ON LAND

Adventures here aren't limited to the sea; there are a plethora of things to do on land. Maui's hiking and horse trails traverse some of the most unique ecosystems on earth. And if knocking around a little white ball is your thing, would-be Tigers can stalk the very greens where the real Tiger plays.

Cycling

Cyclists on Maui face a number of challenges: narrow roads, heavy traffic, an abundance of hills and mountains, and the same persistent winds that so delight windsurfers. On the plus side, many roads, including the Pi'ilani Hwy in South Maui, have bike lanes. Reliable shops include West Maui Cycles in Lahaina, South Maui Bicycles in Kihei and Island Biker in Kahului.

The full-color *Maui County Bicycle Map* ($6), available from bicycle shops, shows all the roads on Maui that have cycle lanes and gives other nitty-gritty details. Consider it essential if you intend to do your exploring by pedal power. There's also a copy on the West Maui Cycles' website (www.westmauicycles.com).

Golf

Flanked by scenic ocean vistas and emerald mountain slopes, golfing just doesn't get much better. The most prestigious of Maui's courses is the Plantation Course (see Kapalua Golf, p81), which kicks off the annual PGA tour. Only slightly less elite are the championship greens at Wailea (p143) and Ka'anapali.

At the other end of the spectrum, you can enjoy a fun round at the friendly Waiehu Municipal Golf Course and at lesser-known country clubs elsewhere around the island.

Pick up the free tourist magazine *Maui Golf Review* for in-depth course profiles and tips on playing specific holes. Another good resource is **Maui Golf** (www.golf-maui.com).

Helicopter Tours

Helicopters go into amazing places that you otherwise might not experience. When you book, ask about seat guarantees, and let it be known you want a seat with a window, not a middle seat. On Maui, winds pick up by midday and carry clouds up the mountains with them. For the clearest skies and calmest ride, book a morning flight. There are four main tours:

West Maui tour (20 to 30 minutes) Takes in jungly rainforest, remote waterfalls and 'Iao Val' this is Maui's prettiest face.

East Maui tour (45 minutes) Highlights Hana, Haleakalā Crater and 'Ohe'o Gulch. Keep this is the rainiest side of Maui. The good news: waterfalls galore stream down the moun you hit clear weather after a rainstorm. The bad news: it can be socked in with clouds.

Helicopter Tour Operators

Company	Tours	Prices
AlexAir (☎871-0792; www.helitour.com)	West Maui	$141-163
	East Maui	$195-225
	Circle Island	$263-304
	East Maui & Moloka'i	$195-225
Blue Hawaiian (☎871-8844; www.bluehawaiian.com)	West Maui	$159-206
	East Maui	$239-283
	Circle Island	$335-413
	West Maui & Moloka'i	$239-283
Sunshine (☎270-3999; www.sunshine helicopters.com)	West Maui	$185-300
	East Maui	$250-375
	Circle Island	$305-455
	West Maui & Moloka'i	$305-455

Circle Island tour (one hour) Combines the West Maui and East Maui tours.

West Maui and Moloka'i tour (one hour) Includes the drama of West Maui as well as a zip along the spectacular coastal cliffs of Moloka'i. Definitely the Big Kahuna of knockout photo ops!

See the table above for recommended helicopter companies. All operate out of the Kahului Heliport, at the southeast side of Kahului Airport. Discounts off the list prices are common; ask when you book or look for coupons online or in the free tourist magazines.

Hiking

The diversity is what makes hiking on Maui so cool. Trails here traverse coastal deserts, twist through bamboo forests and green jungles, and meander across jagged lava fields. The most extraordinary trails are in Haleakalā National Park, where hikes ranging from half-day walks to quad-busting multiday treks meander across the moonscape of Haleakalā Crater. In the Kipahulu ('Ohe'o Gulch) section of the park, a trail leads up past terraced pools ideal for a dip and on to the towering waterfalls that feed them.

In Maui's Upcountry, Polipoli Spring State Recreation Area has an extensive trail system in cloud forest, including the breathtaking Skyline Trail that connects with Haleakalā summit.

North of Wailuku is the lofty Waihe'e Ridge Trail. This wonderful footpath penetrates deep into the misty West Maui Mountains, offering sweeping views of green valleys and the rugged northern coast. Near Ma'alaea Bay, the Lahaina Pali Trail follows an old footpath on the drier western slope of the same mountain mass.

The Kapalua Resort (p81) has opened several fantastic trails offering a range of ry. The Coastal Trail links Kapalua Beach and DT Fleming Beach while the Village Trails meander through an overgrown golf course. For a wonderfully scenic hike (about 7 miles), take the resort's complimentary shuttle to the flora-filled Arboretum Trail, which begins in the mountainous foothills above the resort.

Follow it to the jungle-like Honolua Ridge Trail then link to the easy Mahana Ridge Trail for a downhill ramble to DT Fleming Beach or the Kapalua Resort Center.

Several pull-offs along the road to Hana offer short nature walks that lead to hidden waterfalls and unspoiled coastal views, including the Waikamoi Nature Trail. A longer coastal trail between Wai'anapanapa State Park and Hana Bay follows an ancient Hawaiian footpath past several historic sights, as does the Hoapili (King's Hwy) Trail from La Pérouse Bay on the other side of the island.

Short nature walks that combine bird- and whale watching include the Kealia Pond boardwalk in Ma'alaea and the Kihei Coastal Trail.

One of Maui's top environmental shakers, the **Sierra Club** (www.hi.sierraclub.org/maui), sponsors guided hikes, often educational, to various places around the island. Nonmembers are asked to pay $5 each; carpooling to trailheads may be available. Not only will you be sharing the trails with other eco-minded hikers, but the Sierra Club sometimes hikes into fascinating places that are otherwise closed to the public.

Hiking Considerations

○ Maui has no snakes, no poison ivy and few wild animals that will fuss with hikers. There's only the slimmest chance of encountering a large boar in the backwoods, but they're unlikely to be a problem unless cornered.

○ Be careful on the edge of steep cliffs since cliffside rock in Maui tends to be crumbly. Flash floods are a potential threat in many of the steep, narrow valleys on Maui that require stream crossings. Warning signs include a distant rumbling, the smell of fresh earth and a sudden increase in the stream's current. If the water begins to rise, get to higher ground immediately.

○ A walking stick is good for bracing yourself on slippery approaches, gaining leverage and testing the depth of streams.

○ Darkness falls fast once the sun sets, and ridgetop trails are no place to be caught unprepared in the dark. Always carry a flashlight. Wear long pants for protection from overgrown parts of the trail, and sturdy footwear with good traction. Pack 2L of water per person for a day hike, carry a whistle to alert rescue workers if necessary, wear sunscreen and start early

Horseback Riding

With its abundant ranch land and vibrant cowboy culture, Maui offers some of Hawaii's best riding experiences. Choose a ride based on the landscape you'd like to see, since all are friendly, reputable outfitters.

The most unusual ride, offered by Pony Express (p167), meanders down into the barren hollows of Haleakalā Crater via Sliding Sands Trail. Maui Stables (p229), near Kipahulu, offers rides up the slopes past waterfalls. Makena Stables (p143) takes riders along the volcanic slopes that overlook pristine La Pérouse Bay, while Mendes Ranch (p89) rides high atop the cliffs of the Kahekili Hwy. Families will like the easy rides at Thompson Ranch (p171) in Keokea.

Mountain Biking

If you want to take off into the wilderness on a mountain bike, head to the Upc Experienced downhill riders will find adrenaline-stoked thrills on the Skyline which follows the mountain's spine from Haleakalā National Park into Polin State Recreation Area.

Preserving Hiking Trails

Of special interest to hikers and naturalists is the work of **Na Ala Hele** (https://hawaiitrails.ehawaii.gov), a group affiliated with Hawaii's Division of Forestry and Wildlife. Na Ala Hele was established in 1988 with the task of coordinating public access to hiking trails and also maintaining and preserving historical trails. On Maui, the group has negotiated with private landowners and the military to gain access to previously restricted areas and re-establish abandoned trails. Visit it's website for trail descriptions.

The Na Ala Hele logo signpost – a brown sign that features a yellow hiking petroglyph figure – is marking an increasing number of trailheads. On Maui, Na Ala Hele works out of a small office in the **Division of Forestry and Wildlife** (DOFAW; ✆873-3508; www.dofaw.net) in Wailuku.

Spas

Hawaiian spa treatments may sound a bit whimsical, but they're based on herbal traditions. Popular body wraps use seaweed to detoxify or wild ginger to remedy colds and jet lag. Other tropical treatments sound good enough to eat: coconut-milk baths and Kona-coffee scrubs....mmm.

Most spas are in the large resort hotels, such as the Hotel Hana-Maui (see Honua Spa, p223) and Grand Wailea Resort Hotel & Spa (p135), but if you prefer a more traditional setting consider the Luana Spa Retreat (p223), which offers treatments under a thatched hut in Hana.

Tennis

Singles? Doubles? Or perhaps a lesson? Take your pick at the world-class facilities at Wailea Tennis Club, Royal Lahaina Tennis Ranch in Ka'anapali and Kapalua Tennis. If you just want to knock a ball around, many hotels and condos have tennis courts for their guests and the county maintains free tennis courts at many public parks.

Ziplining

Click. Grab tight. Thumbs up. And whooooosh...you're off. Quick as a flash, Maui's ziplines let you soar freestyle on a series of cables over gulches, woods and waterfalls while strapped into a harness. The hardest part is stepping off the platform for the first zip – the rest is pure exhilaration!

Newest on the scene is Piiholo Ranch Zipline in Makawao. It's winning rave reviews with its 2800ft long final line – Hawaii's longest. It also offers side-by-side zip lines, allowing you to swoop the course alongside up to three of your friends. First on the Maui scene was Skyline Eco-Adventures Haleakalā tour (p167). It often books out months in advance. The company has zipped over to Ka'anapali and opened a second line in the hills above the resort; this one is pricier but easier to book. Kapalua Ziplines (p81) in the West Maui Mountains above Kapalua offers side-by-side dual lines as well as full-moon rides.

Making a flower lei

GREG FLMS/LONELY PLANET IMAGES ©

Greeting. Honor. Respect. Peace. Love. Celebration. Spirituality. Good luck. Farewell. A Hawaiian lei – a fresh garland handcrafted from the islands' rainbow myriad of flora – can signify all of these meanings, and more.

The Art of the Lei

Lei making may be Hawaii's most sensuous – and also transitory – art form. Fragrant and ephemeral, lei embody the beauty of nature and the embrace of the community, freely given and freely shared.

In choosing their materials, lei makers tell a story – since flowers and plants embody place and myth – and express emotions. Lei makers may use feathers, nuts, shells, seeds, seaweed, vines, leaves and fruit, in addition to more familiar fragrant tropical flowers. The most commons methods of making lei were by knotting, braiding, winding, stringing or sewing the raw natural materials together.

Worn daily, lei were integral to ancient Hawaiian society. In the islands' Polynesian past, lei were made part of sacred hula dances and given as special gifts to loved ones, healing medicine to the sick and offerings to the gods, all practices that continue in Hawaii today. So powerful a symbol were they that on ancient Hawaii's battlefields, the right lei could bring peace to warring armies.

Today, locals continue to wear lei for special events, such as weddings, birthdays, anniversaries, graduations and public ceremonies. In general, it's no longer common to make one's own lei, unless you're a devoted member of a *hula halau* (hula school). For ceremonial hula (as opposed to popular competitions or shows for entertainment), performers are often required to make their own lei, even gathering the raw materials by hand.

Modern Celebrations

For visitors to Hawaii, the tradition of giving and receiving lei dates back to the 19th-century steamships that first brought tourists to the islands. In the heyday of cruise ship tourism, disembarking passengers were greeted by local vendors who would toss garlands around the necks of *malihini* (newcomers, or foreigners).

The tradition of giving a kiss with a lei began during WWII, allegedly when a hula dancer at a USO club was dared by her friends to give a military serviceman a peck on the cheek when she placed a flower lei over his head.

In 1927, the poet Don Blanding and Honolulu journalist Grace Tower Warren called for making May 1 a holiday to celebrate lei. The next year, Leonard and Ruth Hawk composed the popular tune 'May Day is Lei Day in Hawaii,' a song that later became a hula *mele* (song). Today, Lei Day is celebrated across the islands with Hawaiian music, hula dancing, parades, lei-making workshops and contests, and more fun.

An armful of lei

Lei Etiquette

o Do not wear a lei hanging directly down around your neck. Instead, drape a closed (circular) lei over your shoulders, making sure that equal lengths are hanging over your front and back.

o When traditionally presenting a lei, bow your head slightly and raise the lei above your heart. Do not drape it with your own hands over the head of the recipient, as this isn't respectful. Let them do it themselves.

o Don't give a closed lei to a pregnant woman, as it may bring bad luck to the unborn child; choose an open (untied) lei or *haku* (head) lei instead.

o Resist the temptation to wear a lei intended for someone else. It's bad luck.

o Never refuse a lei, and do not take one off in the presence of the giver.

o When you stop wearing your lei, don't throw it in the trash. Untie the string and return the lei's natural elements to the earth (eg scatter flowers in the sea, bury seeds or nuts) instead.

Leis in Print

o *Ka Lei: The Leis of Hawaii* (Ku Pa'a Publishing, 1995) by Marie McDonald, a recognized *kapuna* (elder), is an in-depth look at the art of Hawaiian lei making before Western contact and during contemporary times.

o An artful, beautiful blend of botany and culture, *Na Lei Makamae: The Treasured Lei* (University of Hawai'i Press, 2003) by Marie McDonald and Paul Weissich surveys Hawaiian flowers traditionally used in leis and their meaning and mythology.

What's in a Lei?

Lei are a universal language in Hawaii, but some special lei evoke a particular island.

o **O'ahu** The yellow-orange *'ilima* is the island's official flower, and a symbol of Laka, the Hawaiian goddess of hula dancing. Once favored by royalty, an *'ilima* lei may be made of up to a thousand small blossoms strung together.

■ **Hawai'i the Big Island** Lei made from lehua, the pom-pom flowers of the ohia plant, are most often colored red or pink. According to Hawaiian legend, the very first lei was made of lehua and given by Hi'iaka, goddess of healing, to her sister Pele, goddess of fire and volcanoes.

o **Maui** The *lokelani* (pink damask rose, or 'rose of heaven') is a soft, velvety and aromatic flower. It was first planted on the island by early-19th-century Christian missionaries in the gardens of Lahaina. Today it's Maui's official flower, the only exotic species of flora to be so recognized in Hawaii.

o **Lana'i** A yellowish-orange vine, *kaunaoa* is traditionally gathered from the island's windward shores, then twisted into a lei. One traditional Hawaiian chant sings of this plant growing on Lana'i like a feathered cape lying on the shoulders of a celebrated chief.

o **Moloka'i** *Kukui* lei are either made from the laboriously polished, dark-brown nuts of Hawaii's state tree (in which case, they're usually worn by men) or the tree's white blossoms, which are Moloka'i's official flower.

o Kaua'i On the 'Garden Island,' leathery *mokihana* berries that faintly smell of licorice are often woven with strands of glossy, green maile vines. *Mokihana* trees grow in the rain-soaked forests on the western slopes of mighty Mt Wai'ale'ale.

Shopping for Lei

A typical Hawaiian lei costs anywhere from $10 for a single strand of orchids or plumeria to thousands of dollars for a 100% genuine Niihau shell lei necklace. Beware that some *kukui* (candelnut) and *puka* shell lei are just cheap (even plastic) imports.

When shopping for a lei, ask the florist or shopkeeper for advice about what the most appropriate lei for the occasion is (eg for a bride, pick a string of pearl-like *pikake* jasmine flowers), and indicate if you're giving the lei to a man or a woman. Of course, it's okay to buy a lei for yourself anytime!

On Maui you can pick up lei at the gift shop at Kahului's airport, but a better stop is at Whole Foods (Kahului), just a mile from the airport, which sells fresh lei made at Paradise Flower Farms in Kula.

Lei Overboard

When you're leaving the islands, it's tradition to cast a lei into the ocean; if it returns to the beach, it's said, you will one day return to Hawai'i. But don't throw your lei into the water without first removing the string and the bow.

Survival Guide

Big Beach (Oneloa, p139)

PHOTOGRAPHER: GREG ELMS/LONELY PLANET IMAGES ©

Directory

Accommodations

Be it a luxury resort, a rural B&B, a beachside condominium or a national park campground, Maui has accommodations to suit every taste. In this guide we've listed reviews in order of author preference.

Costs Maui has the highest average room rates of any Hawaiian island. That said, costs vary widely depending on which type of accommodations you select and its proximity to the beach.

Price Icons Room rates are for single (s) and double (d) occupancy per night; if there's no rate difference for one or two people, the general room (r) or suite (ste) rate is listed. Unless otherwise noted, breakfast is not included and bathrooms are private.

○ **$** (budget) less than $100

○ **$$** (midrange) $100-275

○ **$$$** (top end) more than $275

Season In this book, room rates given are for the high season of mid-December to

mid-April. Rates are typically up to a third lower outside of peak season. Holiday periods, especially between Christmas and New Year, command premium prices and often book up far in advance.

Booking It's wise to reserve in advance almost any time of the year to lock in a good deal. Many hotels and condos offer year-round internet specials well below the advertised 'rack rates.' To book condos and vacation rentals directly from owners, see **Vacation Rentals by Owner** (www.vrbo.com).

Cancellation Policies Although a reservation guarantees your room, most require a deposit, after which, if you change your mind, there are typically stiff cancellation fees in Maui. Note the cancellation policies and other restrictions before making a deposit.

B&BS & INNS

Maui's B&Bs and inns range from budget options to smolderingly romantic hideaways. If you're considering a B&B, plan ahead. Most are small operations with just a couple of rooms and hence can book out weeks in advance. Some require a minimum stay of a few days. Same-day reservations are hard to get, though there are sometimes last-

minute openings. But always call ahead – B&B owners don't want unannounced visitors disturbing their guests.

In addition to places listed throughout this book, some B&Bs book only through agencies. The following agencies cover B&Bs on Maui.

Bed & Breakfast Hawaii (☏ 822-7771; www.bandb -hawaii.com)

Hawaii's Best B&B (☏ 263-3100; www.bestbnb.com)

Affordable Paradise (☏ 261-1693; www.affordable -paradise.com)

CAMPING

On Maui there's a very clear pecking order when it comes to camping. At the top, offering the best and safest options, are the campgrounds at Haleakalā National Park. After that, the state parks – most notably Wai'anapanapa State Park – are a better option than the county parks.

National Parks Haleakalā National Park has excellent drive-up camping at the summit area and in the seaside Kipahulu section. There are no fees, reservations or permits required for drive-up camping. Haleakalā also offers free backcountry camping on the crater floor

---

Book Your Stay Online

For more accommodations reviews by Lonely Planet authors, check out hotels.lonelyplanet. com/hawaii. You'll find independent reviews, as well as recommendations on the best places to stay. Best of all, you can book online.

with a permit, as well as $75 cabin rentals, though the cabins are in high demand and difficult to score.

State Parks Maui has campgrounds and cabins at Wai'anapanapa State Park near Hana and at remote Polipoli Spring State Recreation Area in the cool Upcountry, as well as tent camping at Pala'au State Park on Moloka'i. Book cabins well in advance to avoid disappointment. Each state park allows a maximum stay of five consecutive nights per month. Tent camping is $18 per night per site. Cabins cost $90. For reservations, contact the **Division of State Parks** (☏ 984-8109; www.hawaiistateparks.org; 54 S High St, Wailuku; ◷ 8:30am-3:30pm Mon-Fri).

County Parks Maui County permits camping at Kanaha Beach Park in Kahului and at Papalaua Beach Park south of Lahaina. Camping is allowed for three consecutive nights and costs $5 to $8 per day ($2 to $3 for children under 18). For reservations, contact the **Department of Parks & Recreation** (☏ 270-7389; www.co.maui.hi.us; 700 Halia Nakoa St, Wailuku; ◷ 8am-1pm & 2:30-4pm Mon-Fri).

Gear If you're going to be camping in the Upcountry or in Haleakalā National Park, bring a waterproof tent, a winter-rated sleeping bag, rain gear and layers of warm clothing. Camping on the beach is another matter entirely – a very lightweight cotton bag and a tent is all you'll need.

Leeward & Windward

Maui's high central mountains trap the trade winds that blow from the northeast, capturing moisture-laden clouds and bringing abundant rainfall to the windward side of Maui. The jungly road to Hana lies smack in the midst of windward Maui and simply gushes with waterfalls.

The same mountains keep clouds and hence rain from reaching the southwest side of the island. So it's in places such as Kihei and Makena that you'll find the driest, sunniest conditions. It's no coincidence that the great majority of Maui's resorts are found on its dry leeward side.

CONDOMINIUMS

❂ Condos are incredibly popular on Maui. Indeed, some top destinations such as Kihei and Napili have far more condominiums than hotels.

❂ Condos are more spacious than hotel rooms, and furnished with everything a visitor needs, from a kitchen to a washer and dryer. They typically work out cheaper than hotels, especially if you're traveling with a group.

❂ In most places condo units are individually owned and then placed in a rental pool, so the furnishings and decor can vary from one unit to the next. Whenever possible, ask to see a few units before settling in.

❂ Maui condos usually have built-in discounts for longer stays: as a general rule the weekly rate is six times the daily rate and the monthly rate three times the weekly.

❂ Don't forget to ask about cleaning fees, which might be tacked onto your bill. These fees are becoming ever more commonplace on Maui.

❂ Some condo complexes are booked only through rental agencies. Others operate more like a hotel with a front desk, though even in these places some units are usually handled by rental agencies.

❂ Most condos, especially those handled through rental agencies, have a three- to seven-day minimum stay.

❂ The following booking agents handle condos and vacation rentals on Maui:

Bello Realty (☏ 879-3328; www.bellomaui.com)

Condominum Rentals Hawaii (☏ 874-5151; www.crhmaui.com)

Kihei Maui Vacations (☏ 879-4000; www.kmvmaui.com)

HOSTELS

There are no Hostelling International (HI) hostels on Maui, but there are a few simple places in older buildings that provide a cheap place to crash. These hostels aren't up to mainland standards, but for travelers on a budget they do provide a dorm bed and kitchen facilities for around $25 per night.

Climate

Haleakalā

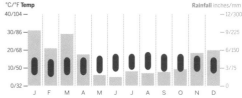

Hana

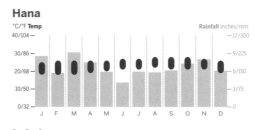

Lahaina

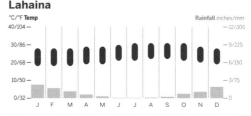

HOTELS

○ It's very common for hotels to discount their published rack rates, especially when booked via the internet. Some hotels discount by the season or day depending on demand, and others throw in a free rental car, so look for specials.

○ Within a particular hotel, the main thing that impacts room rates is the view and the floor you're on. An ocean view can cost 50% to 100% more than a parking-lot view, euphemistically called a 'garden view.'

○ In addition to checking the hotel's website, try these websites for the latest deals:

www.expedia.com

www.hotels.com

www.hotwire.com

www.orbitz.com

www.priceline.com

www.travelocity.com

RESORTS

Maui's top resorts are designed to be pleasure palaces that anticipate your every need and provide 'the best' of everything. They provide myriad dining options, multiple swimming pools, children's programs, nightly

entertainment and spas. At the priciest ones, beach sands are without blemishes, coconut trees are trimmed of drooping fronds and every aspect of your experience managed in a seamless way. They are intentionally contrived visions of paradise – and once you accept that, they're quite nice.

Business Hours

Reviews given in this book list business hours only when they differ significantly from these 'normal' opening hours.

Banks 8:30am-4pm Mon-Fri; some to 6pm Fri and 9am-noon or 1pm Sat

Bars & Clubs To midnight daily; some to 2am Thu-Sat

Businesses 8:30am-4:30pm Mon-Fri

Post Offices 8:30am-4:30pm Mon-Fri; some also 9am-noon Sat

Shops 9am-5pm Mon-Sat, some also noon-5pm Sun; major shopping areas and malls keep extended hours

Courses

○ Want to try your hand at lei-making or hula dancing? Some hotels, most notably the Ka'anapali Beach Hotel in Ka'anapali, offer lessons in a variety of traditional Hawaiian arts to their guests.

○ Hui No'eau Visual Arts Center in Makawao schedules a wide range of courses in arts and crafts for both children and adults.

○ Tantalize the senses at Ali'i Kula Lavender in Kula at a cooking course utilizing lavender.

Customs Regulations

○ For those coming from another country, each adult visitor is allowed to bring 1L of liquor and 200 cigarettes into the USA. You may also bring in up to $100 worth of gift merchandise without incurring any duty.

○ Hawaii is a rabies-free state and there are strict regulations regarding the importation of pets, so don't plan on bringing your furry friend on a short vacation.

○ Most fresh fruits and plants cannot be brought into Hawaii. For complete details, contact the **Hawaiian Department of Agriculture** (☎973-9560; www.hawaii.gov/hdoa).

Gay & Lesbian Travelers

○ Maui is a popular destination for gay and lesbian travelers. The state has strong legislation to protect minorities and a constitutional guarantee of privacy that extends to sexual behavior between consenting adults. That said, people tend to be private so you won't see much public hand-holding or open displays of affection.

○ Gay Maui is not terribly organized. There isn't a big, boisterous 'out' scene. Kihei is the gayest town on Maui, low-key as it is. Although it doesn't have exclusively gay entertainment venues, some Kihei bars and clubs have a gay night, and Kihei has a gay hotel, the Maui Sunseeker.

Both Sides Now (www.mauigayinfo.com) For the full scoop on Maui's gay scene.

Hawaii Gay Travel (☎800-508-5996; www.hawaiigaytravel.com) Arranges travel geared to gay and lesbian travelers.

Pacific Ocean Holidays (☎800-735-6600; www.gayhawaiivacations.com) Vacation packages for gays and lesbians.

Electricity

120V/60Hz

120V/60Hz

International Travelers

○ The **US State Department** (www.travel.state.gov) maintains comprehensive visa information and has application forms that can be downloaded.

○ Depending on your home country, you may not need a visa. The Visa Waiver Program allows citizens of certain countries to enter the USA for stays of 90 days or less without first obtaining a US visa. There are 36 countries currently participating including Australia, France, Germany, Ireland, Italy, Japan, the Netherlands, New Zealand, Sweden, Switzerland and the UK. For a full list of countries and details log onto the State Department's website.

○ With the exception of Canadians and visitors who qualify for the Visa Waiver

Program, foreign visitors to the USA need a visa. To apply, you need a passport that's valid for at least six months longer than your intended stay.

○ Visa applicants may be required to 'demonstrate binding obligations' that will ensure their return home. Because of this requirement, those planning to travel through other countries before arriving in the USA are better off applying for their US visa in their home country rather than on the road.

○ The validity period for a US visitor visa depends on your home country. The actual length of time you'll be allowed to stay in the USA is determined by US officials at the port of entry.

○ Upon arriving in the USA, all foreign visitors must register in the US-Visit program. This entails having their fingerprints scanned and a digital photo taken. For more information, see the **Department of Homeland Security** (www.dhs. gov) website.

Internet Access

○ There are internet cafes in Maui's main tourist destinations. Some hotels offer online computers in their lobbies for guests to use.

○ If you have your own laptop, most Maui hotels and many condos and B&Bs have wi-fi. When wi-fi is available in an establishment, it's marked in this book with a 🛜 symbol.

○ If you bring a laptop from outside the USA, make sure you bring along a universal AC and plug adapter.

Language

Hawaii has two official languages: English and Hawaiian. There's also an unofficial vernacular, pidgin, which has a laid-back, lilting accent and colorful vocabulary that permeates the official tongues. While Hawaiian's multisyllabic, vowel-heavy words may seem daunting, the pronunciation is actually quite straightforward. To learn the basics, including some Hawaiian and pidgin terms, visit www.lonelyplanet. com/hawaiian-language for our free Hawaiian Language & Glossary download.

Legal Matters

Legal Rights Anyone arrested in Hawaii has the right to have the representation of a lawyer from the time of their arrest to their trial, and if a person cannot afford a lawyer, the state must provide one free. You're presumed innocent unless or until you're found guilty in court.

Alcohol Laws The legal drinking age is 21. It's illegal to have open containers of alcohol in motor vehicles, and drinking in public parks or on the beaches is also illegal. Drunk driving is a serious crime and can incur stiff fines, jail time and other penalties. In Hawaii, anyone caught driving with a blood alcohol level of 0.08% or greater is guilty of driving 'under the influence' and will have their driver's license taken away on the spot.

Maps

The maps in this book are sufficient for most exploring. For the most comprehensive road atlas available, pick up a copy of the *Ready Mapbook of Maui County,* which covers virtually every road on Maui, Lana'i and Moloka'i, and is sold in Maui bookstores.

Money

As throughout the USA, the US dollar is the only currency used on Maui.

ATMS, CASH & CHECKS

Major banks such as the **Bank of Hawaii** (www.boh.com) and **First Hawaiian Bank** (www. fhb.com) have ATM networks throughout Maui that give cash advances on major credit cards and allow cash withdrawals with affiliated ATM cards. In addition to bank locations, you'll find ATMs at most grocery stores, mall-style shopping centers and convenience stores.

If you're carrying foreign currency, it can be exchanged for US dollars at the airport and larger banks around Maui. Out-of-state personal checks are not readily accepted on Maui.

CREDIT CARDS

Major credit cards are widely accepted on Maui, including at car-rental agencies and at most hotels, restaurants, gas stations, grocery stores and tour operators. However, many B&Bs and some condos (including some handled through rental agencies) do not accept credit cards.

TRAVELER'S CHECKS

Foreign visitors carrying traveler's checks will find things easier if the checks are in US dollars. Most midrange and top-end restaurants, hotels and shops accept US dollar traveler's checks and treat them just like cash.

Call the following for refunds on lost or stolen traveler's checks on Maui.

American Express
(☎ 800-992-3404)

Thomas Cook
(☎ 800-287-7362)

TIPPING

In restaurants, good waiters are tipped at least 15%, while dissatisfied customers make their ire known by leaving 10%. There has to be real cause for not tipping at all. Taxi drivers are typically tipped about 15% and hotel bellhops about $2 per bag.

Post

o You can get detailed 24-hour postal information by dialing toll-free ☎ 800-275-8777 or going online at www.usps.com.

o First-class mail between Maui and the mainland usually takes three to four days and costs 44¢ for letters up to 1oz and 28¢ for standard-size postcards.

o International rates for postcards and letters are 75¢ to Canada, 79¢ to Mexico and 98¢ to other countries.

o You can have mail sent to you c/o General Delivery at most big post offices on Maui. General-delivery mail is usually

Practicalities

o **Newpapers** Maui's main daily newspaper is the **Maui News** (www.mauinews.com). The **Maui Weekly** (www.mauiweekly.com) covers news and entertainment for all of Maui. **Lahaina News** (www.lahainanews.com) is a weekly newspaper focusing on West Maui.

o **Radio** KPOA 93.5FM (www.kpoa.com) features Hawaiian music with surf reports. Hawaii Public Radio **KKUA 90.7FM** (www.npr.com) features island programs and music.

o **Smoking Regulations** Tobacco smoking is prohibited in enclosed public places, including restaurants and hotel lobbies.

o **TV** All major US TV networks and cable channels available.

o **Weights and measures** As on the US mainland, distances are measured in feet, yards and miles; weights in ounces, pounds and tons.

held for up to 30 days before it's returned to sender. Most hotels will also hold mail for incoming guests.

Public Holidays

When a public holiday falls on the weekend, it's often celebrated on the nearest Friday or Monday instead. These long weekends can be busy, as people from other Hawaiian Islands often take advantage of the break to visit Maui, so if your visit coincides with a holiday be sure to book your hotel and car well in advance.

New Year's Day January 1

Martin Luther King Jr Day Third Monday of January

Presidents Day Third Monday of February

Good Friday March or April

Prince Kuhio Day March 26

Memorial Day Last Monday of May

King Kamehameha Day June 11

Independence Day July 4

Statehood Day Third Friday of August

Labor Day First Monday of September

Discoverer's Day Second Monday of October (celebrated as Columbus Day on the mainland)

Election Day Second Tuesday of November in even-numbered years

Veterans Day November 11

Thanksgiving Fourth Thursday of November

Christmas Day December 25

Safe Travel

HAZARDS & TRESPASSING

Flash floods, rock falls, tsunami, earthquakes, volcanic eruptions, shark attacks, jellyfish stings and yes, even possibly getting brained by a falling coconut — the potential dangers of traveling in Hawaii might seem alarming at first. But as the old saying goes, statistically you're more likely to get hurt crossing the street at home.

Of course, that's not to say that you shouldn't be careful. It's best to educate yourself first about potential risks to your health and safety. This advice becomes even more important when you're engaged in outdoor activities in a new and unfamiliar natural environment, whether that's an island snorkeling spot, a jungle waterfall, a high-altitude mountain or an active (and thus unpredictable) volcanic eruption zone.

Wherever you choose to explore on the islands, remember to mind your manners and watch your step. Hawaii has strict laws about trespassing on both private land and government land not intended for public use. Trespassing is always illegal, no matter how many other people you see doing it. As a visitor to the islands, it's important to respect all 'Kapu' or 'No Trespassing' signs. Always seek explicit permission from the land owner or local officials before venturing onto private or public land that is closed to the public, regardless of whether it is fenced or signposted as such. Doing so not only respects the *kuleana* (rights) of local residents and the sacredness of the land, but also helps to ensure your own safety.

THEFT

Maui is notorious for rip-offs from parked rental cars. It can happen within seconds, whether from a secluded parking area at a trailhead or from a crowded beach parking lot. As much as possible, do not leave anything valuable in your car – ever. If you must, pack things well out of sight *before* you arrive at your destination; thieves wait and watch to see what you put in the trunk.

TSUNAMIS

Tidal waves, or tsunamis as they're called in the Pacific, are not everyday events, but when they do hit they can be deadly. Maui has a warning system, aired through yellow speakers mounted on telephone poles around the island. They're tested on the first working day of each month at 11:45am for about one minute. If you should hear one at any other time and you're in a low-lying coastal area, immediately head for higher ground.

Telephone

If you don't have a cell phone, or you're in a dead zone, pay phones can be found in shopping centers, beach parks and other public places. To make long distance calls consider buying a prepaid phone card at a convenience store or pharmacy.

Toll-free numbers Always dial '1' before toll-free (800, 888 etc) numbers. Some toll-free numbers may only work within the state or from the US mainland, while others work from Canada, too. But you'll only know by making the call.

Agricultural Checks

All luggage and carry-on bags leaving Hawaii for the US mainland are checked by an agricultural inspector using an X-ray machine. You cannot take out gardenia or jade vine, even in lei, although most other fresh flowers and foliage are permitted. You can bring home pineapples and coconuts, but most other fresh fruits and vegetables are banned. Other things not allowed to enter mainland states include plants in soil, fresh coffee berries (roasted beans are OK), cactus and sugarcane.

However, seeds, fruits and plants that have been certified and labeled for export aren't a problem. For more information contact the **Plant Protection and Quarantine Office** (☎ 877-5261; www.aphis.usda.gov).

Important Numbers

Emergency	911
Country code	1
Area code	808
International access code	011

CELL (MOBILE) PHONES

Coverage Cell phone coverage is good on most of Maui, but spotty in remote areas such as the Road to Hana. Verizon has the most extensive cellular network on Maui, but AT&T and Sprint also have decent coverage.

Equipment International travelers, take note: most US mobile-phone systems are incompatible with the GSM 900/1800 standard used throughout Europe and Asia. Check with your cellular service provider before departure about using your phone on Maui.

LONG-DISTANCE & INTERNATIONAL CALLS

Calls to Hawaii If you're calling Maui from abroad, the international country code for the US is '1'. All calls to Hawaii are then followed by the area code 808 and the seven-digit local number.

International calls from Maui To make international calls direct from Maui to any country other than Canada, dial 011 + country code + area code + number. To make calls direct to Canada, dial 1 + area code + number.

Operator Assistance For international operator assistance, dial 0. The operator can provide specific rate information and tell you which time periods are the cheapest for calling.

Calls within Hawaii If you're calling from one place on Maui to any other place on Maui you do not need to dial the 808 area code. However, you must dial 1 + 808 when making a call from one Hawaiian island to another.

Time

Hawaii does not observe daylight saving time. It has about 11 hours of daylight in midwinter and almost 13½ hours in midsummer. In midwinter the sun rises at about 7am and sets at about 6pm. In midsummer it rises before 6am and sets after 7pm.

When it's noon in Maui, the time in other places is as shown below.

PLACE	TIME
Hawaii	Noon
Los Angeles	2pm
New York	5pm
London	10pm
Melbourne	8am next day

Tourist Information

Maui County's tourist organizations have loads of visitor information on their websites and will mail out material to those not online.

Maui Visitors Bureau (244-3530, 800-525-6284; www.gohawaii.com/maui; 1727 Wili Pa Loop, Wailuku) Also represents Lana'i and Moloka'i.

Moloka'I Visitors Association (553-3876, 800-800-6367; www.gohawaii.com/molokai; Kamehameha V Hwy, Kaunakakai)

Destination Lana'i (565-7600, 800-947-4774; www.gohawaii.com/lanai)

Tours

A number of tour-bus companies operate half-day and full-day sightseeing tours on Maui, covering the most visited island destinations. Popular routes include day-long jaunts to Hana, and Haleakalā trips that take in the major Upcountry sights.

Polynesian Adventure Tours (877-4242; www.polyad.com; tours $80-125) A big player among Hawaiian tour companies; offers the greatest variety of tours.

Roberts Hawaii (866-898-2591; www.robertshawaii.com; tours $65-120) Another biggie; more limited options but usually better prices.

Valley Isle Excursions (661-8687; www.tourmaui.com; tours $124) Costs a bit more but hands-down the best Road to Hana tour. Vans take just 12 passengers and guides offer more local flavor and less canned commentary.

Other Tours There are also specialized adventure tours such as whale-watching cruises, snorkeling trips to Lana'i and helicopter tours. Details are in the Activities sections under each town.

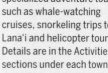

Travelers with Disabilities

○ Maui has decent infrastructure for travelers with disabilities, and most public places comply with *Americans with Disabilities Act* (ADA) regulations.

○ Many of the major resort hotels have elevators, TTD-capable phones and wheelchair-accessible rooms.

○ Major car-rental companies will install hand controls and provide accessible transportation to the vehicle pick-up site with advance notification.

○ Most public buses are wheelchair accessible.

○ The visually impaired are allowed to bring guide dogs into Hawaii without quarantine, provided they meet the Department of Agriculture's requirements.

○ If you have a disability parking placard issued by other states or countries for parking in designated accessible parking spaces, bring it with you – it's valid in Hawaii.

Disability and Communication Access Board (www.hawaii.gov/health/dcab) This website

has the scoop on services for disabled visitors in Hawaii.

Society for the Advancement of Travel for the Handicapped (www.sath.org) A good resource with travel tips and access information for disabled travelers.

Volunteering

Opportunities for volunteering abound on Maui, providing a memorable experience of Hawaii's people and environment that you won't get by just passing through. Some require extended time commitments but lots ask for just a day.

Malama Hawaii (www.malamahawaii.org) Start here to find volunteer opportunities at a wide network of community and nonprofit organizations. Volunteer to do trail maintenance, restore ancient fishponds, clean up wetlands and much more.

Sierra Club, Maui Chapter (www.hi.sierraclub.org/maui) Active on all sorts of fronts. Check out its weekend outings to eradicate invasive plants along Maui's trails.

Hawaiian Islands Humpback Whale National Marine Sanctuary (www.hawaiihumpbackwhale.noaa.gov) Numerous opportunities for volunteers, from reef fish surveys that you can combine with a snorkel outing to student internships.

National Park Service (www.nps.gov/volunteer) Coordinates volunteers at Haleakalā National Park but requires a long-term commitment.

Protect Kahoʻolawe ʻOhana (www.kahoolawe.org) Help restore the uninhabited island of Kahoʻolawe during a five-day trip.

Work

Finding serious 'professional' employment is difficult on Maui since the island has a tight labor market. But casual work, such as waiting on tables at restaurants and working on check-out counters in shops, are positions with a lot of turnover, and hence openings, especially in Lahaina. Folks with language, scuba and culinary skills might investigate better-paying employment with resorts.

Maui News (www.mauinews.com) Classified job ads.

Hawaii Jobs (www.jobshawaii.com) Updated job openings.

Transport

Getting There & Away

✈ AIR

AIRPORTS

❍ Most mainland flights to Maui involve at least one stopover, but direct flights to Maui are possible from some cities, including San Francisco, Los Angeles, Seattle, Dallas, Phoenix and Chicago.

❍ If you don't have a direct transpacific flight into Kahului then you'll be flying into O'ahu at **Honolulu International Airport** (HNL; www.honoluluairport.com) and taking an interisland flight from there. In Honolulu, the terminals for interisland flight and transpacific arrivals are adjacent and connected by shuttle bus.

❍ To reach Lana'i or Moloka'i by air, you'll have to fly via Honolulu or Kahului.

Kahului International Airport (OGG; www.hawaii.gov/ogg) All transpacific flights to Maui arrive in Kahului, the island's main airport.

Kapalua Airport (JHM; www.hawaii.gov/jhm) Off Hwy 30, south of Kapalua, this regional airport has flights to other Hawaiian islands.

Hana Airport (HNM; www.hawaii.gov/hnm) This seldom-used airport in Hana sees only a few flights a week, all by prop plane.

Lana'i Airport (LNY; www.hawaii.gov/lny) This small airport is a few miles outside Lana'i City.

Moloka'i Airport (MKK; www.hawaii.gov/mkk) Moloka'i's main airport.

TICKETS

❍ With so many airlines flying into Hawaii, good airfare deals often pop up. Check both the airline websites and the usual travel websites – the best price could be on either one.

❍ If you're going to Maui on a short getaway, don't rule out package tours – they may cost little more than what an airfare alone would have cost.

Pleasant Holidays (☏ 800-742-9244; www.pleasantholidays.com) This package tour discounter has good deals and departures from several US mainland points.

Air Tech (☏ 212-219-7000; www.airtech.com) Discounted airfares (from $199 one way) between the US west coast and Maui, but you must be flexible; it offers unsold seats at the last minute and doesn't guarantee a specific flight.

Climate Change & Travel

Every form of transport that relies on carbon-based fuel generates CO_2, the main cause of human-induced climate change. Modern travel is dependent on aeroplanes, which might use less fuel per kilometer per person than most cars but travel much greater distances. The altitude at which aircraft emit gases (including CO_2) and particles also contributes to their climate change impact. Many websites offer 'carbon calculators' that allow people to estimate the carbon emissions generated by their journey and, for those who wish to do so, to offset the impact of the greenhouse gases emitted with contributions to portfolios of climate-friendly initiatives throughout the world. Lonely Planet offsets the carbon footprint of all staff and author travel.

SEA

The following cruise lines offer tours to Hawaii with stops on Maui.

Holland America Cruise Line (www.hollandamerica. com) Typically departs from San Diego, Seattle or Vancouver.

Norwegian Cruise Line (www.ncl.com) Operates a cruise between the Hawaiian Islands that starts and ends in Hawaii.

Princess Cruises (www. princess.com) Offers a variety of cruises; most depart from Los Angeles.

Getting Around

If you really want to explore Maui thoroughly, and reach off-the-beaten-path sights, you'll need to have your own wheels. Public transportation is limited to the main towns and tourist resorts.

✈ AIR

Several inter-island airlines connect Maui with its neighboring Hawaiian islands.

The largest, **Hawaiian Airlines**, offers flights in full-bodied planes. Its advantage over the smaller carriers is frequency and dependability of service.

Island Air provides service to the main islands as well as less-frequent connections to Moloka'i and Lana'i. It's the largest commuter airline and offers an extensive schedule, but has a reputation for late and cancelled flights.

Pacific Wings flies prop planes and typically has the best rates and the least restrictions. It's a convenient way to get from Kahului to Moloka'i where the ferry schedule is less than optimal. Another bonus: Pacific Wings' tiny planes fly so low to the ground they almost double as sightseeing planes.

Hawaiian Airlines (☎ 800-367-5320; www.hawaiianair.com) Flies between Maui and the other main Hawaiian Islands.

Island Air (☎ 800-652-6541; www.islandair.com) Flies small 37-passenger planes between Honolulu, Moloka'i, Lana'i and Maui, and is the main carrier at Maui's Kapalua Airport.

Pacific Wings (☎ 888-575-4546; www.pacificwings.com) Flies prop planes between Maui, Moloka'i and Honolulu, and is the only carrier serving Hana.

TO/FROM THE AIRPORT

Shuttle

With either of the following Kahului Airport transfer services you can make advance reservations for your arrival to speed things along. Both services have courtesy phones in the baggage-claim area. Keep in mind you must reserve in advance for your *return* to the airport – and don't wait till the last minute.

Speedi Shuttle (☎ 661-6667, 800-977-2605; www.speedishuttle.com) The largest airport-transfer service on Maui. One plus about Speedi is that it has converted to bio-diesel, using recycled vegetable oil to fuel its vehicles, so if you take it you'll be traveling green-friendly. Fares for one person from Kahului Airport cost $50 to Lahaina, $54 to Ka'anapali, $74 to Kapalua, $35 to Kihei and $40 to Wailea. Add $7 to $10 more per additional person.

Executive Shuttle (☎ 669-2300, 800-833-2303; www.mauishuttle.com) More conventional vehicles, but can be less backlogged. Like Speedi, the price depends on the destination and the size of the group.

Taxi

From Kahului Airport Taxi dispatchers are near the exit of the baggage-claim area. Approximate fares from the airport: to Wailuku $20; to Kihei $35 to $40; to Lahaina $75; to Ka'anapali $90; and to Kapalua $115.

From Kapalua Airport Taxi fares from Kapalua Airport average $20 to Ka'anapali and $25 to $40 to most other places along the West Maui coast. Check with your hotel first, though, as many resorts in Ka'anapali offer free shuttles to and from Kapalua Airport.

᪥ BICYCLE

● Cyclists on Maui face a number of challenges: narrow roads, an abundance of hills and mountains, and the same persistent winds that so delight windsurfers. Maui's stunning scenery certainly will entice hard-core cyclists, but casual riders hoping to use a bike as a primary source of transportation around the island may well find such conditions daunting.

● Getting around by bicycle within a small area can be a reasonable option for the average rider, however. For example, the tourist enclave of Kihei is largely level and now has cycle lanes on its two main drags, S Kihei Rd and the Pi'ilani Hwy.

● The full-color *Maui County Bicycle Map* ($6), available from bicycle shops, shows all the roads on Maui that have cycle lanes and gives other nitty-gritty details. Consider it essential if you intend to do your exploring by pedal power.

● For information on bicycle rentals, see specific destinations around the island.

- Bringing your own bike to Hawaii costs upwards of $100 on flights from the mainland. The bicycle can be checked at the airline counter, the same as any baggage, but you'll need to prepare the bike by wrapping the handlebars and pedals in foam or by fixing the handlebars to the side and removing the pedals.

- In general, bicycles are required to follow the same state laws and rules of the road as cars.

BOAT

- Passenger ferry services connect Maui with Lana'i and Moloka'i. You can buy tickets online, by phone or on the boat. Advance reservations are always a good idea, though they are not required.

Expeditions (☏ 661-3756, 800-695-2624; www.go-lanai. com; adult/child one way $30/20) This ferry is an unbeatable way to island hop between Maui and Lana'i. Spinner dolphins are a common sight with morning sails and whales are sometimes spotted during winter sails. The Lahaina ferry leaves from in front of the Pioneer Inn and arrives at Manele Boat Harbor in Lana'i. Sailing time is about an hour. The boat run includes five roundtrips per day, timed perfectly for day tripping.

Molokai Princess (☏ 866-307-6524; www.molokaiferry. com; adult/child 4-12 $59/30) Operates between Lahaina Harbor and Moloka'i's Kaunakakai Wharf. Unlike the ferry to Lana'i, the Moloka'i ferry schedule is geared

for transporting Moloka'i residents to jobs in Lahaina, which makes it less than ideal for day tripping. It doesn't leave you with enough time to see anything other than Kaunakakai and, truth be told, there's simply not much to see in town. The 90-minute crossing through the Pailolo Channel can get choppy.

BUS

- With the exception of O'ahu, Maui has Hawaii's most extensive public bus system. But don't get too excited – the buses can take you between the main towns, but they're not going to get you to many prime out-of-the-way places, such as Haleakalā National Park, Hana or Makena's Big Beach. And some of the buses, such as the ones between Ma'alaea and Lahaina, make a direct beeline, passing trailheads and beaches without stopping.

- **Maui Bus** (☏871-4838; www.mauicounty.gov/bus) is the island's public bus system. The main routes run once hourly throughout the day and several have schedules that dovetail with one another for convenient connections.

Routes The handiest buses for visitors:

Kahului–Lahaina

Kahului–Wailea

Kahului–Wailuku

Kahului–Pa'ia

Ma'alaea–Kihei

Lahaina–Ka'anapali

Ka'anapali–Napili

Costs Fares are $1 per ride, regardless of the distance. There are no transfers; if your journey requires two separate buses, you'll have to buy a new ticket when you board the second bus. Best deal is a daily pass for just $2. Monthly passes ($45) are also available.

Free Routes Maui Bus also operates a couple of loop routes around Wailuku and Kahului, serving two dozen stops, including major shopping centers, the hospital and government offices. These buses are mainly geared for local shoppers, but are free to everyone – just hop on and see where it takes you!

Carry-on All buses allow you to carry on only what fits under your seat or on your lap, so forget the surfboard.

Resort Shuttles In addition to the public buses, free resort shuttles take guests between hotels and restaurants in the Ka'anapali and Wailea areas.

🚗 CAR & MOTORCYCLE

The majority of visitors to Maui rent their own vehicles.

AUTOMOBILE ASSOCIATIONS

The **American Automobile Association** (AAA; ☏ 800-736-2886; www.aaa-hawaii. com) has its only Hawaii office in Honolulu. Members get discounts on car rentals, some air tickets, hotels and sightseeing attractions, as well as **emergency road service and towing** (☏ 800-222-4357). AAA has reciprocal agreements with automobile associations in other countries, but be sure to bring your membership card from your country of origin.

DRIVER'S LICENSE

An International Driving Permit, obtained before you leave home, is only necessary if your country of origin is a non-English-speaking one.

FUEL & TOWING

❍ When you take a country drive on Maui, you need to be conscious of your fuel gauge. There are no gas stations on several long stretches of road, including the Road to Hana; the Kahekili Hwy between Wailuku and Kapalua; and the Haleakalā Crater Rd to the national park.

❍ Expect to pay about 25% more per US gallon than on the mainland. At the time of research, the average gas price on Maui was about $4 a gallon.

❍ Towing is expensive on Maui. Make sure your car is in good shape before taking off into any remote areas, and be aware that some of these places may be 'off limits' according to your car-rental agreement. Always ask when booking if the company has any road restrictions for its vehicles.

INSURANCE

Liability insurance covers people and property that you might hit. For damage to the actual rental vehicle, a collision damage waiver (CDW) is available for about $15 a day. If you have collision coverage on your vehicle at home, it might cover damages to car rentals; inquire before departing. Additionally, some credit cards offer reimbursement coverage for collision damages if you rent the car with that credit card; again, check before departing.

RENTALS

❍ Be sure to reserve your car in advance, especially if you're traveling during high season or arriving on a weekend when some agencies book out all together. That said, with advance notice, you shouldn't have a problem getting a car on Maui.

❍ Similar to air fares, car-rental rates vary significantly with demand. Rental rates on Maui spike if you pick the car up on a holiday such as Christmas or Thanksgiving.

❍ With advance reservations, the daily rate for a small car ranges from $35 to $50, while typical weekly rates are $175 to $300. Those who book at the last minute are most likely to get the worst rate.

❍ Rental rates generally include unlimited mileage, but confirm that when you book.

❍ If you drop the car off at a different location from where you picked it up, there's usually an additional fee.

❍ One consideration regarding car sizes: if you are going to drive the Road to Hana or around the north side of Maui, these roads are very narrow and driving a wide, full-size car gives you less of a margin than a mid-size or compact vehicle would. You may want to opt for the smallest car you're comfortable in.

Rental Agents Alamo, Avis, Budget, Dollar, Enterprise, Hertz and National all have operations at Kahului Airport. Most of these rental

Driving Distances & Drive Times from Kahului

Average driving times and distances from Kahului are as follows. Allow more time during weekday morning and afternoon rush hours, and any time the surf is up on the North Shore if you're heading that way.

DESTINATION	MILES	TIME
Haleakalā Summit	36	1½ hours
Hana	51	2 hours
Ka'anapali	26	50 minutes
Kapalua	32	1 hour
Kihei	12	25 minutes
La Pérouse Bay	21	50 minutes
Lahaina	23	40 minutes
Makawao	14	30 minutes
'Ohe'o Gulch	61	2¾ hours
Pa'ia	7	15 minutes
Wailuku	3	15 minutes

companies also have branches in Ka'anapali and will pick you up at the nearby Kapalua Airport. Dollar is the only rental agency serving Hana Airport.

The following are contacts for car rentals serving Maui.

Alamo (☏ 871-6235, 800-462-5266; www.alamo.com)

Avis (☏ 871-7575, 800-331-1212; www.avis.com)

Budget (☏ 871-8811, 800-527-0700; www.budget.com)

Dollar (☏ 877-7227, 800-800-4000; www.dollarcar.com)

Enterprise (☏ 877-2350, 800-261-7331; www.enterprise.com)

Hertz (☏ 877-5167, 800-654-3131; www.hertz.com)

National (☏ 871-8852, 800-227-7368; www.nationalcar.com)

In addition to the national chains, there are a couple of local car-rental agencies on the island that are worthy of consideration:

Bio-Beetle (☏ 873-6121, 877-873-6121; www.bio-beetle.com; 55 Amala St, Kahului) This company offers a green alternative to Maui's car-rental scene, with Volkswagen Jettas and Beetles that run on recycled vegetable oil. Plan your outings carefully, though, as you'll need to do all your refueling in Kahului.

Kihei Rent A Car (☏ 879-7257, 800-251-5288; www.kiheirentacar.com; 96 Kio Loop, Kihei) The cars are a bit older than those at the major rental

Hitting the Road

Be aware that most main roads on Maui are called highways whether they're busy four-lane thoroughfares or just quiet country roads. Indeed there are roads in remote corners of the island that narrow down to barely the width of a driveway but nonetheless are designated highways. So when you're scanning a map or planning your day's outing don't let the term 'highway' fool you into thinking you'll be whizzing along.

What's more, islanders refer to highways by name, and rarely by number. If you stop to ask someone how to find Hwy 36, chances are you'll get a blank stare – ask for the Hana Hwy instead.

agencies but this family-owned operation charges competitive rates.

ROAD CONDITIONS & HAZARDS

○ Maui has a lot of ranchland, much of it open pasture, so you'll need to keep an eye out for livestock on the road in rural areas.

○ Narrow, winding or steep roads sometimes wash out after heavy rains. Sections of some roads, including the Road to Hana and the Kahekili Hwy, are particularly susceptible to wash-outs. If it's been raining heavily recently it's best to inquire before setting out.

○ Stay alert for one-lane-bridge crossings: one direction of traffic usually has the right of way while the other must obey the posted yield sign. Downhill traffic must yield to uphill traffic where there is no sign.

ROAD RULES

○ Drivers at a red light can turn right after coming to a stop and yielding to oncoming traffic, unless there's a sign at the intersection prohibiting the turn.

○ A popular bumper sticker here reads: 'Slow Down. This Ain't the Mainland.' Locals will tell you there are three golden rules for driving on the Islands: don't honk your horn, don't follow too closely and let people pass whenever it's safe to do so. Any cool moves like this are acknowledged by waving the *shaka* (Hawaiian hand greeting) sign.

○ Horn honking is considered rude unless required for safety, or for urging cattle off the road.

○ Hawaii requires the use of seat belts. Heed this, as the ticket is stiff.

○ Speed limits are posted *and* enforced. If you're stopped for speeding, expect a ticket as the police rarely just give warnings.

HITCHHIKING

Hitchhiking, though technically illegal statewide, is not unusual on Maui. However, hitchhiking anywhere is not without risks, and Lonely Planet does not recommend it. Hitchers should size up each situation carefully before getting in cars, and women should be wary of hitching alone. People who do choose to hitchhike will be safer if they travel in pairs and let someone know where they are planning to go.

MOPED & MOTORCYCLE

○ You can legally drive both mopeds and motorcycles in Hawaii as long as you have a valid driver's license issued by your home country.

○ The minimum age for renting a moped is 16; for a motorcycle it's 21.

○ Keep in mind that the windward side of Maui generally requires hard-core foul-weather gear, since it rains early and often.

○ State law requires mopeds to be ridden by one person only and prohibits their use on sidewalks and freeways.

○ Mopeds must always be driven in single file and may not be driven at speeds in excess of 30mph.

○ Bizarrely, mopeds can be more expensive to rent than cars.

○ There are no helmet laws in the state of Hawaii, but most rental agencies provide free helmets, and cautious riders will use them.

TAXI

○ On Maui, you can't just flag a taxi down in the street. You need to call ahead for a scheduled pick-up.

○ Pick-ups from remote locations (for instance, after a long through-hike) can sometimes be arranged in advance, though you may have to also pay in advance.

○ Fares are county-regulated. The metered rate costs $6.50 for the first mile and $3 per additional mile.

○ If you opt to tour by taxi expect to pay $60 to $75 per hour, which covers up to six passengers.

The following taxi companies provide service throughout Maui.

Royal Cabs (875-6870)

Sunshine Cabs of Maui (879-2220)

Islandwide Taxi & Tours (874-8294)

A-Z

Glossary

For food terms, see p284

'a'a – type of lava that is rough and jagged

ae'o – Hawaiian black-necked stilt

'ahinahina – silversword plant with pointed silver leaves

ahu – stone cairns used to mark a trail; an altar or shrine

ahupua'a – traditional land division, usually in a wedge shape that extends from the mountains to the sea (smaller than a *moku*)

'aina – land

'akala – Hawaiian raspberry; also called a thimbleberry

'akohekohe – Maui parrotbill

'alae ke'oke'o – endangered Hawaiian coot

'alae 'ula – Hawaiian moorhen

'alauahio – Maui creeper

ali'i – chief, royalty

ali'i nui – high chiefs

aloha – the traditional greeting meaning love, welcome, good-bye

aloha 'aina – love of the land

'amakihi – small, yellow-green honeycreeper; one of the more common native birds

anchialine pool – contains a mixture of seawater and freshwater

'apapane – bright red native Hawaiian honeycreeper

'aumakua – protective deity or guardian spirit, deified ancestor or trustworthy person

'awa – see *kava*

'awa 'awa – bitter

'awapuhi – wild ginger

azuki bean – often served as a sweetened paste, eg as a topping for shave ice

braguinha – a Portuguese stringed instrument introduced to Hawaii in the late 19th century from which the ukulele is derived

broke da mout – delicious; literally, 'broke the mouth'

crack seed – Chinese preserved fruit; a salty, sweet and/or sour snack

e koko mai – welcome

'elepaio – Hawaiian monarch flycatcher; a brownish native bird with a white rump, common to O'ahu forests

grinds – food; to *grind* means to eat

ha – breath

haku – head

hala – pandanus tree; the leaves *(lau)* are used in weaving mats and baskets

hale – house

haole – Caucasian; literally, 'without breath'

hapa – portion or fragment; person of mixed blood

ha'i – high falsetto

hapa haole – Hawaiian music with predominantly English lyrics

hapu'u – tree fern

hau – indigenous lowland hibiscus tree whose wood is often used for making canoe outriggers (stabilizing arms that jut out from the hull)

he'e nalu – wave sliding, or surfing

heiau – ancient stone temple; a place of worship in Hawaii

holua – sled or sled course

honi – to share breath

honu – turtle

ho'okipa –hospitality

ho'olaule'a – celebration, party

ho'onanea – to pass the time in ease, peace and pleasure

hukilau – fishing with a *seine*, involving a group of people who pull in the net

hula – Hawaiian dance form, either traditional or modern

hula 'auana – modern hula, developed after the introduction of Western music

hula halau – hula school or troupe

hula kahiko – traditional hula

'i'iwi – scarlet Hawaiian honeycreeper with a curved, salmon-colored beak

'iliahi – Hawaiian sandalwood

'io – Hawaiian hawk

ipo – sweetheart

ipu – spherical, narrow-necked gourd used as a hula implement

issei – first-generation Japanese immigrants; born in Japan

kahili – a feathered standard, used as a symbol of royalty

kahuna – knowledgable person in any field; commonly a priest, healer or sorcerer

kahuna lapa'au – healer

kahuna nui – high priest(ess)

kalo – taro

kalo lo'i – taro fields

kama'aina – person born and raised or a longtime resident in Hawaii; literally, 'child of the land'

kanaka – man, human being, person; also Native Hawaiian

kane/Kane – man; if capitalized, the name of one of four main Hawaiian gods

kanoa – hidden meaning

kapa – see *tapa*

kapu – taboo, part of strict ancient Hawaiian social and religious system

kapuna – elders

kaua – ancient Hawaiian lower class, outcasts

kaunaoa – a ground-cover vine with yellow tendrils used to make lei

kava – a mildly narcotic drink (*'awa* in Hawaiian) made from the roots of *Piper methysticum*, a pepper shrub

keiki – child

ki – see *ti*

ki ho'alu – slack key

kiawe – a relative of the mesquite tree introduced to Hawaii in the 1820s, now very common; its branches are covered with sharp thorns

kika kila – Hawaiian steel guitar

ki'i – see *tiki*

ki'i akua – *temple images*

kilau – a stiff, weedy fern

kipuka – an area of land spared when lava flows around it; an oasis

ko – sugarcane

ko'a – fishing shrine

koa – native hardwood tree often used in making native crafts and canoes

koki'o ke'oke'o – native Hawaiian white hibiscus tree

kokua – help, cooperation

kona – leeward side; a leeward wind

konane – a strategy game similar to checkers

konohiki – caretakers

ko'olau – windward side

Ku – Polynesian god of many manifestations, including god of war, farming and fishing (husband of Hina)

kukui – candlenut tree and the official state tree; its oily nuts were once burned in lamps

kuleana – rights

kumu hula – hula teacher

Kumulipo – Native Hawaiian creation story or chant

kupuna – grandparent, elder

ku'ula – a stone idol placed at fishing sites, believed to attract fish; if capitalized, the god of fishermen

Laka – goddess of the hula

lanai – veranda; balcony

lau – leaf

lauhala – leaves of the *hala* plant, used in weaving

lei – garland, usually of flowers, but also of leaves or shells

leptospirosis – a disease acquired by exposure to water contaminated by the urine of infected animals, especially rodents

limu – seaweed

lokelani – pink damask rose, or 'rose of heaven,' Maui's official flower

loko i'a – fishpond

loko wai – freshwater fishpond

lolo – stupid, feeble-minded, crazy

lomi – to rub or soften

lomilomi – traditional Hawaiian massage; known as 'loving touch'

Lono – Polynesian god of harvest, agriculture, fertility and peace

loulu – native fan palms

luakini – a type of *heiau* dedicated to the war god Ku and used for human sacrifices

luau – traditional Hawaiian feast

mahalo – thank you

mahele – to divide; usually refers to the sugar industry – initiated land divisions of 1848

mai ho'oka'awale – leprosy (Hansen's disease); literally, 'the separating sickness'

mai'a – banana

maile – native plant with twining habit and fragrant leaves; often used for lei

maka'ainana – commoners; literally, 'people who tend the land'

makaha – a sluice gate, used to regulate the level of water in a fishpond

makahiki – traditional annual wet-season winter festival dedicated to the agricultural god Lono

makai – toward the sea; seaward

make – dead

malihini – newcomer, visitor

malo – loincloth

mamane – a native tree with bright yellow flowers; used to make lei

mamo – a yellow-feathered bird, now extinct

mana – spiritual power

mauka – toward the mountains; inland

mele – song, chant

menehune – 'little people' who, according to legend, built many of Hawaii's fishponds, heiau and other stonework

milo – a native shade tree with beautiful hardwood

moa – jungle fowl

mokihana – an endemic tree or shrub, with scented green berries; used to make lei

moku – wedge-shaped areas of land running from the ridge of the mountains to the sea

mokupuni – island

mo'i – king

mo'o – water spirit, water lizard or dragon

muumuu – a long, loose-fitting dress introduced by the missionaries

na keiki – children

na'u – fragrant Hawaiian gardenia

naupaka – a native shrub with delicate white flowers

Neighbor Islands – the term used to refer to the main Hawaiian Islands outside of O'ahu

nene – a native goose; Hawaii's state bird

nisei – second-generation Japanese immigrants

niu – coconut palm

'ohana – family, extended family; close-knit group

'ohi'a lehua – native Hawaiian tree with tufted, feathery, pom-pom-like flowers

'olelo Hawai'i – the Hawaiian language

oli – chant

'omilu – a type of trevally

olona – a native shrub

'o'o ihe – spear throwing

'ope'ape'a – Hawaiian hoary bat

'opihi – an edible limpet

pahoehoe – type of lava that is quick and smooth- flowing

pakalolo – marijuana; literally, 'crazy smoke'

palaka – Hawaiian-style plaid shirt made from sturdy cotton

pali – cliff

paniolo – cowboy

Papa – earth mother

pau – finished, no more

pau hana – happy hour

Pele – goddess of fire and volcanoes; her home is in Kilauea Caldera

pidgin – distinct local language and dialect, influenced by its multiethnic immigrants

pikake – jasmine flowers

piko – navel, umbilical cord

pili – a bunchgrass, commonly used for thatching houses

pohaku – rock

pohuehue – beach morning glory (a flowering plant)

pono – righteous, respectful and proper

poi – staple Hawaiian starch made of steamed, mashed taro

pua aloalo – yellow hibiscus

pua'a waewae loloa – 'long-legged pigs,' an ancient Hawaiian euphemism for human sacrificial victims

pueo – Hawaiian owl

puka – any kind of hole or opening; puka shells are those that are small, white and strung into necklaces

pukiawe – native plant with red and white berries and evergreen leaves

pulu – the silken clusters encasing the stems of hapu'u ferns

pupu – snack or appetizer; also a type of cowry shell

pu'u – hill, cinder cone

pu'uhonua – place of refuge

raku – a style of Japanese pottery characterized by a rough, handmade appearance

rubbah slippah – rubber flip-flops

sansei – third-generation Japanese immigrants

seine – a large net used for fishing

shaka – hand gesture used in Hawaii as a greeting or sign of local pride

stink-eye – dirty look

taiko – Japanese drumming

talk story – to strike up a conversation, make small talk

tapa – cloth made by pounding the bark of paper mulberry, used for early Hawaiian clothing (*kapa* in Hawaiian)

ti – common native plant; its long shiny leaves are used for wrapping food and making hula skirts (*ki* in Hawaiian)

tiki – wood- or stone-carved statue, usually depicting a deity (*ki'i* in Hawaiian)

tutu – grandmother or grandfather; also term of respect for any member of that generation

'ua'u – dark-rumped petrel

ukulele – a stringed musical instrument derived from the *braguinha*, which was introduced to Hawaii in the 1800s by Portuguese immigrants

'uli'uli – gourd rattle containing seeds and decorated with feathers, used as a hula implement

'ulu – breadfruit

'ulu maika – ancient Hawaiian stone bowling game

wa'a kaulua – an ancient Hawaiian long-distance sailing vessel

wahi pana – sacred place

Wakea – sky father

warabi – fiddlehead fern

wauke – paper mulberry, used to make tapa

wiliwili – the lightest of the native woods

zendo – communal Zen meditation hall

Behind the Scenes

Author Thanks
GLENDA BENDURE & NED FRIARY
A big *mahalo* to Allen Tom of the Hawaiian Islands Humpback Whale National Marine Sanctuary. Thanks also to Jeff Bagshaw of Haleakalā National Park, Glynnis Nakai of the Kealia Pond National Wildlife Refuge, George Kahumoku Jr for welcoming us into his slack key guitar class, Natalie O'Brien for her insights into the Upcountry and David Lefevre for his tips on the Road to Hana. And finally, *mahalo nui loa* to Emily K Wolman, Sasha Baskett and Jennye Garibaldi.

AMY C BALFOUR
Ned Friary and Glenda Bendure, cheers for the wonderful text in *Maui* 3 and for answering my questions. Kudos to my Maui experts: Jay and Erin Habel, Beckee Morrison and the fab women in Kihei's Na'auso Book Club, plus Libby Fulton, Gary Hogan, John Christopher, Judy Heilman, Tim Schools, Sheila Gallien, Collin Chang and local insiders Brayzlee Ilikea Dutro, Keoki Benjamin and Zach Edlao. And a mai tai to mom and grand Eloise.

Acknowledgments
Climate map data adapted from Peel MC, Finlayson BL & McMahon TA (2007) 'Updated World Map of the Köppen-Geiger Climate Classification', *Hydrology and Earth System Sciences*, 11, 163344.

Cover photographs
Front: Big Beach (Oneloa), Giovanni Simeone/4Corners Images
Back: Bamboo forest, Pipiwai Trail, Greg Elms/Lonely Planet Images ©
Many of the images in this guide are available for licensing from Lonely Planet Images: www.lonelyplanetimages.com.

This Book
This 1st edition of Lonely Planet's *Discover Maui* was researched and written by Amy C Balfour, Glenda Bendure and Ned Friary. The Lei chapter was written by Sara Benson. This book is based on the 3rd edition of Lonely Planet's *Maui,* which Ned and Glenda cowrote. The guidebook was commissioned in Lonely Planet's Oakland, USA, office and produced by the following:

Commissioning Editors Jennye Garibaldi, Emily K Wolman
Coordinating Editor Dianne Schallmeiner
Coordinating Cartographer Brendan Streager
Coordinating Layout Designer Paul Iacono
Managing Editors Sasha Baskett, Kirsten Rawlings
Managing Cartographer Alison Lyall
Managing Layout Designers Chris Girdler, Jane Hart
Assisting Editors Gabrielle Innes, Sonya Mithen, Anne Mulvaney, Gabrielle Stefanos
Assisting Cartographers Enes Basic, Marc Milinkovic, Andy Rojas
Cover Research Naomi Parker
Internal Image Research Sabrina Dalbesio

Thanks to Shahara Ahmed, Judith Bamber, Melanie Dankel, Janine Eberle, Ryan Evans, Laura Jane, Jennifer Johnston, Yvonne Kirk, Nic Lehman, John Mazzocchi, Wayne Murphy, Suyin Ng, Piers Pickard, Malisa Plesa, Averil Robertson, Lachlan Ross, Mik Ruff, Rebecca Skinner, Laura Stansfeld, Juan Winata

Our Readers Many thanks to the travelers who wrote to us with helpful hints, useful advice and interesting anecdotes: Don Eastwood, Robert Garretson, Mandy Lam, Meimei Medlock, Milan Moravec, Samantha Smithe

SEND US YOUR FEEDBACK
We love to hear from travelers – your comments keep us on our toes and help make our books better. Our well-traveled team reads every word on what you love or loathed about this book. Although we cannot reply individually to postal submissions, we always guarantee that your feedback goes straight to the appropriate authors, in time for the next edition. Each person who sends us information is thanked in the next edition, and the most useful submissions are rewarded with a free book.

Visit **lonelyplanet.com/contact** to submit your updates and suggestions or to ask for help. Our award-winning website also features inspirational travel stories, news and discussions.

Note: We may edit, reproduce and incorporate your comments in Lonely Planet products such as guidebooks, websites and digital products, so let us know if you don't want your comments reproduced or your name acknowledged. For a copy of our privacy policy visit lonelyplanet.com/privacy.

338

NOTES

NOTES

Index

See also separate subindexes for Activities (p351), Drinking (p352), Eating (p353), Entertainment (p354), Shopping (p355), Sights (p355), Sleeping (p357) and Tours (p358).

000 Map pages

Drinking

Entertainment

Shopping

Sights